The Cambridge Companion to F. Scott Fitzgerald

In this volume, eleven specially commissioned essays by major Fitzgerald scholars present a clearly written and comprehensive assessment of F. Scott Fitzgerald as a writer and as a public and private figure. No aspect of his career is overlooked, from his first novel published in 1920, through his more than 170 short stories, to his last unfinished Hollywood novel. Contributions present the reader with a full and accessible picture of the background of American social and cultural change in the early decades of the twentieth century. The introduction traces Fitzgerald's career as a literary and public figure, and examines the extent to which public recognition has affected his reputation among scholars, critics, and general readers over the past sixty years. This is the only volume that offers undergraduates, graduates, and general readers a full account of Fitzgerald's work as well as suggestions for further exploration of his work.

RUTH PRIGOZY is Professor of English at Hofstra University and Executive Director and co-founder of the F. Scott Fitzgerald Society. She is the author of *F. Scott Fitzgerald: An Illustrated Life*, editor of *The Great Gatsby, This Side of Paradise*, and co-editor of *F. Scott Fitzgerald: New Perspectives*. She has also written many articles on Fitzgerald, Hemingway, J. D. Salinger, D. W. Griffith, and Billy Wilder among others.

CAMBRIDGE COMPANIONS TO LITERATURE

The Cambridge Companion to Greek Tragedy
edited by P. E. Easterling

*The Cambridge Companion to Old English
Literature*
edited by Malcolm Godden and
Michael Lapidge

*The Cambridge Companion to Medieval
Romance*
edited by Roberta L. Kreuger

*The Cambridge Companion to Medieval English
Theatre*
edited by Richard Beadle

*The Cambridge Companion to English
Renaissance Drama*
edited by A. R. Braunmuller and
Michael Hattaway

*The Cambridge Companion to Renaissance
Humanism*
edited by Jill Kraye

*The Cambridge Companion to English Poetry,
Donne to Marvell*
edited by Thomas N. Corns

*The Cambridge Companion to English
Literature, 1500–1600*
edited by Arthur F. Kinney

*The Cambridge Companion to English
Literature, 1650–1740*
edited by Steven N. Zwicker

*The Cambridge Companion to Writing of the
English Revolution*
edited by N. H. Keeble

*The Cambridge Companion to English
Restoration Theatre*
edited by Deborah C. Payne Fisk

*The Cambridge Companion to British
Romanticism*
edited by Stuart Curran

*The Cambridge Companion to
Eighteenth-Century Poetry*
edited by John Sitter

*The Cambridge Companion to the
Eighteenth-Century Novel*
edited by John Richetti

The Cambridge Companion to Victorian Poetry
edited by Joseph Bristow

*The Cambridge Companion to the
Victorian Novel*
edited by Deirdre David

*The Cambridge Companion to American
Realism and Naturalism*
edited by Donald Pizer

*The Cambridge Companion to
Nineteenth-Century American
Women's Writing*
edited by Dale M. Bauer and Philip Gould

*The Cambridge Companion to the Classic
Russian Novel*
edited by Malcolm V. Jones and
Robin Feuer Miller

*The Cambridge Companion to the French
Novel: from 1800 to the present*
edited by Timothy Unwin

The Cambridge Companion to Modernism
edited by Michael Levenson

*The Cambridge Companion to Australian
Literature*
edited by Elizabeth Webby

*The Cambridge Companion to American
Women Playwrights*
edited by Brenda Murphy

*The Cambridge Companion to Modern British
Women Playwrights*
edited by Elaine Aston and Janelle Reinelt

The Cambridge Companion to Virgil
edited by Charles Martindale

The Cambridge Companion to Dante
edited by Rachel Jacoff

The Cambridge Companion to Proust
edited by Richard Bales

The Cambridge Companion to Chekhov
edited by Vera Gottlieb and Paul Allain

The Cambridge Companion to Ibsen
edited by James McFarlane

The Cambridge Companion to Brecht
edited by Peter Thomson and
Glendyr Sacks

The Cambridge Chaucer Companion
edited by Piero Boitani and Jill Mann

The Cambridge Companion to Shakespeare
edited by Margareta de Grazia and
Stanley Wells

*The Cambridge Companion to Shakespeare
on Film*
edited by Russell Jackson

The Cambridge Companion to Spenser
edited by Andrew Hadfield

The Cambridge Companion to Ben Jonson
edited by Richard Harp and Stanley Stewart

The Cambridge Companion to Milton
edited by Dennis Danielson

The Cambridge Companion to Samuel Johnson
edited by Greg Clingham

The Cambridge Companion to Keats
edited by Susan J. Wolfson

The Cambridge Companion to Jane Austen
edited by Edward Copeland and
Juliet McMaster

The Cambridge Companion to Charles Dickens
edited by John O. Jordan

The Cambridge Companion to George Eliot
edited by George Levine

The Cambridge Companion to Edith Wharton
edited by Millicent Bell

The Cambridge Companion to Thomas Hardy
edited by Dale Kramer

The Cambridge Companion to Henry James
edited by Jonathan Freedman

The Cambridge Companion to Oscar Wilde
edited by Peter Raby

The Cambridge Companion to Walt Whitman
edited by Ezra Greenspan

*The Cambridge Companion to
George Bernard Shaw*
edited by Christopher Innes

*The Cambridge Companion to
Henry David Thoreau*
edited by Joel Myerson

The Cambridge Companion to Joseph Conrad
edited by J. H. Stape

The Cambridge Companion to Mark Twain
edited by Forrest G. Robinson

The Cambridge Companion to D. H. Lawrence
edited by Anne Fernihough

The Cambridge Companion to William Faulkner
edited by Philip M. Weinstein

The Cambridge Companion to Virginia Woolf
edited by Sue Roe and Susan Sellers

*The Cambridge Companion to
Ernest Hemingway*
edited by Scott Donaldson

The Cambridge Companion to James Joyce
edited by Derek Attridge

The Cambridge Companion to T. S. Eliot
edited by A. David Moody

*The Cambridge Companion to
F. Scott Fitzgerald*
edited by Ruth Prigozy

The Cambridge Companion to Ezra Pound
edited by Ira B. Nadel

The Cambridge Companion to Robert Frost
edited by Robert Faggen

The Cambridge Companion to Beckett
edited by John Pilling

The Cambridge Companion to Eugene O'Neill
edited by Michael Manheim

The Cambridge Companion to Harold Pinter
edited by Peter Raby

*The Cambridge Companion to
Tennessee Williams*
edited by Matthew C. Roudané

The Cambridge Companion to Tom Stoppard
edited by Katherine E. Kelly

The Cambridge Companion to Arthur Miller
edited by Christopher Bigsby

The Cambridge Companion to Herman Melville
edited by Robert S. Levine

CAMBRIDGE COMPANIONS TO CULTURE

*The Cambridge Companion to Modern German
Culture*
edited by Eva Kolinsky and
Wilfried van der Will

*The Cambridge Companion to Modern Spanish
Culture*
edited by David T. Gies

*The Cambridge Companion to Modern Russian
Culture*
edited by Nicholas Rzhevsky

*The Cambridge Companion to Modern Italian
Culture*
edited by Zygmunt G. Baranski and
Rebecca J. West

THE CAMBRIDGE
COMPANION TO
F. SCOTT FITZGERALD

EDITED BY

RUTH PRIGOZY

Hofstra University

CAMBRIDGE
UNIVERSITY PRESS

CAMBRIDGE UNIVERSITY PRESS
Cambridge, New York, Melbourne, Madrid, Cape Town, Singapore,
São Paulo, Delhi, Dubai, Tokyo, Mexico City

Cambridge University Press
The Edinburgh Building, Cambridge CB2 8RU, UK

Published in the United States of America by Cambridge University Press, New York

www.cambridge.org
Information on this title: www.cambridge.org/9780521624749

First published 2002
Fourth printing 2007

A catalogue record for this publication is available from the British Library

Library of Congress Cataloguing in Publication data
The Cambridge companion to F. Scott Fitzgerald / edited by Ruth Prigozy.
p. cm. – (Cambridge companions to literature)
Includes bibliographical references and index.
ISBN 0 521 62447 9 – ISBN 0 521 62474 6 (pbk.)
1. Fitzgerald, F. Scott (Francis Scott), 1896–1940 – Criticism and
interpretation – Handbooks, manuals, etc. I. Prigozy, Ruth. II. Series.
PS3511.I9 Z575   2002
813´.52 – dc21
[B]
2001025957

ISBN 978-0-521-62447-3 Hardback
ISBN 978-0-521-62474-9 Paperback

For Frances Kroll Ring

With affection, gratitude, and respect from everyone who reveres
F. Scott Fitzgerald as man and artist

CONTENTS

Notes on contributors   *page* xi
Preface   xv
List of abbreviations   xvi
Chronology   xvii

1 Introduction: Scott, Zelda, and the culture of celebrity   1
   RUTH PRIGOZY

2 F. Scott Fitzgerald, age consciousness, and the rise
   of American youth culture   28
   KIRK CURNUTT

3 The question of vocation in *This Side of Paradise*
   and *The Beautiful and Damned*   48
   JAMES L. W. WEST III

4 The short stories of F. Scott Fitzgerald   57
   BRYANT MANGUM

5 *The Great Gatsby* and the twenties   79
   RONALD BERMAN

6 *Tender is the Night* and American history   95
   MILTON R. STERN

7 Fitzgerald's expatriate years and the European stories   118
   J. GERALD KENNEDY

8 Women in Fitzgerald's fiction   143
   RENA SANDERSON

9 Fitzgerald's nonfiction   164
   SCOTT DONALDSON

10 Fitzgerald and Hollywood   189
   ALAN MARGOLIES

11 The critical reputation of F. Scott Fitzgerald   209
   JACKSON R. BRYER

   Bibliography   235
   Index   265

NOTES ON CONTRIBUTORS

RONALD BERMAN is Professor of Literature at the University of California, San Diego. He has published many articles and books about Shakespeare and seventeenth-century drama, and has written *"The Great Gatsby" and Modern Times* (1994), *"The Great Gatsby" and Fitzgerald's World of Ideas* (1997), and *Fitzgerald, Hemingway and the Twenties* (2000).

JACKSON R. BRYER is Professor of English at the University of Maryland, College Park. He is the author of *The Critical Reputation of F. Scott Fitzgerald* (1967; 1984), editor of *New Essays on F. Scott Fitzgerald's Neglected Stories* (1996), *The Short Stories of F. Scott Fitzgerald: New Approaches in Criticism* (1982), and *F. Scott Fitzgerald: The Critical Reception* (1978). He is co-editor of *The Basil and Josephine Stories* (1973), *F. Scott Fitzgerald in His Own Time: A Miscellany* (1971), *Dear Scott/Dear Max: The Fitzgerald–Perkins Correspondence* (1971), the *F. Scott Fitzgerald Newsletter* (annually), and *F. Scott Fitzgerald: New Perspectives* (2000). He is co-founder and President of the F. Scott Fitzgerald Society.

KIRK CURNUTT is Associate Professor of English at Troy State University, Montgomery, Alabama. He is the author of *Wise Economies: Brevity and Storytelling in American Short Stories* (1997) and *The Critical Response to Gertrude Stein* (2000).

SCOTT DONALDSON is a biographer and Louise G. T. Cooley Professor of English, Emeritus, at the College of William and Mary. He has written several books and articles about Fitzgerald, including *Hemingway vs. Fitzgerald* (1999) and *Fool for Love, F. Scott Fitzgerald* (1983). In addition, he edited *Critical Essays on F. Scott Fitzgerald's "The Great Gatsby"* (1984) and *The Cambridge Companion to Ernest Hemingway* (1996).

J. GERALD KENNEDY is William A. Read Professor of English at Louisiana State University and past Chair of the English Department. He is the author of *Imagining Paris: Exile, Writing, and American Identity* (1993) and co-editor (with Jackson R. Bryer) of *French Connections: Hemingway and Fitzgerald Abroad* (1998).

BRYANT MANGUM is Professor of English at Virginia Commonwealth University, Richmond. He is the author of *A Fortune Yet: Money in the Art of F. Scott Fitzgerald's Short Stories* (1991). His essays have appeared in *The Fitzgerald/Hemingway Annual, New Essays on F. Scott Fitzgerald's Neglected Stories, America Literary Realism, Reader's Guide to Literature in English* and many other journals.

ALAN MARGOLIES is Professor of English, Emeritus, John Jay College, City University of New York. He has published numerous essays on Fitzgerald's work and life. He is co-editor of *F. Scott Fitzgerald: New Perspectives* (2000). He is editor of *F. Scott Fitzgerald's St. Paul Plays, 1911–1914* (1978) and Fitzgerald's *The Beautiful and Damned* (1998), co-editor of *F. Scott Fitzgerald: Manuscripts* (1990–1), co-editor of the *F. Scott Fitzgerald Society Newsletter* (annually) and co-founder and Vice-President of the F. Scott Fitzgerald Society.

RUTH PRIGOZY is Professor of English at Hofstra University, New York, and past Chair of the English Department. She is author of the *Illustrated Life of Fitzgerald* (2001), editor of *The Great Gatsby* (1998) and *This Side of Paradise* (1995), co-editor of *F. Scott Fitzgerald: New Perspectives* (2000), and has published numerous essays on Fitzgerald. She is co-editor of the *F. Scott Fitzgerald Newsletter* (annually) and is co-founder and Executive Director of the F. Scott Fitzgerald Society.

RENA SANDERSON is Associate Professor of English at Boise State University, Idaho. She edited *Blowing the Bridge: Essays on Hemingway and "For Whom the Bell Tolls"* (1992), and she has published several studies of Hemingway including "Hemingway and Gender History," a chapter in *The Cambridge Companion to Ernest Hemingway*.

MILTON R. STERN is an Alumni Association Distinguished Professor Emeritus, University of Connecticut, Storrs. He has published books on Hawthorne and Melville and has edited several volumes on American literature. His books on Fitzgerald include *The Golden Moment: The Novels of F. Scott Fitzgerald* (1970), *Critical Essays on F. Scott Fitzgerald's "Tender Is the Night"* (1986, editor), and *"Tender Is the Night": The Broken Universe* (1994).

JAMES L. W. WEST III is Distinguished Professor of English at Pennsylvania State University. His most recent book is *William Styron, A Life* (1998). He is general editor of the Cambridge Edition of the Writings of F. Scott Fitzgerald; two recent volumes are *This Side of Paradise* (1986) and *Trimalchio* (2000).

PREFACE

There have been many collections of essays on F. Scott Fitzgerald, whose reputation has grown steadily since his death in 1940. This particular volume takes note of Fitzgerald's career in terms of both his writing and his life, and presents the reader with a full and accessible picture of each, against the background of American social and cultural change in the early decades of the twentieth century. Fitzgerald's reputation, in the new millennium, is firmer than it has ever been, and we believe that this volume will serve as a guide for all readers who wish to make or renew their acquaintance with the work of this great American writer.

I am grateful to Jackson R. Bryer and Milton R. Stern, who provided some extra help along the way, to Hofstra University for research leave which helped me complete the work, and to Maria Fixell, who helped locate the cover image.

ABBREVIATIONS

AA	*Afternoon of An Author*
ATSYM	*All the Sad Young Men*
B&D	*The Beautiful and Damned*
B&J	*The Basil and Josephine Stories*
F&P	*Flappers and Philosophers*
GG	*The Great Gatsby*
LT	*The Last Tycoon*
LOTLT	*Love of the Last Tycoon*
PH	*The Pat Hobby Stories*
TJA	*Tales of the Jazz Age*
TITN	*Tender is the Night*
TSOP	*This Side of Paradise*
Apprentice Fiction	*The Apprentice Fiction of F. Scott Fitzgerald* (ed. Kuehl)
As Ever, Scott Fitz	*As Ever, Scott Fitz: Letters Between F. Scott Fitzgerald and His Literary Agent, Harold Ober 1919–1940* (ed. Bruccoli and McCabe Atkinson)
Bits	*Bits of Paradise*
Correspondence	*The Correspondence of F. Scott Fitzgerald* (ed. Bruccoli and Duggan)
Crack-Up	*The Crack-Up* (ed. Wilson)
Dear Scott/Dear Max	*Dear Scott/Dear Max: The Fitzgerald–Perkins Correspondence* (ed. Kuehl and Bryer)
Ledger	*F. Scott Fitzgerald's Ledger* (ed. Bruccoli)
Letters	*The Letters of F. Scott Fitzgerald* (ed. Turnbull)
Life in Letters	*F. Scott Fitzgerald: A Life in Letters* (ed. Bruccoli)
Notebooks	*The Notebooks of F. Scott Fitzgerald* (ed. Bruccoli)
Price	*The Price Was High: The Last Uncollected Stories of F. Scott Fitzgerald* (ed. Bruccoli)
Short Stories	*The Short Stories of F. Scott Fitzgerald: A New Collection* (ed. Bruccoli)
Stories	*The Stories of F. Scott Fitzgerald*

CHRONOLOGY

1896   Francis Scott Key Fitzgerald is born on September 24, the first
        surviving child (two others having died) of Edward Fitzgerald
        and Mollie McQuillan, at 481 Laurel Avenue, St. Paul,
        Minnesota.
1898   Edward Fitzgerald's wicker furniture business fails, and the
        Fitzgerald family moves to Buffalo, New York, where
        Edward Fitzgerald is employed by Proctor & Gamble as a
        salesman.
1901   The family moves again, to Syracuse, New York. Later that year,
        Fitzgerald's sister, Annabel, is born.
1903   The family moves back to Buffalo.
1908   After Edward Fitzgerald loses his job in Buffalo, the family returns
        to St. Paul where F. Scott Fitzgerald enrolls in St. Paul Academy.
1909   Fitzgerald's first story, "The Mystery of the Raymond Mortgage,"
        is published in the St. Paul Academy's *Now and Then*.
1911   Fitzgerald enrolls in the Newman School in Hackensack,
        New Jersey. From 1911 to 1913 he writes and produces four
        plays and publishes three stories in the *Newman School News*
        before his graduation in 1913.
1913   Fitzgerald enters Princeton University as a member of the Class
        of 1917. He meets Edmund Wilson and John Peale Bishop. He
        begins to participate in literary and dramatic activities. He writes
        the book and lyrics for a Triangle Club show and contributes
        the lyrics for two others. His stories, plays, and poems are
        published in the *Nassau Literary Magazine* and *Princeton Tiger*
        between 1914 and 1918.
1914   Fitzgerald meets and falls in love with sixteen-year-old Ginevra
        King, from a wealthy Lake Forest, Illinois, family, while on
        Christmas holiday. He would correspond with and see her on
        occasion until she ends their relationship in August 1916.

1915   Fitzgerald leaves Princeton, citing illness, but actually because of his poor grades that resulted from his concentration on extracurricular activities.

1916   Fitzgerald returns to Princeton, planning to graduate in 1918.

1917   Fitzgerald joins the army as second lieutenant in October, reporting to Fort Leavenworth, Kansas, in November for training. He starts work on a novel he calls "The Romantic Egotist."

1918   Fitzgerald is transferred to Camp Taylor in Louisville, Kentucky, in February; some weeks later he completes a first draft of "The Romantic Egotist" and sends it off to Charles Scribner's Sons, publishers. In April, he is stationed at Camp Gordon, Georgia, and in June is transferred to Camp Sheridan near Montgomery, Alabama. He meets Zelda Sayre, popular daughter of an Alabama Supreme Court Associate Justice, at a Montgomery Country-Club dance in July. Scribner's rejects his novel in August; Fitzgerald then revises and resubmits it, but that version is also rejected in October. He is sent to Camp Mills on Long Island, New York, in November, to await overseas duty, but the war's end prevents his departure.

1919   After his February discharge from the army, and now engaged to Zelda, Fitzgerald finds work in an advertising agency in New York City. On a visit to Zelda in June, she breaks their engagement because his future seems insecure to her. Fitzgerald resigns from his job and leaves for St. Paul, where he lives at his parents' house while rewriting his novel. His novel, now called *This Side of Paradise*, is accepted by Scribners in September and he begins to find acceptance for magazine stories that were earlier rejected.

1920   Fitzgerald and Zelda Sayre become engaged again in January. Between January and March, Fitzgerald publishes three short stories and a play in *Smart Set* and two stories in the *Saturday Evening Post*. On March 26, *This Side of Paradise* is published. Fitzgerald and Zelda Sayre are married on April 3 in the rectory of St. Patrick's Cathedral in New York City. They live in Westport, Connecticut, from May to September. *Flappers and Philosophers*, his first short-story collection, is published in September. The couple move to New York City in October.

1921   The Fitzgeralds travel abroad in England, France, and Italy from May to September. In August they return to St. Paul, where in October their daughter Frances Scott (Scottie) is born.

1922 Fitzgerald's second novel, *The Beautiful and Damned*, is published in March and his second collection of stories, *Tales of the Jazz Age*, appears in September. In October, the family moves to a rented house in Great Neck, Long Island, a wealthy community about twenty-five miles from New York City.

1923 In April, Fitzgerald's play, *The Vegetable*, is published, but in November it fails in a try-out production in Atlantic City, New Jersey.

1924 The Fitzgeralds embark for France in April, and reside in St. Raphael on the French Riviera. During that summer, Zelda and Edouard Jozan, a French aviator, are romantically attached, which Fitzgerald sees as a serious betrayal. In late October, the family travels to Italy where Fitzgerald revises his new novel.

1925 On April 10, *The Great Gatsby* is published. A few weeks later, the Fitzgeralds rent a Paris apartment. In May, Fitzgerald meets Ernest Hemingway at the Dingo Bar in Montparnasse. In July, Fitzgerald meets Edith Wharton at her home outside Paris.

1926 A third collection of short stories, *All the Sad Young Men*, is published in February. The Fitzgeralds return to the Riviera where they reside until they sail back to America in December.

1927 Scott and Zelda leave Scottie with his parents and travel to Hollywood, where he has been hired to write a screenplay for a flapper film, "Lipstick," which is never produced. He meets a beautiful young actress, Lois Moran, to whom he is visibly attracted. In March, the Fitzgeralds rent a large home, Ellerslie, near Wilmington, Delaware, and Zelda begins to take lessons in ballet.

1928 In April, the Fitzgeralds return to Paris, where Zelda continues her ballet lessons. They return to Ellerslie in September.

1929 In March, the Fitzgerald family returns to Europe, traveling to Italy and the Riviera before renting an apartment in Paris in October. Zelda resumes her ballet lessons in Paris.

1930 The Fitzgeralds travel to North Africa in February and then return to Paris, where in March friends notice Zelda's intense concentration on ballet. Fitzgerald tries to focus on his new novel, and writes a number of short stories that defray their expenses. In late April, Zelda suffers her first nervous breakdown and enters the Malmaison Clinic outside the city. Several weeks later, she is moved to Valmont Clinic in Switzerland and in June to another Swiss clinic, Prangins. Fitzgerald lives in Switzerland during the summer and fall.

1931   Fitzgerald returns to the United States for his father's funeral in February. He visits Montgomery to inform Zelda's family of her condition. On his return to Europe at the end of the month, she is considerably improved, and by September, after her release from Prangins, they move back to Montgomery, where they rent a house. In the fall, Fitzgerald accepts Metro-Goldwyn-Mayer's offer to go to Hollywood to work on a screenplay for Jean Harlow.

1932   Zelda's condition deteriorates at the beginning of the year and in February, she is admitted to Phipps Clinic at Johns Hopkins University Hospital in Baltimore. Fitzgerald returns to his daughter in Montgomery. In May, Fitzgerald rents La Paix, a house near Baltimore, where Zelda, on her release from Phipps in June, joins him. Her novel, *Save Me the Waltz*, which she completed while at Phipps, is published.

1933–4   After completing his novel, *Tender is the Night*, Fitzgerald moves from La Paix to a town house in Baltimore in December 1933. His novel is published the following April. Zelda has another breakdown in January 1934 and is admitted to Sheppard-Pratt Hospital outside Baltimore. In March she enters Craig House in Beacon, New York, but is sent back to Sheppard-Pratt in May.

1935   Fitzgerald, ill, stays at a hotel in Tryon and then in Asheville, North Carolina. *Taps at Reveille*, his fourth collection of short stories, is published in March. In September he moves to an apartment in downtown Baltimore, and then moves to Hendersonville, North Carolina, for the winter, where he starts writing the *Crack-Up* essays.

1936   Zelda is hospitalized in Asheville in April, and in July, Fitzgerald returns to the Grove Park Inn in Asheville where he had stayed previously. Fitzgerald's mother dies in September.

1937   Fitzgerald moves to the Oak Park Inn in Tryon for six months; in need of money, he accepts an offer from Metro-Goldwyn-Mayer studios for a six-month contract in Hollywood. In July, he meets gossip columnist Sheilah Graham, and they begin a relationship that lasts until his death. In the summer he starts the script for *Three Comrades* (the only screen credit he would receive). The studio renews his contract in December for another year.

1938   Fitzgerald moves several times in California, from the Garden of Allah Hotel, to Malibu, to Encino, where he lives in a cottage on the estate of actor Edward Everett Horton. His MGM contract is not renewed in December.

1939 In February 1939, producer Walter Wanger hires him to work with writer Budd Schulberg on a script for a new film, *Winter Carnival*. The two go to Dartmouth College where Wanger fires Fitzgerald for drinking. He recovers in a New York City hospital, returns to California, and works as a freelance scriptwriter. In October, he begins work on a new novel about Hollywood.

1940 Zelda is released from Highland Hospital in North Carolina in April and returns to Montgomery to her mother's home. Fitzgerald dies of a heart attack on December 21, 1940, at Sheilah Graham's apartment in Hollywood. He is buried in Rockville Union Cemetery, Maryland, on December 27.

1947–8 Zelda reenters Highland Hospital in November and dies in a fire there on March 10, 1948.

1975 F. Scott Fitzgerald and his wife, Zelda, were reburied in the cemetery of St. Mary's Church in Rockville, Maryland. In 1986, their daughter Scottie was buried with her parents.

I

RUTH PRIGOZY

Introduction: Scott, Zelda, and the culture of celebrity

F. Scott Fitzgerald is one of the most recognized figures in American literary and cultural history, not only as one of the major writers of the twentieth century, but also as a man whose life story excites the fascination of a public that knows him primarily as the author of *The Great Gatsby*. Any study of Fitzgerald's career must trace its familiar trajectory: early success, then public oblivion, and finally posthumous resurrection; had he lived a few years longer, he might have proved the exception to his own belief that there are no second acts in American lives. Fitzgerald's life and work were intertwined from the very beginning; his career spanned one of the most turbulent eras of the century, and from the very start he was part creator, part victim of the new culture of celebrity which accompanied the rise of modern technology. His fame and his marriage coincided, and so today, as in the 1920s, the names of F. Scott and Zelda Fitzgerald are linked in public perception; indeed, for the last three-quarters of a century they have been indissolubly tied to American popular culture.

Scarcely a week passes that we do not notice an allusion to one or both of them in our mass media. In a bestselling paperback mystery, a leading character marries a beautiful but hopelessly mad woman who slashes the bathroom mirror with lipstick before shattering it, and then collapses bleeding on the floor. He later tells his friend, "I've got Zelda for a wife" (Patterson, *Escape the Night*, 1984, 31). In a 1970s film, *Getting Straight*, the protagonist, played by Elliott Gould, rebels against his questioners at an MA oral examination when they state that Nick Carraway and Gatsby have a homosexual relationship, that Jordan Baker is probably a lesbian, and that Fitzgerald, Gould's favorite author, was driven by "a terrible need to express homosexual panic through his characters." The candidate, outraged yet afraid at first to offend his mentors, finally retorts, "It's possible . . . but it's gonna be a surprise to Sheilah Graham. Sheilah is not gonna believe that." (Sheilah Graham was Fitzgerald's lover during the last three years of his life.) He then explodes in fury, throws away his academic career, salvaging his soul in the process.

And in the fall of 1993, the Turner Network presented *Zelda*, a barely fictionalized television drama on the Fitzgeralds' troubled marriage, with the glamorous Natasha Richardson in the title role and Timothy Hutton as Fitzgerald. (Both actors playing the diminutive Fitzgeralds are over six feet tall, suggesting perhaps contemporary media inflation of celebrities.) The three examples, drawn from three mass media, are not unique. Fitzgerald has been played on the screen by Gregory Peck (1959), on television by Jason Miller (Tuesday Weld was Zelda, [1976]), and countless one-man and one-woman shows have played throughout the country purporting to disclose the inner struggles of either Scott or Zelda. For better or worse, mostly worse, they are part of our lives, appropriated probably forever into mainstream American culture.

Why Scott and Zelda? Other major American writers from Mark Twain and Jack London to Ernest Hemingway have entered the public's consciousness without the spousal link. Indeed, although she was a more talented writer than Zelda, there has never been, to my knowledge, a conference dedicated to Martha (Gellhorn) and Ernest Hemingway. Clearly the Fitzgeralds' lives together had a mythic quality, and their symbiosis made both their successes and their tragedies, like the actors who impersonate them today, larger than life. As Mary Gordon has remarked, "The case of Zelda and Scott Fitzgerald... as creator and object of creation, may be unique in the history of literature – at least in the history of literary married couples" (Introduction, Zelda Fitzgerald, *The Collected Writings*, xvii). Further, they were extraordinarily attractive, and both worked studiously at developing public personalities that at first enchanted and later repelled the audience they had always courted. Fitzgerald had, as Scott Donaldson has noted (*Fool for Love*, 190), a "histrionic" personality, which coincided with Zelda's lifelong need for self-dramatization. So they became popular culture icons, and the story, so irresistible in its dimensions, has become fixed in the imagination of a mass public larger and more curious than they had ever imagined. There is another dimension to the connection between the Fitzgeralds and American popular culture: Fitzgerald knew and liked that culture, he drew on the stories of his youth to retell episodes from his own life, he was a fan of movies, musical comedy, popular songs, songwriters and stars, and the study of the Fitzgeralds and popular culture involves a dialectic between their public performance and public image on the one hand and their use of popular culture in their creative language on the other.

Popular culture may be over-simply but usefully referred to as one "well-liked or widely favored by many people" (Storey, *Introductory Guide*, 7). Certainly in twentieth-century America it has been a commercial culture created for mass consumption, and a culture whose "texts and practices... are seen as forms of public fantasy... a collective dream world" (Storey,

Introductory Guide, 11). Popular culture is not a fixed entity; it emerged after the industrial revolution and the urbanization of America, and because it is not historically fixed, it is highly responsive to economic and social change. It is often distinguished from "high culture," but the cross-over is not only from "high" to "popular" but the reverse as well. (And we have not even mentioned the category of "pulp" which too has managed to infiltrate formerly fixed categories.) Popular culture, in the world of the twenties, meant the illustrated magazines (a negligible element in contemporary life), newspapers, bestsellers, drama, radio, and movies. As technology grew and shifted throughout the twentieth century, television largely supplanted popular magazines and forced changes in movies and the moviegoing public. Thus, any discussion of the Fitzgeralds and popular culture inevitably reflects the changes in that culture throughout the twentieth century.

The relationship between the Fitzgeralds and American cultural life may be traced through three stages that reflect their popular image in the twentieth century: first, the creation of the legendary couple in the mass media of the 1920s and their disappearance during the Depression; second, the Fitzgerald revival of the 1950s signaled by the almost simultaneous publication of Budd Schulberg's *The Disenchanted* and Arthur Mizener's *The Far Side of Paradise*, and lasting through the 1960s; and third, the revisionist legend, propelled by Nancy Milford's biography of Zelda, from the 1970s to the present day. In the uneasy alliance between a writer and the vast audience to which he or she aspires, the relationship between a successful writer and the public is never simple. Whether he or she courts its favor and develops the kind of persona suitable to a mainstream audience, like Hemingway,[1] Fitzgerald, and Mailer, or rejects it and remains personally unrecognizable like Bellow or in an extreme case, Salinger (although his hermetic existence exerts its own fascination on an admittedly smaller public), the public arena is seductive, the rewards for personal notoriety great, and the temptations eternal. For Fitzgerald, there was never a doubt.

The Fitzgeralds create a legend

That Scott and Zelda Fitzgerald throughout their life together were acutely conscious of their public image, is attested to by their scrapbooks, into which they pasted newspaper articles about themselves as well as brief mentions, photographs from magazines and newspapers together with others from their own collections, reviews of Fitzgerald's books, films adapted from books and stories, theater reviews of his play and dramatic adaptations, Zelda's varied artistic endeavors, and even advertisements which alluded to either of them. Near the end of his life, Fitzgerald pasted in his scrapbook clippings which compared other writers to him, or even mentioned his name in passing, heading the page, "The Melody Lingers On" (Bruccoli *et al.*, *Romantic Egoists*, 204–5). From the start, immediately following the success of *This Side of Paradise* (1920), the Fitzgeralds courted public attention, and in that quest, the press was a strong ally in creating their public personas. Today we are accustomed to manipulation of the press by celebrities, but in the twenties, only a skilled self-publicist could dictate the form his public image would take, and the Fitzgeralds had an innate instinct about their own popular appeal. Critics have noted that even a close friend of Fitzgerald, Alex McKaig, was distrustful of the couple's antics – even those likeliest to provoke a storm of criticism. He wondered if the couple's brawls were "all aimed to hand down the Fitzgerald legend" to a public eager to read of their exploits.[2] After Scott's death, Zelda wrote to Scottie, "Daddy loved glamour & I also had a great respect for popular acclaim" (quoted in Mellow, *Invented Lives*, 491), so it is fair to conclude that much of what they did in those apparently unthinking times in the twenties was in some way aimed at keeping their image alive for the public and further enhancing their legend.

James Mellow's description of their "invented lives" is only half the story; popular culture itself dictated the terms of that invention, and Fitzgerald was, from childhood, adept at self-promotion. In "My Lost City" (1932), he remembers how the "offices of editors and publishers were open to me, impresarios begged plays, the movies panted for screen material. To my bewilderment, I was adopted...as the arch type [*sic*] of what New York wanted." He recalls that he

> was pushed into the position not only of spokesman for the time but of the typical product of that same moment. I, or rather it was "we" now, did not know exactly what New York expected of us and found it rather confusing. Within a few months after our embarkation on the Metropolitan venture we scarcely knew anymore who we were and we hadn't a notion what we were. A dive into a civic fountain, a casual brush with the law, was enough to get us into the gossip columns... ("My Lost City," *Crack-Up*, 27)

And he reveals what the publicity, the notoriety, the public life meant to him: success is linked with "eternal youth" (33). The narrator of that and other autobiographical essays, Fitzgerald's literary persona, is recasting earlier events as part of a lifelong pattern of constructing a popular image; we cannot take at face value his apparent bewilderment at his notoriety. As Budd Schulberg has noted, "He himself had been a prime mover in this god-making and god-smashing" (*Four Seasons*, 142).

Fitzgerald was a keen observer of the cultural marketplace. He once suggested to Scribners that they reprint Scribner titles in low-priced editions, suggesting that "known titles in the series" would "carry the little known or forgotten"(*Life in Letters*, 57–8). He decided to remake his image before *Gatsby* appeared, writing to his editor at Scribners, Maxwell Perkins, "I'm tired of being the author of *This Side of Paradise* and I want to start over" (*Life in Letters*, 84). He was an expert judge of advertising, and directed his publisher where to advertise his books, and what kind of blurbs, if any, were to be printed on the jackets. And he advised Ernest Hemingway, no amateur at creating his own legend, that a published Hemingway parody "would make you quite conscious of your public existence" (*Life in Letters*, 151). His investment in his self-created image was so great that we can comprehend and sympathize with his outrage over Zelda's effort to tell their story in *Save Me the Waltz*: "My God, my books made her a legend and her single intention in this somewhat thin portrait is to make me a non-entity" (*Life in Letters*, 209). So intent was Fitzgerald on controlling the public's perception of him, that he wrote suggesting to Perkins in 1933 how his new novel should be advertised so as to preserve the precarious balance he always sought between the popular figure and the serious writer:

> For several years the impression has prevailed that Scott Fitzgerald had abandoned the writing of novels and in the future would continue to write only popular short stories. His publishers knew different and they are very glad now to be able to present a book which is in line with his three other highly successful and highly esteemed novels, thus demonstrating that Scott Fitzgerald is anything but through as a serious novelist. (*Life in Letters*, 241)

What was the public image of the Fitzgeralds in the 1920s, and how did it arise? Clearly, the daily press, in feature stories, news articles (public relations pieces), photos and gossip columns, and the popular magazines with their lavish illustrations, were the prime shapers of the legend of F. Scott and Zelda Fitzgerald.

From the outset, the Fitzgeralds readily granted interviews to reporters. Their physical attractiveness was a key element in their successful seduction of the media. One reporter marvels at the "blue-eyed, frank-faced, fastidiously dressed author" (Bruccoli and Bryer, *In His Own Time*, 256), and another notes Zelda's beauty, concluding, "The two of them might have stepped, sophisticated and charming, from the pages of any of the Fitzgerald books" (Bruccoli and Bryer, *In His Own Time*, 278). A woman reporter confesses archly after noting how handsome Fitzgerald is, "My interest was perhaps a bit more than professional" (Bruccoli and Bryer, *In His Own*

Time, 278). Thomas Boyd's 1922 description is representative of the journalist's vision of the author:

> His eyes were blue and clear; his jaw was squared at the end which perceptibly protruded; his nose was straight and his mouth, though sensitive looking, was regular in outline. His hair which was corn-colored, was wavy. His were the features that the average American mind never fails to associate with beauty. But there was a quality in the eye with which the average mind is unfamiliar. (Bruccoli and Bryer, *In His Own Time*, 247)

That last quality is, of course, intellect, or genius, and Fitzgerald sought to portray himself as both hedonistic and intellectual at the same time. Boyd concludes, "To be with him for an hour is to have the blood in one's veins thawed and made fluent" (Bruccoli and Bryer, *In His Own Time*, 252). Years later, when Fitzgerald could no longer control the press and his own public persona, he was to read Michel Mok's notorious description which stands in such stark and painful contrast to those of a decade earlier: "His trembling hands, his twitching face with its pitiful expression of a cruelly beaten child" (Bruccoli and Bryer, *In His Own Time*, 294).

As the image of the fun-loving Fitzgeralds captured the public imagination, Fitzgerald would consistently remind readers that he was a serious writer. (Later, when his exploits became less attractive, and his need for the money that his stories brought in became greater, he tried to distance himself from the image he had so consciously created in the early 1920s, and to remind his public that he was a writer first.) Even in the earliest interviews, he called attention to his drinking, which was not nearly the problem then that it would become in just a few years. On the one hand, he boasts of drinking, and on the other asserts that he does not let it interfere with his artistry. He cannot drink and write, he tells Boyd, "For me, narcotics are deadening to work. I can understand anyone drinking coffee to get a stimulating effect, but whiskey – oh, no" (Bruccoli and Bryer, *In His Own Time*, 253). In "The Author's Apology," which appeared in the third printing of *This Side of Paradise* (April 1920) distributed to the American Booksellers Association convention, however, Fitzgerald, under an extremely flattering photograph, advises them to "consider all the cocktails mentioned in this book drunk by me as a toast to the American Booksellers Association" (Bruccoli and Bryer, *In His Own Time*, 164). In 1926, he was quoted in the *New Yorker*, "Don't you know I am one of the most notorious drinkers of the younger generation?" (Bruccoli and Bryer, *In His Own Time*, 443). And in 1929, he published a clever, tongue-in-cheek "A Short Autobiography" in the *New Yorker*, tracing his life from 1913 through the present in terms of varied alcoholic beverages consumed through the years.

The same interview pattern was repeated so frequently that it seems clear it was orchestrated by the Fitzgeralds and the press. After answering the obligatory questions on the current state of flapperdom, Fitzgerald would launch a stream of apparently spontaneous observations on the state of the world, on marriage, on the modern woman, on writers both classical and modern, on the Leopold–Loeb case, and even on the future of America from a Spenglerian perspective. His magazine pieces attempt to shock (mildly, of course) the mass-audience readership, but more important, to establish Fitzgerald as the authority on male–female relationships of the era, unafraid to reject the sexual codes which were no longer as widely held as both he and the reporters would have the reader believe. The Fitzgeralds were challenging public notions of sexual morality in the traditionally conservative, pseudo-rebellious fashion characteristic of the popular media. None of their apparently outrageous remarks would have been truly shocking to the audience reading their breezy comments in *Metropolitan,* or the *New York Evening World.* Indeed, remarks like, "I believe in early marriage, easy divorce and several children" (Bruccoli and Bryer, *In His Own Time,* 184) are thrown out for their shock effect with no serious discussion of their implications. He was not a bit perturbed when a reporter said, "He is an actor...vivacious, imaginative, forceful – slightly imbalanced. The latter is his chief charm" (Bruccoli and Bryer, *In His Own Time,* 416). Fitzgerald played at publicity with childlike ingenuousness, little suspecting that a sensation-seeking biography seventy years later would devote pages to his public and probably facetious confession of a "pedentia complex" (Bruccoli and Bryer, *In His Own Time,* 416), his exaggeration of his psychological quirk as a four-year-old-child (*Ledger,* 155). As in *Vanity Fair* articles today, the reader's interest is piqued, but the "shocking" revelations generally prove to be far less revealing than the headlines and advertising suggest. In this particular instance, the biographical accuracy of Jeffrey Meyers's discovery of Fitzgerald's "foot fetish" and all of its psychosexual implications is highly questionable. He writes, to confirm his assertions, that Frances Ring (Fitzgerald's secretary during his last years) told him that Fitzgerald "always wore slippers and never went about in bare feet" (Meyers, *Scott Fitzgerald,* 13). Mrs. Ring told me[3] that she was asked by this biographer what kind of clothes Fitzgerald wore, and she replied, that because he arose late and preferred to work before he dressed, he usually wore a bathrobe and slippers during the day. She was horrified, she says, to find her words distorted to support the lurid conjectures of her interviewer. She also explains Sheilah Graham's remarks about Fitzgerald's not taking his shoes and socks off at the beach (Graham, *Rest of the Story,* 33) as stemming not from a "mysterious shyness" (he had told Sheilah about his childhood complex), but from his extreme hypochondria in his last years. He was always worried about TB, about colds, about flu, and indeed, did not play tennis and swim with Sheilah at their Malibu home. In support of Mrs. Ring's version, we should look at the photographs of Fitzgerald with bare – and well-formed – feet clearly displayed at the beach in four photographs reprinted in Bruccoli et al., *The Romantic Egoists*, in Hyères in 1924 (117), in Vevey in 1930 (177), at Lake Annecy in 1936 (181), and at Myrtle Beach in 1938 (219). Thus do myths begin and grow until they enter into popular culture. This particular one is foolish and irrelevant, but it is a good example of the kind of mythologizing to which the lives of the Fitzgeralds have been subjected over the years.

Interviews with Zelda and her own pieces for the popular press from this period are designed to reinforce the public's perception of the two Fitzgeralds as overgrown children having a riotous good time, very much in love, and happily married. Her apparent unconventionality (masking the real disturbances she experienced) is part of her charm, and in no way threatens her marriage or her role as wife and later mother. Indeed, Zelda is for her public the new flapper grown up. (The flapper was the new young woman of the 1920s, considered bold and unconventional.) One of the popular essays published under Fitzgerald's name, but written by Zelda, states that flapperdom is a necessary brief period in a young woman's development that will better prepare her to be safely settled as wife and mother. Zelda writes (in Scott's name), "I believe in the flapper as an artist in her objective field, the art of being – being young, being lovely, being an *object*" (italics mine) (Bruccoli and Bryer, *In His Own Time*, 398). In another flapper piece, she argues that if women are allowed to be free and to express themselves fully when young, there will be fewer divorces and women will be content to marry and settle down (Bruccoli and Bryer, *In His Own Time*, 392). Zelda publicly presents herself as a partner in the Fitzgeralds' life-as-extravaganza. Her tongue-in-cheek review of *The Beautiful and Damned* offers as the reason why people should purchase the book the "aesthetic" one that "there is the cutest cloth-of-gold dress for only three hundred dollars in a store on forty-second street" (Zelda Fitzgerald, *Collected Writings*, 387). Zelda never challenges the frivolous, Southern belle persona publicly. (All of the interviewers comment admiringly on her Southern drawl, her indolence around the house, her easy charm.) And as early as 1924, both of the Fitzgeralds were eager to tell the world that Zelda was a writer too, with a "queer decadent style. Scott incorporates whole chapters of his wife's writing into his own books" (Bruccoli and Bryer, *In His Own Time*, 419). Just as everything else they wrote and enacted for public consumption is exaggerated, if not a set of elaborate fantasies, we should note that the source of contemporary mythology surrounding Fitzgerald's putative use of Zelda's material lies in the couple's public role-playing, as fabricated as everything else they concocted for public consumption in those days. That mythology is no less suspect than such early Fitzgerald public pronouncements as "I am a pessimist, a communist (with Nietschean overtones), have no hobbies except conversation – and I am trying to repress that" (Bruccoli and Bryer, *In His Own Time*, 270). Similarly, in a 1928 interview (where he again boasts of his drinking prowess), he informs the reporter that "happiness consists of the performances of all the natural functions, with one exception – that of growing old. Sunday, Washington, D.C., cold weather, Bohemians, the managing type of American woman, avarice, and dullness are his principal dislikes" (Bruccoli and Bryer, *In His Own Time*, 282). His confessional public pronouncements in the 1920s, so essentially different from those of the 1930s, must be seen, for the most part, as coyly self-conscious celebrity exaggerations.

Magazine illustrations and photographs in newspapers and magazines also helped feed the Fitzgeralds' mythmaking enterprise. Perhaps the most characteristic shot of the couple was originally published in *Hearst's International* in 1923 (Bruccoli *et al.*, *Romantic Egoists*, 105) along with the often reproduced photo of the family in their Paris apartment at Christmas. The Fitzgeralds were not only good-looking, but they were ideally suited to the 1920s' need for models illustrating the culture of youth, and they exploited their own personal appeal accordingly. Their pictures accompanied the movie magazine articles written during their 1927 trip to Hollywood. Magazine illustrations of Fitzgerald's fictional heroes all look like taller versions of Fitzgerald, and all of his characters, whether true to the story or not, are dressed in elegant evening clothes. John Held Jr. cartoons accompany their dual articles on "What Became of Our Flappers and Sheiks" for *McCall's* (October, 1925, Bruccoli *et al.*, *Romantic Egoists*, 132–3), and James Montgomery Flagg's glamorized drawing of Scott and Zelda accompany the *College Humor* 1928 essay, "Looking Back Eight Years" (Bruccoli *et al.*, *Romantic Egoists*, 162–3). The headline for a Westport, Connecticut, newspaper photograph of the Fitzgeralds in 1920 is "Illustrating His Own Title!" (Bruccoli *et al.*, *Romantic Egoists*, 72). The caption continues, "This fortunate youngster has won not only an enviable reputation as a writer but also an undeniably charming wife to share with him the joys of 'This Side of Paradise'." The comic essay, "The Cruise of the Rolling Junk" for *Motor* magazine (1924), is accompanied by photos of the Fitzgeralds in matching white touring outfits which were to scandalize observers in small Southern towns on the route to Montgomery (Meyers, *Scott Fitzgerald*, 69). Fitzgerald's famous profile adorned advertisements for his novels, and in the advertisement for *Scribner's Magazine*'s serialization of *Tender is the Night*, "Richard Diver: A Romance" (January 1934, Bruccoli *et al.*, *Romantic*

Egoists, 194), the portrait forever links the author and the hero of his novel. Further publicity photographs for the novel use *both* Fitzgeralds, in recognition of the public's memory of the couple when both commanded attention. Perhaps the most memorable illustration of the Fitzgeralds was Reginald Marsh's drawing for the drop curtain of *Greenwich Village Follies* showing Zelda's dive into a downtown New York fountain and Fitzgerald with a group of young literary celebrities riding down Seventh Avenue. Photographers and illustrators could not resist their appeal; as John Dos Passos described them, "There was a golden innocence about them and they both were so hopelessly good looking" (Mellow, *Invented Lives*, 161). Virtually every reporter commented on his coloring, her complexion, their eyes, and their style. Zelda was, in those years, Scott's equal in physical attractiveness, and the combination of outrageous behavior, youthful exuberance, and personal beauty secured their place in the public eye.

Their public image was further enlarged by the gossip columnists who reported their exploits, by occasional editorials criticizing Fitzgerald's "attempts to be an aristocrat" (Louisville *Courier-Journal*, April 4, 17, 1922; Bruccoli and Bryer, *In His Own Time*, 410), and above all by the impression they made on their circle of friends and acquaintances who would remember, with Donald Ogden Stewart, "I felt like some embarrassed spectator caught by the unexpected rising of the curtain on the stage of a comedy in which the two stars were competing for the spotlight" (*Fitzgerald/Hemingway Annual* [1971], 179); or with Gilbert Seldes, who recalled, "The two most beautiful people in the world were floating toward me" (Milford, *Zelda*, 127). As Scott himself wrote in sad retrospection,

> There'd be an orchestra
>   Bingo! Bango!
> Playing for us
>   To dance the tango,
> And people would clap
>   When we arose,
> At her sweet face
>   And my new clothes.   (*Crack-Up*, 159)

Fitzgerald's early magazine pieces are pseudo-confessionals where he eagerly seizes on whatever print opportunities are available to define himself for his public. Thus "Who's Who – and Why" (1920) (his first public print appearance for a mass audience – readers of the *Saturday Evening Post*) also marks the beginning of his self-created legend, shrewdly rewriting the text of his life so that, for example, there is no hint of his dismal performance at Princeton. The essay is a brief autobiography culminating in an account of his brilliant success, written as though in dazed wonder, but there is considerable calculation behind the simple recitation (*Afternoon*, 83–6). Similarly, his mock confessionals, "How to Live on $36,000 a Year" (*Saturday Evening Post*, April 5, 1924) and "How To Live on Practically Nothing a Year" (*Saturday Evening Post*, September 20, 1924) are ironic and humorously self-deprecating, yet convey the excitement, a "kind of unconscious joy," the couple experienced in those early years. Their self-revelation was itself self-creation in its most extreme form. The author's stated fear in 1922 of "conventionality, dullness, sameness, predictability" (Bruccoli and Bryer, *In His Own Time*, 213), his lack of patience with the older generation, his distaste for the parasitic leisure class, the diatribe against education for women, along with his advice to insure that the new generation will avoid the fate of its elders, is Fitzgerald's way of seizing public attention at the outset, and then, forced by the confessions themselves, to continually raise the stakes, until the lives of the Fitzgeralds (which later would include their daughter) soon became the popular myth they had always planned, but larger, and ultimately more destructive to them than they could realize at the outset. Fitzgerald quotes in "My Lost City" (*Crack-Up*, 28) a headline he read years earlier "in astonishment": "Fitzgerald Knocks Officer This Side of Paradise." He notes his difficulty remembering this and other exploits from the heady period of his success, admits ruefully how ephemeral that success was, and at the same time, he attempts to cast an elegiac glow on events that might have been too humiliating and self-destructive to report unless they were transmuted into a portion of the ongoing legend of his life.

The Fitzgeralds were equally aware of other popular media. As a young boy, Fitzgerald was captivated with the theater, and described in his scrapbook his first appearance in a play, "The Coward" (1913) as "The great event" (Bruccoli *et al.*, *Romantic Egoists*, 18). The theatrical season in New York in the 1920s was particularly exciting to a young man who had long worshiped musical comedy and had written his own at Princeton. Zelda's love of the theater was as intense as Scott's, and her self-dramatization was integral to her personality at a young age. When these two people at the height of their success met the Broadway of the 1920s, the effect on both was electric. They saw Ina Claire, Theda Bara, Marilyn Miller, and the Barrymores, and in their delight at the dramatic spectacles, they were moved to enact dramas of their own. A public greedy for stories about celebrity hijinks relished the dramatic antics of the Fitzgeralds which gossip columnists painted in expectedly sensational colors. Today we cannot dissever the real from the fabricated, so successful were they at self-publicizing. But they have surely provided fodder for the few contemporary biographers seeking to sensationalize and in the process trivialize their lives.

Fitzgerald's interest in the theater remained unabated throughout his lifetime, although his involvement in Hollywood drew his attention to that popular medium. He was enormously pleased by the success of Owen Davis's stage version of *Gatsby*, directed by George Cukor in 1926 ("Cukor's Breakthrough," McGilligan, *George Cukor: A Double Life*, 52), particularly since the theatrical world "had not anticipated such a shrewd adaptation" by a playwright "best known for his hundreds of cheap melodramas and Hippodrome extravaganzas" (*George Cukor: A Double Life*, 52). The play had a substantial run, 113 performances, some compensation for the failure of his own work, *The Vegetable* (1923), which had a disastrous opening night when the audience walked out during the second-act fantasy (Bruccoli, *Some Sort of Epic Grandeur*, 187).

Fitzgerald was a movie fan too. As Schulberg has noted, he "believed in film as an ideal art form for reaching out to millions who might never have read a serious novel" (*Four Seasons*, 98). Movies, for Fitzgerald, were foremost a popular entertainment. He declared in 1921, "I like to see a pleasant flapper like Constance Talmadge or I want to see comedies like those of Chaplin's or Lloyd's. I'm not strong for the uplift stuff. It simply isn't life to me" (Bruccoli and Bryer, *In His Own Time*, 245). He was always looking for opportunities to see his work adapted for film, remarking to Perkins in 1924 that he thought he had hard luck with the movies. "I must try some love stories with more action this time," he wrote (*Life in Letters*, 82). Before the publication of *Gatsby* he was interested in moving-picture bids, and in 1936, he proposed to Harold Ober a movie about a ballet dancer based on Zelda's life (*Life in Letters*, 297). "Of course," he wrote, "the tragic ending of Zelda's story need not be repeated in the picture. One could concede to the picture people the fact that the girl might become a popular dancer in the Folies Bergère" (*Life in Letters*, 296). He proposed an alternative ending that reveals how well he understood the popular marketplace: "One could conceive of a pathetic ending à la Hepburn in which because of her idealism she went on being a fifth rate 'figurine' in ballets all over Europe – this to be balanced by a compensatory love story which would make up for her the failure of her work" (*Life in Letters*, 296). Fitzgerald maintained a lifelong admiration for D.W. Griffith (Prigozy, "From Griffith's Girls to *Daddy's Girl*"). He recalls in 1935 how as a young author in the 1920s he had tried to interest Griffith in a film about Hollywood and a studio romance (*Life in Letters*, 297), indicating how apt a student he was of public taste, for shortly thereafter such self-reflexive films as *What Price Hollywood?* (1932) and *A Star Is Born* (1937) showed how accurately he took the public pulse. Beginning with the sale of "Head and Shoulders" (1920) to Metro Studios for $2,500 as a vehicle for the popular actress, Viola Dana (produced as *The Chorus*

Girl's Romance, 1920), Fitzgerald was tireless in seeking opportunities to see his fiction translated into film. Indeed, in the same year, he sold the options for "Myra Meets His Family" (1920) and "The Offshore Pirate" (1920), and signed a contract with Metro for future film rights to his short stories. His lifelong association with Hollywood would last until his death. In 1939, whether it was true or not, he was proud to inform Harold Ober that Alfred Hitchcock had put him at the top of his list as a possible writer for *Rebecca* (*Life in Letters*, 297).[4]

Fitzgerald's connection with movies extended beyond film adaptations of his own work. He and Zelda wanted to play the leads in a possible adaptation of *This Side of Paradise*, and during his 1927 Hollywood sojourn, Lois Moran arranged a screen test for him which proved unsuccessful. As Alan Margolies has pointed out, screenwriter Edwin H. Knopf and director King Vidor believed that the lives of Scott and Zelda Fitzgerald could provide material for a popular movie. An early version of the 1935 film, *The Wedding Night*, with Gary Cooper and Helen Vinson, and featuring Anna Sten, was known as "Broken Soil," and it was based on their lives – indeed their names are Scott Fitzpatrick and Zelda; the author in the screenplay has as his publisher Scribners, and his first book is titled *This Side of Heaven*. As Margolies tells us, both Knopf and Vidor knew Fitzgerald from the late 1920s into the 1930s, and although the filmed version differs from the early screenplay, there is still some resemblance to the famous couple (Margolies, "F. Scott Fitzgerald and *The Wedding Night*," 224–5). The story of Fitzgerald and Hollywood has been told many times, including Fitzgerald's allusions to movies in many fictional works. But that the Fitzgeralds as a couple would themselves become the subject of popular films – in their own time and years later – is another illustration of their absorption into American popular culture.

Fitzgerald was aware that he was no longer a literary or public celebrity in the 1930s, although brief items about the Fitzgeralds' several moves in the early thirties found their way into mostly local newspapers. He was deeply concerned about his reputation both as popular and serious writer, desperate for the public attention that had attended him so devotedly a decade earlier. As Scott Donaldson has suggested, *The Crack-Up* essays were in part public confession, in part an effort to recast his private life into a public image with which readers who might have forgotten him could identify (Donaldson, "The Crisis of Fitzgerald's 'Crack-Up'"). Letter after painful letter to Zelda, to Perkins, to Ober attempt to explain the public's neglect. On the one hand, he would tell Zelda, in 1940, that "a whole new generation grew up in the meanwhile to whom I was only a writer of Post stories" (*Life in Letters*, 466), and on the other, in the same year, he would tell her of a "new idea...a comedy series which will get me back into the big magazines – but my God I am a forgotten man"(*Life in Letters*, 439). To Perkins, he would write, "But to die, so completely and unjustly after having given so much" (*Life in Letters*, 445). He is mourning, of course, his neglect as a serious writer, but again, he is looking for any way back into public favor – even taking the route of the "commercial" stuff he claimed had destroyed his reputation. In his last letters, he frequently linked the public image of the Fitzgeralds with the unaccountable public neglect. He wrote to Zelda in 1940, "It was partly that times changed, editors changed, but part of it was tied up somehow with you and me – the happy ending" (*Life in Letters*, 467, 469).

Both the Fitzgeralds were largely forgotten in the 1930s, save for brief newspaper accounts of the 1934 exhibition of her paintings. As one biographer has noted, "The press was less interested in the work than in the resurrection of a legendary figure from the Jazz Age" (Mellow, *Invented Lives*, 427), and photographs of Zelda in *Time* magazine were not flattering. Accounts of the exhibition all noted that Zelda had been released from a mental institution to attend the opening.

And Scott Fitzgerald's brush with the press in the 1930s took the form of the notorious interview with the *New York Post*'s Michel Mok in 1936, who established the picture of the writer that would remain with the public for years to come: a foolish, drunken failure whose degradation was matched only by that of his mad, suicidal wife. Anthony Powell, meeting Fitzgerald in 1937, noted, "It was almost as if he were already dead; at best risen from the dead, and of somewhat doubtful survival value" (Dardis, *Some Time in the Sun*, 3). Powell was then surprised to discover that the mythical failure was very much alive, sober, and anything but the broken man he and the few who still recalled the writer expected. Even Sheilah Graham, who was to create a new public Fitzgerald mythology for later generations, remembered him at their first meeting only as a figure out of the past:

> I thought, he's the writer of the gay twenties, of flaming youth, of bobbed hair and short skirts and crazy drinking – the jazz age. I had even made use of his name: in SHEILAH GRAHAM SAYS when I wanted to chide women for silly behavior, I described them as passé, as old-fashioned F. Scott Fitzgerald types, though I had never read anything he wrote. (Graham, *Beloved Infidel*, 174)

Ironically, Fitzgerald was to spend the most memorable days of his last years with one of that great public who knew him only by his popular reputation, one who had never read his books.

It is now part of the legend that when Fitzgerald died in 1940, he was remembered as "the best chronicler of a short and parochial chapter in

American history," "part and parcel of the twenties," who "dramatized an American state of mind, wild and reckless, and when it petered out, as much from emptiness as anything else, he, too, petered out – tragically and completely" (Bryer, *Critical Reputation*, 202–4). His genius was trivialized in the *New York Times*, which described his "real talent which never fully bloomed" (Bruccoli and Bryer, *In His Own Time*, 469). Friends of Fitzgerald paid tribute to the forgotten author in a special edition of the *New Republic* (February 17, 1941), remembering him fondly, with Glenway Wescott, as "a kind of king of our American youth" in the 1920s (Kazin, *F. Scott Fitzgerald: The Man and His Work*, 116). Budd Schulberg, reminiscing in the same issue, connected Fitzgerald's rise and fall to the massive social upheavals of his era (one of the first of many attempts to connect Fitzgerald's life to American history): "My generation thought of F. Scott Fitzgerald as an age rather than as a writer, and when the economic strike of 1929 began to change the sheiks and flappers into unemployed boys or underpaid girls, we consciously and a little belligerently turned our backs on Fitzgerald" (Kazin, *The Man and His Work*, 110). Fitzgerald finally achieved in death a new, if smaller public life, as our American failure – and the legend of Fitzgerald, the failure – would haunt the second stage of Fitzgerald's life in popular culture. By the 1950s, not only would the public meet the failed alcoholic writer, but they would be reintroduced to his wife, now a pathetic madwoman whose life had literally gone up in flames.

The Fitzgerald revival in the 1950s

The Fitzgerald revival in the 1950s was inaugurated by Budd Schulberg's best-selling novel, *The Disenchanted* (1950), a thinly veiled portrait of Fitzgerald as a failed alcoholic has-been writer, Manley Halliday, who accompanies a young man – like Schulberg himself – to a college winter carnival to write a screenplay. The book was a huge success, and was followed almost immediately by Arthur Mizener's scholarly biography, *The Far Side of Paradise* (1951). Schulberg and Mizener were in close contact, and much of the material in the Mizener book about the Hollywood years was in fact the product of a Mizener–Schulberg collaboration which Sheilah Graham felt it necessary to correct in both *Beloved Infidel* (1958) and in *The Rest of the Story* (1964). Schulberg was happy then, and has been since, that the "one-two punch" of these books "brought to Scott...the new generation of readers, admirers, and enthusiastic critics he had been hoping for in vain throughout the thirties"(Schulberg, *Four Seasons*, 140), and indeed, Schulberg has been actively involved in contemporary tributes and conferences devoted to Fitzgerald.

The Schulberg and Mizener books stressed Fitzgerald's great success and equally stunning failure, and they stimulated ruminations among scholars and journalists about the price of success and failure in America. Indeed, America in the 1950s was embarking on a postwar period of expansion; as in Fitzgerald's own youth, life seemed to be starting all over again as if we could put behind us the traumas of a war, the dropping of the atomic bomb, and the revelations of the Holocaust. New York City was once again a magnet that drew young writers and artists. (Dan Wakefield has recently compared his youthful days as a writer in New York with Fitzgerald's in *New York in the Fifties*, [1992]). Treatises on the lonely crowd and the man in the gray flannel suit led to speculation on the meaning as well as the price of success in America. Undoubtedly, as Malcolm Cowley has suggested, Fitzgerald's "was a story that appealed to something deep in the American psyche" (Cowley, "The Fitzgerald Revival," 12). For Americans, he suggests, the words "success" and "failure" had always been weighted, the question "Will I be a success?" giving way to "Mightn't it be better to be a failure, that is, to fall from some dizzy height and yet in the end to be better than those who kept on rising?" By 1950 Scott and Zelda had become "the hero and heroine of an American legend" (Cowley, "The Fitzgerald Revival," 12). Leslie Fiedler's 1951 essay, "Some Notes on F. Scott Fitzgerald" (Fiedler, *An End to Innocence*, 174–82), was written during the revival spurred by the Schulberg and Mizener books, and he asked why we had seized on Fitzgerald as a great writer. Discounting, as too many of the popular sociologists and psychologists of the era consistently did, the brilliance of the writing, Fiedler attributes the revival to nostalgia for the 1920s, but beyond everything else the seduction of his failure for the American public. Quoting Schulberg's line, "Nothing fails like success," he feels that for American artists, whose prototype was Poe, "Nothing succeeds like failure," that "Fitzgerald *willed* his role as a failure" (176). Fiedler links Fitzgerald's failure to his great flaw, alcoholism, decries the author's penchant for "composing himself," and concludes, "when the lives of Scott and Zelda are forgotten, or when they have become merely chronologies without the legendary distortions and pathos, his books will be less rewarding" (178). The words "success" and "failure" in the 1950s would become associated with Fitzgerald as with no other American writer. In his recent book on Fitzgerald and Hemingway, Matthew Bruccoli quotes from "Prince" Michael Romanoff, whose description of Fitzgerald in Lillian Ross's 1950 *New Yorker* article became the popular starting point for a discussion of Fitzgerald in the 1950s: "Scott Fitzgerald was a failure as a success – and a failure as a failure" (Bruccoli, *Fitzgerald and Hemingway*, 7). Unquestionably, the Schulberg and Mizener books forced that legend into popular culture mythology, while at the same time, writers like J. D. Salinger and Dan Wakefield were responding to the words behind the image. And I should mention here that the revelations by Mizener about Zelda Fitzgerald's insanity and death served both to keep her image alive and to enhance the mythology of Fitzgerald's all too public rise, fall, and posthumous resurrection.

Schulberg's *The Disenchanted* introduced the subject of glamorized failure, in the scene when Manley Halliday is dying and thinks, "Take it from me, baby, in America nothing fails like success" (388), and Halliday is the consummate American failure. In the 1950s and subsequently, Schulberg stated that Halliday was a composite of many writers he knew (particularly with regard to popular culture – "unlike my Manley Halliday . . . Scott was quite the opposite of a film snob," [*Four Seasons*, 97]), but the book was so superficially accurate that readers and reviewers accepted it as a barely fictionalized account of Fitzgerald's last years. It was a bestseller, and brought Fitzgerald's name back into the arena of popular culture.[5] Author James M. Cain praised the novel in the *New York Times*, while disparaging Fitzgerald's artistry. However, Alfred Kazin in the *New Yorker* (November 4, 1950) perhaps spoke for many writers and scholars when he challenged Schulberg's portrait: "Schulberg pities Fitzgerald, but he does not really approve of him, with that approval which starts from creative sympathy and understanding. That is the trouble with the book all along." Burke Wilkinson's laudatory essay in the *New York Times Book Review* (December 24, 1950) surveyed the writer's career and hailed Schulberg's book for reintroducing Fitzgerald to the American reading public. But *The Disenchanted* and the Mizener biography also spawned new criticism of the Fitzgeralds' lives, as in the *New Leader* (March 12, 1951), which intoned, "The secret of the problem of F. Scott Fitzgerald is that the author and his wife actually believed that money could buy happiness" (Bryer, *The Critical Reputation*, 219).

One of the more interesting contributors to the popular Fitzgerald mythology in the 1950s was his old friend, Ernest Hemingway. In January 1951, *Life* magazine ran an article on the Mizener biography, which was being serialized in the *Atlantic*, and included five pages of photographs of pages from Fitzgerald's scrapbooks. Hemingway was outraged by the captions and headings which the *Life* editors wrote, particularly the subheading, "The rediscovered novelist of the 20s was beset by drink, debt, a mad wife" (quoted in Bruccoli, *Fitzgerald and Hemingway*, 219). Hemingway's anger at the article which criticized writers and artists of the twenties, although it did not mention him, led him to write to Harvey Breit of the *New York Times Book Review* and to Malcolm Cowley castigating the "Schulberg–Mizener axis" (Bruccoli, *Fitzgerald and Hemingway*, 222). Publicly, he responded only by citing as among six titles he would like to have read had they been published, "*Longevity Pays: The Life of Arthur Mizener* by F. Scott FitzGerald, and *The Schulberg Incident* by F. Scott Fitzgerald" (Bruccoli, *Fitzgerald and Hemingway*, 222). Whatever outrage Hemingway might have felt at the time, it did not prevent him from adding to the public mythology of Fitzgerald the failure. Whatever Hemingway's motives,[6] his portrait of Fitzgerald, very precise, and very damning, particularly the last line of the description, "The mouth worried you until you knew him and then it worried you more" (Bruccoli, *Fitzgerald and Hemingway*, 149), fed into the image of Fitzgerald created by Mizener and Schulberg. And because those memories of Fitzgerald were published in *Life* (April 10, 1964), they were assured a wide readership. Hemingway's dislike and distrust of Zelda Fitzgerald, whom he described as "more jealous of [Scott's] work than anything" (Bruccoli, *Fitzgerald and Hemingway*, 183), as well as Hemingway's conviction that he knew she was crazy at the outset, enhanced her image as one of the prime causes of Fitzgerald's failure. As if that were not sufficient to garner public attention, Hemingway's remarks about the size of Fitzgerald's male organ generated a very public debate in the pages of *Esquire* (December 1966, 188). Entitled "Scott, Ernest and Whoever," it was an unprecedented controversy to which *Esquire* editor, Arnold Gingrich, and Sheilah Graham added their perspectives. *Getting Straight* certainly indicates the extent to which the debate had become part of Fitzgerald's popular culture persona. One of the first plays on the friendship between Fitzgerald and Hemingway, *Before I Wake*, opened at the Greenwich Mews Theater on October 13, 1968. Ninety-five percent of the dialogue was drawn from the letters between the two writers and to others commenting on each other. Both writers were now in the public domain.

In 1958, the dramatic version of *The Disenchanted* opened on Broadway to generally excellent reviews (December 3, 1958, Coronet Theater). Again, the Fitzgerald-as-failure story became public entertainment; critics described it as "the story of the waning life and ebbing faculties of F. Scott Fitzgerald" (John Chapman, *Daily News*, December 4, 1958); or "He and his wife led a gay life. He made money fast, and she spent it faster. Eventually, both were broken physically" (Robert Coleman, *Daily Mirror*, December 4, 1958); or "the destruction of a writer haunted by the past, possessed by the demons of the present, weary, disillusioned, overwhelmed on every side by the practical realities that he has never faced" (Brooks Atkinson, *New York Times*, December 4, 1958). But the film version was never made, largely as the result of efforts by Sheilah Graham and Scottie Fitzgerald, who threatened legal action (Graham, *Rest of the Story*, 14). (Schulberg has indicated that he and Graham, after a long misunderstanding, reviewed the events which she had challenged and mended fences [*Four Seasons*, 122].)[7]

Sheilah Graham's book, *Beloved Infidel* (1958), a genuinely moving account of Fitzgerald's last years with her, attempted to offer a corrective to the Schulberg–Mizener version of that period, and to tell the public about their love. It too became a bestseller, and was made into a 1959 Cinemascope film which Schulberg describes as "just as screwed up as *Winter Carnival*" (*Four Seasons*, 142). Articles by Frances Ring (1959) and Budd Schulberg (1962) in *Esquire* responded to public fascination with Fitzgerald's Hollywood years, and Calvin Tompkins's well-received *Living Well Is the Best Revenge* (1971) shed light on the Fitzgeralds' sojourns on the French Riviera with Gerald and Sara Murphy. Andrew Turnbull's 1962 sympathetic biography of Fitzgerald was widely reviewed throughout the United States and became a bestseller. Although it was a warm response to Turnbull's boyhood friendship with the author, it did little to dispel the contemporary popular view of the author.

Perhaps the best contemporary view of the Fitzgeralds as they appeared to the American public in these years is that of Wakefield, who recalls meeting a friend accompanied by a girl identified as "Zelda." It was not her name but "she could have passed for a twenties flapper that night. She loved the legend surrounding Zelda and Scott Fitzgerald, our generation's idols of literary glamor and doom" (*New York in the Fifties*, 39–40). In the seventies, both the glamor and the doom would be held up to new scrutiny as the scholarly world joined the media marketplace to create a new image of Scott and Zelda Fitzgerald that has persisted to the present.

The revisionists: 1970 to the present

Public perception generally lags behind that of critics and scholars. During the early 1970s, the influence of Hemingway's and of Sheilah Graham's revelations shaped the popular culture images of the Fitzgeralds, even though Nancy Milford's revisionist biography, *Zelda*, was published in 1970, creating a new interpretation of the couple which has lasted until the present. Thus, the early 1970s television dramatization of their lives on ABC-TV with Jason Miller and Tuesday Weld presented the story of the Fitzgeralds and of Sheilah Graham according to the accepted biographies of the 1960s. Nancy Milford's frankly feminist book drew upon new material to cast Zelda in the light of an artist whose talents were thwarted by her husband, who was fearful that she would use material drawn from their lives together that properly belonged to him as the established writer and financial support of the family. In her introduction, she proclaims her emotional involvement with her subject: "Reading Zelda's letters to her husband moved me in a way I had never been moved before"(xiii). (I might add here that one might be equally moved by *his* letters to her and others, revealing his desperation about earning enough to support her and their daughter, and by Sheilah Graham's memoir of her desperate efforts to save his life and work.) Milford paints Zelda as "the American girl living the American dream," who "became mad with it" (xiv). Milford passes quickly over the many mental illnesses in the Sayre family, choosing to stress Zelda's relationship with Scott as the chief contributor to her breakdown, although she does provide sufficient instances of Zelda's youthful bizarre escapades to raise questions about her mental and emotional balance. Unfortunately, she relies upon Sara Mayfield's biased memories (later appearing in Mayfield's *Exiles From Paradise*) which recall Zelda as not mentally ill (for her, Scott was the unbalanced one), and as the true genius of the family. Milford's book appeared at a crucial period for women in America, indeed, at the beginning of the women's movement, which needed heroines, particularly women whose creativity had been stifled by a patriarchal society. What figure better fits that paradigm than Zelda Fitzgerald, and what better male oppressor than F. Scott Fitzgerald? Scottie Fitzgerald Smith perhaps put it best in her comment on the phenomenon of her mother's new status in life and letters:

> I was surprised when Women's Lib finally became part of our national consciousness to find that my mother was considered by many to be one of the more flamboyant symbols of the movement. To a new generation, the generation of her grandchildren, she was the classic "put down" wife, whose efforts to express her artistic nature were thwarted by a typically male chauvinist husband ... Finally in a sort of ultimate rebellion, she withdrew altogether from the arena; it's a script that reads well and will probably remain a part of the "Scott and Zelda" mythology forever, but is not, in my opinion, accurate. (Preface, Zelda Fitzgerald, *The Collected Writings*, v)

Scottie was correct, of course, for to the revisionists, Zelda was a literary talent of the first rank. Mary Gordon sees her work as a *Bildungsroman*, "a female self coming to maturity in the age of the flapper" (Gordon, Introduction, Zelda Fitzgerald, *The Collected Writings*, xxi). Gordon sides with Zelda in her accusations against her husband, and advises that we should apply new criteria to Zelda's writing, "discarding the notion that the formal, finished and pared down is aesthetically superior to the associative and fragmentary" (xvii), that we give a more "open" reading to her work, "to make a place for the 'You see what I means,' and the 'Can't you understands'" (xvii). Feminist critics have been unwilling to look at the Fitzgeralds' troubled relationship from both perspectives: he *had* to support his family; he was the professional writer; he had been working on *Tender is the Night* for years (interrupted by his having to earn money to pay for her care), and was understandably disturbed by her use of the same material for her book. They had both concocted the story of his use of her work years earlier; it now became an issue for her. Was she, as Hemingway asserted, deeply jealous of her husband's success, or was she a writer who deserved recognition in her own right? (Considering their publicly created personas, that judgment would have been difficult to make in any event.) It is insufficient, but accurate, to state that there are passages of brilliant writing in her stories and her novel, but that she is finally a highly gifted amateur who would not have received the recognition now accorded her had she not first been married to F. Scott Fitzgerald, with him experienced the heady success of the twenties, collapsed pathetically in the thirties, and died tragically in the forties.

But the new image of the Fitzgeralds was intriguing to the popular audience which now had not only Scott's failure to relish, but his abuse of Zelda and her emergence as a heroine-victim as well. This last image, along with that of her abusive, manipulative alcoholic husband, has been kept alive in American popular culture – in film, in theater, in the popular press, and notably in popular biographies like those of Milford, Mayfield, Mellow, and Meyers.

Among the many dramatizations based on the lives of the Fitzgeralds according to the new gospel, the most representative is perhaps that by Tennessee Williams, who creates in Zelda his own double, as he did in Blanche Du Bois: the troubled, misunderstood Southern belle, confined to a mental institution. Williams's play, *Clothes For a Summer Hotel*, opened in 1980, and drew heavily on material in Milford's book, with Scott complaining, with regard to *Save Me the Waltz*, "Didn't I have to pay for her treatment, for Scotty's Vassar?" (Williams, *Clothes For a Summer Hotel*, 34). Scott and Zelda reminisce about their fame, their picture in *Cosmopolitan*, and Zelda mourns their "storybook marriage, legendary. Yes, well, legends fade" (74). She concedes their marriage had been as Scott described it, a "monumental error, and that it had been a mistake for us ever to have met"(74). As the reviewers noted, this is a ghost play which offers "no more about the Fitzgeralds and their companions than we might have picked up from stray accounts over the years without ever having cracked one of the novels or books about the pair" (Douglas Watt, *N.Y. Daily News*, March 27, 1980). One reviewer found it hard to find Zelda, the central character, sympathetic: "For much of the play she wears a shabby tutu, which has a forlornly comic sense of grace, quite undone by the dancers' leggings on her thighs . . . For the most part, she whines. She nags Scott or taunts him. It is hard to find her tragic or even sympathetic" (Howard Kissel, *Women's Wear Daily*, March 27, 1980). Other figures from the Fitzgerald legend appear – Gerald Murphy, Ernest Hemingway, Mrs. Patrick Campbell – but the play simply rehashes the popular mythology with little of the poetry Williams usually brings to his drama. Joel Siegel, reviewing the play on television, said "Until I double-checked my Playbill I was sure I'd walked into a play about Ed and Pegeen Fitzgerald by Tennessee Ernie" (New York, ABC-TV News, March 26, 1980).

In her 1985 memoir, Frances Ring noted Fitzgerald's entry into the world of television, his stories and novels providing material for countless adaptations which she describes as "Scott's lucrative life after death" (*Against the Current*, 145). In the fall of 1993, Turner Network Television's dramatization of the lives of the Fitzgeralds accurately reflects their image in popular culture today. The TV play (based largely on the Milford biography) opens with their meeting at a dance in Alabama in 1918. From that moment and throughout the film, Scott is rarely, if ever, shown without a flask or a glass. In their first encounter, Zelda, whose daring is her most notable attribute, says, "I've always wanted to swim naked" and promptly sheds her clothes; their naked swim is the equivalent of the classic "meet cute" Hollywood scenarios from the 1930s and 1940s. Every aspect of their lives is reduced, trivialized, exaggerated, vulgarized, and Maxwell Perkins, Hemingway, and Edmund Wilson are bit players in this sordid tale of a couple of losers. Throughout, their sexual lives are held up to scrutiny, as are their Jazz Age escapades and their troubled marriage. The obligatory sequences depicting Scott's lack of sympathy for Zelda's artistic endeavors, and her relationship with the French aviator are familiar, yet somehow strange, episodes in this visual medium which cruelly caricatures the couple. When Zelda says, "Scott and I don't believe in self-preservation" and jumps from the roof of a villa into a pool (followed by Scott), we can only laugh at the gross lack of subtlety that has made their lives into television trash. But it does tell us what F. Scott and Zelda Fitzgerald signified in American popular culture by the 1990s: a morality tale directed at the excesses of the 1980s which so resembled those of the 1920s. The Fitzgeralds are thus portrayed for the general public as object lessons, paradoxically combining popular rebelliously radical notions of female victimization with failure to conform to broadly acceptable norms of behavior.

Undoubtedly several recent biographies have contributed to the skewed popular culture vision of F. Scott and Zelda Fitzgerald. For James Mellow, Fitzgerald's life interferes with judging his art, and he consistently denigrates Fitzgerald's short stories, simplistically taking the author's rationalizations for truth. Because Mellow is unsympathetic to Fitzgerald the person, he draws upon several versions of a story (without any direct evidence) to portray the writer as a thoroughly unsympathetic drunk. Mellow describes several versions of an episode involving Hemingway and Fitzgerald after the Hemingways' visit at Fitzgerald's home at Ellerslie. There are so many accounts that any conclusion would seem questionable, yet Mellow quotes in detail the versions (by Sara Mayfield and A. E. Hotchner in particular – neither of whom is notably reliable) particularly damaging to Fitzgerald. Matthew J. Bruccoli, in *Fitzgerald and Hemingway: A Dangerous Friendship*, has found no supporting evidence for either Mayfield's or Hotchner's descriptions of the event (101–2).

The meeting was first described in an unfinished section Hemingway intended for *A Moveable Feast*. The only evidence of the trip is from a letter Hemingway wrote thanking Fitzgerald for his hospitality at Ellerslie, apologizing for arriving too early at the Philadelphia train station, and referring to a "cop" who was "very nice" even though he had Fitzgerald "in his hands" (102). But Mellow fills in sensational details, all damaging to Fitzgerald. He trots out the old homosexuality stories, and provides grim details about Scott and Zelda's charges and countercharges regarding sexual performance. His disapproval makes his biography truly reflective of its title, *Invented Lives*. Sara Mayfield's biography is so biased that it cannot be taken seriously, so it is fruitless to linger on such foolish conclusions as Scott's being responsible for Zelda's madness, or that *he* had the split personality, that he encouraged her to be dependent on him and kept her in hospitals so that he might be free (a charge made by members of her family), that *Save Me the Waltz* is superior to *Tender is the Night*, or the incredible conclusion that she was the genius, he the mere talent.

Jeffrey Meyers's biography is the latest assault on the couple, as it assiduously digs out whatever "dirt" he believes lies under an already picked-over corpse. Thus his psychosexual diagnoses, his sensationalized "discoveries" of Fitzgerald's past flames, and his incapacity to portray either of the Fitzgeralds as the creative figures they were, leave the reader repelled. He has turned Scott and Zelda into tabloid personalities, Roseanne and Tom Arnold of the Jazz Age.

All of these biographies have turned the writer and his wife into vulgarized figures easily recognized by a mass public which does not distinguish between great talent and dross, so intermingled are they today in the pages of *People* and *Vanity Fair*, and even *The New Yorker*.

The future of the Fitzgeralds in popular culture

Is dismal vulgarization to be the final incarnation of the Fitzgeralds in American popular culture? Probably not; in fact, the tide has already turned. There has been, for the past fifteen years, a strong link between academics and the mass market. As the film *Getting Straight* suggests, the mass market may turn on recent "revelations" and reject them in the name of common sense. And even the academics themselves may discern the excesses that biographers with biased agendas have committed. The Meyers book was rejected both by critics and the public, and at the Hemingway–Fitzgerald Conference in Paris (1994), the only standing ovation was accorded Frances Ring, who advised us to "pour the gin down the drain" and to think of what the Fitzgeralds really were and what they accomplished:

> She was more than a pretty face and he was more than a handsome playboy. She had a sharp intelligence and creative gifts that were adrift in an aimless sea. She was a product of the era in which she lived when women were dependent "girls" or obedient wives... Why make comparisons? They were two different people linked by the public spectacle of their marriage, but still separate in the degrees of their talent. A writer was all he ever wanted to be... But she drifted in and out of the arts. Her painting reflected her exaggerated erratic personality, decorative though it was. And her obsession with the ballet ultimately defeated her. Yes, she was searching desperately for some gratification of her very own and it was a valid search, but it was her illness, not Scott, that interfered with achievement.[8]

Mrs. Ring recalls Fitzgerald at the end, and asserts, "He wasn't finished. He wasn't a failure though he was poor... He believed in his talent; he believed in *The Last Tycoon*. So let us give him credit for his own resurrection and let's finally pour the gin down the drain."

On what would have been Fitzgerald's ninety-eighth birthday, Garrison Keillor and a group of St. Paul residents led a birthday parade and celebration before dedicating the Fitzgerald Theater in the city of his birth. The announcement of the dedication states, "Fitzgerald was a beautiful writer, his best writing as graceful and truthful as ever, and he was a heroic man who was defeated and kept on fighting." Perhaps we have all tired of the old stories and are ready to look more charitably on a great writer and his talented wife whose personal lives held both laughter and sadness, and whose gifts deserve to live in the glow of that public affirmation they so tirelessly sought.

As the foregoing suggests, the evolving popularization of the Fitzgerald icon was shallowly concerned with sensationalism and fleeting celebrity, much more so than with the reality of Fitzgerald's art. But as the following chapters suggest, the art is what has lasted and will continue to last. The cult of celebrity in America might have devolved into Andy Warhol's pronouncement about every man's fifteen minutes of fame, but the serious attention that has been paid to Fitzgerald's work, justly – if, deplorably, posthumously – guarantees that his superb writing will be the rock on which his fame and name will endure. The significance and depth of Fitzgerald's work are examined, but by no means exhausted, in the following chapters.

Taken together, they reveal why what he sought so fervently when he was young, to be a personality, was nothing compared to what he sought with greater fervor as he matured: to be a true artist. Unfortunately, perhaps, for him, he succeeded in his youthful wish. Fortunately for the realm of distinguished literature, he also succeeded, and brilliantly, in his larger vision. With this in mind, we turn now to the chapters themselves.

Fitzgerald was, from the start of his career, associated with the youth culture that developed in the 1920s, a major emphasis in his first novel, *This Side of Paradise* (1920), and many of his short stories. Kirk Curnutt explores this culture and shows how its fetishization of youth affected Fitzgerald's consciousness of premature aging, central to his tragic sensibility. Curnutt develops his thesis by tracing the historical origins of the new youth culture, and then examining its profound effect on Fitzgerald's work, from his first novels and stories to his last writings just before his death in 1940.

Curnutt's chapter provides a fine background to James L. W. West III's discussion of Fitzgerald's two early novels, *This Side of Paradise* and *The Beautiful and Damned* (1922). West focuses on the central questions that beset so many young people coming of age in the 1920s: "What does one do with one's life? What can give meaning and purpose to one's hours and days?" Those questions by young men and women lead to corollary concerns about love and marriage. West's emphasis on the importance of work as a theme in both novels illuminates Fitzgerald's concerns about the danger of idleness and drift, the enervating effect of money, and the allurement of alcohol – all central to his later work.

Throughout his career, Fitzgerald wrote short stories, and Bryant Mangum outlines the author's career as a short story writer beginning in adolescence and ending with his death. Many of the concerns we trace in this volume are reflected in the short stories, and Mangum provides a thorough examination of Fitzgerald as a serious short story writer, referring to the myth of the two Fitzgeralds, the serious writer, and the popular personality. He also describes Fitzgerald's own awareness of the role the stories played in maintaining his popular image, discussed in detail above. He illuminates, in particular, Fitzgerald's lifelong effort to reconcile the roles of professional author and literary artist.

Ronald Berman's provocative chapter on *The Great Gatsby* explores Fitzgerald's masterpiece against the background of contemporary American issues and philosophy, and traces many of the aspects of the novel to their origins in the changes that were occurring in American culture. He describes the secular theology that underlies Jay Gatsby's ideas, and illuminates the world of objects and things in a burgeoning consumer society that affect the language, imagery, and direction of the novel. Like Curnutt, Berman explores the notion of "drift," but here in the world of the novel and in the writings of contemporary philosophers.

Milton R. Stern traces the style of Fitzgerald's *Tender is the Night* (1934), which changes from the poetic prose of *Gatsby* to the "gossamer evocativeness" of the new novel which focuses on a broad range of themes (some discussed by Curnutt and Berman in different contexts): war, the fathers, the new woman, American history, and the international theme. Stern's chapter is a thorough examination of the composition, revisions, and reception of the novel, but it is more than that: it is a probing study of the novel that reveals the sweeping changes in a world affected by a brutal war and a convulsive peace.

J. Gerald Kennedy, in his discussion of Fitzgerald's expatriate years, extends Stern's examination of the international theme by focusing on the fifteen stories that reveal the effects of expatriate life on Fitzgerald's work. By reading these stories as a "virtual sequence," Kennedy shows that we witness "the emergence of a larger, composite narrative of displacement and cultural encounter that delineates national identity as it critiques American naivete and excess." Through his careful examination of these stories, Kennedy reveals Fitzgerald's awareness of the irreversible consequences of expatriation, and again, of the effects on his writing of evolving historical events.

Another cultural icon popularized by Fitzgerald, as we have noted, was the flapper, who, according to Rena Sanderson, represented a new philosophy of romantic individualism, rebellion, and liberation. Sanderson shows how Fitzgerald used the figure as a symbol not only of a new order, but also of social disorder and conflict. Her wide-ranging study of women in Fitzgerald's fiction describes the author's very complex and evolving view of women by examining his major works in their most revealing contexts, both cultural and personal.

Many of the issues raised at the outset of this Introduction are reiterated, with a somewhat different emphasis, in Scott Donaldson's intriguing study of Fitzgerald's nonfiction. Donaldson discusses the celebrity status Fitzgerald partially created, and then focuses on the "lyrical magic and emotional power" of those autobiographical essays of the early 1930s which match in artistry his most lasting fiction. Donaldson sheds new light on the less known *Esquire* pieces from the late 1930s, and examines those last brief, haunting vignettes, some fact, some fiction, that reflect his sense of his own life's story.

Although Alan Margolies discusses Fitzgerald's last years in Hollywood, his focus is on Fitzgerald's interest in film throughout his life. He demonstrates how Fitzgerald used his knowledge of Hollywood in several short stories as well as in *The Beautiful and Damned* and *Tender is the Night*, and then traces the relationship between his use of film in fiction and his actual screenplays, which contain biographical elements concerning his experiences in the film capital. Finally, Margolies provides a unique analysis of the strengths and weaknesses in Fitzgerald's filmscripts, and completes our discussion of his short stories with an examination of the Pat Hobby pieces for *Esquire*.

Jackson R. Bryer's detailed commentary on the scholarly reputation of Fitzgerald reinforces the judgments by contributors to this volume, as he traces the evolving attention the author has received, particularly in the last decades of the twentieth century. Bryer's discussion indicates that Fitzgerald today is undoubtedly one of the handful of truly great writers of the twentieth century, and that his reputation, which he worked to secure during his first years of success, has exceeded even his own early hopes and expectations. His celebrity, in this volume, resides in his achievements as an American writer whose masterpieces continue to be passed on to new generations of readers throughout America and the world.

NOTES

1 For a thorough discussion of Hemingway's public personality and celebrity, see John Raeburn's *Fame Became of Him*.
2 See Nancy Milford, *Zelda*, p. 109, and James Mellow's account, in *Invented Lives*, p.123.
3 Telephone interview, October 7, 1994.
4 Movies made from Fitzgerald stories during his lifetime also include *The Offshore Pirate*, *The Beautiful and Damned*, and *The Great Gatsby*. He also wrote titles (to convey dialogue), a scenario, and a screenplay for three silent movies in 1923–4 (Meyers, *F. Scott Fitzgerald*, 168). After his death, five films were made from his works or from works about him: *The Great Gatsby* (1949; 1974); *The Last Time I Saw Paris* from "Babylon Revisited" (1954); *Beloved Infidel* (1959); *Tender is the Night* (1962); and *The Last Tycoon* (1976).
5 Tom Dardis comments on Schulberg's role in creating what Dardis sees as an inaccurate picture of Fitzgerald in Hollywood, and ponders Schulberg's motives, which he finds suspect. See Dardis, *Some Time in the Sun*, 26.
6 Ruth Prigozy, "A Matter of Measurement."
7 Schulberg regards Andrew Turnbull's account of the *Winter Carnival* episode – his trip to Dartmouth with Fitzgerald while they were working on the film with that title – as stemming from "pure malice," its errors later inherited by Henry Dan Piper, in *F. Scott Fitzgerald: A Critical Portrait*.
8 Frances Ring, "The Resurrection of F. Scott Fitzgerald" talk published in *The F. Scott Fitzgerald Society Newsletter*, 5 (October 1995): 1–4.

2

KIRK CURNUTT

F. Scott Fitzgerald, age consciousness, and the rise of American youth culture

"At Your Age," a relatively unknown 1929 short story published in the *Saturday Evening Post*, contains all the trademark elements that F. Scott Fitzgerald's readers had come to expect by the end of the Jazz Age: there is a handsome, sympathetic hero embarrassed by his conventional, middle-class background; an irrepressible flapper whose flamboyant petulance symbolizes the frivolity of youth; a contemptuous, vain rival who steals the girl away with a flashy car; a doting, dull mother flummoxed by her daughter's anti-traditionalism; and even talk of petting parties, those scandalous teenage necking extravaganzas that *This Side of Paradise* first brought to public attention nearly a decade earlier. And yet "At Your Age" departs from the familiar Fitzgerald formula in at least one significant way. Unlike Amory Blaine, Dexter Green, or Jay Gatsby, Tom Squires loses the girl not because he is too poor, but because he is too old. At fifty, Tom is attracted as much to Annie Lorry's age as to her beauty or social status. She is for him a veritable fountain of youth, reviving memories of "the warm sureties" of his own adolescence and reintroducing him to "the very terminology of young romance" (*Price*, 288). The pathos of the story arises from Tom's belief that age is a mind set, not a chronological measure. "I am not old," he assures himself. "At fifty I'm younger than most men of forty" (*Price*, 278). But when Annie betrays him with a swain thirty years his junior, he is stunned by the foolishness of his Ponce-de-Léon pretensions. Chastising her in a parental tone, he realizes "with a shock that he and her mother were people of the same age looking at a person of another." By story's end, Tom resolves to act his age: "He had lost the battle against youth and spring, and with his grief paid the penalty for age's unforgivable sin – refusing to die" (*Price*, 291).

One exclamatory passage in particular captures Tom's obsession with juvenescence: "Youth, by heaven – youth! I want it near me, all around me, just once more before I'm too old to care" (*Price*, 279). The statement aptly glosses Fitzgerald's entire corpus, for throughout his writing his fixation with youth is a central concern. At its most basic, age provided Fitzgerald a measure of self-worth. As long as he believed himself young, he embodied the promise of early achievement. "I was always interested in prodigies because I almost became one," he recollected at the ripe old age of 23. "I think [I] was one of the ten youngest in my class at Princeton" (*Correspondence*, 59–60). Seventeen years later, he described why he valued precocity over maturity: "The man who arrives young believes that he exercises his will because his star is shining," he writes in "Early Success" (1937). "The man who only asserts himself at thirty has a balanced idea of what will power and fate have each contributed, the one who gets there at forty is liable to put the emphasis on will alone" (*Crack-Up*, 89). Youth was an ambrosial gift from the gods, a divine favor that marked the triumph of destiny over hard work. Even before Fitzgerald's premature death in 1940, John Peale Bishop remembered how his former Princeton pal believed "he must produce from an early age," lest he deem himself a failure: "I complained to him that I thought he took seventeen as his norm, making everything later a falling off. For a moment he demurred, then said, 'If you make it fifteen, I will agree with you' " (Bishop, "The Missing All," 108).

Unfortunately, most critics ignore the cultural background of Fitzgerald's age consciousness, describing his obsession with youth as a personality flaw that distracts from the maturity of his craft. Yet his attitude toward growing old reflects a broader fetishization of youth that proved endemic to twentieth-century popular culture. "Time was when age meant dignity, authority, and power, while youth meant helpless slavery," sixty-two-year-old Charlotte Perkins Gilman lamented in 1922. "Age as age claimed respect, the elders assuming that wisdom accrued with the passage of time with no effort on their part. . . . But now the scene changes – changes beyond recognition. Age [now] stands as the rear-guard of an advancing society." Appreciating the significance of youth in Fitzgerald's writing necessitates looking beyond personal pathology to a broader conflux of modern attitudes toward the life cycle. It requires understanding why, in Gilman's phrase, "the hour of the aged has passed, and the hour of youth has come" (Gilman, "Vanguard," 349).

The forces responsible for this century-long "youthquake" are broad and diverse. As many historians have noted, the definition of adolescence as a distinct transitional period in the life cycle did not exist outside of the upper classes until the 1890s, when a range of institutions charged with overseeing the moral development of maturing youth arose in response to increasing patterns of industrialization and urbanization that eroded familial oversight over children. Compulsory public schooling, child-labor laws, and even extracurricular outlets like the Boy Scouts and the YMCA segregated teens from adult culture, granting them their own social space by stratifying them into age-specific cohort groups that encouraged intra-generational identification.[1] As social scientists began distinguishing the psychosocial peculiarities of this new category of experience from pre-pubescence and adulthood, the idea of adolescence as a liminal stage of life took shape. Whereas children were once trained to emulate adults from an early age, the new ideal insisted that the teen years were a unique developmental period fraught with turbulence. And while Victorian moralists insisted on a strict regime of moral policing to ensure proper entry into adulthood, modern thinkers promoted an indulgent attitude that encouraged teens to formulate their identities through peer affiliations. By the 1920s, the first youth to grow up under this conception of adolescence entered the public eye as a distinct subculture, replete with its own slang, styles, and rites of passage. The sudden prominence of the younger generation excited public concern and launched a decade-long debate over the morality of its fads and fashions. The scrupulous attention fixed on youth also created a demand for spokesmen to mediate the widening generation gap – a role that no one in this period played better than Fitzgerald.

Teenagers themselves constituted only a segment of this emerging youth culture, however. The signs and symbols by which adolescents flaunted their youth entered the public domain where they risked appropriation by those who may not have been young but nevertheless wished to appear young. As Fitzgerald remembered in "Echoes of the Jazz Age" (1931), the "children's party" of the early 1920s was eventually "taken over by the elders, leaving the children puzzled and rather neglected and rather taken aback" (*Crack-Up*, 15). A legion of self-help gurus insisted that youth did not belong exclusively to the young; it was an attitude, a life style available to those who knew the secret of not succumbing to senescence. As Hollywood films, music, and novels popularized the orgiastic credo of "ain't we got fun," the fashion, health, and cosmetic industries seized upon the youth appeal to claim their wares could imbue consumers with the vitality of young people. This enculturated pursuit of youth quickly transformed attitudes toward aging. Whereas the journey of life once symbolized a pilgrim's progress from innocence to experience, growing old during the Jazz Age came to resemble planned obsolescence – an unsolicited invitation to irrelevance. Reading Fitzgerald's work against this backdrop allows better recognition not only of the influences that shaped his own anxieties toward aging but also why the 1920s – and nearly every decade since – has seemed such an exclusive "affair of youth" (*Crack-Up*, 15).

Young man blues: rewriting the adolescent experience

When *This Side of Paradise* was published in 1920, readers were shocked by the realism of Fitzgerald's portrait of teenage life. Here was a hero, Amory Blaine, who drank, flunked out of Princeton, and was even caught in an Atlantic City hotel room with a scantily clad underage girl. Most strikingly, the novel failed the major prerogative of young-adult fiction, for instead of illustrating the civic responsibilities of adulthood, it ended ambivalently, its protagonist no longer a boy but not quite a man, uprooted from the past but uncertain of the future. "I know myself, but that is all," Amory confesses in a closing monologue (*TSOP*, 260). As Fitzgerald declared in an unpublished foreword, "whether [the] hero really 'gets anywhere' is for the reader to decide."[2] According to the *Chicago Daily Tribune*'s Burton Rascoe (April 3, 1920), *Paradise* offered "the only adequate study that we have had of the contemporary American in adolescence and young manhood" (Bryer, *Critical Reception*, 3–4). Popular books about growing up like Owen Johnson's *Stover at Yale* (1912) or Booth Tarkington's *Seventeen* (1916) suddenly seemed superficial by comparison. Amory might be "a prig, a snob, [and] an ass," but "youth is all these things rather than the amiable baby Mr. Tarkington pictures him as being. Moreover, at 17 a youth has, despite the evidence of Mr. Tarkington, begun to think . . . to have ideas, worries, ambitions – unless he is fated for a life of utter stupidity and automatic action" (Bryer, *Critical Reception*, 3–4). While Johnson and Tarkington portrayed youth as adults wanted to see them, Fitzgerald showed teens as they saw themselves – as restless, hungry for experience, prone to temptation and excess. As the *St. Louis Post-Dispatch* warned, *Paradise* promised a rude awakening for parents who believed their children lived in a Louisa May Alcott world. This was "no book for a daughter to put in the hands of her mother!" (Bryer, *Critical Reception*, 2).

Of course, the *outré* aspects of *Paradise* today seem more precious than shocking, but before 1920 revelations of deviant behavior among middle-class youth were few and far between. Rarer still was the novel's unapologetic attitude, which not only took these indulgences for granted but boasted of them. Traditionally, Fitzgerald's *provocateur* stance has been credited to influences such as naturalism, Freudian psychology, and the modernist *Bildungsroman* like James Joyce's *Portrait of the Artist as a Young Man*, all of which encouraged darker, more complex portraits of maturation. Yet aesthetic innovations alone do not account for *Paradise*'s realism. Rather, the idea of adolescence itself was undergoing a redefinition that effectively antiquated roseate novels like *Stover* and *Seventeen*. Victorians had defined youth as a moral apprenticeship in which children learned the prevailing ideals of *politesse* essential to bourgeois respectability. Fictional teens like Horatio Alger's genteel heroes were expected to model for young readers the appropriate responses to various ethical quandaries. Such youth perforce lacked psychological conflict, for had their authors dwelt too intently on the emotional complexities of adolescence, they would have contradicted their own insistence that rigorous self-discipline alone could shepherd young people through the maturation process.

By the early twentieth century, the Victorian image of pious, obedient youth competed against a new conception of adolescence as an awkward, troubled age, one inherently prone to deviance and rebellion. According to G. Stanley Hall, whose massive 1904 study *Adolescence* lent scientific legitimacy to the burgeoning notion of the "terrible teens," youth was a time of "storm and stress" in which young people were overwhelmed by conflicting emotions and impulses. "Youthful dements wrestle with great problems and ideas," Hall wrote. "But their powers are inadequate and they grow mentally dizzy, confused and incoherent" (*Adolescence*, I, 310–11). While Victorians condemned this confusion as a sign of moral frailty, Hall expressed unprecedented empathy (if not envy) for his subjects. Essentially a Romantic, he defined adolescent development as a Rousseauian struggle between natural youth striving to retain primitive instincts and a civilized adult world excessively reticent in its passions and creativity. The teenager was the father of the man for Hall, for while maturity made one "prematurely old and too often senile in heart," youth bristled with "the hot life of feeling" that adults failed to appreciate (II, 59). The imperative of growing up was *not* to police impulses but to resist their repression, for if forced to mature too quickly, adolescents would find the salutary energy of youth enervated. The main legacy of Hall's theory was a new "magnanimity and a large indulgent parental and pedagogical attitude" toward adolescents, "especially toward juvenile offenders" (I, 339), whose tendency toward transgression was ameliorated from a moral threat into a search for self-expression. As this new leniency redrew the norms of acceptable behavior, the "amiable baby" was succeeded by the rebel without a cause whose alienation and disquietude marked an intuitive quest for ethical certitude amid adult hypocrisies.

Fitzgerald owed his early success to the fact that adolescent and postadolescent readers were ripe for fiction that substantiated the newfound confusion and complexity associated with teenage life. As *The Bookman* recognized, *Paradise* was "a convincing chronicle of youth by youth" because Fitzgerald was not "looking back to [youth's] problems with a wistful patronage" but was "still in the thick of the fight, and [writing with] the fierceness of combat" (Bryer, *Critical Reception*, 26). By tracing Amory's emotions through triumph and tragedy, the novel documented the "instability and fluctuation" of youth's temperament, illustrating how, as Hall argued, teens are torn between a "genius for extracting pleasure and gratification from everything" and an antithetical tendency toward "pain and disphoria" (*Adolescence*, II, 75, 77). Moreover, by ending his story with his hero "grown up to find all Gods dead, all wars fought, all faiths in man shaken" (*TSOP*, 260), Fitzgerald defined adolescence as a process of emotional *and* historical accommodation. Ultimately, Amory does not know how to grow up because the lessons imbibed from role models prove ineffectual in the modern age. By suggesting that young people bear the brunt of cultural change, *Paradise* vividly endorsed Hall's thesis that "modern life is hard, in many respects increasingly so, on youth" (*Adolescence*, I, xiv). In fact, Amory's descent into disillusionment and *ennui* seemed such a confirmation of the Hallsian notion of the "dangerous teens" that the *San Francisco Chronicle* suggested *Paradise* could pass for "an additional chapter [of] G. Stanley Hall's *Adolescence* or a psychopathological case record" (Bryer, *Critical Reception*, 28–9).

Although Fitzgerald's novels after *Paradise* center on characters at the cusp of their thirties, much of his short fiction also features adolescents like Amory who must weather the storm and stress of growing up. Among the best of these "juveniles" are the Basil and Josephine stories, a series of fourteen tales written between 1928 and 1931 that treat teen courtship and popularity rituals with empathetic depth and dignity. Although its plots were based on incidents from the author's own boyhood, the series was actually modeled on Tarkington's *Penrod* and *Seventeen,* which Fitzgerald had enjoyed in his youth. Indeed, feeling the stories were too "full of Tarkington," he declined to collect them in book form in the mid-1930s, fearing, as he wrote his editor Maxwell Perkins, that the "inevitable comparisons" would undermine his reputation (*Dear Scott/Dear Max*, 199). Because he wrote these pieces for the highly remunerative *Saturday Evening Post*, Fitzgerald disparaged them as hack work and was perhaps incapable of appreciating just how they transcended their inspiration. Tarkington had popularized a facile image of youth called the "mooncalf," usually a boy caught in the throes of a romantic delirium that renders him a comic figure. While the humor was more sentimental than satirical, the adolescent's weepy, dreamy disposition was exaggerated to cartoonish proportions to emphasize his immaturity and demonstrate how "seventeen cannot always manage the little boy alive under all the coverings" (*Seventeen*, 243). Although Fitzgerald appreciated Tarkington's skills as a humorist, he condemned the mooncalf as a dishonest representation of youth: "It is a pity," he wrote in 1922, "that the man who writes better prose than any other living American was brought up in a generation that considered it a crime to tell the truth" ("Three Soldiers," in Bruccoli, *F. Scott Fitzgerald on Authorship*, 72).[3]

Abandoning the demeaning mooncalf stereotype in his short stories allowed Fitzgerald to focus on the liminality of the adolescent experience and examine, like Hall, the conflict between impulse and discipline. Basil Duke Lee and Josephine Perry are simultaneously naive and knowing, part child and part adult. Both are aware of burgeoning carnal desires that, even if they culminate only in kisses, are nevertheless foreign to *Seventeen*'s Willie Baxter and his belle, Miss Pratt. (As if to reassure readers of her pre-pubescent asexuality, Tarkington inflicts Willie's paramour with a cloying penchant for baby talk.) Fitzgerald's teens must also confront serious character flaws that threaten the evolution of their personalities. For Tarkington, Basil's vanity or Josephine's selfishness would occasion slapstick humor, for whenever Willie preens for Miss Pratt, he inadvertently trips into dessert trays or sits on wet paint. Yet Fitzgerald refrains from reducing adolescence to a risible foible, treating it instead as a series of formative developmental challenges. In the final Basil story, "Basil and Cleopatra," the hero longs "to be older, less impressionable, less impressed"; to do so, however, he must outgrow his attraction to the frivolous, popular girls who, over the course of eight tales, repeatedly prove unworthy of his affection (*B&J*, 207). The five-story Josephine series ends on a sadder note. In "Emotional Bankruptcy," the heroine must admit that her "vast, tragic apathy" and narcissism render her unfit for mature love. Her flippant attitude toward romance leads her to the realization that, although not yet eighteen, she "has nothing to give" and can't "feel anything at all" (*B&J*, 326–7). In both cases, Fitzgerald insists on the adolescent's capacity for epiphany. Basil and Josephine not only gain valuable insight into themselves, but the stories hint that they will never look upon the world as innocently as they once did.

Fitzgerald's most intriguing departure from the mooncalf tradition involves his revision of Tarkington's patronizing narrative stance toward young readers. In *Seventeen*'s final pages, Willie is forever separated from his love when Miss Pratt's family relocates. As the boy rebukes a neighbor girl for mocking his anguish, the narrator intrudes to report that, a decade later, she and Willie will marry, and their matrimonial bliss will prove to the mooncalf what he can't now bear to believe – that at seventeen he is too immature to recognize true love. Such interjections convey the benevolent condescension with which Tarkington dismisses adolescent emotions. Significantly, when Fitzgerald indulges in editorial asides, he directs his comments *to adults* unsympathetic to the teenage point of view. In "First Blood," the introductory Josephine story, he describes his heroine's urge to kiss a suitor she barely knows: "Josephine was never either ashamed or plaintive ... She did not plan; ... she merely let herself go, and the overwhelming life in her did the rest." Rather than condemn her abandon, Fitzgerald criticizes those who would judge her: "It is only when youth is gone and experience has given us a sort of cheap courage that most of us realize how simple such things are" (*B&J*, 235). Instead of encouraging adolescents to think like adults, Fitzgerald insists that older readers recognize that youth are instinctual, impulsive creatures for whom restraint seems an unfair impediment to mapping their own moral boundaries. By addressing a different implied audience than Tarkington, Fitzgerald made it clear that his sympathy lay with youth who, he implies, need latitude, not lecturing from elders.

In soliciting this adult understanding, Fitzgerald was not simply creating a more nuanced portrait of teen psychology than *Seventeen* allowed. He was also reversing the values traditionally attached to youth and maturity by idealizing the former as a standard that adults invariably fail. Youth for Fitzgerald marked the apogee of one's romantic promise; once that peak was reached, aging exiled one into the cold, mundane world. In portraying age this way, Fitzgerald drew from a common pool of imagery that equated growing up with the Biblical story of the fortunate fall. Hall's *Adolescence* also alluded to the fall to describe adulthood: "Perhaps the myth of Adam of Eden describes this epoch. The consciousness of childhood is molted, and a new ... consciousness needs to be developed" (II, 72).

For Fitzgerald, postlapsarian imagery accentuated the plot of the "initiation" or "coming-of-age" story to which he repeatedly returned. In tale after tale, a young man dispossessed of his dreams through a sudden twist of fate gains archetypal insight into the vanity of human desire. For several of his protagonists, including Amory, George O'Kelly in "The Sensible Thing" (1924), and Andy in "The Last of the Belles" (1929), a failed first love brings about this unwanted initiation. Others, whether Dick Diver, Anthony Patch, or Charlie Wales in "Babylon Revisited" (1931), fall prey to dissipation and find themselves nostalgic for the carefree fun they once took for granted. Whatever the catalyst, the effect of these experiences is always the same: Fitzgerald's heroes feel suddenly, irrevocably old. The conclusion of "Winter Dreams" (1922) dramatizes this realization through explicit *felix culpa* imagery as Dexter Green is shocked to learn that his former love's beauty has faded: "The dream was gone. Something had been taken from him ... The gates were closed, the sun was gone down, and there was no beauty but the gray beauty of steel that withstands all time. Even the grief he could have borne was left behind in the country of illusion, of youth, of the richness of life, where his winter dreams had flourished" (*Stories*, 145). Few passages better convey the revelatory power of this analogy between the fall and aging.

For Fitzgerald, there was simply no climax to a story more cathartic than a sudden yearning for the lost paradise of youth.

Anthems for doomed youth: defining a jazz generation

Fitzgerald and Hall were not alone in employing postlapsarian images to describe modern youth. By the 1920s, the first generation raised under Hall's definition of adolescence was subjected to numerous editorials assessing its fallen state. (As late as 1919, the *New York Times Index* did not even include *youth* as a category heading. The 1922 *Reader's Guide to Periodical Literature*, meanwhile, lists roughly twenty times more entries on the topic than its 1918–19 edition.) As titles like "Elder Not Better" and "Youngsters vs. Oldsters" suggest, commentators were divided along generational lines, with adult "grundies" condemning wild young people while self-proclaimed spokesmen for the latter bragged of their frankness. The older generation's anxiety arose from a simple question: could indulged, cynical youth grow up into productive, moral adults? As Paula S. Fass argues, Fitzgerald served a mediating role in this debate. While his fiction "threw the behavior of America's youth in the public's face," it also lamented their alienation from "an older order [of] values and standards" that "had been rendered conspicuously inoperative." While providing an insider's perspective on his generation's mind set, he also assured older readers that youth "were less a threat to [America's] former stability than an ongoing reminder that it had passed" (Fass, *The Damned and the Beautiful*, 28). We know we have fallen, Fitzgerald was insisting, but we do not know if we can get up.

No rite of passage depicted in Fitzgerald's fiction excited as much comment as petting, a term that in polite circles referred to the relatively innocent art of "making out" but among young people themselves intoned a broader range of non-coital intimacies. *This Side of Paradise* owed its initial notoriety to its claim that "Victorian mothers" had no "idea how casually their daughters were accustomed to be[ing] kissed" and that a "popular girl . . . met before eight" at a dance might "possibly kiss before twelve" (*TSOP*, 61–2). Several early stories almost taunt adults with the threat of promiscuous necking. "Bernice Bobs Her Hair" (1920) begins at a country-club dance where "a great babel of middle-aged ladies with sharp eyes and icy hearts" police the "barbaric" dancing of the younger set, blissfully unaware that the "more popular, more dangerous, girls" are being "kissed in the parked limousines" of these same "unsuspecting dowagers" (*Stories*, 25–6). At such moments, Fass argues, Fitzgerald was telling "readers what they most feared but wanted to hear again and again in different and ever more alarming ways" (*The Damned and the Beautiful*, 28).

Yet petting scenes were not meant just to shock. They also conveyed youth's unabashed interest in sex and its belief that Victorian repression was unhealthy. By insisting that recreational kissing did not lead to "cocktails, opium . . . and sheer perversity," Fitzgerald illustrated how, as he wrote in a 1924 article, petting offered "an introduction to life" that was "intended by nature to ameliorate the change between the married and unmarried state." Rather than weaken morality, premarital foreplay would "lessen a roving tendency after marriage," for "a girl who knows before she marries that there is more than one man in the world but that all men know very much the same names for love is perhaps less liable after marriage to cruise here and there seeking a lover more romantic than her husband."[4] Within a decade, this argument became commonplace in advice guides and parenting manuals that encouraged adults "to accept the healthy conditions of our unsegregated modern adolescence" and recognize that "petting-parties" were "a natural and wholesome part of growing up emotionally."[5] The key word here is *natural*: although Fitzgerald's work sensationalized petting and provoked scandal, it opened a cultural dialogue through which erotic intimacy became an accepted rite of passage in an adolescent's growth.

Fitzgerald also examined the related issue of early marriage, a phenomenon that concerned the media almost as much as petting. In the 1920s, couples began to enter matrimony at a younger age than their parents. Fitzgerald and his own bride, Zelda Sayre, fell only slightly short of the decade's median marriage age when they wed at twenty-three and nineteen respectively in April 1920.[6] As the chronological boundaries of the new adolescence were extended to the mid- and late-twenties, trepidation arose over youth's ability to reconcile expectations of marital bliss with the realities faced by most unions. These expectations were fueled by romanticized images of young love prevalent in films and sentimental fiction, including Fitzgerald's more sugary *Post* stories. Such images not only established a new ideal of domestic passion but often intimated that premarital sex and birth control were appropriate means of searching out the perfect partner. As a 1930 study noted, tales of true romance depicted a "new attitude toward [a couple's] preliminary trial union" that arose not from a "desire for promiscuity, but rather [from] the wish to make certain . . . that [a man and woman] are really suited to each other" (Blanchard and Manasses, *New Girls for Old*, 220). Traditionalists, upset to learn that youth believed sexual experimentation was healthy, found themselves in an awkward position. While praising youth's commitment to the institution of marriage, they discouraged early entry into that responsibility. As a favorite phrase of the era insisted, it was better to "wait" than to "mate."

Fitzgerald's treatments of youthful marriage court both points of view. His commercial fiction generally promotes a *carpe diem* attitude toward young love. Gloria Patch in *The Beautiful and Damned* describes the marital ideal of many girls her age: "Marriage was created not to be a background but to need one. Mine is going to be outstanding. It can't, shan't be the setting – it's going to be the performance, the live, lovely, glamorous performance, and the world shall be the scenery" (*B&D*, 147). Stories like "The Offshore Pirate" (1920), "The Unspeakable Egg" (1924), and "Rags Martin-Jones and the Pr-nce of W-les" (1924) insist that this theatrical dimension is essential to young romance. In each case, conventional and boring suitors prove themselves heirs to Valentino by concocting elaborate seduction ruses; the more outlandish their schemes, the more the young women are assured of an intriguing, adventurous marriage. Meanwhile, sentimental confections like "Love in the Night" (1925) and "The Adolescent Marriage" (1926) rewrite Tarkington's *Seventeen* by valuing the intuitiveness of puppy love over mature, reasoned affection. Whereas Willie Baxter's crush on Miss Pratt proves transitory, the infatuations of Fitzgerald's adolescent couples weather separation and economic misfortune without enervating their intensity. Both stories insist that a first love is one's true love, for the "unreal, undesirous medley of ecstasy and peace" of adolescent passion is "unrecapturable" in middle age (*Stories*, 310).

Equally often, however, Fitzgerald cautions against the disappointments of early marriage. Barely six months after their wedding, Anthony and Gloria Patch discover the "breathless idyl" of first love is an "extortion of youth" that quickly flees "on to other lovers" (*B&D*, 156). Similarly, "Babylon Revisited," "One Trip Abroad" (1930), and "What a Handsome Pair!" (1932) all suggest that the self-absorption of adolescence is incompatible with marital felicity. "The Adjuster" (1925) offers his most didactic take on the subject. After barely three years, Luella Hemple has grown bored with her spouse and complains she deserves better. Her husband hires a mysterious specialist whose therapy consists mainly of telling Luella to grow up. Not surprisingly, she rebels against his prescriptions. "I want the light and glitter," she insists. "There can't be anything wrong in wanting to have things warm." But Dr. Moon speaks of duty, not desire: "Happy things may come to you in life, but you must never go seeking them any more. It is your turn to make the fire." When Luella demands to know his true identity, he offers a cryptic response: "I am five years" (*TJA*, 158–9). A brief coda confirms the doctor's wisdom, for within a half decade, Luella learns to sacrifice her youth for the "mature kindness" and selflessness a successful marriage requires. While the story hardly subscribes to the Fitzgerald stereotype of wild youth, it does voice the sentiments of many columnists who questioned the viability of the new romantic conception of matrimony.

In assessing these new attitudes toward sex and marriage, Fitzgerald fixated in particular on the liberties afforded to the female sex. He was certainly not alone in discoursing on the subject. Throughout the decade, observers were startled by the plethora of self-described flappers, "It" girls, and baby vamps claiming to modernize femininity. Fitzgerald recognized that a girl's access to new freedoms rested on her ability to blur the distinction between the child and adult. The "hard-boiled baby," he told an interviewer in 1927, combined the "carefree, lovable child who rules bewildered but adoring parents with an iron hand" with the "pretty, impudent, superbly assured" *femme fatale* who is "as worldly wise, briefly clad and 'hard-berled' as possible."[7] *Tender is the Night* describes the ideal body type that resulted from this age blending: "Her resemblance," Fitzgerald writes of a minor acquaintance of the Divers, "was rather to one of John Held's flat-chested flappers than to the hierarchy of tall languid blondes who had posed for painters and novelists since before the war" (*TITN*, 291). The passage suggests how the new woman eschewed the feminine icon of her mother's generation, the Gibson Girl, because her Rubenesque proportions conveyed matronly stolidness. By contrast, the sleek, boyish figure limned by Held (whose work illustrated three Fitzgerald book jackets) projected joyous, unrestrained movement. As a psychologist of the era observed, the flapper's "long slender limbs and undeveloped torso" also suggested "immaturity": "If modesty has departed from [her] legs, it has moved upwards to the body, where any display of the (formerly so much admired) characteristics of the fuller figure is discountenanced. The bosom must be small and virginal and maturity . . . is concealed as long as possible" (Flügel, *The Psychology of Clothes*, 161–2).

The idea that physical and emotional immaturity advanced women's liberation offended older feminists like Charlotte Perkins Gilman, who condemned flappers for abandoning their major duty: "By a strong, well informed, rigidly selective motherhood the young women of today could cleanse the human race of its worst inheritance by a discriminating refusal of unfit fathers . . . [But] as women [these girls] dress, their facial decoration, their behavior, show no hope of better motherhood, which is what they are women for" (Gilman, "Vanguard," 353). But what Gilman failed to recognize – and what Fitzgerald's fiction documents – is that young women felt their freedom inexorably tied to their youth. As Gloria Patch understands, the world is hers as long as she is young, which is why she prefers to act eighteen instead of twenty-two (*B&D*, 64). Zelda Fitzgerald made the same point more explicitly in a 1925 *McCall's* article: "I believe in the flapper as an artist in her particular field, the art of being – being young, being lovely, being an object... [Her] sole functions are to amuse and to make growing old a more enjoyable process for some men and staying young an easier one for others" (*Collected Works*, 393).

Fitzgerald's early work is a virtual hymn to these functions. His prototypical heroine, whether Rosalind Connage in *Paradise*, Sally Carrol Happer in "The Ice Palace," or Nancy Lamar in "The Jelly-Bean," is self-consciously immature, petulant, and selfish. "She wants what she wants when she wants it and she is prone to make every one around her pretty miserable when she doesn't get it," Fitzgerald writes in *Paradise*. "But in the true sense she is not spoiled. Her fresh enthusiasm, her will to grow and learn, her endless faith in the inexhaustibility of romance, her courage and fundamental honesty – these things are not spoiled" (*TSOP*, 170–1). G. Stanley Hall voiced a similar judgment in 1922 when he wrote that the flapper's "sublime selfishness," carelessness, and "the fact that she never seems to realize what it means to clean up after herself" were "affectations" by which she was "simply trying out all the assortments of temperamental types, dispositions, and traits of character, as she often tries out styles of handwriting before she settles upon one" ("Flapper Americana Novissima," 780). For both writers, the flapper's appreciation for the romance of life sanctioned her outlandish behavior. By modeling her exuberance, she taught peers how to maximize their pleasure.

Yet Fitzgerald also recognized that the fantasy of endless youth must inevitably confront the reality of aging. In his novels in particular, flappers typically enjoy an extended adolescence only to discover suddenly that their decadent, indulgent fun has irreparably weathered them. Although Gloria Patch aspires "to be young and beautiful for a long time" (*B&D*, 270), dissipation and marital discord exhaust these precious qualities. After a decade's worth of living out the role of baby vamp, she is despondent to learn on her twenty-ninth birthday that she looks too old to convincingly play that part in the movies. Because she can pass for "a woman of thirty," the film studio suggests she is better suited for "a small character... supposed to be a very haughty rich widow" (*B&D*, 403). In *Tender is the Night*, Rosemary at first fulfills the flapper's function by resuscitating Dick Diver's youth. "You're not middle-aged," she assures him when he complains of their age difference. "You're the youngest person in the world" (*TITN*, 106). But while Rosemary invigorates his adolescent passions, Dick's "father complex," his quasi-incestuous attraction to young girls, allows him to see her only as a child. During their initial infatuation, he is haunted by gossip that the teenage Rosemary was caught *in flagrante delicto* on a train; four years later, upon consummating their affair, he demands full knowledge of her sexual history. At both moments, Dick cannot reconcile her sexuality with the *ingénue* she portrays in films like *Daddy's Girl*, in which she appears "*so* young and innocent...embodying all the immaturity of the race" (80). While he tries to explain the abrupt ending of their friendship by claiming that "Rosemary didn't grow up" (321), his affection for her is doomed the minute he realizes that she is indeed an adult. Once he understands that her apparently naive innocence is a cinematic illusion, Dick simply has no use for Rosemary.

Of course, Fitzgerald's most affecting portrait of the aging flapper is Daisy Buchanan in *Gatsby*. Although worn cynical by her husband's constant infidelity, Daisy strives at twenty-three to remain the same frivolous teenager who fell in love with Jay Gatsby five years earlier. To maintain her self-image, she affects contrived, exaggerated gestures that accentuate her childishness, occasionally even speaking in the same baby talk as Miss Pratt in *Seventeen*. But whereas Tarkington employed this affectation to convey his heroine's innocence, in *Gatsby* it underscores Daisy's desperate denial of her role in her lover's demise. As long as she believes herself young and carefree, she can be careless without consequence. Thus when Tom and Gatsby square off at the Plaza Hotel to demand Daisy choose between them, she pines to escape into youth: "We're getting old," she announces as music seeps into their suite from a nearby ballroom. "If we were young we'd rise and dance" (*GG*, 135). In the novel's closing indictment of Tom and Daisy's "vast carelessness," Nick implicitly ties the couple's ability to retreat and "let other people clean up the mess they had made" to their unwillingness to acknowledge their lost youth. When Jordan Baker accuses *him* of mistreating her, Nick acknowledges the connection between age and complicity that the Buchanans cannot admit: "I'm thirty. I'm five years too old to lie to myself and call it honor" (186). Equating maturity with guilt, Nick suggests that Daisy's desire to remain young is not born the hope of preserving youth's ephemerality but her immature need to evade adult responsibilities.

Forever young: age consciousness and the youth market

Fitzgerald's work also reveals awareness of a third aspect of youth culture prevalent in the 1920s: the emergence of youth as a marketplace commodity. With a fervor equal to their editorial counterparts, era advertisers began courting the under-thirty market with campaigns that appealed to youth's sense of distinction from elders. In 1925 a professor of advertising psychology explained this targeting of adolescent consumers: "Young people not only rule the market as far as their own purchases are concerned, but they have a powerful influence upon all family purchases...The resistance to new ideas to be met in the young is less than in the old, hence the widespread appeal to the young in current advertising" (Poffenberger, *Psychology in Advertising*, 583). These appeals involved the creation of trademark logos like the Arrow Collar Man and the Jantzen Girl (the nation's first swimsuit model) that glowed with athletic vitality and aristocratic sophistication. The flapper also provided an all-purpose spokeswoman for everything from tourism to deodorant. The Fisher Body Girl is perhaps the most extreme example of her appropriation by advertisers; celebrating automobile designs by equating car and female frames might seem an absurd (and sexist) stretch, but, as Roland Marchand notes, the flapper exuded a sleek mobility that made the "woman on the move" motif, the "image of women in actual or impending motion," a coveted symbol among motor companies (*Advertising the American Dream*, 182). By claiming to embody a similar aura of youthful energy, consumer goods across an array of product lines formed a network of identification that allowed youth from disparate backgrounds to define themselves as part of a homogeneous generational constituency. A boy lacking the financial resources to attend college could nevertheless look collegiate with the right polo shirt, baggy tweeds, and knickers. In this way, youth culture confirmed the power of mass culture to promulgate life styles across a national expanse previously segregated by region, class, and ethnicity.

Fiction proved a popular medium in this expanding youth market. Only five years before *This Side of Paradise* was published, *Saturday Review of Literature* founder Henry Seidel Canby had complained that publishers were indifferent toward the campus novel.[8] But after *Paradise* sold fifty thousand copies, the world of the co-ed became a common literary setting. While many of the resulting books merely relocated the typical sentimental romance plot to an academic locale, other college novels like Percy Marks's *The Plastic Age* (1924) or Kathleen Millay's *Against the Wall* (1929) were serious critiques of the pedagogical imperatives of higher education, often portraying the university as a "prison," with "administrators [as] smooth, cold wardens...faculty [as] tired and uninspired" and "thinking [as] dangerous" (Marchalonis, *College Girls*, 129). But while critics protested its condemnation of elitism and pedantry, campus fiction inspired intense reader loyalty. Students at the University of Illinois were so devoted to a Midwestern variation on Fitzgerald's debut novel, Lynn and Lois Montross's *Town and Gown* (1923), that when a lukewarm review appeared in the student newspaper, the editor found himself on the receiving end of a month-long barrage of angry letters. Another novel that rivaled *Paradise* in sales and influence, Warner Fabian's *Flaming Youth* (1923), proved such a phenomenon that even Fitzgerald was compelled to write the author. "Who in the devil are you?" he playfully demanded during a brief correspondence with Fabian.

"Do you know at least a dozen people have asked me if I wrote *Flaming Youth*? I wish I had but I'm sure I didn't" (*Correspondence*, 131).

Readers could be forgiven for assuming Fitzgerald had authored the novel, for the press so persistently identified him with flappers and slickers that he was often credited with creating youth as a market niche. Much-circulated declarations like his 1920 claim that "an author ought to write for the youth of his own generation, the critics of the next, and the schoolmasters of ever afterward" ("Author's Apology," in Bruccoli, *F. Scott Fitzgerald on Authorship*, 35) not only implied that an artist's primary loyalty was to his peers; they also suggested that his peers constituted an ideal target market. In at least one light comedy, "Dice, Brassknuckles & Guitar" (1923), he poked fun at the commodification of youth with a tale of a self-professed "jazz master" who opens an institute to train debutantes in flapper etiquette. "Parents innocently assumed that it was a sort of musical and dancing academy," Fitzgerald writes. "But its real curriculum was transmitted from Santa Barbara to Biddeford Pool by that underground associated press which links up the so-called younger generation" (*Stories*, 248). More often, Fitzgerald was on the receiving end of parody for bringing this "underground associated press" into the mainstream. In a *Saturday Evening Post* piece, Dorothy Parker satirized what many saw as his entrepreneurial savvy in writing about his generation. Fitzgerald may not have "invented youth . . . but he was well up in the van when it came to cashing in on the idea." He and his fellow littérateurs "don't regard being young as one of those things that are likely to happen to anybody. They make a business of it." Parker even offered some attention-grabbing titles sure to propel future exposés on debauched youth into bestsellerdom: *Annabelle Takes to Heroin*, *Gloria's Neckings*, and *Suzanne Sobers Up*, she insisted, all "broadcast the grim warning that conditions are getting no better rapidly and that decadence, as those outside the younger generation know of it, is still in its infancy" (Parker, "Professional Youth," 14, 156–7).

The fascination with youth's life style also engendered fads and fashions aimed at adults anxious to avoid feeling old. By the mid-1920s, much popular discourse was insisting that age was a matter of psychology, not chronology. As *Forum Magazine* assured its audience, "A youthful spirit can dominate gray hair or wrinkled hands, if it is not cramped and cumbered by the mental limitations of 'years'. Remember always, *don't act your age*" (Lutes, "The Art of Not Growing Old," 246). Teenagers scoffed at the sight of mothers in knee-high skirts and rolled stockings. "The old girls are doing it because youth is," one flapper told the *New Republic*. "Everybody wants to be young, now – though they want all us young people to be something else. Funny, isn't it?" (quoted in Bliven, "Flapper Jane," 66). Yet the coveting of youth nevertheless created demand for an array of wrinkle creams, vitamins, and bizarre surgical remedies. An extreme example of the latter, known as the "Steinach operation" and practiced even by eminent sages like William Butler Yeats, required severing a man's vas deferens so testosterone was not ejaculated in the sperm but remained in the bloodstream to rejuvenate the spirit.[9] Such curatives dramatize just how desperately consumers wanted to believe that the biological clock could be turned back. Fitzgerald's "The Curious Case of Benjamin Button" (1922) dramatizes the productivity many presumed possible if only youth's energy and maturity's wisdom could be synchronized. A man who emerges from the womb at seventy and grows progressively younger throughout his life hits his peak just when middle age should slow him down. Yet Button at forty possesses the vigor of twenty; he even beats out boys younger than his own son for a spot on the Harvard football squad. For many commentators, capitalizing on youthfulness in this fashion wasn't a supernatural fantasy but the end result of a positive, vitalist outlook on life.

This pursuit of youth inspired a reciprocal anxiety about the age at which one officially became "out of date." The significance of certain milestones (thirty and forty most often) became a subject of endless conjecture. The groundwork for this trend was laid as early as the 1880s, when scientists like George Miller Beard began formulating laws on "the relation of age to work." Beard calculated that most statesmen, military leaders, and artists peaked before forty, a time when "their brains have begun to degenerate, and the fires of youth have spent half their force" (*American Nervousness*, 22). (His life subsequently validated his assertion; after concocting it in his mid-thirties, Beard was dead by forty-four.) By 1905, age sensitivity was so acute that an address by Johns Hopkins University professor William Osler (a former instructor of Gertrude Stein's) ignited outrage for satirically endorsing euthanasia for sexagenarians. When tabloids claimed that his comments prompted some two dozen elderly suicides, a shaken Osler was forced to explain in the *New York Times* that he was merely promoting compulsory retirement for aged workers incapable of competing with youth's productivity.[10] The age discrimination that Beard and Osler advocated was *de facto* employment policy by the 1920s; in the advertising and public relations industry, it was a common belief that men over thirty-five were unfit for the hectic pace and pressure of agency life. When a leading ad agency executive voiced this opinion in a 1931 *Printer's Ink* interview, his comments incited an angry response from one reader: "The man of forty-five has a hard enough time as it is now. Stop telling the world that as a copywriter he lacks potency. What is to become of the upper-middle-aged if this stuff is kept up?" (quoted in Marchand, *Advertising the American Dream*, 242). Despite such rebuttals, the belief that the end of one's twenties marked the ebbing of promise and potential persisted. According to Howard Chudacoff, as chronological milestones "became a rite of passage ... provoking introspection about one's individual history and schedule," growing older occasioned the pervasive assumption that life's "greater rewards ... were to be had at previous ages" (*How Old Are You?*, 132).

Far from an aberration then, Fitzgerald's age consciousness was the product of a culture in which aging became synonymous with deterioration and degeneration. More than any author of the era, he was obsessed with the symbolism of age milestones, often making their passage the dramatic crux of his plots. *The Beautiful and Damned* might well be subtitled "Countdown to Thirty," for Anthony and Gloria so dread the onslaught of middle age that their descent into decadence seems an effort to squander their youth before time can claim it. The story is often interrupted by editorial asides that echo popular assessments of the stages of life: "It is in the twenties that the actual momentum of life begins to slacken, and it is a simple soul indeed to whom as many things are significant and meaningful at thirty as at ten years before. At thirty an organ-grinder is more or less a moth-eaten man who grinds an organ – and once he was an organ-grinder!" (*B&D*, 169). In a similar fashion, Anson Hunter in "The Rich Boy" (1926) fears that turning thirty will imbue him with "the fussy pessimism of a man of forty," so to maintain his sense of vitality and possibility, he dedicates himself to acting twenty by immersing himself in a frivolous, pseudo-collegiate world of drinking parties and debutante balls (*Stories*, 348–9). *Tender is the Night* also attributes characters' behavior to their age. As Nicole Diver dresses for an adulterous rendezvous with Tommy Barban, Fitzgerald compares her desire for romance to a teenage girl's: "Attractive women of nineteen and of twenty-nine are alike in their breezy confidence ... The former are ages of insolence, comparable the one to a young cadet, the other to a fighter strutting after combat." Because she is not yet thirty, Nicole is excused from accounting for "the subsequent years when her insight will often be blurred by panic, by the fear of stopping or the fear of going on. But on the landings of nineteen or twenty-nine she is pretty sure that there are no bears in the hall" (*TITN*, 313). (Nicole in this way recalls Gloria in *Beautiful*, who staves off her fear of growing old by acting like a teenager, until at twenty-nine she realizes she looks *older* than her age.) In defining the significance of age milestones, Fitzgerald inverts (if not mocks) the advice of youth gurus like the *Forum Magazine* author who extolled her audience to act as youthful as possible. However we might fancy ourselves young, he insists, the moment at which we are unmasked as old and decrepit is always imminent.

Fitzgerald's deterministic belief in the stages of life turns even grimmer in his notebooks, where he often ascribes his professional failures to senescence. A prescient couplet suggests how deeply aging shaped his sense of his own capability: "Drunk at 20, wrecked at 30, dead at 40 / Drunk at 21, human at 31, mellow at 41, dead at 51" (*Notebooks*, 189). Age consciousness is even a recurring motif in the reminiscences of his contemporaries. In her autobiography *What is Remembered*, Alice B. Toklas recalls Fitzgerald visiting Gertrude Stein's famous atelier at 27, rue de Fleurus on his thirtieth birthday: "One afternoon he said, You know I am thirty years old today and it is tragic. What is to become of me, what am I to do? And Gertrude told him that he should not worry, that he had been writing like a man of thirty for many years" (*What is Remembered*, 117). Even if the story were true – and its veracity seems doubtful since Fitzgerald was in southern France, not Paris in September 1926 when he passed this particular milestone – it is unlikely that Stein's response would have comforted him much. The idea of premature aging was simply too central to his tragic sensibility.

The glorification of youth prevalent in Fitzgerald's writing suggests the extreme to which American popular culture denigrates adulthood. The fixation with adolescence apparent in *This Side of Paradise, The Beautiful and Damned, The Great Gatsby, Tender is the Night*, the short stories, and essays not only reflects this denigration but also has helped sustain it in the American imagination since the 1920s. In 1953, Van Wyck Brooks cautioned against resurgent interest in Fitzgerald by warning that "the cult of youth" he celebrates might "fill [readers] with a fear of growing old that... precludes at the outset any regard for the uses of growing up" (*The Writer in America*, 69). Other Eisenhower-era critics – one thinks of Leslie Fiedler and Ihab Hassan in particular – also cited Fitzgerald as an example of the American intellect's arrested development. To minimize his importance, they depicted him as a harbinger of the beats, "J.D.s" (juvenile delinquents), and Elvis Presleys of their time – which may not be as frivolous a legacy as they intended the comparison to seem. The rise of culturalist approaches to literature has helped us better appreciate the multifarious uses that the category "youth" serves in the popular arena. Adolescence as a tempestuous stage of ethical accommodation and adjustment dramatizes the unsettling celerity of change that characterized the twentieth century; the adolescent, meanwhile, marks the space within which we debate these transforming social attitudes toward sex, marriage, and work, among other issues. Rather than rebuke Fitzgerald for failing to mature, we ought to recognize how deeply his corpus registers the struggle to grow up in a culture that demonizes growing old.

NOTES

Quotations in this chapter are from the 1934 edition of *Tender is the Night*, the 1991 edition of *The Great Gatsby*, and the 1995 edition of *This Side of Paradise*. For details, see Bibliography.

1 For the emergence of youth as a distinct subculture in America, see Joseph F. Kett, *Rites of Passage* 245–72.

2 This piece is printed under the title "Preface" in the 1995 Cambridge University Press edition of *This Side of Paradise*. See 393–5.

3 In *Tender is the Night*, Fitzgerald also parodies the mooncalf's self-debasing romanticism while describing Dick Diver's attraction to Rosemary Hoyt. In pursuing this nineteen-year-old actress, Dick succumbs to "the fatuousness of one of Tarkington's adolescents" (103) and, by compromising the aristocratic superiority of his character, initiates his long fall into mediocrity.

4 See "Why Blame It on the Poor Kiss if the Girl Veteran of Many Petting Parties Is Prone to Affairs After Marriage?" originally published in *New York American* 52 (February 24, 1924): 3. The piece is reprinted in Bruccoli and Bryer, *F. Scott Fitzgerald in His Own Time*, 179–84. For this particular passage, see 183.

5 See Floyd Dell, "Why They Pet," *Parent's Magazine* 6 (October 1931): 63. It is worth noting that Fitzgerald routinely dismissed Dell's 1920 novel *Mooncalf* as a pale imitation of his own *Paradise*.

6 See John Modell, *Into One's Own: From Youth to Adulthood in the United States, 1920–75*. Modell notes that "the 1920s were a decade in which rather regularly, younger cohorts could look forward to somewhat younger marriages than their immediate predecessors [those of the 1910s] and to distinctly younger marriages than in the generation of their parents" (110).

7 Quoted in Margaret Reid, "Has the Flapper Changed? F. Scott Fitzgerald Discusses the Cinema Descendants of the Type He Has Made So Well Known," *Motion Picture Magazine* (July 1927). Reprinted as "Flappers Are Just Girls With a Splendid Talent for Life," in Bruccoli and Bryer, *F. Scott Fitzgerald in His Own Time*, 277–81. For this quote, see 280.

8 See Canby's *College Sons and College Fathers*, 97.

9 For an overview of this and other strange remedies, see Thomas Cole, *The Journey of Life: A Cultural History of Aging*, 181ff.

10 See Carol Haber and Brian Gratton, *Old Age and the Search for Security: An American Social History*, 163–5.

3

JAMES L. W. WEST III

The question of vocation in *This Side of Paradise* and *The Beautiful and Damned*

The histories of composition for F. Scott Fitzgerald's first two novels, *This Side of Paradise* (1920) and *The Beautiful and Damned* (1922), resemble each other very little. *This Side of Paradise* was an inspired cut-and-paste job, a merging of bits and pieces of a failed novel (called "The Romantic Egotist") with some short stories, a handful of poems, and a one-act play. Fitzgerald assembled the book during the summer of 1919 in a desperate attempt to prove himself as an author and as a prospective husband for Zelda Sayre, his golden girl. He produced the manuscript in a rush of improvisation, revised it quickly, submitted it to Charles Scribner's Sons in the early fall of 1919, had it accepted, and saw it into print the following spring.

The Beautiful and Damned, by contrast, was a carefully planned piece of literary composition. After a false start that produced "May Day"(1920), one of his finest stories, Fitzgerald settled down and wrote *The Beautiful and Damned* from start to finish. He sought advice about the novel from his friend Edmund Wilson and from Maxwell Perkins, his editor at Scribners, and he took their suggestions seriously, revising and polishing throughout. The narrative was serialized in *Metropolitan Magazine* beginning in September 1921, then published in book form in the spring of 1922. *The Beautiful and Damned* reads much more like a conventional novel than does *This Side of Paradise*. The narrative is coherent; the characters are consistent (as they are not in *This Side of Paradise*); and the themes are carefully articulated throughout. That does not make *The Beautiful and Damned* the better book: it lacks the verve and energy of *This Side of Paradise*, but it makes up for its deficiencies by providing readers with a blueprint for character types and moral questions that would preoccupy Fitzgerald for the rest of his writing career.

Stylistically *This Side of Paradise* seems daring; it mixes genres in a fashion that even today looks unconventional, shifting from fictional narrative to rhymed or free verse, then moving to drama dialogue and slipping toward the end into interior monologue. The writing itself is by turns glib and confessional, sophisticated and callow, arrestingly beautiful and disappointingly flat. Fitzgerald has been praised (and faulted) for fashioning such a mongrel of a book, but the manuscript of the novel reveals that he created its many surfaces largely by accident. He was determined somehow to incorporate into the manuscript all of the good writing, and some of the less good, that he had on hand from his apprentice years. He therefore stitched and spliced with abandon. The poems that pop up from time to time, for example, were nearly all left over from his undergraduate years at Princeton, and the sections in drama dialogue were taken from a play typescript that was sitting on his desk. Other sequences began life as short stories, then were thriftily recycled as novel chapters or subchapters. Thus what appears to be bold in *This Side of Paradise* – its mixture of genres and styles – is not really as daring as one might think.

The Beautiful and Damned also contains unconventional writing, but Fitzgerald seems here to have been looking back at his first novel and trying to imitate himself. He borrowed techniques which had been praised in *This Side of Paradise* but which, on their second outing, seem artificial and a little stale. The best example is "A Flash-Back in Paradise," a section in Book One, chapter 1, in which Gloria Gilbert, the heroine-to-be of the novel, is introduced as one of the speakers in an odd supernatural event which is rendered as a drama script. Gloria, we learn, is to be born on earth where she will be known as a "ragtime kid," a "flapper," a "jazz-baby," and a "baby vamp" (*B&D*, 29). This section of drama dialogue, and others in the chapters that follow, seem to be obvious efforts by Fitzgerald to repeat himself and perhaps to give the book some kind of current appeal.

This Side of Paradise, published in March 1920, was well received by the press. There were some naysayers, but not many; most of the notices were upbeat and positive. "My, How that boy can write!" gushed one of the more enthusiastic reviewers (Bryer, *Critical Reception*, 1). Sales moved quickly, passing the 40,000 mark by the end of 1920 and leveling off eventually at about 48,000. This was not a remarkably high figure for the times – indeed, Fitzgerald never published a true bestseller during his career – but it was a commendable tally for a first novel. Perhaps as a result, the publication of *The Beautiful and Damned*, in March 1922, was a much-anticipated literary event. Scribners was ready this time with a first printing of 20,000 copies (only 3,000 copies of *This Side of Paradise* had been in stock for its publication day), and the publisher mounted a strong advertising campaign. Reviews, though mostly favorable, were less enthusiastic than the notices for *This Side of Paradise*. One senses some disappointment, as if Fitzgerald had not delivered on his initial promise. Despite these notices, *The Beautiful and Damned* sold briskly, prompting a second impression of 20,000 and a third of 10,000 for a final figure of 50,000 copies – just a little higher than the mark set by *This Side of Paradise*.

The two novels can be said to stand in sequence: the first marks the end of Fitzgerald's literary apprenticeship while the second signals his beginnings as a professional. *This Side of Paradise* is crowded with characters and themes; it is a *Bildungsroman* that asks more questions than it answers and leaves its hero poised on the edge of adulthood. *The Beautiful and Damned*, by contrast, has a more limited cast of characters and is focused on a shorter list of themes. It traces its protagonist from young adulthood to a kind of early senility, brought on by too strong an attachment to money and too great a fondness for alcohol.

The settings for the two novels are worth remarking on. *This Side of Paradise* is set largely in the Midwest and at Princeton – locales that Fitzgerald knew well from his childhood and college years. The pace is meandering and relatively slow, providing time and leisure for the hero to find himself. *The Beautiful and Damned*, on the other hand, is set almost entirely in New York City and its environs; much of the action, in fact, occurs on the grid of central Manhattan, up and down Fifth Avenue, then as now the center of American acquisitiveness. New York, of course, is also the cultural capital of the nation, with its great museums and libraries and concert halls, but none of this seems to interest the protagonists, Anthony Patch and Gloria Gilbert. For them, the allurements are hotels, bars, cabarets, movie theaters, and retail stores.

A major theme that stands out in both *This Side of Paradise* and *The Beautiful and Damned* has to do with the matter of vocation. What does one do with one's life? What can give meaning and purpose to one's hours and days? This question was much on Fitzgerald's mind while he was writing *This Side of Paradise*, and he continued to ruminate about it in *The Beautiful and Damned*. The comments about vocation that he makes in the first novel are carried forward into the second, providing a link between the two and a central theme that illuminates many other questions in the two books.

"Vocation" comes from the Latin *vocatio*, a word which carries the literal meaning of "calling." This is not the same thing as work, a more specific word with overtones of the mundane and financial. For Fitzgerald, the idea of vocation was crucial: one had literally to be called or summoned to meaningful efforts in life. Fitzgerald recognized, however, that the pressures in American culture were designed to channel one relentlessly away from one's natural calling and into the pursuit of money and status. His characters therefore face a dilemma: is there a worthwhile role for them to play in society? Can they discover and pursue it?

Fitzgerald applied the question of vocation largely to his male characters, but he saw that women too needed meaningful roles in life. One of his best insights in both *This Side of Paradise* and *The Beautiful and Damned* was that women of the upper classes really had only one socially approved activity, at least during their young years, and that was the procurement of an acceptable husband. Isabelle Borgé, the pretty charmer in Book One of *This Side of Paradise*, is fully aware of this: she knows that the game of flirtation that she and Amory are playing will "presumably be her principal study for years to come" – that is, until she marries and settles into the privileged life of a society woman (*TSOP*, 68). One senses that this role will suit Isabelle, but other young women in *This Side of Paradise* do not find it as attractive. Rosalind Connage is frankly bored with the whole business (to her mother's great frustration), and Eleanor Savage is angry and bitter about what is required of her. Gloria Gilbert, the most important female in *The Beautiful and Damned*, is openly in search of a husband. Like many of Edith Wharton's young women (Undine Spragg from *The Custom of the Country* comes to mind) Gloria lives in a fashionable New York hotel where she is on display, a beautiful item of merchandise available to a socially qualified man. Her business, and that of her sister debutantes, is to be alluring to suitors. "The average debutante spent every hour of her day thinking and talking about what the great world had mapped out for her to do during the next hour," Fitzgerald tells us (*B&D*, 35). And most of what was mapped out had as its purpose the acquisition of a suitable mate.

Gloria achieves her goal early in *The Beautiful and Damned* when she captures Anthony, whom she presumes to be in line to inherit old Adam Patch's millions. After their marriage, her only activity seems to be self-indulgence; her deterioration, caused by idleness and alcohol, is one of the least pleasant aspects of the novel. After marriage she prods Anthony, hoping that he will choose some career or goal that will give structure to both of their lives. (Her only professional possibility is to get into the movies, a long shot that she chooses not to play.) And yet one cannot condemn Gloria, or the young women in *This Side of Paradise*, too severely. The influences on them of money and class are simply too strong, and they have no alternative models among older women of their social stratum to follow.

Amory Blaine and Anthony Patch are the same in one respect: both are waiting for money to settle upon them. Both have incomes from family property; neither has to take a job or enter a profession straight out of college. Amory is from a wealthy family, and in the early parts of *This Side of Paradise* he can reasonably expect to possess the Blaine fortune some day. But his mother (another woman without vocation) mismanages the family finances, squanders much money in idle pleasures and travel, and leaves half of what remains to the Catholic Church. By the end of the novel Amory is deprived of his inheritance, stripped of the protection that money can bring. One senses, in *This Side of Paradise*, that this will be a good thing. (At least it is an effective plot device.) Amory gradually loses his financial prospects in the same way that he sheds his youthful illusions and beliefs, and by the final scene he has only himself to rely on. Of course Amory is not without resources; he possesses intangibles of talent, ambition, and imagination. Surely he will take these and make something of himself, if only he can find a place in American society that has a use for him.

For Amory this is a significant problem. "How'll I fit in?" he asks his friend Tom D'Invilliers. "What am I for? To propagate the race?" (*TSOP*, 200). In college Amory had ambition, though it was unfocused; after the war and the failure of his romance with Rosalind, he feels deflated. "What a pleasure it used to be to dream I might be a really great dictator or writer or religious or political leader," he tells Tom. Now all such desires have vanished, leaving Amory adrift. "The world is so overgrown that it can't lift its own fingers," he muses, "and I was planning to be such an important finger ... " (*TSOP*, 198).

Anthony, also drifting, is a paler and less attractive version of Amory. He has lived for so long with the assumption that he will one day be rich that he has failed to develop any purpose for himself – other than a vague desire to write. The question of what he is to do, what his vocation is to be, comes up repeatedly in *The Beautiful and Damned*. One sees it as early as the first page of the narrative, where Fitzgerald tells us of Anthony, "He considered that he would one day accomplish some quiet subtle thing that the elect would deem worthy and, passing on, would join the dimmer stars in a nebulous, indeterminate heaven half-way between death and immortality" (*B&D*, 3). The ironic and faintly mocking tone of the sentence, though, alerts us to the fact that Fitzgerald has little confidence in Anthony's ability to identify that "quiet subtle thing" that he can and will do.

The question of Anthony's future vocation becomes a leitmotif in *The Beautiful and Damned*, a question that is periodically taken up, considered, and put down unresolved. "Now that you're here you ought to *do* something," his grandfather tells him, "accomplish something" (*B&D*, 15). But Anthony vacillates and can offer only murmured comments about his intention to write a book on the Middle Ages. This bothers Anthony, to be sure: "If I am essentially weak," he thinks, "I need work to do, work to do" (55). But no plan materializes, and he spends his time in idleness and drinking, "making careers out of cocktails" as Fitzgerald puts it (56). Even Gloria gets in on the questioning. "What *do* you do with yourself?" she asks him in one of their early scenes, and he can only answer: "I do nothing" (65). After their marriage he continues the pretense of working on his book, but she sees through his subterfuges. "Work!" she scoffs. "Oh, you sad bird! You bluffer! Work – that means a great arranging of the desk and the lights, a great sharpening of pencils" (212) – but little else.

Fitzgerald, with his prep-school and Princeton background, must have known many men of this type – men who were waiting for inheritances. They had attended the proper schools, had found mates and married, and had settled back into the protection of family money, waiting for it to descend upon them. Fitzgerald must have been able to observe carefully the ways in which prospective wealth influenced character and sense of purpose in these men. Some of the most memorable characters in his early stories, in fact, are of this type: Philip Dean, the rich boy early in "May Day" (1920) who refuses to lend money to Gordon Sterrett; Knowleton Whitney, the prospective heir in "Myra Meets His Family" (1920); and Percy Washington, the scion of the family in "The Diamond as Big as the Ritz (1922)." In all of those characters, the anticipation of money has produced a curious enervation and an insensitivity to the needs and desires of others. These characters please only themselves, wait for their money, and drift.

In both novels, the American educational system bears much of the blame for the predicaments of these protagonists. Neither Princeton (for Amory) nor Harvard (for Anthony) teaches its students usable skills – or, more important for them, a sense of social duty and purpose. Fitzgerald seems to believe that colleges such as these two, which cater to the elite of American society, need to instill a version of *noblesse oblige* in their charges. Graduates need some notion of how inherited wealth might be deployed to make society better, or at least to free the possessor to develop artistically or intellectually. But neither Princeton nor Harvard provides these ideals: the students seem bored and insular, caught up in campus activities and social games, largely oblivious to the world beyond the boundaries of academe.

In a true aristocracy, Fitzgerald suggests, men such as Amory and Anthony would be groomed for leadership, as would their counterparts in other families. But in American society, these young heirs are trained only to accumulate further. We do not see in either *This Side of Paradise* or *The Beautiful and Damned* a group of older men who serve as examples for what might be done with money and influence. Amory's father is weak and inept, dominated by his exotic wife; Anthony's father is equally colorless and ineffectual. Only old Adam Patch shows energy and drive, but in typical American fashion he has channeled his power into do-goodish causes and has made himself into a crank. Bloeckman, the other strong male in *The Beautiful and Damned*, has directed his considerable talents toward the movies, and toward remaking himself from an upwardly mobile Jew into an assimilated entrepreneur. One can commend him (certainly he is a better focused man than Anthony), but Bloeckman lacks social refinement and is too obviously interested in money, appearances, and women to be wholly admirable.

Both Amory and Anthony have one vocation open to them: writing. Both are skilled with words, and both have some successes in college with the pen, but neither has the discipline or focus to move forward from there. In *The Beautiful and Damned* we do have the example of Richard Caramel, Anthony's friend who makes a mark in literature, but after a promising start he is corrupted by the lure of magazine money, and at the end of the novel he has lost the sense of literary purpose that he had as a young man. Part of the trouble for Amory and Anthony, and for Richard as well, is that authorship in America is not and has never been truly a profession. It requires no degrees or certifications; it has no apprentice system (as medicine and law do, for example); it provides no strata of ranks and titles; and its emoluments are slim and sporadic. Authors drift into and out of the craft of writing, performing it rather as one might do cottage labor. True professions provide their members with protection from the harsher aspects of capitalism; writing, by contrast, leaves its practitioners vulnerable to every evil of the system. Amory sees writing as something he might someday do, if he decides that he has something worthwhile to say, but one has trouble believing at the end of *This Side of Paradise* that Amory will write anything of consequence very soon. For Anthony it is slightly different: writing is that thing which he claims to be doing, whenever anyone asks him what direction he means to take in life. Writing is therefore a useful concept for Anthony, a word he can employ when questioned about his future vocation, but it is little else.

Perhaps the major problem for both young men is their sense of the ultimate futility of effort. In *This Side of Paradise* this feeling is lightly and cynically expressed, but it is there all the same – in Amory's frustration with religion, with education, and with romance. Amory fails at all that he attempts and concludes, in the end, that no system or arrangement of beliefs will give order and purpose to his life. In *The Beautiful and Damned* the themes of futility and absurdity are more strongly stated, probably because Fitzgerald was much under the sway of such thinkers as H. L. Mencken, Theodore Dreiser, and Joseph Conrad during the period in which he wrote the book. Gloria is allowed to state the moral: "There's only one lesson to be learned from life," she says. "What's that?" asks Anthony's friend Maury Noble. "That there's no lesson to be learned from life," she answers (*B&D*, 255).

Lack of vocation and purpose for Amory and Anthony opens the door to a common problem among both writers and the wealthy: alcoholism. With

Amory this is not yet a significant issue; we see him drinking in many scenes but drunk in only one. This is the protracted bender in "Experiments in Convalescence," the second chapter in Book Two of the novel, when he uses alcohol (in rather a stagy way) to dull the pain of his rejection by Rosalind. All the same, one can say that alcohol permeates *This Side of Paradise*; it is always there as a lubricant and support. One finishes the novel wondering whether Amory will avoid its snares.

The *Beautiful and Damned*, for its part, is an astute study of the effects of alcohol on personality and character. Idle and without vocation, Anthony slips into a rhythm of drinking that blunts his will and clouds his judgment. Both he and Gloria come to rely on drink for stimulation and distraction; like many alcoholics they learn to arrange their days and weeks around the consumption of spirits. "Liquor had become a practical necessity to their amusement," we learn (*B&D*, 278), and the consequences of this dependency are grave. Fitzgerald is especially good at charting the progress of their imbibing – from merely social drinking to frequent weekend binges to a final cycle of drunkenness and inanition. The ceremonies of preparation, procurement, consumption, and inebriation are charted with great exactitude.

Self-absorption is yet another problem shared by the characters in *This Side of Paradise* and *The Beautiful and Damned*. Amory is his own chief subject; he never grows weary of self-observation and is consequently hindered by his vanity and pride. At the end of the novel he seems to be moving away from self-study toward a more socially responsible behavior, but we never see him achieve it in the narrative. Anthony and Gloria are self-absorbed in a different way; with no purpose other than to wait for Adam Patch's money, they become preoccupied with each other. Gloria is Anthony's principal study, just as Anthony is hers. They feed on each other – physically and emotionally – but the relationship has no way to replenish itself. By the end of the narrative each character has drained and exhausted the other, and they have slipped into silly quarreling and empty discussions of emotion. No circle of friends or family sustains them: "No one cares about us but ourselves, Anthony," observes Gloria to her bored husband (*B&D*, 227).

If *This Side of Paradise* is a better novel (or at least a more satisfying one) than *The Beautiful and Damned*, it might be because Amory is unsuccessful at love. He fails to win Rosalind, whom he adores, losing her to a wealthy rival named Dawson Rider. This gives an edge to his romantic disappointment that the reader can feel, a sorrow that carries through to the last line of the book – and even beyond. Amory loses his dream girl and must now make his way into adulthood without her. He can only keep her memory alive and her image pure in his imagination. In *The Beautiful and Damned*, by contrast, Anthony wins the object of his desires. According to his plans (always vague), life should go perfectly from there: love should endure, and money should arrive. But neither of these things comes to pass, and Anthony must watch as Gloria loses her youth and appeal, and as their marriage disintegrates. Perhaps Anthony, who like Amory is a romantic, would have been happier if he had not captured the woman of his dreams.

These various concerns – the importance of vocation, the danger of idleness, the allurement of alcohol, and the enervating effect of money – continued to draw Fitzgerald's attention in the years to come, in the stories and novels that we think of today as his best. Tom and Daisy Buchanan in *The Great Gatsby* (1925) are rendered morally corrupt by wealth and lack of vocation: Tom ("the polo player" to Jay Gatsby) reads racist literature and pursues vulgar women; Daisy seems capable only of light, bantering conversation. Anson Hunter in "The Rich Boy" (1926) is emotionally deadened by his money and status, unable to commit himself to another human being or to surrender his sense of social superiority. Charlie Wales in "Babylon Revisited" (1931) loses his vocation and consequently turns to alcohol: "You know I never did drink heavily until I gave up business and came over here with nothing to do," he tells Lincoln Peters, his brother-in-law (*Stories*, 393–4). And Dick and Nicole Diver in *Tender is the Night* (1934) embody nearly all of these themes. Dick has strayed from the medical profession, which gave order and purpose to his life, and now drifts about with Nicole, increasingly dependent on her money. This leaves him vulnerable to alcohol, which he comes to rely on for stimulation and comfort.

This Side of Paradise and *The Beautiful and Damned* can be read as preliminary statements in the Fitzgerald canon, early novels in which the author introduces his major themes and his most memorable character types. But these two novels are also considerable achievements in themselves, searching examinations of the importance of vocation in American life, where ease and riches have always been the material of our dreams. Without a calling, Fitzgerald tells us, we risk deterioration and ruin. Alcohol and idle pleasure cannot sustain us, nor can wealth. We must have purpose and vocation to give direction and consequence to what we do.

NOTE

Quotations in this chapter are from the 1922 edition of *The Beautiful and Damned* and the 1995 edition of *This Side of Paradise*. For details see Bibliography.

4

BRYANT MANGUM

The short stories of F. Scott Fitzgerald

In an all-too-brief professional career of approximately twenty years, Fitzgerald wrote 178 short stories, most of them for sale to commercial magazines of the 1920s and 1930s. Thirty-nine of these stories were collected in four separate volumes, one accompanying each of the four novels which Scribners published during Fitzgerald's lifetime: *Flappers and Philosophers* (1920) was the companion volume for *This Side of Paradise* (1920); *Tales of the Jazz Age* (1922) for *The Beautiful and Damned* (1922); *All the Sad Young Men* (1926) for *The Great Gatsby* (1925); and *Taps at Reveille* (1935) for *Tender is the Night* (1934). In addition, he wrote a play, *The Vegetable*, published by Scribners in 1923, and scores of nonfiction pieces, many of which appeared in commercial magazines during his lifetime. At the time of his death he was working on an elaborately conceived novel, *The Last Tycoon*, which was published posthumously in 1941 as a fragment with Fitzgerald's own notes. When he was not writing for publication, Fitzgerald wrote about his life and about his observations on life in his ledger and in his notebooks, both of which are now available in book form. In spare moments he wrote letters – letters to Maxwell Perkins, his editor at Scribners; letters to his literary agent Harold Ober; letters to literary acquaintances, friends, and family – letters, often about his writing, which now fill four substantial volumes. Above all else Fitzgerald was a writer, a literary artist, who early shared with Edmund Wilson his immodest goal of becoming "one of the greatest writers who ever lived" (Bruccoli, *Some Sort of Epic Grandeur*, 70).

By "one of the greatest writers," Fitzgerald seems at least at the beginning to have meant "one of the greatest novelists," regarding the writing of short stories as something that he had to do to support himself while he wrote the novels that, as he saw it, would be his main literary legacy and the primary exhibit of his greatness as a writer. In 1925 Fitzgerald explained to Ernest Hemingway that writing short stories for popular magazines was "whoring but that he had to do it as he made his money from the magazines to have money ahead to write decent books" (Hemingway, *A Moveable*

Feast, 153). He soon learned, of course, that short story writing could be quite profitable. As he remarked to Ober in 1922, "By God + Lorimer [editor of the *Saturday Evening Post*, which published most of Fitzgerald's stories in the twenties], I'm going to make a fortune yet" (*As Ever, Scott Fitz*, 36), a prediction that in retrospect was not far off the mark. In 1925, for example, he earned over $11,000 from short stories, nearly three times as much as he made from book royalties during that year; in 1930, his income from stories was over $25,000, which accounted for more than 80 percent of his total earnings for the year. His lifetime earnings from the sale of stories to magazines amounted to approximately $250,000, over half the amount of his total earnings from all sources, including royalties and scriptwriting in Hollywood, combined.[1] Understandably, he complained off and on all of his life to friends and acquaintances that his "popular" efforts earned such disproportionately high prices in relation to his "serious" fiction.

However, Fitzgerald's public attitude toward his story-writing reflected in comments like those above to Ober and Hemingway was in fact misleading, perhaps deliberately so, in its depreciation of the value of his stories, the writing of which played such an extraordinary role in the development of his talent as a literary artist. Partly because of his attitude, but also because the four story collections that Scribners published as companion volumes to his novels contained stories from slick popular magazines that had paid Fitzgerald handsomely for his contributions, contemporary critics were quick to find weaknesses in his story collections, frequently damning individual stories as potboilers. For example, H. L. Mencken, who often praised Fitzgerald and who published some of his best early stories in the *Smart Set*, referred to the flapper "confections."[2] A frequent refrain in the reviews of the second collection, *Tales of the Jazz Age*, was that Fitzgerald had already received high prices for many of the stories contained in the volume, a view expressed in one reviewer's observation that Fitzgerald was making "financial hay while the popular sun is shining."[3] And though the contemporary reception of *All the Sad Young Men* was much more favorable than that of any preceding Fitzgerald story volume, the litany of such phrases as "uneven," "popular magazine fiction," and "money-making" continued to appear, unfairly so, it seems, for this extraordinary collection, particularly in view of the fact that Fitzgerald had taken pains to exclude his most popular stories from the volume. In a similar vein, *Taps at Reveille*, the final collection of stories, elicited backhanded compliments including one which praised Fitzgerald for being "entertaining... [and] slickly so."[4] With each collection of stories, praise for occasional brilliant performances, as in the case of such stories as "May Day," "The Ice Palace," "The Diamond as Big as the Ritz," "The Rich Boy," "Winter Dreams," and "Babylon Revisited," was typically diluted with criticism of the slickness of other selections. After Fitzgerald's death the myth – originating, among other places, in contemporary reviews of his story volumes – that there was "Fitzgerald A," who was the serious writer, and "Fitzgerald B," who brought "home the necessary bacon," persisted.[5] And even a decade after Fitzgerald's death, Arthur Mizener in his *The Far Side of Paradise* (1951), maintained that the stories were Fitzgerald's inferior output, the creation of which had presented moral conflicts that would "haunt his career from beginning to end" (Mizener, *Far Side*, 94).

Now, over a century after Fitzgerald's birth and nearly a half-century after Mizener's pioneering critical biography, virtually all of Fitzgerald's 178 stories have been collected in hardbound volumes, six books devoted exclusively to his short fiction have been published, and more than a hundred articles or chapters devoted to the stories have appeared in books and scholarly journals. And whereas Matthew J. Bruccoli could observe accurately in 1979 in his introduction to *The Price Was High: The Last Uncollected Stories of F. Scott Fitzgerald* that "the role of the stories in Fitzgerald's development as a writer is still not properly understood";[6] and whereas Jackson R. Bryer in his *The Short Stories of F. Scott Fitzgerald: New Approaches in Criticism* (1982) could properly lament the dearth of scholarly attention that the stories had received to that point (xi), the last decade of Fitzgerald scholarship has established a solid foundation upon which one can begin to make an accurate appraisal of Fitzgerald's short story canon. This relatively brief time of intensified scrutiny of the stories has firmly established a number of well-documented conclusions about the stories, some of them rather predictable, some much less so. First, many of the stories praised in Fitzgerald's lifetime for their artistic brilliance have been shown to be, if anything, more carefully conceived and artfully crafted than they had been thought by Fitzgerald's contemporaries to be. Alice Hall Petry, for example, in her book-length study of the stories collected in the four volumes during Fitzgerald's lifetime, discovers layers of complexity in such stories as "The Ice Palace," "The Diamond as Big as the Ritz," and "May Day," as well as in such well-known, but less often examined ones as "Benediction" and "The Adjuster" (Petry, *Fitzgerald's Craft of Short Fiction*, xi), complexities like those which John A. Higgins began to explore in his *F. Scott Fitzgerald: A Study of the Stories* (1971). And in a somewhat different vein, new studies, particularly those contained in Bryer's *New Essays on F. Scott Fitzgerald's Neglected Stories*, have pointed to underexamined and undervalued performances, among them, "The Spire and the Gargoyle," "Dalrymple Goes Wrong," "Benediction," "Outside the Cabinet Maker's," and "Jacob's Ladder."

Also in the course of analyses such as those contained in Bryer's *The Short Stories of F. Scott Fitzgerald: New Approaches in Criticism*, a number of scholars have begun to examine subtle connections between related stories not obviously connected to each other. While some individual stories were conceived of as part of a series (those in the Basil Duke Lee and Josephine Perry series, or the Pat Hobby series, for example), others are connected less directly, and their connections had for decades after Fitzgerald's death been largely overlooked. Lawrence Buell's study of Fitzgerald's "fantasy stories," "The Diamond as Big as the Ritz," "The Adjuster," "The Curious Case of Benjamin Buttons," and others, is one of a number of studies which have explored subtle, previously ignored connections between stories, as is C. Hugh Holman's analysis of the Tarleton, Georgia, trilogy, including "The Ice Palace," "The Jelly-Bean," and "The Last of the Belles" (Bryer, *New Approaches*, 23–38; 53–64). And finally, the stories have entered the era of post-structuralist analysis and gender studies, revealing further evidence of their timeless value in documenting the degree to which they address, sometimes with surprisingly post-modernist vision, enduring aspects of the human condition. Susan F. Beegel, for instance, applying to the short stories a perspective used earlier by Sarah Beebe Fryer in her study of the novels, *Fitzgerald's New Women: Harbingers of Change*, examines the degree to which a story often regarded as simply "humorist" like "Bernice Bobs Her Hair" provides in fact a serious contribution to the discourse in contemporary women's studies (Bryer, *New Essays*, 58–73).

Any examination of Fitzgerald's short story canon must, of course, take into account those issues referred to above, many of them prompted as they have been by careful analysis undertaken in light of late twentieth-century critical theory; it must acknowledge the richness of Fitzgerald's very best stories; it must search for undiscovered strengths in the neglected stories; it must find connections in those stories not ordinarily connected in an effort to examine tropes that wind through the body of Fitzgerald's fiction, short and long; and it must examine the degree to which Fitzgerald's short fiction, often through subtext, both deconstructs post-World War I values and also speaks to issues that transcend the modern. Any thorough study, however, must also be undertaken with an eye on inclusiveness: it must account for, or at least be able to account for, the place of every single story, the weakest and the strongest, in Fitzgerald's overall development as a professional writer and literary artist. Ultimately it must work toward reconciling the existence of "Fitzgerald A" and "Fitzgerald B," and finally keep open the possibility that the two Fitzgeralds, the short story writer and the novelist, may finally have been in much closer touch with each other than conventional wisdom has thus far placed them.

It is thus important in considering Fitzgerald's short stories to acknowledge from the beginning that he was a literary artist who was also a professional writer. The relationship between his short story writing and his novel writing in the development of his literary artistry could easily serve as a paradigm for the central dilemma of professional authorship, described by William Charvat in *The Profession of Authorship in America* in this way:

> The terms of professional writing are these: that it provides a living for the author, like any other job; that it is a main and prolonged, rather than intermittent or sporadic, resource for the writer; that it is produced with the hope of extended sale in the open market, like any article of commerce; and that it is written with reference to buyers' tastes and reading habits. The problem of the professional writer is not identical with that of the literary artist; but when a literary artist is also a professional writer, he cannot solve the problems of the one function without reference to the other. (Charvat, *Profession*, 3)

Early in his career Fitzgerald grasped the seemingly conflicting demands on the literary artist who is also a professional writer, and he spent much of his life reconciling them.[7]

Indeed, in a retrospective look at his career immediately preceding the publication of *This Side of Paradise*, Fitzgerald notes the point at which he recalls becoming aware of the required structure of a professional author's life: "While I waited for the novel to appear, the metamorphosis of amateur into professional began to take place... the stitching together of your life in such a way that the end of one job automatically becomes the beginning of the next" (*Crack-Up*, 86). In practical terms this meant, for the moment, that Fitzgerald, until *This Side of Paradise* began earning money, needed to support himself by writing short stories that would pay his bills. With this realization, he began a cycle that would continue until his death: he would write stories to sustain himself and his family between novels – novels, as it turns out, whose royalties rarely provided him more than a brief respite from story writing. On one level, then, throughout his life Fitzgerald continued writing stories, as he told Hemingway, "to have money ahead to write decent books" (Hemingway, *Moveable Feast*, 153). On another level, he came to what was perhaps the even more important realization that he could use the stories as a workshop for subjects, themes, and techniques that he would continue to develop in later stories and novels. The foundation for this use of the magazines as a workshop for later works was established long before *This Side of Paradise* went to press in the earliest years of his apprenticeship.

Fitzgerald's apprenticeship began when he was thirteen, with the 1909 publication in St. Paul's Academy's *Now and Then* of a detective story, "The

Mystery of the Raymond Mortgage"; it ended with the 1917 publication in Princeton's *Nassau Literary Magazine* of what is clearly the most complex of his juvenile pieces, "The Pierian Springs and the Last Straw." The thirteen stories of Fitzgerald's apprenticeship were scattered among *Now and Then*, the *Newman News* (the Newman School's literary magazine), and the *Nassau Literary Magazine*. Few would argue that there are neglected masterpieces among Fitzgerald's apprenticeship stories though there are clearly brilliant moments in many of them. Nor would one likely suggest that there are startling connections between any single juvenile story and Fitzgerald's best mature work, a point noted by John Kuehl in his introduction to *The Apprentice Fiction of F. Scott Fitzgerald*: "the points of similarity . . . are scattered rather than clustered; no one juvenile work shares themes, characters, and techniques with any single work written during maturity" (*Apprentice Fiction*, 15). What one can see by following the apprenticeship stories chronologically, however, is Fitzgerald's intuitive development in rather clear stages of the talent that would reach its high point in *The Great Gatsby* and *Tender is the Night*, as well as in many of the extraordinary stories that cluster around these novels.

The four earliest stories, which appeared in *Now and Then*, show a young Fitzgerald experimenting with first- and third-person points of view, and managing particularly well in the first-person narratives such as "The Room with the Green Blinds" to approach what Malcolm Cowley referred to as "double vision" (Kazin, *F. Scott Fitzgerald: The Man and His Work*, 146): his ability to immerse the reader in experience at an emotional and sensory level, while at the same time allowing him to stand back at a distance and criticize the experience intellectually. In the three *Newman News* stories, on the other hand, Fitzgerald seems less concerned with technical matters than with developing the leisure-class material that will later become his trademark, focusing particularly in two of the stories, "A Luckless Santa Claus" and "The Trail of the Duke," on the *femme fatale*, who will figure prominently in *This Side of Paradise* and in such flapper stories as "The Offshore Pirate" and "Rags Martin-Jones and the Pr-nce of W-les," to name two of more than a dozen. While all three of the *Newman News* stories have trivial plots, they are important in marking the point in Fitzgerald's life when he laid claim to what he came to consider his material: youth, wealth, and beauty; and they are noteworthy in pointing ahead to the kind of brilliant prose passages that were the saving grace of even his weakest stories, prose that would lead Dorothy Parker to comment that, though Fitzgerald could write a bad story, he could not write badly. Even the earliest stories of his apprenticeship contain such passages, among them this one from "The Trail of the Duke": "Inside, through screen, window and door fled the bugs and gathered around the lights like so many humans at a carnival, buzzing, thugging, whirring... In the flats that line upper New York, pianos (sweatting [*sic*] ebony perspiration) ground out ragtime tunes of last winter and here and there a wan woman sang the air in a hot soprano" (*Apprentice Fiction*, 54).

Not surprising, of course, is the fact that Fitzgerald's most sophisticated apprenticeship stories are the ones he wrote while an undergraduate at Princeton, those six stories that appeared in the *Nassau Literary Magazine*, several of which were later revised and published in the *Smart Set* (e.g., "Tarquin of Cheepside," "The Ordeal," "Babes in the Woods") and some of which were incorporated with changes into *This Side of Paradise* after their publication in both the *Nassau Lit* and the *Smart Set* (e.g., "Babes in the Woods"). Though the *Nassau Lit* stories reveal a developing writer aware of intricacies of point of view and a writer, by this time, settled already into his leisure-class subject matter, they are perhaps distinguishable from the earlier stories mainly in their possessing a characteristic attitude that Fitzgerald would later take toward his material, an attitude that he would call his "stamp" of "[t]aking things hard": "That's the stamp that goes into my books so that people can read it blind like Braille," he later remarked (Bruccoli *et al.*, *Romantic Egoists*, 27). This stamp is most evident in two of the best of these stories, "The Spire and the Gargoyle" and "Sentiment and the Use of Rouge," in which main characters "take hard" the lack of money and the transient quality of beauty.

It is, of course, unlikely that Fitzgerald consciously set out during the various phases of his apprenticeship to focus narrowly and systematically on a single aspect of his talent such as experimentation with subtleties of viewpoint; it is furthermore unlikely that he then proceeded to another, such as the claiming of an exclusive domain of material – youth, wealth, and beauty; or that he finally and knowingly marked all that he wrote with his "stamp" of "taking things hard." It is true, however, that by the time he made the transition from amateur to professional, by the time he sold his first novel to Scribners and his first stories to the *Smart Set* and the *Saturday Evening Post*, the foundations of his mature talent – double vision, his material, and his stamp – were in place, granted of course that they would require and receive much refinement in the years to follow. In retrospect Fitzgerald had established with his apprenticeship stories a pattern by which he would develop themes, subjects, and techniques in his short stories that he would later experiment with and refine in novels and other stories. His extensive borrowing and reworking of earlier material for *This Side of Paradise*, in fact, led one critic to refer to the novel as "The Collected Works of F. Scott Fitzgerald" (Bryer, *Critical Reception*, 22). As he became more sophisticated, especially during and after the composition of *The Great Gatsby*, the "borrowing" became more subtle, as in the case of a story like "Winter Dreams," which he referred to as "A sort of 1st draft of the Gatsby idea" (*Dear Scott/Dear Max*, 112). Later, as his alcoholism dulled the edge of his ability to compose freshly, particularly in the instance of his numerous revisions of *Tender is the Night*, he actually lifted complete passages from the cluster stories and used them unaltered in the novel, a fact which ultimately strengthened the novel as it limited the number of stories that he could consider including in *Taps at Reveille*, since he did not want to be accused of selling warmed-over fare.

From beginning to end, the relationship between Fitzgerald the short story writer and Fitzgerald the novelist was complex and integral. But about this relationship one is safe in making this general observation: he was at his best as a novelist during the time he was also writing his best short stories, during those periods when solving the problems of the professional writer seemed quite often to coincide with solving the problems of the literary artist. In the months during which Fitzgerald waited for *This Side of Paradise* to appear, and indeed during the two-year period leading through the publication of the first and second story collections, *Flappers and Philosophers* and *Tales of the Jazz Age*, the problems of the one did not seem to coincide with the problems of the other, and Fitzgerald's transition into the profession of authorship was bumpy, a period of uncertainty regarding the audience for which he was writing and about the suitability of various subjects that he wished to explore in his short stories. Clearly he was buoyed up by the sale of his gimmicky flapper story, "Head and Shoulders," to the *Post* and even more excited by the sale of its movie rights for $2,500, but he was frustrated by the fact that "The Ice Palace," the second story bought by the *Post* and perhaps his best story to date, was delayed in its publication, apparently on hold until the magazine was able to sandwich it between the lighter flapper stories, "Bernice Bobs Her Hair" and "The Offshore Pirate." He was also baffled that Ober, who had become his agent in November 1919, had difficulty placing such "realistic" stories as "The Smilers" even with serious publications like *Scribner's Magazine*. His frustration led him to write Ober, asking, "Is there any market at all for the cynical or pessimistic story except the *Smart Set* or does realism bar a story from any well-paying magazine no matter how cleverly it's done?" (*As Ever, Scott Fitz*, 7). His difficulty in placing his excellent "realistic" story, "May Day," which he finally sold to the *Smart Set* for a mere $200, must have provided a sobering answer, to which would be added the frustration he experienced when Ober had no luck selling the brilliant story, "The Diamond as Big as the Ritz" for a good price to a popular magazine like the *Post* and Fitzgerald virtually had to give it to the *Smart Set* for $300.

The obvious lesson regarding his short story writing that Fitzgerald was learning during this early period of exploration was that the magazines paying the highest prices for his stories, like the *Post*, preferred, with some exceptions, his light, entertaining, gimmicky stories, particularly his flapper stories. The more serious stories, especially those that had a naturalistic bent like "May Day" and the weak but deterministic "Dalrymple Goes Wrong," could be sold, but usually only to low-paying, if more prestigious, publications like the *Smart Set*; and it was these stories, again with some exceptions, that such magazines preferred. The literary implications of these facts are clear: first, in order to earn money Fitzgerald appropriated subjects and settings with which he had always been comfortable – youth, the wealthy, and the glamorous – and packaged them in stories that would entertain a middle-brow reading audience, stories like "Myra Meets His Family," "The Camel's Back," and "The Popular Girl." But secondly, in order to please the audience he regarded as highbrow, those who might read the *Smart Set* and not coincidentally Mencken, who edited it, Fitzgerald experimented with literary naturalism, moving toward a "meaninglessness of life" philosophy that he seemed never able to embrace fully. His flirtation with naturalism led him to produce perhaps a half-dozen stories, among them "The Four Fists," "The Smilers," "The Lees of Happiness," and "May Day," this latter the sole triumph of his experimentation with naturalism. It finally led to what is usually regarded as his weakest novel, *The Beautiful and Damned*.

Of the thirteen published stories available for inclusion in *Flappers and Philosophers*, Fitzgerald selected eight that accurately represented the range of stories he had written in the first year of his professional career, and consequently the volume sharply underscored the tension between the popular audience for which he had been writing and the "literary" one. Two of the stories were from the *Smart Set*: "Benediction," a reworked version of "The Ordeal" from the *Nassau Lit* and one of the best stories in the collection; and "Dalrymple Goes Wrong," a weak naturalistic tale that Fitzgerald, usually a very good judge of the quality of his work, thought of at the time as "the best story I ever wrote" (*As Ever, Scott Fitz*, 5). Two of the stories, "The Cut Glass Bowl" and "The Four Fists," were from *Scribner's Magazine*, and are both serious, but self-consciously symbolic and overly didactic. The remaining four are from the *Post*: three of them, "Bernice Bobs Her Hair," "The Offshore Pirate," and "Head and Shoulders," are ingenious flapper stories, and at least the first is worthy of the serious critical scrutiny it has, in fact, begun to receive; and finally "The Ice Palace" is a masterful North–South contrast, the first of what will be a trilogy set in Tarleton, Georgia, and unquestionably the best story in the volume.

It is fair to say that Fitzgerald during the year of the publication of *This Side of Paradise*, the year leading up to *Flappers and Philosophers*, was more sharply focused on the concern of the professional writer to earn a living than that of the literary artist to create works of lasting merit. As he struggled with the novel that would become *The Beautiful and Damned* he entered a dark, thankfully brief, period of his story writing, working under the spell of "the meaninglessness of life" philosophy that was for most of 1920 and 1921 the guiding light of his stories and of the novel in progress. "May Day" is the single great artistic triumph of his flirtation with naturalism, which also accounts for such relatively weak stories as "The Lees of Happiness," "His Russet Witch," and "Two for a Cent." Even "The Jelly-Bean," an underestimated piece and the second of his three Tarleton stories, was weakened by the deterministic philosophy. "The Diamond as Big as the Ritz," which Fitzgerald wrote "utterly for my own amusement," escapes the spell of naturalism and stands with "May Day" as the saving grace of the 1920–1 period.

When the moment came to assemble stories for *Tales of the Jazz Age* he was able to anchor the volume with "May Day" and "The Diamond as Big as the Ritz," but he was forced to dip into the cache of his undergraduate pieces for "Jemina," "Tarquin of Cheepside," and "Porcelain and Pink," and into the previously uncollected store of his earliest flapper stories, retrieving from it the light, frothy "The Camel's Back," which he perhaps saw as balancing such darker stories as "The Jelly-Bean," "His Russet Witch," and "Two for a Cent" (all written for *Metropolitan Magazine* under contract), "The Curious Case of Benjamin Buttons" (rejected by *Metropolitan* and published in *Collier's*), and "The Lees of Happiness," a story from the *Chicago Tribune* which chronicled a popular writer's decline into a vegetable state. The bright side of this bleak period, from which came *The Beautiful and Damned* and his weakest story collection, *Tales of the Jazz Age*, is that he had during this time returned to a serious consideration of his role as literary artist, trying out what he regarded as a coherent theory for literary art and human behavior subscribed to by Frank Norris and Theodore Dreiser, among other naturalists admired by Fitzgerald, though as it turned out, this was a theory not well suited to Fitzgerald either artistically or temperamentally. Ironically, by trading on the early popularity of his stories about flappers and young love, he had gained a measure of financial freedom and the security of knowing that *Metropolitan* would buy a fixed number of his 1920–1 stories before they could know, of course, that these stories were leading Fitzgerald toward a literary dead end. There has been much critical debate about the process that led the author of *The Beautiful and Damned* and of the stories in *Tales of the Jazz Age* to make what seems to have been an almost magical leap in three short years to the composition of his masterpiece, *The Great Gatsby*. Granted there was energy and originality in *This Side of Paradise*; there were also isolated bursts of virtuosity in stories like "The Ice Palace," leading up to the first story collection, *Flappers and Philosophers*; and there were extended works of extraordinary promise from the group of stories that finally worked their way into *Tales of the Jazz Age*, most notably "May Day" and "The Diamond as Big as the Ritz." Nevertheless, Fitzgerald's early stories had only been related loosely to his novels, and then primarily in shared general subject, philosophy, and mood. After the publication of *Tales of the Jazz Age*, he began to reconcile the demands of professional writer and literary artist, skillfully using the stories he wrote for commercial magazines as a proving ground for ideas for novels, and also drawing upon narrative strategies and themes from his novels for subsequent stories, as he does, for example, in the case of "The Rich Boy," which immediately follows *The Great Gatsby* and whose point of view and subject matter clearly grow out of the novel. Perhaps the most important story for understanding the leap that Fitzgerald was about to make in the direction of *The Great Gatsby* after *All the Sad Young Men* is "Winter Dreams," written in September 1922 and the final story published under the terms of his contract with *Metropolitan* before that magazine went into receivership. With this story Fitzgerald began his break from the dark, deterministic stories that surrounded *The Beautiful and Damned* and began to look forward to *The Great Gatsby*, which he would complete in 1925. This "1st draft" of *The Great Gatsby* is a pivotal story in Fitzgerald's use of the popular magazines as a workshop for his novels, demonstrating as it does his growing awareness of the fact that he can experiment with ideas in his stories that will be developed and refined later in longer works.

With few exceptions, the eighteen stories that lie between "Winter Dreams" and "The Rich Boy" show Fitzgerald using the commercial magazines in precisely this way; on the one hand earning from them enough money to carry him through the publication of *The Great Gatsby*, while on the other using them as a place to experiment with his evolving ideas, particularly those about romantic illusions and the American Dream. For this purpose he used two major short story markets he had cultivated in his first two years as a professional writer: the contract market, which he had discovered through his experience with *Metropolitan*, and the *Saturday Evening Post*, which had essentially been outbid by *Metropolitan* for Fitzgerald's stories and which had not published one of his stories for two years. In December 1922 Fitzgerald signed a contract with the Hearst organization, by which he was paid $1,500 for an option on his 1923 story output with a guarantee that Hearst's would buy at least six stories at $1,875 per story. Of the six stories Fitzgerald wrote under the terms of this contract, the two that most clearly illustrate his working through of ideas he would refine in *The Great Gatsby* are "Dice, Brassknuckles & Guitar," and "'The Sensible Thing'" (bought by Hearst's, but exchanged for another story and finally published in *Liberty*). In the first of these, Jim Powell of Tarleton, Georgia, embarks on a quixotic quest to rescue Amanthis from what he sees (wrongly as it turns out) as her loneliness, and is told by her at the end that "You're better than all of them put together, Jim" (*Price*, 63), a comment similar to one that Nick makes to Gatsby near the end of the novel. In the second, "'The Sensible Thing'," George must leave Jonquil at what he perceives to be the irrecoverable golden age of their love to earn the money that will let him come back into her life. When he returns, he discovers that the original love is lost, never to be regained, a situation clearly anticipating Fitzgerald's treatment of Gatsby's relationship with Daisy. Typically, and again with few exceptions, the 1923 stories written with Hearst's in mind are serious ones in which Fitzgerald treats, with varying degrees of succcess, serious, novel-related topics. In 1924 he returned for the first time in two years to the *Saturday Evening Post* and published in that magazine four stories dealing with success and American business. In these stories, "Gretchen's Forty Winks," "The Third Casket," "The Unspeakable Egg," and "John Jackson's Arcady," Fitzgerald became the *Post*'s resident expert on the American Dream, trying out in them ideas that would inform not only Gatsby's experiences in the novel, but also George Wilson's and Mr. Gatz's as well. A third market for the *Gatsby* cluster stories was the *American Mercury*, a glossier version of the by-then-defunct *Smart Set*, which published "Absolution," one of the most important stories of the period and the one referred to by Fitzgerald as a "prologue" to *The Great Gatsby* (Piper, *F. Scott Fitzgerald: A Critical Portrait*, 104). The publication of this story illustrates how committed Fitzgerald had become to the idea of using all of his work-in-progress, in this case a discarded prologue to a very early draft, which does not survive, of the novel that would become *The Great Gatsby*. The main exceptions to Fitzgerald's advances in reconciling the conflicting demands of professional authorship and literary artistry during this period bounded by *Tales of the Jazz Age* and *All the Sad Young Men* come near the end of his completion of the novel, a time during which he reverted to old, tried material and produced such weak stories as "The Pusher in the Face," "One of My Oldest Friends," and "Not in the Guidebook" for *Woman's Home Companion*.

What can be known for certain is that by the end of the crucial 1923–5 period, devoted to the time-consuming writing and producing of his play, *The Vegetable*, and also writing and publishing some twenty short stories, Fitzgerald had managed also to create his masterpiece, *The Great Gatsby*.

This novel succeeds in large part because he had developed a mastery of his craft far exceeding that in evidence in his first two novels. In *The Great Gatsby* Fitzgerald constructs a story that operates on many levels and at varying levels of abstraction. On one level it is the simple story of Jay Gatsby's love for Daisy Buchanan, a love story reminiscent of the one in " 'The Sensible Thing' "; on another it is a story of the American Dream, of the infinite promise that with hard work one can achieve the best that America has to offer, a subject he had dealt with in the *Post* success stories; and on another, it is a story of the ideal quest, which he had worked with earlier in "Winter Dreams." Through skillful use of narrative point of view Fitzgerald manages in the novel to sustain the tension in the various levels of the story and communicate to the reader the kind of double vision that he himself had. And through his use of unforgettable images such as the eyes of T. J. Eckleburg and the Valley of Ashes he was able through the novel to convey, in Maxwell Perkins's words, a "sort of sense of eternity" (*Dear Scott/Dear Max*, 84).

There are various schools of thought regarding Fitzgerald's maturation as an artist during this time, particularly regarding the role of the short stories in his progress toward *The Great Gatsby*. One school, of which James E. Miller is a spokesman, attributes the leap largely to conscious aesthetic considerations such as Fitzgerald's decision to abandon the artistic principle of "saturation" (evidenced in *This Side of Paradise* and in early, expansive stories) in favor of the Jamesian principle of "selected incident," or to his absorption of Conradian principles related to point of view (Miller, *F. Scott Fitzgerald: His Art and His Technique*). Another line of thought articulated by Milton R. Stern, among others, attributes the leap both to Fitzgerald's increased aesthetic awareness and to a growth spurt in Fitzgerald's maturity as well as a general broadening of his vision (Stern, *The Golden Moment*). This latter argument is elaborated upon with particular application to the short stories by Petry, who focuses sharply on "Fitzgerald's changing perception of his wife and his increasingly astute understanding of his own responsibility for their troubled relationship [which] had a direct and immediate impact on his art" (Petry, *Fitzgerald's Craft*, 6). This changing perception, as Petry sees it, accounts in large part for the radical improvement in the stories in *All the Sad Young Men* over those in *Tales of the Jazz Age*. To these observations must be added another, perhaps in part an extension of the ideas mentioned above, but worth emphasizing in regard to the stories. Fitzgerald, during the 1922–5 period, began for the first time in his professional career to see the demands of the professional writer to be, if not precisely the same as, then at least not entirely incompatible with, those of the literary artist, as the stories selected for inclusion in *All the*

Sad Young Men clearly demonstrate. Four of the stories, "Winter Dreams," "Absolution," " 'The Sensible Thing'," and "The Rich Boy," have direct ties to *The Great Gatsby* and are among the strongest of Fitzgerald's 178 stories. Four additional ones, "Hot & Cold Blood," "Gretchen's Forty Winks," "The Baby Party," and "The Adjuster," though weaker, all deal with serious, *Gatsby*-related subjects such as lost ideals, strained marriages, and material success. Conspicuously absent from *All the Sad Young Men* are the gimmicky flapper stories so often singled out for criticism in reviews of earlier volumes, a consideration which no doubt figured in Fitzgerald's decision to omit "Dice, Brassknuckles & Guitar," an important, though at least on its surface, commercial, *Gatsby* cluster story, from *All the Sad Young Men*.

In the years separating this third collection from his fourth and final one, *Taps at Reveille* – years during which Fitzgerald carried *Tender is the Night* through eighteen complete drafts to publication in 1934, during which his wife suffered two major mental breakdowns, and during which Fitzgerald himself battled on and off with alcoholism – he managed to publish an astonishing fifty-six stories, all but eight of them in the *Saturday Evening Post*, and many of them, including "Babylon Revisited," among the finest of his career. Having shopped around for markets for his stories in the six years leading up to *The Great Gatsby* and *All the Sad Young Men*, Fitzgerald, during the period leading up to *Taps at Reveille*, settled into a sustained relationship with the *Post*, which was the mouthpiece of middle America during the 1920s and 1930s. He became, according to Ober, a virtual employee of the *Post*, primarily because it paid the highest prices for fiction of any magazine in America (*As Ever, Scott Fitz*, 192). During these years Fitzgerald earned prices ranging from $2,000 to $4,000 per story from the *Post*, and it came to serve as an ideal, predictable, and lucrative workshop for ideas, characters, and settings that he was developing for *Tender is the Night*.

The seventeen *Tender is the Night* cluster stories that appeared in the *Post* indeed reflect the extraordinary complexity of the novel itself, which explores through shifting viewpoints the intersecting stories of the American psychiatrist Dick Diver and his schizophrenic wife Nicole, tracing Dick's tragic decline into emotional bankruptcy as it simultaneously documents Nicole's ascent to greater emotional stability and independence. In five of the stories, "Love in the Night," "A Penny Spent," "Majesty," "The Bridal Party," and "The Hotel Child," Fitzgerald develops the European setting, particularly the French Riviera, that will provide the backdrop for much of the novel. In some cases, as in "Love in the Night," he experiments with specific scenes such as the Privateer yacht scene in the story that he will develop into the T. F. Golding yacht episode in the novel, an important one in which Nicole meets Tommy Barban again for the first time in five years. Eight other stories, "Jacob's Ladder," "Magnetism," "The Rough Crossing," "The Swimmers," "Two Wrongs," "One Trip Abroad," "Indecision," and "A New Leaf," are essentially dress rehearsals for characters in *Tender is the Night*, in which Fitzgerald explores interactions between characters in the Dick–Nicole–Rosemary and Dick–Nicole–Tommy triangles in the novel. An additional group of four stories, "The Love Boat," "At Your Age," "Babylon Revisited," and "On Schedule," are close thematically to the novel, sharing particularly, as in "Babylon Revisited," the novel's mood of loss and regret, and in the other three stories the sadness of lost youth brought into high relief through relationships between older men and younger women, explored in the novel in the Dick–Rosemary relationship.

The *Tender is the Night* cluster stories are perhaps the most significant group of stories that Fitzgerald ever wrote when they are considered together and in the context of his uniting in them the concerns of the professional writer and literary artist. They show him in many cases walking a thin line between the demands of contemporary popular readers and discriminating critics, a feat all the more impressive given typical biases of his *Post* readers in the 1920s and 1930s against frank treatment of such subjects as alcoholism and suicide ("The Swimmers"); expatriation ("Majesty"); disillusionment ("The Love Boat"); and dissipation ("One Trip Abroad"), among others. But Fitzgerald, who had already written in *The Great Gatsby* one of the strongest indictments of American materialism and who was about to write in *Tender is the Night* a poignant prophesy of the decline of Western civilization, had indeed developed by the time of these stories a mastery of the craft that enabled him at least at times in magazine stories like many of these to write honestly, as his artistic conscience dictated, and at the same time to entertain an audience that seems in retrospect a rather unlikely one upon whom to try out his serious *Tender is the Night* subjects and themes.

The stories that cluster around *Tender is the Night*, of course, account for only seventeen of Fitzgerald's *Post* contributions in the *Taps at Reveille* period; and the story of his success with this magazine, which reached a high point around 1930 with "Babylon Revisited," as well as his gradual loss of it, marked in 1937 by his final *Post* story, " 'Trouble'," is complex. In the first several years of the period, during which he was publishing the serious novel-related stories such as "Jacob's Ladder" and "Magnetism" in the *Post*, Fitzgerald also began working on a group of retrospective stories dealing with the subject of adolescence. Among these are "Presumption," "The Adolescent Marriage," "A Short Trip Home," and "The Bowl." And though none of them, arguably with the exception of "The Bowl," ranks high in his story canon, these stories, all containing young protagonists, foreshadow and, in fact, pave the way for the Basil Duke Lee–Josephine Perry stories, which were unquestionably popular successes, and in the cases of several individual stories, artistic triumphs.

The eight Basil Duke Lee stories taken together comprise a novelette of growth, chronicling the social and moral development of a resourceful boy, a romantic hero, not unlike Amory Blaine in *This Side of Paradise* (or Fitzgerald for that matter) in his adolescence. Typically, Basil's adventures involve a beautiful, rich girl, Basil's arch rival, and usually a situation that leads him to some conclusion about life that he has not thought about before. In one instance from "The Captured Shadow," for example, Basil knowingly allows a small boy to catch the mumps so that the boy's family – in particular, his attractive sister, who is scheduled to play the lead in one of Basil's plays – will not be able to leave town on vacation; and though Basil is successful with his plotting, he comes through the experience wiser, as he does in virtually all of the stories. Fitzgerald's success in this series comes mainly from his ability to entertain with the ingenious and hilarious situations in which he places Basil. As Ober told him, "I shall never be satisfied until I hear more about Basil, and I think everyone who reads the stories feels the same way" (*As Ever, Scott Fitz*, 116). But the stories succeed also because Fitzgerald is able to distance himself aesthetically from his subject in a way he had not been able to do with Amory Blaine, whom Basil in superficial ways resembles. Fitzgerald maintains this same kind of ironic stance in relation to Josephine Perry, the adolescent protagonist of five *Post* stories that chronologically follow the Basil series, though Josephine is by no means simply a female version of Basil. Whereas Basil was largely a sympathetic figure, who progressively endeared himself to the reader as he grew toward self-knowledge in episode after episode, Josephine is a spoiled rich girl who moves step by step toward the condition referred to in the title of the final story of the series, "Emotional Bankruptcy," a state of emotional depletion which most readers will agree she has earned through her snobbishness and insensitivity to others.

In addition to the unquestionable artistic value of these stories is the fact that they played an important role in Fitzgerald's maintaining the *Post* as a workshop for his novel. The early adolescence stories were scattered among the early *Tender is the Night* cluster stories; the Basil stories, published as they were almost back-to-back in 1928, in effect provide audiences with a one-year break from the dark novel-related stories such as "The Rough Crossing" and "The Swimmers"; and the Josephine stories appear in a kind of alternating pattern with the bleakest of the *Tender is the Night* stories such as "One Trip Abroad," and "A New Leaf." While there is no correspondence that reveals why Fitzgerald, in the midst of composing *Tender is the Night*, suddenly also began writing retrospective stories about adolescence, a partial explanation is that he knew these stories would be acceptable to *Post* editors because they would be popular with the magazine's readers, a fact that he could not count on with the novel-related stories, which often pushed the limits of what was acceptable for a popular magazine. Thus these adolescence stories gave Fitzgerald a guaranteed income during an important period of the composition of the novel, and they allowed him to practice his craft, particularly that part of it related to narrative viewpoint and aesthetic distance, considerations of great significance in his most ambitious novel, *Tender is the Night*.

With the final Josephine story, "Emotional Bankruptcy," Fitzgerald had begun to blend the serious concept of emotional depletion that is at the heart of Dick Diver's story in the novel with his entertaining narratives about adolescence, and from approximately the time of this story forward he seemed, for whatever combination of reasons, to lose a sense of the tastes of his popular magazine audience that he was never able fully to regain. Between "Emotional Bankruptcy" and the publication of *Taps at Reveille*, he published twenty more stories in the *Post*, but virtually all of them lacked the spark of his *Tender is the Night* cluster stories and the Basil and Josephine stories. Most of the works of the period of Fitzgerald's declining popularity with the *Post* are characterized by a retrospective quality that had, even as recently as 1928, worked to Fitzgerald's advantage, as is evidenced by "The Last of the Belles," in which Fitzgerald reached back into his early Tarleton, Georgia, series (including "The Ice Palace," "The Jelly-Bean," and "Dice, Brassknuckles & Guitar") and retrieved Ailie Calhoun, one of his most memorable heroines. But by 1933, even the best of his retrospective stories such as "More than Just a House," lack freshness and are characterized by blurred focus and multiple plots, not always clearly related to each other. There is about his stories in the years immediately preceding *Tender is the Night* an almost desperate quality that one senses results from Fitzgerald's searching for stories that he once wrote with such seeming effortlessness, stories that he could not now quite find. He attempted, for example, a series of loosely related stories involving the medical profession, including "Her Last Case," "Zone of Accident," and "One Interne," but was unable to sustain it. The *Post* began rejecting more and more of his submissions, and his prices for individual stories began steadily dropping from $4,000 to $3,500 to $2,500, and finally to $2,000, which was the price he earned for his last *Post* story.

With the disappointment of his gradual but inevitable loss of the *Post* and the even more devastating critical reception of *Tender is the Night* (published in 1934), Fitzgerald clearly wanted to assemble the strongest possible story collection to serve as a companion volume for the novel. The Fitzgerald–Perkins correspondence outlines several alternatives for constructing what would become *Taps at Reveille*, including the possibility that it could be an omnibus volume containing strong selections from the three previous story volumes, supplemented by the best of his work since the last one (*Dear Scott/Dear Max*, 195–201). Finally, following the precedent set by those three volumes, they agreed to use only stories from the fifty-six published since 1926. Perkins favored a collection consisting primarily of Basil and Josephine stories, an idea that Fitzgerald opposed since he did not want critics to consider the book as his next novel. He also objected to filling the volume with his *Tender is the Night* cluster stories, since many of them had been stripped of scenes and passages that had been included in the novel, and would, if included, leave him open to criticism that he was recycling material. The two finally agreed on a volume that would include some of the Basil and Josephine stories (to be scattered through the volume rather than run as units), a few *Tender is the Night* cluster stories, and assorted selections representing the magazine work that Fitzgerald had done outside those two groups since *All the Sad Young Men*.

The volume that was finally published contained four *Tender is the Night* cluster stories: "Babylon Revisited," which was unquestionably the strongest story in the collection; and "Majesty," "Two Wrongs," and "Crazy Sunday," the last of these a strong story with ties both to *Tender is the Night* and *The Last Tycoon*. Interestingly, "Majesty" and "Two Wrongs" are among the weakest of the novel-related stories, and there is no question that the inclusion of "One Trip Abroad," "The Swimmers," or "The Rough Crossing," all too clearly linked to *Tender is the Night* in Fitzgerald's eyes, in the place of either of them would have strengthened the volume. Five of the eight Basil stories were included, as were three of the five Josephine stories, which meant that they occupied more than half the volume. Outside of these groups Fitzgerald understandably chose "The Last of the Belles," his beautifully nostalgic farewell to the South. The remaining choices, however, are curious: "One Interne," from the aborted series of *Post* stories about the medical profession; "Family in the Wind," one of the long rambling stories that manifests the lack of focus and disjointedness that caused Fitzgerald to lose the *Post*; "A Short Trip Home," one of the adolescence stories which precedes the Basil and Josephine stories and weaker than "The Bowl," which might have replaced it; and finally, "The Night Before Chancellorsville" and "The Fiend," two relatively short pieces that had appeared in *Esquire*, for which Fitzgerald had just begun to write – stories exhibiting what would become known as his sparser, more economical "new manner," but nevertheless stories weaker than numerous ones whose place they took in *Taps at Reveille*.

Whether by accident or design Fitzgerald had assembled each of his short story volumes in such a way that it would be representative of the various kinds of stories he had been writing since the volume that preceded it. In this, *Taps at Reveille* clearly is no exception; it does, however, differ from earlier volumes in foreshadowing, perhaps eerily so, the direction that his short story writing career would take in the years leading up to his death in December 1940. *Taps at Reveille* had been published in March 1935. As it went to press, Fitzgerald completed work on "Zone of Accident," which would be the dead end of his series about the medical profession, represented in *Taps at Reveille* by "One Interne." Also, while the collection was in press, he devoted two months to writing "The Passionate Eskimo" and "The Intimate Strangers," the first two of what would become a group of stories written for the *Post* but rejected because of weaknesses evident in such *Taps at Reveille* stories as "Family in the Wind" and published finally in slick magazines such as *McCall's*, *Liberty* and *Collier's*, generally considered a step down from the *Post*. Then in December, he tried to launch a new series of stories about Gwen Bowers, a young girl approximately his own daughter's age, a series clearly inspired by his success with the Josephine Perry stories. The *Post* bought the first two stories but rejected the third, in effect ending the series. His last success with the *Post* was bittersweet, a pilot for a series of stories about a nurse whose nickname, "Trouble," provided the title for the first story and with sad irony predicted the series' fate. There would be no sequel to this story, which earned for Fitzgerald only his 1925 price of $2,000; and though he would try many times after "'Trouble'" to regain his favorite popular audience, he was never again able to write a story the *Post* would accept.

The two *Esquire* selections in *Taps at Reveille* ("The Fiend" and "The Night Before Chancellorsville") point to what would emerge as the dominant force in Fitzgerald's career as a short story writer in the last years of his life. Fitzgerald had sent these two stories to *Esquire* after its editor, Arnold Gingrich, had accepted a collaborative essay, largely the work of Zelda Fitzgerald, in early 1934. And Gingrich, who had long been an admirer of Fitzgerald's work, encouraged him to send virtually anything he wrote for publication in *Esquire*. He would pay Fitzgerald "[$]200–250 for a mere appearance (1,000 to 2,000 words in any genre)," Fitzgerald reported to Ober (*As Ever, Scott Fitz*, 291). In the years that followed, Fitzgerald's work would appear in *Esquire* forty-five times, thirty-six of these in the form of what could loosely be called short stories. All of these stories were written in Fitzgerald's "later style," which was characterized by pared-down prose, uncomplicated story lines, and generally sparse description – in essence all of those things that his *Post* stories had not been. While the *Post* stories, for example, had averaged 6,000 words, the *Esquire* stories were typically 2,000 words. And while the *Post* stories were heavily plotted and neatly resolved at the end, the *Esquire* stories were often built around a single, simple episode which was often left unresolved. In effect, Fitzgerald was able in the stories that he wrote with *Esquire* in mind to write as he chose to, knowing that his work would be published. The final effect of this latitude on Fitzgerald's artistic development is debatable, but some of the immediate results were positive. In one of the shorter of these sketches, the 1,200-word "The Lost Decade," Fitzgerald artfully captures his main character's feeling of disorientation after he has come back from being "every-which-way drunk" for a decade by rendering his sensory experience of feeling a building's granite and the texture of his own coat. In the longer "Design in Plaster," he focuses on a single night in the life of Martin Harris, whose extraordinary frustrations in life are brought into high relief by the immediate dilemma of his having a broken shoulder. Thus with these two stories, to which can be added two others, "Financing Finnegan" and the later Pat Hobby story, "A Patriotic Short," Fitzgerald added good stories to the body of his work. Unfortunately these strong stories are the exception, and far more of the *Esquire* sketches lack redeeming value, as in the case of one of the weakest, "Shaggy's Morning," a stream of consciousness narration from a dog's point of view which fails utterly to make it clear why his reflections are worth reading about.

In the final year of his life Fitzgerald conceived of the idea of writing a series of stories about a "scenario hack" named Pat Hobby, whose sad predicament represented a caricature of what Fitzgerald feared he himself might become. The seventeen stories he developed in this series probably stand, if considered together, as Fitzgerald's most worthwhile artistic achievement to emerge from his *Esquire* contributions. The individual Pat Hobby stories typically follow a pattern in which Pat starts at a low point in his life, finds an angle that seems worth pursuing to improve his plight, and then sinks again into failure. In a characteristic story, "Pat Hobby's Secret," for example, Pat comes close to success when he becomes the only one who knows the secret ending for a script whose writer has just been murdered; but his success is undermined when he develops amnesia, in part because he has witnessed the murder of the writer, and thus he loses the contract that he would have had if he had recalled the ending. In the strongest story of the Pat Hobby series and one of the best of his *Esquire* pieces, "A Patriotic Short," Fitzgerald uncharacteristically gives Pat a past, which effectively draws the reader into his character much more deeply than usual, and in the process hints at what Fitzgerald might have done with this series if he had not been so reliant on turning the stories out quickly for the $250 that he seemed always to need so desperately in that last year.

Gingrich, understandably, defended the Pat Hobby stories as evidence that Fitzgerald was turning out "good copy" in the year before his death, and that these stories were his "last word from his last home" (*PH*, ix–xxiii). There is no question that *Esquire* provided an outlet for his story writing that he seemed unable to find elsewhere. However, if one takes a broad view of Fitzgerald's twenty-year career, it becomes clear that the close relationship between his short story writing and his novel writing that he had spent his entire professional life developing is absent during the *Esquire* years. The composition dates of the Pat Hobby stories, after all, coincide with the composition period of *The Last Tycoon*, which Fitzgerald was laboriously working on when he died. Yet all that the Pat Hobby stories share with the novel is their Hollywood setting, whose particulars never seem to overlap. And clearly, there are no dress rehearsals for Monroe Stahr, Kathleen, or Cecelia Brady in the *Esquire* stories, as there were many dress rehearsals for Dick and Nicole Diver and Rosemary Hoyt in the stories leading up to *Tender is the Night*.

One might reasonably conclude, with only the thirty-six *Esquire* stories and *The Last Tycoon* fragment on which to form a judgment, that Fitzgerald himself ultimately gave up on reconciling the roles of professional author and literary artist that seemed for so much of his life to be a primary goal. The Pat Hobby stories, however, do not turn out to be Fitzgerald's only "last word from his last home," and there is good reason to believe that in that final year, more diligently than he had since his *Tender is the Night* cluster stories, Fitzgerald was working to reestablish the popular magazines as his "more orderly writer's notebooks" for *The Last Tycoon*. Two stories, written in 1939 and 1940 and published posthumously, show him with vintage sparkle shaping for a popular audience other than *Esquire* his serious material from *The Last Tycoon*: "Discard," published by *Harper's Bazaar* in 1948, presents a convincing study of the corrupt Hollywood that Stahr was to be up against in the novel, and "Last Kiss," billed by *Collier's* as a story that "contain[s] the seed that grew into the novel *The Last Tycoon*, which Fitzgerald was writing when he died,"[8] indeed contains counterparts to Stahr and Kathleen, as well as echoes of their lost love. There is no correspondence to suggest how Fitzgerald planned to market "Last Kiss," but his exchanges with Ober concerning "Discard" indicate that he wrote this story for *Collier's*, which declined it, and then rewrote it for the *Post*, which also finally rejected it for the reason, Ober concluded, that it was still too subtle for a popular audience (*As Ever, Scott Fitz*, 410–16). But, of course, he would continue to work on it, Fitzgerald must have promised, and they would, of course, continue to hope that he might succeed – that he might be at last what he had long ago become, and what even his short stories alone have probably made him, "one of the greatest writers who ever lived."

NOTES

1 All figures related to Fitzgerald's earnings are taken from his *Ledger*.
2 H. L. Mencken, *Smart Set* (December 1920), 40. Reprinted in Jackson Bryer, ed., *F. Scott Fitzgerald: The Critical Reception*, 48.
3 "Too Much Fire Water," *Minneapolis Journal* (December 10, 1922), 12. Reprinted in Bryer, ed., *The Critical Reception*, 162.
4 Arthur Coleman, "Stories by F. Scott Fitzgerald Are Merely Entertaining," *Dallas Morning News*, March 24, 1935, 8. Reprinted in Bryer, ed., *The Critical Reception*, 339.
5 T. S. Matthews, *New Republic* (April 10, 1935). Reprinted in Alfred Kazin, ed., *F. Scott Fitzgerald: The Man and His Work*, 108.
6 Page xii. Bruccoli was first to develop the "cluster story" concept and explore it in his *The Composition of "Tender Is the Night."*
7 For a full discussion of the role of the popular magazines in Fitzgerald's literary career, see Bryant Mangum, *A Fortune Yet: Money in the Art of F. Scott Fitzgerald's Short Stories.*
8 "Last Kiss," *Collier's* (April 16, 1949), 16.

5

RONALD BERMAN

The Great Gatsby and the twenties

The Great Gatsby, published in 1925, seems to speak directly to its current audience about love and existential freedom. Yet the ideas we bring to the story may not be the ideas that the story brings to us. The book was written before most of its readers were born. It inhabits a different world, with barriers between men and women, Protestants, Catholics, and Jews, rich and poor, capital and labor, educated and half-literate. It was a more defined and morally harder world then: at no point in the novel does Daisy Fay Buchanan ever appeal to the transcending authority of love, or Jay Gatsby to that of equality. Social judgment matters more. Daisy knows that life has many things more permanent than love, and Gatsby knows, or Fitzgerald knows for him, that equality is only a political virtue.

Part of the meaning of the text can be explained by sources, influence, background. Research on these things has concentrated on three broad issues: the novel's development from Fitzgerald's earlier writing about love and money; the influence of other writers like Joseph Conrad and T. S. Eliot; and its powerful retelling of the story of Scott and Zelda. Fitzgerald's own "Winter Dreams" (1922) and "'The Sensible Thing'" (1924) are both about men who need money, in love with women inaccessible without it. The first of these stories "examines a boy whose ambitions become identified with a selfish rich girl." Part of it was absorbed into *The Great Gatsby*: "Indeed, Fitzgerald removed Dexter Green's response to Judy Jones's home from the magazine text and wrote it into the novel as Jay Gatsby's response to Daisy Fay's home."[1] He also cannibalized an extraordinary passage ("All night the saxophones wailed the hopeless comment of the 'Beale Street Blues'" [*GG*, 218]) from "Diamond Dick and the First Law of Woman" (1924) in order to fit it into a description of Daisy Fay Buchanan as the goddess of jazz. Both "Winter Dreams" and "'The Sensible Thing'" describe the loss of idealism, and the grand romantic theme of recapturing the vanished past which is so much a part of Fitzgerald's work.

There are a number of external sources, and Fitzgerald's debt to Joseph Conrad has been well handled: *Almayer's Folly* (1920), for example, is about "the hero's futuristic dream set in an ironic time perspective; his apprenticeship aboard the yacht of an old adventurer who has become rich, which marks his initiation into his dream; the young woman who seems to embody, but then repudiates, the dream" (Long, *The Achieving of "The Great Gatsby"*, 118). Fitzgerald read widely, and traces of that reading can be seen in the text. His novel, according to Richard Lehan (*"The Great Gatsby": The Limits of Wonder*), echoes *The Ordeal of Mark Twain* (1922) by Van Wyck Brooks, *The Waste Land* (1922) by T. S. Eliot, even *The Education of Henry Adams* (1918). One of the classics of literary criticism, Lionel Trilling's *The Liberal Imagination*, makes a convincing case for it being the last in a great series of novels beginning in the early nineteenth century about the rise from poverty to wealth. The protagonist of Balzac, Stendhal, and Dickens tries to conquer the social world of London or Paris. He is able to do so because under the new industrialism, money has taken the place of class. So, what used to be a fairytale, the peasant turning into a prince, becomes a historical possibility. However, these novels are cautionary because success breeds its enemies.

Nowhere is this more true than in a series of novels that was much closer to home. The Horatio Alger stories about starting poor and ending rich were very much on Fitzgerald's mind. They are less innocent than they seem. One of their principal messages is that getting rich is easier than being accepted. Alger's working-class heroes in books like *Sink or Swim* (1870) or *Strong And Steady* (1871) must fight for their success. Money is not the problem: the social order is against them, usually personified by a rich man's son who understands that when poor boys rise, rich boys have less space to breathe in. Fitzgerald had a lifelong interest in the theme, and his works feature antagonistic figures like Braddock Washington of "The Diamond as Big as the Ritz" (1922), Anson Hunter of "The Rich Boy" (1926), and Tom Buchanan of *The Great Gatsby*. They are all figures of control and exclusion. They are all threatening – and in each of their stories are responsible for at least one death.

Source studies on the lives of Scott and Zelda cover much of Fitzgerald's fiction. Some leading biographies should be consulted, especially Matthew J. Bruccoli's *Some Sort of Epic Grandeur* (1981) and Scott Donaldson's *Fool for Love* (1983). They establish the connections not only between the events of the Fitzgeralds' lives, but the way in which they interpreted those events. There is a useful biographical interpretation of the short stories, Alice Hall Petry's *Fitzgerald's Craft of Short Fiction* (1989). James R. Mellow's biography *Invented Lives* (1984) suggests that if art came out of the lives of Scott and Zelda their lives were also consciously shaped by art – a process somewhere between creativity and public relations that has been native to the American scene since Samuel Clemens became Mark Twain.

But, as far as sources are concerned, there may now be too much emphasis on the evolutionary aspect of Fitzgerald's work, the silent assumption being *post hoc, ergo propter hoc*. Mutation matters as much. Fitzgerald agreed with his friend and critic Edmund Wilson, who had encouraged him to forget his earlier writing, and move on to new plots, characters, and ideas. In fact, he instructed his editor Max Perkins to have the jacket for his 1926 volume of stories *All the Sad Young Men* "show transition from his early exuberant stories of youth which created a new type of American girl to the later and more serious mood which produced The Great Gatsby and marked him as one of the half dozen masters of English prose now writing in America" (*Life in Letters*, 122). (A nice assessment on both points. There is much in *The Great Gatsby* that does not have a literary history. It is as accurate and self-justifying as a photograph – something often encountered in its pages.)

The Great Gatsby uses much contemporary historical material. The choice of place and subject, for example, was itself a statement. In 1924, H. L. Mencken, then the most influential American critic, identified the life of post-war New York City as one of the new subjects of the novel. That life was monied, vulgar, noisy, chaotic, and immoral, hence more interesting than anything that could be served up by the literature of gentility. He was fascinated by the same New York crowds that provide the background for Fitzgerald. He too understood their figurative meaning. The frenzied life of Manhattan, its open pursuit of sex, money, and booze was, Mencken wrote, a "spectacle, lush and barbaric in its every detail, [which] offers the material for a great imaginative literature." A new kind of American novel might not only capture the moment but also understand a new experience in American history, the replacement of Victorian public conscience by modern subjectivity. As Mencken put his advice to writers, the New York scene – democracy in its current incarnation – "ought to be far more attractive to novelists than it is."[2]

Sinclair Lewis's *Main Street* (1920) and *Babbitt* (1922) had recently been deserved successes, both of them making the bestseller list. But, despite their example and his own capabilities, Fitzgerald decided to cover new ground. He and his main characters break with provincialism. An enormous amount of the telling of his story is about New York as well as about Gatsby. One of the reasons for the interest of the novel is his description of the city, and any study of the language must take that into account.

The modern moment had after all found its correlative: the great literary and artistic movement of the century's beginnings saw the social world from the urban, dislocated point of view of *The Waste Land*. Modernism provided Fitzgerald, Hemingway, and other writers not only with new tactics but a new sensibility. For example, as Susan Sontag writes of cityscape in photography, "bleak factory buildings and billboard-cluttered avenues look as beautiful, through the camera's eye, as churches and pastoral landscapes. More beautiful, by modern taste" (Sontag, *On Photography*, 78). Ezra Pound had written about the aesthetic power of city lights; Hemingway began his description of Paris in *The Sun Also Rises* (1926) with its "electric signs" (14); Blaise Cendrars theorized that billboard-cluttered avenues had really for the first time made urban landscape visually interesting.[3] Ordinary things were accepted – welcomed – by Modernist writers. They challenged the high seriousness of art and artiness. One of the great moments of twentieth-century fiction comes in 1929 with the sharp, clear description in *A Farewell to Arms* of a bowl of *pasta asciutta* eaten in a dugout without forks. In *The Great Gatsby* Fitzgerald writes with authority about ads, photos, automobiles, magazines, and Broadway musicals as if these things too fuel the energies of art: "the cars from New York are parked five deep in the drive, and already the halls and salons and verandas are gaudy with primary colors and hair shorn in strange new ways and shawls beyond the dreams of Castile" (*GG*, 34). Production, entertainment, style, and consumption are native subjects of Modernism, often displacing what is merely natural. And in the case of a certain billboard featuring Doctor T. J. Eckleburg – both symbol and sign of the times – they become part of the weave of a great American novel.

Like any other intellectual movement, Modernism had its sacred texts: from its use of Baudelaire to that of T. S. Eliot it was self-referential. We can see the hand of the leading modern writers in *The Great Gatsby* and *The Sun Also Rises*: Hemingway writes a reprise of a scene from *Madame Bovary* (1857), and Fitzgerald brings *Almayer's Folly* up to date. Throughout Fitzgerald's deeply symbolic novel we become aware of how far we have gone from the values of realism. As for subject, Mencken may have wanted a Great American Novel on social life in New York, but when it came out he did not recognize it. I think that he expected something that might have been called *Prohibition on Broadway*. He did not expect a romance, or a myth as powerful as that of *The Waste Land* – what Nick Carraway calls "the following of a grail" (*GG*, 116–17). As for style, Fitzgerald's novel of New York is nowhere more Modernist than in its impressionism. Expecting hard-edged delineation of the manners and mores of the Jazz Age, we find instead evocations of yellow cocktail music and trembling opal and a moon produced out of a caterer's basket. The Jazz Age is there, but the story is its own telling.

The Great Gatsby is a recollection of events that took place in the summer of 1922. Jay Gatsby, who began life as Jimmy Gatz, has moved steadily upward in an offbeat version of Making It in America. He has been farm-boy, student, and fisherman; steward and mate for the rich and mindless Dan Cody; eventually the brave and decorated Major Jay Gatsby. He has loved and lost Daisy Fay, and understands that in order to get her back he needs a good deal of money. When we meet him he is a "success" – but as a bootlegger and possibly as a swindler. We enter the story in its last stage, along with the narrator, Nick Carraway. A number of lives become swiftly entangled: Gatsby with Daisy Fay Buchanan; her husband Tom with Myrtle Wilson; Nick with Daisy's friend, Jordan Baker.

Things look simple at the beginning: Nick Carraway, like Gatsby himself, wants to change his life through success. It is a grand American motif. However, getting to where you want to go is not at all simple: Jordan cheats at golf, Myrtle leads a double life, even the unseen but much-heard-of Walter Chase is "very glad to pick up some money" (*GG*, 104) with few questions asked. Nick quickly understands that the glittering social world he has come to conquer is built on ambiguities. One begins to expect that, after having "been everywhere and seen everything and done everything"; after becoming, as Daisy describes herself, "sophisticated" (17). But Nick does not expect the entire texture of lives and human relationships to be affected, and that is the point of his story. These characters are more than the sum of their own experiences: they constitute America itself as it moves into the Jazz Age. There is a larger story which swirls around them, and its meaning is suggested by Fitzgerald's unused title for the novel: *Under the Red, White, and Blue.*

The Great Gatsby is about American issues. Just before Fitzgerald came of age, Walter Lippmann had stated that "those who are young to-day are born into a world in which the foundations of the older order survive only as habits or by default" (Lippmann, *Drift and Mastery*, xvii–xviii). And, soon after the publication of *The Great Gatsby*, John Dewey was to write that "the loyalties which once held individuals, which gave them support, direction, and unity of outlook on life, have well-nigh disappeared."[4] The world of *The Great Gatsby* is a version of the new social world feared by the tradition of American moralists from William James to John Dewey. It is a world of broken relationships and false relationships; a world of money and success rather than of social responsibility; a world in which individuals are all too free to determine their moral destinies. Daisy warns Nick and the reader about the way this world is when she says, "I think everything's terrible anyhow" (*GG*, 17). Because she believes that, she is free to act any way she wants.

One issue of the novel is loyalty to love, another is loyalty to friendship. Nick himself exemplifies loyalty to people and ideas, while Daisy and Tom have freed themselves from troublesome conscience – and from even more troublesome self-awareness. They will be loyal neither to idea nor person. But their characters have not been chosen arbitrarily by Fitzgerald. Americans had long been advised of the perilous subjectivity of their lives. The strong tradition of social philosophy in America, its Public Philosophy, was known for concern with day-to-day issues. Few things better exemplify this than Josiah Royce on the need for loyalty, or William James on the moral life. There were the lectures and writings of Walter Lippmann, George Santayana, and especially John Dewey, all intensely focused on the American scene. In these works are thoughtful accounts of the good life as opposed to the way we live now; there was Walter Lippmann's account of the American Dream (bearing very little relationship to current ideas about it); and there were deliberations about the way that Americans think, or refuse to think, about the implications of that dream. These works called the nation to account for the way it made and spent money, about its class relationships, about the state of American national character. Here is how Josiah Royce described the basic subject of Public Philosophy just before Fitzgerald went to Princeton:

> Since the war, our transformed and restless people has been seeking not only for religious, but for moral guidance. What are the principles that can show us the course to follow in the often pathless wilderness of the new democracy? It frequently seems as if, in every crisis of our greater social affairs, we needed somebody to tell us both our dream and the interpretation thereof. We are eager to have life ... But what life?[5]

Readers who come to Fitzgerald's novel and to the twenties are inclined to think that the oft-mentioned subject of the American Dream is a matter of personal freedom and financial success. However, early twentieth-century thinkers like Josiah Royce and Walter Lippmann wrote about that dream in much more idealistic terms. They related it to the building of the nation in the eighteenth century, and to the qualities of character that implied. But Royce, for one, had recently written that the American Dream was getting difficult even to discern, much less to reconstruct. Perhaps it had already been lost. Were there even models left for Americans to understand? Milton R. Stern agrees, in *The Golden Moment*, that the possibility of even *understanding* the dream had diminished:

> The poor, naive, believing son of a bitch. He dreamed of a country in the mind and he got East and West Egg. He dreamed of a future magic self and he got the

history of Dan Cody. He dreamed of a life of unlimited possibility and he got Hopalong Cassidy, Horatio Alger, and Ben Franklin's "The Way to Wealth." What else could he imitate? (Stern, *The Golden Moment*, 247)

For Fitzgerald himself (and this has something to do with the title he finally chose for his novel) the dream was quite literally about the quality of greatness. It meant displaying in private life those daring unselfish qualities that had made America possible. To be "great" in this novel means to continue an American tradition. And American greatness was definitely on Fitzgerald's mind in the twenties. We are fortunate that he defined it in the conclusion of his short story "The Swimmers" (1929):

> France was a land, England was a people, but America, having about it still that quality of the idea, was harder to utter – it was the graves at Shiloh and the tired, drawn, nervous faces of its great men, and the country boys dying in the Argonne for a phrase that was empty before their bodies withered. It was a willingness of the heart. (*Short Stories*, 512)

It would be difficult to understand *The Great Gatsby* without that last line. But, as good as it is, it is not entirely original. It comes from a good deal of reading about the nature of Americans.

First, the opposite of this idea: against Royce's panoramic vision of national development, responsibility, and obligation, a character like that of Tom Buchanan is a compendium of American failures: he is rich with no conscience, moralistic without being moral, exclusionary, racist, and, above all, true only to himself. As for *his* American dream, that seems undisclosable. He is Royce's nightmare and the nightmare of the Public Philosophy, a classic figure of *ressentiment* and of absolute, selfish subjectivity. How is Gatsby himself to be measured?

The values that Fitzgerald recalled from the years before the Jazz Age did not consist wholly of moral prohibitions. William James did indeed preach fully conscious responsibility for American moral decisions; George Santayana did lecture the American public about its responsibility to create a meaningful social order; and John Dewey did repeatedly outline the conditions for an informed public adapting to necessary social change. But more was implied than public morality. James, in a letter to H. G. Wells that has become part of American intellectual history, once remarked on the new and alarming "worship of the bitch-goddess SUCCESS" in America (Cotkin, *William James, Public Philosopher*, 91). He saw that prosperity and power might in themselves become trivial and boring. Life demanded intense powers of imagination – even of romantic love and devotion. He argued for dedication to people and ideas, and against the state of mind which lost itself in meaningless subjectivity. Life demanded goals, sacrifice, and a certain amount of risk. In fact, James once wondered idly if the last heroes in America might not be outside the law, choosing not to be prudentially middle class. So far as he could see, there was nothing wrong (although excess would clearly be dangerous) in Americans dedicating themselves emotionally to a cause, and losing themselves in it. The characters of *The Great Gatsby* enact many a drama scripted by American philosophy, and its language mirrors the language of debate about a country becoming ever more monied and less heroic, less true – except for Jay Gatsby – to the grand passions of its past.

Gatsby has the capacity for the pursuit of happiness. He believes in his dream and in Daisy as its object. Except for Nick Carraway and poor George Wilson he is the only figure in the novel to have a passion for belief, and to care deeply about someone else. He may be wrong about the kind of happiness that is possible, and about the woman who represents that happiness, but he has committed himself to the dream. Gatsby's pursuit of Daisy against impossible odds is perhaps the final form of the American will to wring a new life from destiny.

Of course, Gatsby is imperfect: in spite of his idealism, his idea of the good life seems merely to be the acquisition of money, things, property. Possibly the most famous literary possession of the twentieth century is his car, in "a rich cream color, bright with nickel, swollen here and there in its monstrous length with triumphant hatboxes and supper-boxes and tool-boxes, and terraced with a labyrinth of wind-shields that mirrored a dozen suns" (*GG*, 51). In this book we tend to see the sun as it is reflected by produced things. Gatsby's house (like Myrtle's apartment) is a showcase of consumption. And yet: an enormously shrewd essay by George Santayana in 1920 (entitled "Materialism and Idealism in American Life") had pointed out that materialism and idealism do not necessarily cancel each other out. Gatsby is materialistic because Americans do not have many other alternatives. Material life offers one of the few recognized ways in which the American can *express* his idealism. This is how Santayana puts the issue:

> For the American the urgency of his novel attack upon matter, his zeal in gathering its fruits, precludes meanderings in primrose paths; devices must be short cuts... There is an enthusiasm in his sympathetic handling of material forces which goes far to cancel the illiberal character which it might otherwise assume... his ideals fall into the form of premonitions and prophecies; and his studious prophecies often come true. So do the happy workmanlike ideals of the American. When a poor boy, perhaps, he dreams of an education, and presently he gets an education, or at least a degree; he dreams of growing rich, and he grows rich... He dreams of helping to carry on and to accelerate the movement of a vast, seething progressive society, and he actually does so. Ideals clinging so close to nature are almost sure of fulfillment; the American

beams with a certain self-confidence and sense of mastery; he feels that God and nature are working with him. (Santayana, *Character and Opinion in the United States*, 108–9)

Money, after all, has been only a means to express otherwise inchoate ideas. Santayana was convinced that this was a kind of secular theology, which is not a bad way to approach Jay Gatsby's own ideas. One of the central themes of Fitzgerald's novel is the application of religious feeling to secular experience; one of the central themes of Santayana is the representativeness of this American conception. Perhaps William James said it best: "faith based on desire is certainly a lawful and possibly an indispensable thing" (James, *The Will to Believe*, 29). For us, the secular and religious have been long intertwined.

What are the obstacles to Gatsby's dream, apart from intractable human nature, time, and chance? Gatsby does not want only to be a success, he wants to be a gentleman. Meyer Wolfshiem reminds us several times that he has fulfilled *both* of his desires, but Wolfshiem turns out to be less than a reliable judge. One of the most important things for readers at the beginning of a new century to remember is that democratic life was different in 1922. Throughout Fitzgerald's novels and stories we see aspiration meeting rejection. The text refers to a democracy that current readers may not recognize; it is defined by caste. Nick, Wolfshiem, Tom, and even Myrtle Wilson have an ideal social type in mind. So does Gatsby. We might be disposed to think that, especially in America, a self-made man would be proud of his achievement. But Gatsby hides his past – although it has been interesting enough to have provided the material for a dozen novels. He begins life on a worked-out farm, learns how to read and think with not much help, goes on his *wanderjahre*, becomes irresistible to women, rescues a yacht from disaster, tops it all off by becoming (Basil Duke Lee dreams of this) a gentleman criminal. If this reminds us of famous lives and books, it is intended to. Every literary-biographical theme we can imagine has been part of his forgotten life: there are echoes of David Copperfield, Julien Sorel, Compton Mackenzie, Horatio Alger, Joseph Conrad, even Raffles, the suave society crook admired by Fitzgerald and also by George Orwell when they were schoolboys. But this adventurous story remains profoundly uninteresting to Gatsby, although it fascinates Nick.

Gatsby does not want to be praised for what he is, but for what he is not. In this, he represents the tensions of the early twenties. Wolfshiem has virtually no social class – he is almost dizzyingly beyond conceivable arrangements – but he thinks about Gatsby being "a perfect gentleman" and "a man of fine breeding" (*GG*, 57). Myrtle Wilson has married her husband

George "because I thought he was a gentleman." She pumps gas, but says the same thing as Wolfshiem about the ideal social type: "I thought he knew something about breeding" (30). Her friend Lucille McKee, who is by no means Mrs. Astor, has dropped a suitor, she says, because "he was way below me" (29). Even Tom Buchanan, with his delusions of science and art and all that, wants badly to assert patrician responsibility, and assert the values of his social class.

When Gatsby says, "Here's another thing I always carry" (53), it is final proof that his early life has disappeared, a photo "of Oxford days" showing that he has always belonged, so to speak, among his peers. Gatsby is not only the leading man of the Jazz Age but the last great figure of the gentleman hero. He understands and accepts that inequality is characteristic of his democratic moment. Unfair, but there is a benefit: his character is thickened, made more intense, by obsolete qualities of courtesy, thoughtfulness, and honor. Whether dealing with Nick Carraway or Daisy or with a girl who has torn her gown at his party, he has that nobility unknown to West Egg, forgotten by East Egg, and by our national memory. The irony of the novel is that he has become far more of a gentleman than his social adversaries – "the whole damn bunch" (120) of them – who have no use for honor. But, by succeeding, he has made himself vulnerable. By retreating from loyalty and honor, Tom and Daisy have protected their unfeeling lives.

Before *The Great Gatsby*, Fitzgerald dealt with the educated and literate world. He told us possibly more than we want to know about the privileged life of Princeton and its college-boy weekends in Manhattan. The creation of Jimmy Gatz, Myrtle Wilson, and George Wilson shows how far his understanding developed. In his correspondence with Max Perkins, his editor at Scribners, Fitzgerald went so far as to state that Myrtle Wilson was a more achieved character than Daisy Fay Buchanan. There are reasons for that: Daisy and Gatsby do not have the same hard delineation as their surrounding cast. They are partly mythical and even allegorical, so that the quality of diffusion is understandable. Myrtle belongs to the everyday world; Fitzgerald's tactic in establishing her is to describe in detail her relationship to that world – and to allow her to reveal her taste and style. Daisy, rarely described directly, is part idea; Myrtle, often described directly, is understood through her countless acquisitions. Her apartment has as much to say about her conception of herself as Gatsby's palace has to say about his:

> The apartment was on the top floor – a small living room, a small dining room, a small bedroom and a bath. The living room was crowded to the doors with a set of tapestried furniture entirely too large for it so that to move about was to stumble continually over scenes of ladies swinging in the gardens of

Versailles... Several old copies of "Town Tattle" lay on the table together with a copy of "Simon called Peter" and some of the small scandal magazines of Broadway. Mrs. Wilson was first concerned with the dog. A reluctant elevator boy went for a box full of straw and some milk to which he added on his own initiative a tin of large hard dog biscuits – one of which decomposed apathetically in the saucer of milk all afternoon. (*GG*, 25)

When we see Myrtle's arrangements we see the inside of her mind. There are many things that are admirable about her but, like Gatsby, she has never understood essential models of style. He wants to be a gentleman, she wants to be a lady: what are the odds? Myrtle, who is blue-collar, has surrounded herself with the artifacts of the middle class. She does not understand even these things very well, which argues that her understanding of Tom, who exists many levels above the middle class, is itself deficient. Everything about the apartment suggests that Myrtle, like Gatsby, has gotten her ideas about style and class from the mass market. Not only are the magazines and books in plain sight; the furnishings are a demonstration of what she has learned from newsstand culture. One of Fitzgerald's tactics in the scene of Myrtle's apartment is to quantify to the limits of comprehension. There are more objects and things described in this apartment than the mind can easily register. Myrtle has tried to *accumulate* her social character. She has installed the tapestried furniture because it provides her with a self-image that is more grandiose than we might guess at first sight, when all she seems to have is carnal intelligence. She has bought books, magazines, furniture, pictures, and a "police dog" (24) because of the urgings of advertisements which promise status through acquisition. Her catalogue of all the things she's "got to get" – a massage, a wave, a collar for the dog, a wreath, an ash tray – is a blueprint for becoming what she knows she is not (31). But, as Stern suggests, even the possibilities of imitation have diminished. That word "small," repeated four times in a paragraph, says something about great expectations compressed into limited psychological space.

It might be as difficult to cover the language of *The Great Gatsby* as it would to do full justice in brief space to each of its characters. But there are some major patterns, relationships, and repetitions drawing attention to the work they do. The narrative itself is tactically repetitive: we find ourselves continually walking through Gatsby's house; seeing Tom and Daisy's place again; reading the small biographies embedded in the novel which refract point after point of the main story. Key ideas and words are mentioned in repeated sequence:

a promise that she had done gay, exciting things just a while since and that there were gay, exciting things hovering in the next hour. (11)

"it's very romantic outdoors . . . It's romantic, isn't it, Tom? . . . Very romantic."
(16)

"She told me it was a girl, and so I turned my head away and wept. 'All right,'
I said, 'I'm glad it's a girl. And I hope she'll be a fool – that's the best thing a
girl can be in this world, a beautiful little fool.' " (17)

"It just shows you . . . It just shows you . . . It just shows you." (135)

Fitzgerald was a student of speech patterns, and these show how people
without much verbal agility tend to repeat themselves while they believe they
are explaining themselves. In the last of these citations, Mr. Gatz thinks that
the connection between things is real and visible; saying that it is, makes it
so for him. One of those "It just shows you" belongs to Nick, politely drawn
into this frail world of belief and assent. Daisy has romance on her mind,
but what we hear is the increasingly flat, reiterated tone of a phrase that does
not have a place among those using it. The more it is repeated, the less it
means, as when Tom tiredly agrees ("Very romantic" [16]) about something
that to him means nothing. Daisy's voice may be golden, but not her speech:
she is often at a loss for words, and can express sincerity or the appearance
of sincerity only through repetition.

The book's imagery has drawn the most attention from critics, but I think
it difficult to rely solely on imagery as a criterion. There are many visual
descriptions of people and things, but they are counterbalanced by the failure of perception which is so large a theme in the narrative. To see things
unclearly is, Fitzgerald implies, about as close as we get to essences. And, the
failure of perception in this story seems to me to correspond to the nature of
human relationships. Nick sees things unclearly because almost no relationship holds true. What matters as much as the object perceived is the mist and
darkness in which it is viewed. (Nick calls history itself a "vast obscurity"
[141], and this sense of impeded understanding applies to the way that we
understand ourselves within the present moment.)

The book's language is famously about color and its implications.
Fitzgerald wrote that Gatsby's house was "gaudy with primary colors" (34)
and the text itself is full of them. It has long been argued that each color
stipulated has some meaning: a good place to look over the categories is
Robert Emmet Long's The Achieving of "The Great Gatsby." Green, for example, is the color of hope, of the green light at the end of a mysterious
dock, of "the . . . green breast of the new world" (GG, 140). The novel is
full of unmediated yellows, implying always in the background the color
of gold and the theme of Midas who turned all he touched into gold.
Colors frame each other: "high in a white palace the king's daughter, the
golden girl" (94). Yellow is also the color of transmutation, and it appears

at intervals, as in the novel's third chapter, to suggest the alchemical powers of great wealth. The creation of a golden world is, evidently, only a matter of intention:

> his station wagon scampered like a brisk yellow bug to meet all trains... Every Friday five crates of oranges and lemons arrived from a fruiterer in New York... On buffet tables, garnished with glistening hors d'oeuvre, spiced baked hams crowded against salads of harlequin designs and pastry pigs and turkeys bewitched to a dark gold... and now the orchestra is playing yellow cocktail music... two girls in twin yellow dresses... With Jordan's slender golden arm resting in mine we descended the steps. (33–6)

We are intended to recognize that money can make the world over, an idea occupying Fitzgerald's imagination since at least 1922, when he published "The Diamond as Big as the Ritz." But color is impermanent; and not necessarily evidential: a white daisy with its golden heart may be supremely deceptive. There is an allegorical moment at Gatsby's first party in which a chorine is singing: "the tears coursed down her cheeks – not freely, however, for when they came into contact with her heavily beaded eyelashes they assumed an inky color, and pursued the rest of their way in slow black rivulets" (42). It is a reminder about surfaces, and all of the metaphorical applications of the idea of surfaces.

The novel is "time-haunted," permeated with hundreds of references to the escape of memory from our lives (Bruccoli, *New Essays on "The Great Gatsby"* 10–12). Throughout, these references to the passage of time convince us of an underlying argument. The novel operates under two different schemes of time, human and cosmic. For example: a powerful irony is generated when the time-bound consciousness of Daisy Buchanan – "What'll we do with ourselves this afternoon," cried Daisy, "and the day after that, and the next thirty years?" (*GG*, 92) – is set against the machinery of the uncaring cosmos. Sun, moon, sky, and stars are in *The Great Gatsby* not entirely because they are the counters of romanticism but because they correct the impressions of Nick and Jordan and, especially, of Jay Gatsby, who want to think that we can in fact see life "beginning over again" (7). The further we get into the narrative, the less comfort there is in nature.

There is a powerful opposition beneath the skin of the novel between the language of navigation and will, and that of drift and unconsciousness. That opposition comes from Public Philosophy. Language reflects some of the national themes that I have mentioned. The description of vital energy, for example, implies strength of character. That energy in Jay Gatsby, in Myrtle Wilson, and, from time to time, in Nick Carraway, suggests the ability to lead a life of feeling. It states the intensity and emotional commitment that are so rare among others in this story. So, when we see Gatsby at rest – as near to rest as he gets – we see his readiness for experience:

> He was balancing himself on the dashboard of his car with that resourcefulness of movement that is so peculiarly American – that comes, I suppose, with the absence of lifting work or rigid sitting in youth and, even more, with the formless grace of our nervous, sporadic games. This quality was continually breaking through his punctilious manner in the shape of restlessness. He was never quite still; there was always a tapping foot somewhere or the impatient opening and closing of a hand. (51)

"Vitality," "energy," and the "restlessness" that Gatsby displays are common terms of the early twentieth century. Their cognates are used, as in the speeches and writings of Teddy Roosevelt, to typify American character and its creative possibilities. Always in motion, Gatsby is intended to remind us of qualities praised not only by novelists, but by those who believed that in order to have a moral life one had first to have great energy, concentrated will, and high resolution. Against the language of this passage we need to pose the language describing others in the text. They are sensed through terms of indolence, inertia, withdrawal, and even paralysis. Daisy Fay Buchanan's languor ("What do people plan?" [13]) shows the life of the Lotos-eaters. Jordan seems not only situationally "bored" but existentially; and she is, of course, too wise or, like Daisy, perhaps too "sophisticated" to dream. Background figures are sick, silent, "lethargic," or paralytically drunk. All display the dull unconsciousness of mind without will that T. S. Eliot had stamped upon the year 1922.

Fitzgerald picked up the national implications of personal and cultural "drift" in unexamined lives:

> Why they came east I don't know. They had spent a year in France, for no particular reason, and then drifted here and there unrestfully wherever people played polo and were rich together. This was a permanent move, said Daisy over the telephone, but I didn't believe it – I had no sight into Daisy's heart but I felt that Tom would drift on forever seeking a little wistfully for the dramatic turbulence of some irrecoverable football game. (8–9)

The term "drift" is inherited from William James, who called it the complete opposite of moral consciousness; and from Walter Lippmann, who had used it as part of the title of a famous book, *Drift and Mastery*. Fitzgerald reminds his readers of debates very much unfinished: Lippmann had said that if you did not *use* your freedom you hardly deserved it. And, indeed, you would not have it long. When Fitzgerald describes Tom and Daisy and the rest he brings back to his audience Lippmann's contemptuous line about Americans who have become a "nation of uncritical drifters," mindless and self-absorbed (Lippmann, *Drift*, xvii). A fatal lack of energy is implied, and, necessarily, of any moral tension. The language tells us, a long time before Tom and Daisy and Jordan ever make their decisions, how those decisions are likely to be made.

Fitzgerald opposes harmony and dissonance, literally and figuratively. For example, Gatsby's first party begins formally, but by evening's end, "most of the remaining women were now having fights with men said to be their husbands." One particular song ends in "gasping broken sobs," and we exit to a "bizarre and tumultuous scene" of collision amid the "harsh discordant din" of auto horns (*GG*, 42–4). Those "caterwauling horns" are not merely background noise, they constitute a cultural metaphor. Amanda Vaill's biography of Gerald Murphy, Fitzgerald's much admired friend, shows that this particular sound was in the Modernist domain by the mid-twenties. Murphy collaborated with Fernand Léger on a film of *Ballet mécanique* which featured the sound of machinery, including the "automobile horn" (Vaill, *Everybody Was So Young*, 189). The harsh, blaring noises of its uncaring mechanical "moving objects" were perfectly calculated to represent not only the tone but the moral dissonance of industrial life.

In Fitzgerald's novel, assonance on every level of meaning is displaced by dissonance. The extraordinary scene at the Plaza Hotel is built around the interruption of rhythm or predictive expectation. Nick, Daisy, Jordan, Tom, and Gatsby overhear a wedding – very much a symbolic event in this story – on the floor below their rented suite. But the wedding's music is overpowered by "compressed heat exploded into sound." The "portentous chords of Mendelssohn's Wedding March" are quite literally drowned out by a much less mellifluous and harder-edged "burst of jazz" (*GG*, 99–100). From this point on the novel's lyrical language becomes broken, dissonant. In fact, Nick describes words as "babbled slander," while Gatsby exits to "clamor" and "tumult" (106), implying the failure of meaning and intention. The new, broken rhythms are the equivalent of operatic themes. But there are further implications. The people at both of Gatsby's parties (and at Myrtle's party also) represent "New York," not simply a place but an idea. "New York" is itself dissonant, it being widely understood in the twenties that the city is no longer entirely white, native, or Christian. In fact, "the most fundamental charge being brought by its critics against New York is the charge that here is an 'alien' city, literally un-American and anti-American in its make-up... the city has gone foreign" (Merz, *The Great American Band Wagon*, 235–6). That is one of the reasons why the language of the novel applied to the life of New York is harsh, discordant. Names matter a great deal, and such drastically unfamiliar aggregates of syllables as Wolfshiem and Da Fontano and the Bembergs and Beluga the tobacco importer are objects of suspicion not only to Tom Buchanan but to the framers of the Immigration Bill of 1924, the year of the novel's composition. The splendid procession of names that begins Fitzgerald's fourth chapter implies the uneasy presence in America of those who have come (all too recently) from the wrong parts of Europe. In Manhattan, Nick and Jordan hear that "foreign clamor on the sidewalk" (*GG*, 106) which has made everyone uneasy. It is in the course of things that "Gatz" from *Mitteleuropa* should become the anglophone "Gatsby." Lily Shiel (Fitzgerald's Jewish-Cockney lover, with a name difficult to scan) herself became Sheilah Graham, metrically-socially a happier choice.

Breakdown is characteristic of both story and language. We begin with harmonic, rhythmic statement, with long, assured, and sweeping sentences, with language that easily imitates music: "And so with the sunshine and the great bursts of leaves growing on the trees" (*GG*, 7). But things move inexorably from harmony to chaos. Starting with the sober, careful, and practiced enunciations of Jay Gatsby we go to another mode featuring the "harsh discordant din" and "violent confusion" and exhaustion which dominate the later telling and experiencing of the story. The language changes from rhythmic precision of statement to cacophony. We move from day to night – and from the description of dreams to that of nightmares. Harmony and discord have the same relationship to each other as expectation and reality. Dissonance in the text is proleptic, and keeps urging us to foresee the ending: those sad, wailing horns of W. C. Handy's *Beale Street Blues* (1916) that we hear about in the text accompany a lyric: "bus'ness never closes til somebody gets killed."

NOTES

Quotations in this chapter are from the 1991 edition of *The Great Gatsby*. For details see Bibliography.

1 Matthew J. Bruccoli, in *The Short Stories of F. Scott Fitzgerald*, ed. Bruccoli, 217. All citations from the stories are from this edition.

2 "Totentanz," in *A Second Mencken Chrestomathy*, ed. Terry Teachout, 181. Mencken's essay is from *Prejudices: Fourth Series*.

3 Cited by Marjorie Perloff, *The Futurist Moment*, 9.

4 From Dewey, *The Public and its Problems* (1927). Cited by Christopher Lasch in *The Revolt of the Elites*, 84.

5 "William James and the Philosophy of Life," *The Basic Writings of Josiah Royce*, 2 vols., ed. John J. McDermott, I: 212, 215. The essay was delivered as a lecture in 1911, so that the war it refers to is the Spanish-American War of 1898.

6

MILTON R. STERN

Tender is the Night
and American history

In the very young Fitzgerald's first novel, *This Side of Paradise* (1920), the driving engine was an impulse toward lyricism and extended evocative description – what the fledgling author thought of as "poetic" language, often included for its own sake. In his second novel, *The Beautiful and Damned* (1922), the driving force changed. The more seasoned young author began to concentrate on objective circumstance and the forward motion of narrative, but the book was less rich in the signature Fitzgerald element of extraordinary evocative power. In his third novel, *The Great Gatsby* (1925), Fitzgerald's genius, luck, and artistic experience succeeded brilliantly in combining the impelling energies of the first two books. His structural method was the presentation of each concrete event within a progression of related events, a series of meals and parties, by means of hauntingly evocative patterns of language that intricately reflected events upon each other – themes that Fitzgerald called "elaborate and overlapping blankets of prose."[1] In the process of combining lyrical description with objective circumstance he mastered the connections between themes and narration. He discovered how to build a story out of tightly controlled and intricately woven patterns to express ideas. The expression itself grew from his remarkable power with evocative language.

But Fitzgerald would not again write a novel composed so fully of such lush and haunting "overlapping blankets of prose." Except for a few instances (such as the description of the final break between Nicole and Dick or the famous depiction of Nicole's shopping) in *Tender is the Night* (1934), there are no extended passages of what Fitzgerald had thought of as "poetic." In the years between *The Great Gatsby* and *Tender is the Night*, Fitzgerald clearly felt the influence of what American literary style had evolved into by the 1930s; that influence continued to train his trademark evocative genius toward narrative momentum without extended rhetorical flights. A rich history of literary, intellectual, social, and political influences provided an inevitable context for Fitzgerald's style in his economic dependence on magazine short fiction during the Depression and in his attempts to write for the Hollywood studios. His fiction took on more tints of the realism that increasingly had characterized American fiction since the Civil War and also merged with the existentially energized anti-sentimentality of language and event that had characterized American fiction since World War I. *Tender is the Night* suggested the hardboiled humor, favored by *Esquire* magazine, with which Fitzgerald was to characterize his last published efforts, the Pat Hobby stories; it also suggested the style with which he was to compose the compelling, beautiful fragment of *The Last Tycoon* (1941). Seen within the totality of Fitzgerald's work, in Fitzgerald's mature stylistic journey *Tender is the Night* is as gigantic a landmark as *The Great Gatsby*.

It took a while before readers began to discover the book's enormous wealth: it was not especially well received upon publication on April 12, 1934, but by the close of the twentieth century, it had become admiringly recognized, appreciated, and praised as one of America's great books. Yet it also had suffered badly from ideologically distorting criticism and simplistic readings stemming from an overidentification of Fitzgerald's work with his life and times during the Jazz Age. He named the age, which featured Roaring Twenties expatriates – not only artists and writers, but also the idle rich such as those who people his fourth novel. In the 1930s *Tender is the Night* was often dismissed because the surfaces of its materials were shallowly seen as the intellectual and moral substance of the book, just another story about playboys and playgirls with not enough serious work to make them significant in what had become an economically grim "real world."[2]

In the creation of Dick and Nicole Diver, Fitzgerald used aspects of his own life: his friends, especially Gerald and Sara Murphy; Zelda's affair with a French naval officer; her breakdowns; his own youthful exultations and expectations; his own high promise; his own great social charm; his own weariness and disillusion following his spent early success; and his own destructive alcoholism and his frequent nastiness when he was drunk. Nevertheless, the fictional character of the "spoiled priest,"[3] Diver the doctor was by no means an autobiographical photograph of the spoiled priest, Fitzgerald the author. Yet, some contemporary (1934–40) reviews insisted on identifying Diver as Fitzgerald and thereby helped consign the book, its characters, and its author to the detritus of a wanton pre-Depression past best forgotten as frivolity.[4]

As a result of this equation of historical fact with fictional recreation, contemporary readers identified Dick Diver as a thoroughly contemporary man of the 1920s (when the action of the book takes place) and the 1930s (when most contemporary readers and reviewers too quickly read and reviewed it). Scott and Zelda, victims of their own notoriety, became such one-dimensionally popularized national properties that even today many casual readers respond to *Tender is the Night* the way contemporaneous reviewers did. There is little or no popular inkling that Fitzgerald or any of his characters might also have belonged, as both he and Diver did, to an old-fashioned, pre-war age of manners and courtesy, when gentlemen and ladies wore pince-nez spectacles, divorce was taboo, and girls saved their virginity for marriage.

Some first-time readers still dismiss Dick Diver as a social idler: a cosmopolitan companion and a charming host parasitically living on the Warren wealth and self-indulgently avoiding the work he had intended to do. Some even see Diver as a gigolo who married Nicole for her money. No assumptions could be more mistaken, yet they arise understandably from the subtlety with which Fitzgerald made his hero out of the intricacy and complexity of human personality, as well as from the shallow preconceptions of Fitzgeraldiana with which some readers dimly make out his hero. The mistaken identification of Dick also arises from what Fitzgerald came to see as a structural problem concerning the way the novel begins.

The text of *Tender is the Night* presents special and vexing problems, and "when this story begins"[5] is especially problematical. Fitzgerald worked intermittently on the novel for nine years, with some long, bitter, and extremely distracting lapses. In the wearisome and worrisome process he created three versions and seventeen drafts of what became *Tender is the Night*. But he remained insecure about how "this story begins" as he kept rewriting it, completing the version that was serialized in *Scribner's Magazine* during the winter and spring of 1933–4. Still uneasy, he made changes, sometimes frantically, in the serial version in preparation for its publication as a book. He continued to make changes in the proofsheets of the book right up to publication. In response to the book's cool reception, by May of 1936 certainly, and probably earlier, Fitzgerald returned to doubting the clarity of the novel's time sequences and he began to think anew about changes.

He prepared what amounts to an eighteenth draft, making changes in the order of scenes in one of his copies of the first edition, revising "when this story begins." Almost five years after the first edition, on the day before Christmas 1938, Fitzgerald wrote to his friend and editor, Maxwell Perkins, that the book's "great fault is that the true beginning – the young psychiatrist in Switzerland – is tucked away in the middle of the book" (*Letters*, 281). Fitzgerald was restating the doubts and difficulties he had experienced with Book I in various drafts of the novel, long before book publication and critical reception. But although until his death Fitzgerald apparently maintained his intention of an eighteenth draft, in the financial straits of the Depression no publisher would undertake what Fitzgerald called his "final version."[6] He died without fully completing the changes in the book as he wanted it.[7] What he wanted was the long, steady "dying fall" of Dick Diver from his transcendent possibilities at "the book's true beginning" to the suffocatingly understated sense of loss in the book's last two paragraphs. "The first part, the romantic introduction," Fitzgerald wrote to H. L. Mencken shortly after the book was published,

> was too long and too elaborated largely because of the fact that it had been written over a series of years with varying plans, but everything else in the book conformed to a definite intention and if I had to start to write it again tomorrow I would adopt the same plan... That is what most of the critics fail to understand (outside of the fact that they fail to understand and identify anything in the book): that the motif of the "dying fall" was absolutely deliberate and did not come from any diminution of vitality but from a definite plan. (*Letters*, 510)[8]

Whatever else can be said by revisionist or anti-revisionist commentators, Fitzgerald's uncompleted revision clearly emphasizes the dying fall. In either version the last two chapters are irresistible examples of Fitzgerald's creation of overpowering evocativeness out of relative stylistic sparseness.

In parody or in earnest, the styles of the two other American giants of Fitzgerald's time, Hemingway and Faulkner, have been imitated or echoed. But Fitzgerald's style remains inimitable, for it is woven out of a gossamer evocativeness – Fitzgerald called it "hauntedness" – that is the essence of the impeccable diction with which his treatment of golden moments, memory, expectations, love, and loss become so moving. But whether in "blankets" or in comparative spareness, the major artistic function of Fitzgerald's evocative language is to organize the coherent narrative motifs that create his themes. The complex interweaving of themes in *Tender is the Night* is among the richest of aesthetically and intellectually satisfying performances in American literature.

Consider the pattern of nationality and race that begins near the opening of the novel and that initiates the theme of America and Europe. This "international theme" pervades American literature, and in *Tender is the Night* it is substantively (certainly not stylistically) reminiscent of the early Henry James. In an early humorous passage Tommy Barban reads names from *The New York Herald*:

> "Well, what nationality are these people?" he demanded suddenly, and read with a slight French intonation, "'Registered at the Hotel Palace at Vevey are Mr. Pandely Vlasco, Mme. Bonneasse' – I don't exaggerate – 'Corinna Medonca, Mme. Pasche, Seraphim Tullio, Maria Amalia Roto Mais, Moises Teubel,

Mme. Paragoris, Apostle Alexandre, Yolanda Yosfuglu and Geneveva de Momus!' She attracts me most – Geneveva de Momus." (*TITN*, 21)

With his half-American Tommy Barban reading opaque and mysterious names with "a slight French intonation," Fitzgerald begins to establish a pattern of confusion and disintegration attendant upon the disappearance of reliably established identity. By itself the instance is merely a funny moment at the beach. But in its preparation for other appearances of the theme, the significance of this moment expands as part of the totality of the novel's ideas. Thus, much later in the book, when Mary North becomes Mary Minghetti, the presentation of her second husband has a prepared context in which the presentation and the context enrich each other:

> "Conte di Minghetti" was merely a papal title – the wealth of Mary's husband flowed from . . . southwestern Asia. He was not quite light enough to travel in a Pullman south of Mason-Dixon; he was of the Kabyle-Berber-Sabaean-Hindu strain that belts across north Africa and Asia, more sympathetic to the European than the mongrel faces of the ports. (266)

By itself, this Portrait of Hybrid might be comic, like the names Tommy reads on the beach. But within the expanding context of identities, especially because Mary had been the wife of an Abe ironically associated with Lincoln, it takes on dark undertones of the racism and exclusionary class consciousness that characterizes the international Warren world – a warren indeed! – within which Dick exists. In deliberate affront to what his world and he himself have become, both of which he has come to despise, the older, ruined Dick uses racist slurs that the altruistic young Doctor Diver would have abhorred. His language becomes one of the signs of the extent to which his – and his world's – disintegration has progressed.

The themes are many and complex. They include war (the book's central metaphor for moral chaos and the destruction of humane values and relationships), identity (the overall theme), wealth, the movies, acting, swimming, the New Woman, the fathers, Europe and America, priestliness, past and present, sun and moon, heat and coolness, black and white, as probably the most prominent, though there are several more. This chapter can only suggest the essential nature of the novel, and will touch on the international theme via the companion themes of war, the fathers, and the New Woman. It is helpful to place these themes in the context of *Tender is the Night*'s relation to Western history surrounding World War I. The essential setting of the book is post-war Western-world confusion as that world undergoes disintegrations and refashionings in a morass of identity. *Tender is the Night* is not a great American historical novel. Rather, it is a great American novel about history, a chronicle of post-war loss of the kinds of identities associated with stable societies, social altruism, and personal responsibility. The story of Dick Diver is a microcosm of that history.

Dynamic and accomplished, young Dick Diver is nevertheless vulnerable in his contradictions. He is a self-sacrificial enthusiast, an unworldly naif, and yet a sophisticated man of brilliant studiousness. He is a romantic of deep feeling and yet a man of strong self-discipline. He is youthfully exuberant and extravagantly hopeful, yet restrained by a deep sense of moral obligation. He is highly educated and internationally traveled, yet, for all of Yale and Johns Hopkins and Oxford and Zurich, he begins his story as a shining-eyed kid from the country, an idealistically optimistic young American, fresh from the dewiness of his family's pioneer history and his father's ministerial background. He is bursting with limitless expectations and promise. He is yet to discover the extent to which his world is heir to legacies from fathers other than his own.

Fitzgerald develops a dualism in the legacy of the fathers, both American and European. The good European fathers leave a legacy of magnificent knowledge and civilization; the bad ones are internationally indistinguishable from the American Warrens. The bad American fathers represent a continuing legacy of "the forces of lust and corruption"(*TITN*, 74) in the historical America. Sid Warren, the founder of his dynasty, was a rough "white-eyed" crook. But the good American fathers, the Divers, represent the legacy of the idea of America, a dream of goodness and transcendent self. Home, America, is a romantically hypothesized history that is all innocent youth and world-redeeming service. Dick Diver's father was an honest minister who believed in service and courtesy and lived by the great words he preached. "Dick loved his father – again and again he referred judgments to what his father probably would have thought or done" (211).

Because of what he associates with these determining "Diver" aspects of Americanness, Fitzgerald defines Dick's vulnerability as a self-annihilatingly romantic need to be used and to be loved. It was with the great words and great concepts and great idealism that Dick arrived at the snakepit of historical actualities epitomized by the operative America and Europe of a present day that has emerged from the international war. His charm lay in his endless need to serve and be useful, to put into action his desire to redeem, to heal, to create love.

> Dick got up to Zurich on less Achilles' heels than would be required to equip a centipede, but with plenty – the illusions of eternal strength and health, and of the essential goodness of people – illusions of a nation, the lies of generations of frontier mothers who had to croon falsely that there were no wolves outside the cabin door. (123)

From the very beginning of his story Dick had intuited that "the price of his intactness was his incompleteness," and that if he were to reach the power of his full maturity in the hard actualities of a fallen world, his education required some disillusioning finishing strokes of experience: he had been too lucky; "he must be less intact, even faintly destroyed" (122). Nevertheless, at the end of his story, when there was nothing left to believe in and little left of the man he used to be, even then he still responded to the corrupt "new" world with a deeply instilled exercise of

> the old fatal pleasingness, the old forceful charm, [that] swept back with its cry of "Use me!" ... because it had early become a habit to be loved, perhaps from the moment when he had realized that he was the last hope of a decaying clan... Wanting above all to be brave and kind, he had wanted, even more than that, to be loved. So it had been. So it would ever be, he saw... (308)

Diver is a very mixed hero. His genuinely heroic qualities and transcendent possibilities are used up and thrown away not only by the corrupt world around him but also by his own outworn pre-war romantic idealism, whose erosion was to lead increasingly to his alcoholism and his descent into oblivion. Fitzgerald makes the name Diver connote at least two ideas. One is Dick's deep diving into learning, discipline, creativity, and the moral identity Dick learned from his father and aunts, all metaphorically suggested by Dick's superb aquatic abilities in his younger days. The other is the dying fall, Dick's long dive into disintegration and oblivion, metaphorically related through the swimming theme with the older, dissipated, and exhausted Dick's inability to perform aquatically. The totality of the dive is indicated in Fitzgerald's hint of priapic overtones in making the man who once had been "Lucky Dick," the "big stiff" (122), go limp, repeatedly unable to "rise" on the aquaplane (290–1). We can measure the life of Dr. Richard Diver as a paradigm of the larger context of the international theme of history. Europe's "Vienna was old with death" (121–2), but the novel presents America's Diver in his young manhood and gives us a picture of a vigorous American post-war youth: "twenty-seven years old, a fine age for a man, indeed the very acme of bachelorhood" (121). Dick "swam in the winter Danube" and "had done the flying rings at New Haven" (122). We see him bicycling and climbing mountains. He is unselfconsciously attractive, handsome, and strong. His superior mind is as clear as his bright blue eyes, and it creatively absorbs and completely retains bookful after bookful of medical studies (122). This Oxford Rhodes Scholar from Yale, who is also a Johns Hopkins M.D., is in the expectant, hopeful, healthy prime of his energy, planning transcendently to cure the sick post-war world by being "a good psychologist – maybe to be the greatest one that ever lived."

"That's very good – and very American," replies the Swiss Franz Gregorovius (138), who earlier had remarked on Dick's "unaging American face" (124) and who was to remark that Dick can get away with large and visionary new medical ideas because "You are an American" (146). From the outset Dick exemplifies America in the fresh morning of its vigor and idealistic expectations. In Franz's littered study, which is full of smoke, stuffy and dark with "the Swiss piety" of the world of Franz's father and grandfather, Dick opens wide a French window to let in fesh air and "a cone of sunshine" (126). No stuffy old world aristocrat conformist with gold-headed walking-stick and pince-nez he. Just as Dick is associated with young energy, Europe, on the other hand is at once associated with the decayed old world of aristocracy "when this story begins." Gausse's Hotel is on the Mediterranean, situated "about half way between Marseilles and the Italian border" with an "English clientele." It stands amidst "a dozen old villas rotted like water lilies" (8), on a vacation coast that for years had been played in by the visiting pre-revolutionary Russian nobility, now moribund and "never coming back any more" (19). And in contrast to the zest with which Dick had swum the winter Danube, on this European shore of cane-strutting, be-monocled and be-pince-nezed Europeans, only one man "came down to the beach in a blue bathrobe and with much preliminary application to his person of the chilly water, and much grunting and loud breathing, floundered a minute in the sea" (7) and then left.

But as he does throughout the book, Fitzgerald leaves nothing one-dimensional. For "when this story begins" with Rosemary's entrance, Dick Diver does in fact use both gold-headed cane and eyeglasses – pince-nez, no less. Fitzgerald mentions the glasses only twice (174, 216), their pearl-mounted black cord only once (216), and Dick's walking-sticks only three times (87, 95, 272–3). The casual throwaway of these details – the most surprising and unexpected of all details for the presentation of a post-war, modern, young American hero – is in itself an indication of the extent to which much of the amalgam of associations in Fitzgerald's mind and times belonged to a pre-war world of customs and manners, as did his protagonist's. Because Fitzgerald and his writings are too closely identified with the 1920s and 1930s, commentators seldom note that the author and his works emerge from a pre-war background compounded of nineteenth-century sensibilities.[9] From that background Fitzgerald took as givens images and attitudes that lend his work subtle pre-war undertones. The very minor but significantly representative details of canes and eyeglasses are elements of what in many ways is a *fin-de-siècle* "feel" in this very twentieth-century post-war novel. As walking-sticks and monocles were disappearing in the first four decades of the twentieth century, pince-nez, which had been common, came to designate people of aristocracy or of solid substance and achievement. In the 1920s they designated people who were not of the modern moment only but who retained something of a more old-fashioned pre-war world. Even "plain" Calvin Coolidge changed from blackrimmed eyeglasses to "a pair of small pince-nez with a gold nosepiece and a long black cord" for a Presidential presence, and P. G. Wodehouse humorously found pince-nez appropriate for "1) good college professors, 2) bank presidents and 3) musicians."[10] All the American Presidents of Fitzgerald's lifetime emerged from a pre-World War I world. Franklin Roosevelt, whom Fitzgerald admired, was one of the last American aristocrats who could wear pince-nez without looking silly (as had also been true of his kinsman, Theodore Roosevelt, and "The War President," Woodrow Wilson), and wear them FDR did, throughout the years Fitzgerald was completing *Tender is the Night*. The point of paying attention to this detail is that it reveals a pervasive and general background sense of a decorous pre-war world in which, for all its murderous corruptions and hypocrisies, the assumed values of manners, courtesy, honor, and politeness in a stable and predictable society were elegantly summed up by walking-sticks and a fashion in eyeglasses. Dick is not just young American Dick in the Roaring Twenties: he is also Doctor Diver, who was formed by nineteenth-century forebears and who has some very old-fashioned virtues and ideas of morality – just as, astonishingly but essentially, did F. Scott Fitzgerald. Unlike the work of most of Fitzgerald's best-known contemporaries, *Tender is the Night* is not generally thought of as a war novel because it is not set in the war. But no novel written in the so-called "lost generation" more deeply or centrally probes the significance of the war's legacy. Like the American and European fathers, both the pre-war and post-war worlds have conflicting qualities within themselves. Both worlds are postulated against the book's dominant background, World War I.

World War I changed the human universe, quite literally. The Western world, especially, was never the same again. The war was the last cataclysmic gasp of British and French empire; it was the devastating interruption of an attempt at German empire; it brought about fundamental change in governmental structures and social foundations. In its aftermath of enveloping cynicism and profoundly anarchic disillusion, it gave enormous impetus to everything anti-establishmentarian, socially and politically, and to everything existential, personally and culturally. On the political level the war was the violent midwife at the chaotic births of the Russian Revolution, of Italian Fascism, and of German Nazism, all of which Fitzgerald lived to see. It brought about the modern totalitarian state at the same time that in large measure it destroyed popular acquiescence in pre-war governmental and social systems fixed in the absolutes of a conformist underclass and a privileged peerage and moneyed class. In America the war brought about a hysteria of superpatriotic backlash, which Fitzgerald captured in his story, "May Day" (1920), against the radically dissenting impulses born of angry post-war disillusion. The upheaval of the war was such a wrench from the past that it dissolved the very structures of beliefs and values that had been the shibboleths by which vast populations had regulated their lives.

Perhaps the most important war death of all was one that went unnoticed, or at least unnamed at the time: the demise of the belief of the eighteenth- and nineteenth-century Western world in perfectibility. The ongoing twenti- eth century was to encompass a tension between *realpolitik* and what was left of perfectibilitarian hope; it would take the remainder of the century and the horrors and aftermath of World War II to bury the fond hope of com- plete human redemption. Dick Diver, F. Scott Fitzgerald, and "the American Century" were born in an idealistic expectation of perfectibility that had been a certitude of the good fathers. Diver and Fitzgerald came to recognize the loss, tragedy, and adulthood attendant upon its death, not even know- ing the name of the corpse. But Fitzgerald, like Diver, knew its features in the very marrow of his life and, lovingly mourning, came to reject its some- time promise as an illusion ironically fundamental to the resplendent idea of America.

Accompanying Rosemary Hoyt and Abe North during a visit to the trenches between Beaumont Hamel and Thiepval, Dick sums up Fitzgerald's profound sense of the massive change World War I effected in human history and behavior. He defines the motivation for sacrifice characterized by the dif- ference in mass loyalties before and after the battle that had been fought in those trenches.

"This land here cost twenty lives a foot that summer," Dick explained to Rosemary.[11]

> "See that little stream – we could walk to it in two minutes. It took the British a month to walk to it – a whole empire walking very slowly, dying in front and pushing forward behind. And another empire walked very slowly backward a few inches a day, leaving the dead like a million bloody rugs. No Europeans will ever do that again in this generation."
>
> "Why, they've only just quit over in Turkey," said Abe. "And in Morocco – "
>
> "That's different. This western-front business couldn't be done again, not for a long time. The young men think they could do it but they couldn't. They could fight the first Marne again, but not this. This took religion and years of plenty and tremendous sureties and the exact relation that existed between the classes . . . You had to have a whole-souled sentimental equipment going back further than you could remember. You had to remember Christmas, and postcards of the Crown Prince and his fiancée, and little cafés in Valence

and beer gardens in Unter den Linden and weddings at the mairie, and going to the Derby, and your grandfather's whiskers."

"General Grant invented this kind of battle at Petersburg in sixty-five" [interposed Abe].

"No, he didn't – he just invented mass butchery. This kind of battle was invented by Lewis Carroll and Jules Verne and whoever wrote 'Undine,' and country deacons bowling and marraines in Marseilles and girls seduced in the back lanes of Wurtemburg and Westphalia. Why, this was a love-battle – there was a century of middle-class love spent here. This was the last love-battle."
(*TITN*, 61–2)

When Abe mocks Dick by saying, "You want to hand over this battle to D. H. Lawrence," Dick replies in a way that reveals his romanticism and its related old-fashioned idealization of a historical legacy from his minister-father's American context. The legacy extends from the pathfinding seventeenth century to the immediate pre-war past, and Dick nostalgically identifies it with altruism, stable values, and a predictable world: "'All my beautiful lovely safe world blew itself up here with a great gust of high explosive love,' Dick mourned" (62).

But in weaving his international theme into the war theme, Fitzgerald suggests that however far back we look, even in the seventeenth- and eighteenth-century American context of Dick's father's forefathers (the "Divers, Dorseys and Hunters . . . [t]hese dead" with "their weather-beaten faces with flashing blue eyes, the spare violent bodies, the souls made of new earth in the forest-heavy darkness of the seventeenth-century" [213]), in historical actuality we find a catalogue of wars, each unfolding into the next. He uses the American Civil War in Dick's father's life as an adumbration of World War I and he hints of seventeenth-century violence and the American Indian wars as adumbrations of the Civil War. Abe's drunken involvement with Swedish and American blacks in Paris is referred to as a war between hostile and friendly Indians (111, 115), and the event of Peterson's murder is at once merged with the Civil War. Caught up in the mess Abe's alcoholic lunacy has created, Dick refuses to give Abe anything more to drink. Abe "waved his finger reproachfully at Dick. 'But remember what George the Third said, that if Grant was drunk he wished he would bite the other generals'" (113). Indian wars, the Revolutionary War via George the Third, and the Civil War all become one in Abe's drunken deterioration, which foreshadows Dick's own dissolution. At "the true beginning" of Dick's story Fitzgerald suggests the connections by telling us that Dick, "the hero, like Grant lolling in . . . Galena, is ready to be called to an intricate destiny" (123). And to indicate that the elaborately patterned war references are not accidental, at the very end of Dick's story and the demise of his grand destiny, Fitzgerald symmetrically and ironically rounds off his narrative with Nicole dismissively thinking that Dick's "career was biding its time, again like Grant's in Galena . . . "(321).

As the war motif makes all the pasts prologue to the international present, so Abe North's degeneration prefigures Dick Diver's: the brilliantly creative young American who promises a whole new world of wonders dives into disintegration. Reciprocatingly, the developing illumination of Dick's decline sheds some shadowy light backwards on Abe's collapse, which Fitzgerald deliberately leaves unspecified as a non-diversionary part of the general background of Dick's history. And as Fitzgerald ties Abe to Dick, he ties them both to America, so that their personal histories become metaphors for national history. Like America itself they both began in revolutionary new visions, romantic expectations, and brilliantly transcendent promise. The nationally ideal and idealized self-sacrificially altruistic icons are summed up in heroes like Abraham Lincoln, who stood forth to bring national unity and moral redemption. Abe of the North (in one draft of the novel Abe North was Abe Grant) marries a woman named Mary. He has a "slow and shy" voice, a sad face, "the high cheekbones of an Indian, a long upper lip and . . . deepset . . . eyes"(13). Although in many details Abe North was in part consciously modeled on Fitzgerald's friend, Ring Lardner, he clearly is also a type of Lincoln.

But when this disintegrated Abe becomes involved in the fate of black people, the ironic result is the death and imprisonment of blacks. It is typical of Fitzgerald's fine touch that the black who loses his freedom at the hands of this ironically and tragically offered latter-day Great Emancipator is named Freeman. The corruption of the legacy of Lincoln in the legacy of the Grant administration is encompassed in the devolution from the great Abe of the North to an Abe North whose drunken ruin of his great promise is the debauched national heritage after the war. With Abe Lincoln, Abe North, U. S. Grant, and Lucky Dick all in intricate association, the long, diving "dying fall" of Dick Diver is a paradigmatic expression of Fitzgerald's tragic sense of America's and the Western world's history.

The suggestions of America's wars are brought up to date and interwoven with World War I through subtle references to war, weapons, and combat that pepper the novel and are associated with everyone in the story. Dr. Richard Diver gradually and against all his discipline and intentions had "somehow permitted his arsenal to be locked up in the Warren safety-deposit vaults" and his "spear had been blunted" (209) during a long campaign in which, he came to realize, he had "wasted eight years teaching the rich the ABCs of human decency" (210).

Shortly after the opening of Dr. Diver's European history, the moment that expresses the very beginning of Dick's and Nicole's lovemaking has as

its background the blast of field artillery. For this romance the guns fire
to save things, to break up hail clouds that threaten to bring destruction
to the vineyards. In ironic parallel, shortly before the close of Dr. Diver's
European history, the moment that expresses the very beginning of Tommy's
and Nicole's lovemaking has as its background the blast of naval artillery.
For this romance the guns of a United States battleship fire to recall the
sailors from their shoreleave of whoring, boozing, and – as the scene makes
explicitly clear – fighting. But for both romances the background is an echo
of war. The juxtaposition is ripe with the historical complexities and ironies
of Fitzgerald's implicit comments.

There is not enough space here to instance each reference to war and
weapons, but a few will indicate Fitzgerald's conscious artistry. Rosemary's
lovelocks are "an armorial shield" (8); her mother is named Speers and
Mrs. Speers's two husbands were army officers (16); the capitalist lord,
Devereux Warren, is so economically and politically powerful that he is
able to commandeer a United States Navy cruiser during wartime to bring
his daughter to Europe for treatment (134); Tommy Barban, the victor with
a "martial laugh" (205), is a professional soldier who has "worn the uni-
forms of eight countries"(34); Abe pretends to be General Pershing (83);
Dick has war nightmares (188) and awakens to the slow memorial march of
war veterans (208); Dick's favorite patient, the dying woman with eczema,
is a victim of women's battles with men (191–3); Dick feels that the atmosphere in a restaurant where he is dining is consecrated by the presence of
the "gold star muzzers" who have come to Europe to visit their sons' graves
(105); Dick's skill as a host acutely aware of his guests' psychological needs
is cast in terms of generals moving armies (31, 83).

Among the many war references are two central instances, both related to
the emergence of the "New Woman." In one, the scene in which the hungover
Abe is leaving Paris at the Gare Saint Lazare, Maria Wallis, a woman with
"helmet-like hair," shoots her lover "through his identification card"(88). A
porter discussing the event with his friend says, "Tu as vu sa chemise? Assez
de sang pour se croire à la guerre" (90). ("Did you see his shirt? So much
blood you'd think it was the war.") That is the only appearance of Maria
Wallis in the novel; however, the scene not only unites the motifs of identity
and war (the war shoots identities to pieces), but it is the central scene in
which Dick, unable for once to take care of things in his endless combat with
circumstances, loses dominance as the omnipotent manager of all situations.
It is the first forewarning that Dick might have a less controlling place than
Nicole in the rampaging chaos of the new post-war society, and that the
world in which Baby Warren of the international set inherits the power has
supplanted the altruistic and moral aspect of the young America from which

Dick had come. Everything has changed with the shots of Maria Wallis's revolver: "as if nothing had happened, the lives of the Divers and their friends flowed out into the street. However, everything had happened" (90).

The second central battle scene is the final confrontation between Dick and Nicole. Even before Rosemary first comes to Dick's beach, Dick has recognized that the unremitting need for his incessant nurturing of Nicole is draining him empty and leaving him starved for the self he once was and the love he once imagined. Also he has come to the recognition (the rising waves of the silent, bitter, interior laughter that characterize his sardonic feelings at the end of the novel) that the fault is his, too, for being such a romantic fool as to imagine that he could heal the world's trauma or that he could cure Nicole and, as her lover and husband, remain immune to the process. Diver the doctor knows that the ultimate act he can make to effect Nicole's final independence, and thus the completion of her cure, is to direct her into one more sexual transference – from himself to another man, just as he had begun her cure by directing her transference from her father to himself. Dick Diver the husband is agonized by what Dr. Diver the healer knows. In the last few of the approximately twelve years of marriage[12] he has to allow himself to acknowledge the resentment he feels about what life with Nicole and her world has done to him. He has to harden himself against her in order to be able to bring her to free herself from him, thus giving her the supreme gift of her own self. For him it has become "difficult now to distinguish between his self-protective professional detachment and some new coldness in his heart . . . he had learned to become empty of Nicole, serving her against his will with negations and emotional neglect" (176). His growing distaste for his Warren-life helps him to undertake the battle of his greatest and most self-sacrificial cure. Fitzgerald brilliantly avoids heavy-handed sentimentality in developing the action. Readers must be alert to the subtle but several implications (most of them in Nicole's own fleeting thoughts) that Dick knows beforehand what is going to happen between Nicole and Tommy Barban, and that he plans her freedom (see especially 294–5). His only self-protection is to wince and say to Nicole, "Don't tell me about it. It doesn't matter what you do, only I don't want to know anything definitely" (305).

In his exhausted state, deep in the stale human contaminations of the world's immemorial social and sexual corruptions, Dick has a desperate need for the beauty of freshness and innocence. His adolescently frantic attraction to new love, exemplified by dewy youth, is what makes the Rosemary story such an integral part of the novel's plot. Dick's is no mere midlife crisis, no seamy middle-aged lust for young flesh. Dick has been reduced to his recognition that he has given himself, with all the ridiculousness of a Don

Quixote, to the salvation of an unsalvageable world not worth saving. His bitter resentment of the baby-new, blithely free Nicole, whom he has liberated at every cost to what he had been, is surpassed only by his ridicule and loathing of himself – he should have known better in the first place, but he had had the bad luck to fall in love. All that is left to him in his last battle is a lashing out – a symptomatic racism, xenophobia, a short-tempered nasty honesty, and that hideously hilarious internal giggle – at what a farce his world and life have become.

The two pages in which Nicole observes Dick in his pain and in which he initiates the final battle between them, after which he leans his defeated head on the parapet, is one of the most excruciating and passionately moving scenes in American literature. The break itself is cast in the imagery of war. It is a summation of all the wars and major motifs in the book: between past and present, between the sexes, between wealth and dependence, between new irresponsible freedom and old responsibilities, between obliviously destructive selfishness and old courtesies and honor, between free amorality and reliable morality, between impulsive gratification and thoughtful self-discipline, between the fathers, both American and European, who left a legacy of sexual chaos and destruction of identity and the fathers, both American and European, who bequeathed a rich legacy of culture and highly responsible identity. Nicole fights fiercely, using

> her unscrupulousness against his moralities – for this inner battle she used even her weaknesses – fighting bravely and courageously with the old cans and crockery and bottles, empty receptacles of her expiated sins, outrages, mistakes. And suddenly, in the space of two minutes she achieved her victory and justified herself to herself without lie or subterfuge, cut the cord forever. (306–7)

She discards Dick. The "household...was hers at last... The case was finished. Doctor Diver was at liberty" (307). All the old hopes of the Diver legacy have been used for the victory of the Warren legacy. And in the process of this war the new Nicole Warren is born, or rather she becomes "what she had been in the beginning"(302): the untrammeled adventurer with her "white crook's eyes" is at last set free to inherit the "broken universe of the war's ending" (253) with her money. If "my eyes have changed it's because I'm well again. And being well perhaps I've gone back to my true self – I suppose my grandfather was a crook and I'm a crook by heritage, so there we are" (297).

Interwoven with the ubiquitous "daddy's girl" motif, the theme of the birth of the New Woman, like the theme of the fathers or the international theme, is as pervasive as the central metaphor of war. It is one of the most pointed patterns of significance in *Tender is the Night*. It was a prominent theme in much of the fiction that arose from the legacy of World War I, which released smoldering feminist energies. The most popular of the new heroines in Fitzgerald's day was Hemingway's Lady Brett Ashley. In American fiction her ground had been prepared by many writers predating and culminating in Kate Chopin, Edith Wharton, and Theodore Dreiser. Europe had created its variations on the theme for the literary moment, all the way back from Lysistrata to Emma Bovary, Hedda Gabler, Nora Helmer, and then to the most celebrated Lady Chatterley, who made her debut six years before the Warren girls.

In the old pre-war world that Nicole, Rosemary, and Mary North had been born into, women who were comfortable in that world's comfortable values had identities comfortably prepared for them. Fitzgerald contemplates these American women:

> The trio of women at the table were representative of the enormous flux of American life. Nicole was the grand-daughter of a self-made American capital-ist and a grand-daughter of a count of the House of Lippe Weissenfeld. Mary North was the daughter of a journeyman paper-hanger and a descendant of President Tyler. Rosemary was from the middle of the middle class, catapulted by her mother onto the uncharted heights of Hollywood. Their point of resem-blance to each other, and their difference from so many American women, lay in the fact that they were all happy to exist in a man's world – they preserved their individuality through men and not by opposition to them. They would all three have made alternatively good courtesans or good wives not by the accident of birth but through the greater accident of finding their man or not finding him. (57)

Along with its legacy of hypocrisy and corruption the past also had offered a world in which men were supposed to have had a role and an identity that women could rely on and in which women were supposed to have had a role and an identity that men could rely on: "Up to a point that was right: men were for that, beam and idea, girder and logarithm... [men and women] opposite and complementary" (199).

But the war tore off the surface suppositions of the comfortably respectable world and exploded them to shreds. They could not be reassembled by the "gray-haired men of the golden nineties who shouted old glees at the piano" in the 1920s, allowing Dick to pretend for a moment "that the world was all put together again" (182). The world will change most ironically for Mary, Rosemary, and Nicole, and so will they. In the internationalized, chaotic post-war world American Mary North, in becoming the Contessa di Minghetti, with her power and hauteur of wealth and position, becomes, like her Himadoun sisters-in-law, even more of a feudal subject to "her man" than she ever had been to Abe. In that same world, the innocent young American Rosemary will become as sexually free a woman as she is economically free, yet will be a Hollywood sex object who will take her choices from an endless supply of Signor Nicoteras. And American Nicole, foreseeing her own procession of men to play with, "none of whom she need obey or even love" (299), chooses her Frenchified Barbarian, the totally overmastering male. As for the despicably corrupt English Lady Caroline Sibly-Biers, who brings Mary North di Minghetti into her bisexual escapades, old Gausse sums up their entire new world by kicking the bottom of Lady Caroline as hard as he can, sending her deservedly sprawling, as he says to Dick: "I have never seen women like this sort of women. I have known many of the great courtesans of the world, and for them I have much respect often, but women like these women I have never seen before" (312).

In the ironic, historical view of *plus ça change plus c'est la même chose* with which he contemplates the international, intersexual chaos of the privileged classes, celebrities, and adventurers in the Western post-war world, Fitzgerald presents a crowded roomful of avant-garde women, both heterosexual and lesbian, malicious, some with necks and heads "like cobras' hoods" (78). They are clustered in a futuristic modern-world "Frankenstein" (78) of a house whose interior is as "perverted as a breakfast of oatmeal and hashish" (77). Outwardly unchanged, it is the old palace of the Cardinal de Retz and it stands in the – perfect irony – rue Monsieur.

Irony becomes inescapable, as when "war" and "the New Woman" merge in the climactic mating of Tommy and Nicole: in her anarchic new sexual (and supposedly all other) freedoms she is depicted as the bound sexual trophy of the conquering warrior:

> Symbolically she lay across his saddle-bow as surely as if he had wolfed her away from Damascus and they had come out upon the Mongolian plain. Moment by moment all that Dick had taught her [the moral burdens of discipline, self-control, responsibility, and order] fell away and she was ever nearer to what she had been in the beginning, prototype of that obscure yielding up of swords that was going on in the world about her. Tangled with love in the moonlight she welcomed the anarchy of her lover. (302)

The old familiar Western world is replaced by new and alien ("Mongolian") perspectives of a different world – "She liked his bringing her there to the eastward vision" (302). Historically, the idea of the New Woman by no means centered exclusively on sexual activity. But in the post-war ferment, sex, as a salient symbol of the type and the movement, rose like skirt hemlines in a repudiation of the hypocritical old double sexual standard, with concomitant insistence on the sexes' equal rights and statures in all political, economic, and social identities.

Fitzgerald's picture of the New Woman is not an anti-feminist pastiche; rather it is anti- the identity-destroying moral chaos that the Warren world offered as freedom to all sexual identities. Fitzgerald never had any argument with women's struggle for the vote, for better working conditions, for equal rights, and equal opportunities. His correspondence indicates that as someone responsive to the American 1930s vision of Marxism in a decade of rising national discontent, he was sympathetic to the struggles of those who were oppressed. But those specifics were not his materials. Within his own context, Fitzgerald focused not on the woman's movement as such but on the extent to which it was an emblematic function of fundamental change. Unhappily, he saw that change taking place in a world in disintegration, blindly and mistakenly declaring itself free of everything in the past. And the consequences of that supposed liberation continued crazily to victimize everyone.

Consequently, Fitzgerald incorporated complexities and multiple ironies concerning the liberation of the New Woman, as a central concern that he inextricably interwove with all the other themes, especially those of war, the fathers, the movies, and babylike immaturity. Tommy looks at the newly free Nicole who now is his ward. Fittingly, Tommy is the barbarian dominator who belongs in the licentious post-war world and is Fitzgerald's prototype of the fascist. He measures Nicole and says, "You are all new like a baby" (300). It is an ironic sign of the post-war insanity that with his mastery of women by means of "all the old Languedoc peasant remedies" (300) – phallic and oral puns intended – Tommy should be the one to scoff at "all this taming of women"(298). What he means by untamed women is limited entirely to sexual abandon.

With the post-war woman as new as a baby, Fitzgerald adds dimensions to the theme of identity in the shifting social values of the war's aftermath. Women are liberated – but into what? Women are new, like babies, and can now become anything their men have become – but what is that? What Fitzgerald put into *Tender is the Night* is his sense that if old values and old beliefs like "'good instincts,' honor, courtesy, and courage" (212) are gone; if old communities have lost their meaning and are replaced only with personal access to money and empowerment; then men and women alike have only their own selfish desires and personal perspectives to constitute both reality and morality. Fitzgerald saw this as especially true of the very rich in the rampaging capitalism of the post-war decade. "'You've got too much money,'... [Tommy] said impatiently [to Nicole]. 'That's the crux of the matter. Dick can't beat that'" (298).

One of Fitzgerald's intuitions about the historical meaning of the war and its aftermath is that women inevitably will be more free and no longer content merely "to exist in a man's world." But because men and women have become freed into an anarchic amorality bereft of the disciplined adult's sense of consequences and obligation, they are reduced to infantile irresponsibility. The practice of that fundamental irresponsibility in the world of privilege is demonstrated by Devereux Warren, when he places the mess he has created – and plenty of American money – in old Dr. Dohmler's professionally competent hands: "look here, Doctor, that's just what you're for. I have a hurry call to go home!" (135). Such assertive irresponsibility depersonalizes human beings, no matter how rare or precious they might be, into conveniences of lust, power, or money. The display of that irresponsibility is breathtakingly continued by Sid and Devereux's true Baby Warren, the real daddy's girl, when she says in reply to Nicole's protestations that the Dr. Diver she has just cast away had been a good husband to her for many years, "That's what he was educated for" (318). Baby always had wanted to buy a nice doctor who would take care of Nicole and relieve the Warrens of any responsibility: "I can't understand... what we're supposed to do" (159).[13]

The criminal irresponsibility of the Warrens is a benchmark of their international set's rootlessness. Unlike the Divers' American rootedness in "the low forested clayland of Westmoreland County" (213), for the Warrens and their playmates everywhere is home, and there is no home. Home is Chicago, Rome, London, the Riviera, Switzerland. Home is someone's yacht or a transoceanic liner where one "is a citizen of a commonwealth smaller than Andorra" (213). Home is a "Balkan-like state composed of... Europeanized Americans who... could scarcely have been said to belong to any nation at all" (292). "Home!" roared Nicole in another onset of her father-generated madness. "And sit and think that we're all rotting and the children's ashes are rotting in every box I open? That filth?" (198). Rot and filth indeed, and Fitzgerald misses no chances: Devereux's wormfilled legacy is in the French of his given name. De[s] véreux literally means of maggots – belonging to that which is maggoty. In this rootlessness of identity the "emergent Amazons" (185) triumphantly take their places in the post-war world the Warren fathers have left them. *Daddy's Girl* Rosemary and "daddy's girl" Nicole discover that in their young girlhoods they had both lived on the same street in Paris. The name of that street is rue des Saints-Pères (73).

Because it is men like Nicole's and Baby's father who end up owning America, the popular culture of America has become irresponsible and venal, a stew of immature sentimentality. Fitzgerald makes that observation another dimension of the intertwined father and baby motifs. Rosemary's role of "Daddy's Girl," as different as it was from poor Nicole's (but even at that, the movie displayed "a father complex so apparent that Dick winced for all psychologists" [74]) is sign and consequence of the society that pays homage to the fabulous Warren wealth and the transmittal of all its origins and consequences to America in a debased popular culture. Daddy's girl on the silver screen:

> there she was – so young and innocent... there she was – embodying all the immaturity of the race, cutting a new cardboard paper doll to pass before its empty harlot's mind...
>
> Daddy's girl. Was it a 'itty-bitty bravekins and did it suffer? Ooo-ooo-tweet, de tweetest thing, wasn't she dest too tweet? Before her tiny fist the forces of lust and corruption rolled away; nay, the very march of destiny stopped; inevitability became evitable; syllogism, dialectic, all rationality fell away. (74)

Dick had resented "the nursery footing" (89) on which Rosemary had kept the beginning of their affair, and, in one of Fitzgerald's most complicated inversions, Nicole continued to get sustenance by "dry suckling at... [Dick's] lean chest" (285) long after he had any nourishment to give her.

The triumphant babies need not be suckling infants or Shirley Temple "ickle durls" (181). Fitzgerald displays a bitter merger of the ideas of the Warren fathers, infantile immaturity, the New Woman, and combat in the scene in which Baby Warren defeats the American consul and bullies him into putting on his hat and going forth to get Dick out of the Roman jail – because "We're people of considerable standing in America" (240).

> The mention of his hat alarmed the Consul who began to clean his specta-cles hurriedly and to ruffle his papers. This proved of no avail: the American Woman, aroused, stood over him; the clean-sweeping irrational temper that had broken the moral back of a race and made a nursery out of a continent, was too much for him. He rang for the vice-consul – Baby had won. (240)

But America is not alone in the Western world's legacy of chaos from the Warren fathers. With a sentimentality full of movie-screen clichés (256), Devereux "was gracefully weakening and sinking" (255) in a luxurious suite in the Hôtel des Trois Mondes, a name that suggests both international-ism and the sexual demi-monde. His suite is "the same size as that of... [the European father] Señor Pardo Ciudad Real" (255). "Warren... [had been] a strikingly handsome man... a fine American type in every way, tall, broad, well-made... and he had that special air about him of hav-ing known the best of this world" (132). Ciudad Real was "a handsome iron-gray Spaniard [from Chile], noble of carriage, with all the appurte-nances of wealth and power"(251). They are twin citizens of the same world and they have both made a mess of their children's lives. The Spaniard repeatedly had tried to whip his son, Francisco, "the Queen of Chile" (252), out of homosexuality. The father's brutality, money, doses of Spanish Fly, and forced trips to whorehouses only sank his irreclaimable son more deeply into the sexual demi-monde – Señor Pardo Ciudad Real also has a daddy's "girl." Internationally the "new" children assume their freedom within the corrupt legacy their parents have left, and Baby rules the scene.

As for the truly good American fathers and guardians, with their legacy of "'good instincts,' honor, courtesy, and courage," they die: "Good-by, my father – good-by, all my fathers," says Dick at his father's grave (213). But the corrupting American fathers live on: instead of dying as he was supposed to, Devereux Warren "picked up his bed and walked" (258). The legacy of the great, pioneering, creative European fathers is now the monumental, centuries-old mausoleum of an enormous cultural heritage, depressingly seen from the window of Franz's study (139). What was a magnificent legacy is now a weighty dead hand of authority. So a European good-by to all those fathers. (The novel is a litany of goodbyes: to the good fathers, to all that was fresh, like Gstaad, or responsibly disciplined, like Mrs. Speers.) But like Devereux Warren the international fathers continue their destructive way in the world: the Australian father of Von Cohn Morris is nastily one with the Warrens and Pardo Ciudad Real. What remains onstage with the inheritors at the end as "a ghost of the past" (253–4) is the homosexual, Royal Dumphrey. So too the McKiscos endure and triumph (214), as does Mrs. Abrams (291).

Gatsby died – he lived with the terrifying probability of complete disillusion only for that one brief, final afternoon of his life. He did not have to live on after learning "what a grotesque thing" existence seemed to be once he had discovered what cheats the objects of his unattainably transcendent dream had been and what a fool he had been for "living too long with a single dream."[14] "Lucky Dick" Diver, another American believer in transcendent possibility, who also had a "heightened sensitivity to the promises of life" (*GG*, 6) fleshes out in pain what Gatsby would have had to bear had he had to linger on, as Dick did, moving from one small nothing town to a smaller one. *Tender is the Night* is Fitzgerald's continuation of his moral history of his age, completing the international story where *The Great Gatsby* left off.

In *Tender is the Night* Fitzgerald was writing out of his own mature power and experience, knowing yearningly that there never was an American Eden, knowing sadly that the corrupting actualities of human life had always betrayed what Nick Carraway had called that "last and greatest of all human dreams" (*GG*, 143), knowing darkly that America will be America only as long as it understands that dream, knowing hauntingly that it is no less than an impossible dream of the fulfillment of the best and most creative human aspiration in a world whose idealizations thereby become real. But Fitzgerald's generative paradox is that impossible as is its attainment, without the constant reinvigoration of that dream, America is lost, along with the promise of its youth, "somewhere back in that vast obscurity... where the dark fields of the republic rolled on under the night" (*GG*, 144). Or "almost certainly," as Nicole dismissively surmises about Dick's whereabouts, somewhere "in a very small town... almost certainly in that section of the country in one town or another" (*TITN*, 321). The materials of all of Fitzgerald's major fictions are dreams, love, money, and marriage. In *Tender is the Night* they are complicated by incest and madness and hugely enlarged by an international setting. But madness and incest are not what the novel is about. It is about a world in transition, when established values crumble, when human society's ideas of goodness, stability, and moral purpose are lost in corruption, and when the emerging society has not yet discovered a reason or a way to regain them. *Tender is the Night* is about the moral chaos attendant upon violent, if inevitable, change in the Western world in the twentieth century – and perhaps in all human worlds in all places and times. The tale of a dying fall is told in the story of one good man ruined in that process of change and, in his way, representative of it, in all its sad and tremendous history.

NOTES

1 To H. L. Mencken, May 4, 1925; in Andrew Turnbull, ed., *The Letters of F. Scott Fitzgerald*, 480.

2 For an overview of critical responses to Fitzgerald's work, see Jackson Bryer, *Critical Reputation of F. Scott Fitzgerald*; his *Supplement to The Critical Reputation*; and his *F. Scott Fitzgerald, The Critical Reception*.

3 In his "General Plan" for the novel, Fitzgerald made clear that he was creating a talented hero with the highest calling, destroyed by a combination of his own idealistic character and the destructive world around him. "The novel should do this: show a man who is a natural idealist, a spoiled priest, giving in for various causes to the ideas of the haute bourgeoisie, and in his rise to the top of the social world losing his idealism, his talent, and turning to drink and dissipation. Background one in which the leisure class is at their truly most brilliant and glamorous." An easily available source of the "General Plan" is Appendix B in Arthur Mizener's *The Far Side of Paradise*.

4 For an overview and discussion of critical responses to *Tender is the Night* see Bryer, cited above. See also Milton R. Stern, "Introduction" to *Critical Essays on F. Scott Fitzgerald's "Tender is the Night,"* ed. M. R. Stern; and Stern, *"Tender is the Night": The Broken Universe*, esp. chapter two.

5 F. Scott Fitzgerald, *Tender is the Night*, ed. Matthew Bruccoli, 7. Until Cambridge University Press completes its definitive edition of Fitzgerald's works, there is no universally received edition of *Tender is the Night*. But Bruccoli's edition is dependable and was the best of any at the close of the twentieth century. All

further references to this text will be indicated by parentheses in the body of the chapter.

6 On the front endpaper of the copy of *Tender is the Night* that Fitzgerald was rearranging for his eighteenth draft he had written, "This is the *final version* of the book as I would like it" (italics his).

7 The standard study of the composition of the first edition is by Matthew Bruccoli, *The Composition of "Tender Is the Night"*. See also Bruccoli, "Material for a Centenary Edition of *Tender Is the Night*," in *Critical Essays*, ed. Stern; and Bruccoli (with Judith S. Baughman), *Reader's Companion to F. Scott Fitzgerald's "Tender Is the Night"*. For an argument in favor of the "final version" and a summation of critical arguments about it see Stern, "Tender Is the Night: The Text Itself," in *Critical Essays*, ed. Stern, 21–31. Special mention must be given to Malcolm Cowley, who first edited and published the "final version" in 1951. See his "Introduction" to *Tender is the Night*, in *Three Novels of F. Scott Fitzgerald*. Both the first edition and the "final version" require some basic emendations to correct faulty and confusing time sequences; some corrections have been made by Bruccoli in the edition used here for citation.

8 In *Letters*, ed. Andrew W. Turnbull, see pp. 240–1, 242, 309–10, 346, 362–3, 510 (especially), and 538. In *The Correspondence of F. Scott Fitzgerald*, ed. Matthew Bruccoli and Margaret M. Duggan, 329, see the 1:29 p.m. wire to Maxwell Perkins, in which "TRIAL OFF" obviously was intended to be "TRAIL OFF."

9 A very notable exception is Ronald Berman's *"The Great Gatsby" and Fitzgerald's World of Ideas*.

10 Quoted in Dora Jane Hamblin, "What a Spectacle," 100. See also Richard Corson, *Fashions in Eyeglasses*.

11 They are on the site of the first Battle of the Somme, which began on July 1, 1916, and lasted through November. Before the battle was over, more than three million French, British, and German combatants had fought over no more than a pitiful 200 square miles, at a cost of one and one quarter million casualties. The part of that small territory that included Beaumont Hamel and Thiepval was manned by the British, with the French in the rest of the area to the south. The British piece of "this land here" comprised all of about fifty square miles.

12 The time sequence is problematical. Fitzgerald gave Topsy and Lanier the ages of nine and eleven, which Bruccoli edited down to six and eight (*TITN*, 264). Also, Fitzgerald specified that five years elapsed between the time Rosemary left the Riviera and her return to it, but Bruccoli reduces the interval to four years (287). He does this to clear the calendar and make the book end in 1929. However, at the beginning of the book, the children's conversation and singing suggests that they were about four and six, or three and five at the youngest, which would be in keeping with the ages Fitzgerald assigned them at the end of the book, five years after Rosemary had left the Riviera. The Divers would have had to be married about twelve years. There are several contradictory time indications in the novel. See Bruccoli's discussions in his edition of *Tender* and in his *Reader's Companion*.

13 See also pp. 160–1, 184, and 223.

14 F. Scott Fitzgerald, *The Great Gatsby*, ed. Ruth Prigozy, 128. All further references are to this edition.

7

J. GERALD KENNEDY

Fitzgerald's expatriate years and the European stories

During the peak of his contemporary popularity, F. Scott Fitzgerald lived abroad – mostly in France – for five years and eight months, much of that time pursuing a frenzied social life that impeded his literary work. His European travels included lengthy stays from May 1924 through the end of 1926 and then from March 1929 through September 1931, as well as a five-month sojourn in mid-1928. On foreign shores he experienced misery and elation: his wife Zelda's romance with French aviator Edouard Jozan; completion, publication, and celebration of his third novel, *The Great Gatsby* (1925); new friendships with Ernest Hemingway and with Gerald and Sara Murphy; innumerable alcoholic binges and embarrassments; false starts on a fourth novel and increasing self-doubts; domestic rivalry and acrimony; Zelda's first nervous breakdown and treatment; his hotel life and fugitive magazine fiction. Only after returning to the US did Fitzgerald publish *Tender is the Night* (1934), a work that despite its flaws plumbs the paradoxes of desire more profoundly than did *Gatsby*. Understandably, *Tender* has preoccupied scholars and biographers seeking insight into the author's life abroad, for its thinly veiled treatment of the Fitzgeralds' domestic calamities, set against the crazy violence of post-war Europe, reveals much about the author's own identification with expatriate culture. But the many short stories set at least partly in Europe likewise merit closer attention, less for their biographical connections than for their representations of the American migration to Europe after World War I.[1]

Fitzgerald's years abroad of course figure in a broader interpretive paradigm, popularized by Malcolm Cowley and elaborated by a host of modern critical studies beginning with George Wickes.[2] This model of expatriate life celebrates "exile" (a term of contested applicability) as the enabling adventure that provided both the fictional raw material and the displacement essential to a Modernist point of view. Yet as Caren Kaplan insists, "all displacements are not the same" (Kaplan, *Questions of Travel*, 2). Distinguishing exile from expatriation, immigration, travel, and tourism, she comments that "Euro-American middle-class expatriates adopted the *attributes* of exile as an ideology of artistic production" (28, my emphasis). Kaplan adds that their "imperative of displacement" privileged distance as "the best perspective on a subject" (36). Most provocatively, she claims that the "voluntary homelessness" of expatriates such as Cowley, Hemingway, and Fitzgerald indicates their "lack of commitment" to social or political causes: "More and more like voyeurs of the decadent and exotic, the expatriates *see* 'others' and 'otherness' but do not yet divine their roles as actors in the production of the world they believe they are simply observing" (47). Revising Cowley's observation that the expatriates had a "spectatorial" relationship to post-war Europe, Kaplan accuses Fitzgerald and his cohorts of being politically unconscious, disengaged from the socioeconomic realities playing out around them. Their experience abroad brought this group "not to a fuller understanding of the histories and particularities of the places they have traveled through," Kaplan writes, "but to a will to power that consolidates nationalist identities and confirms a repressive hierarchy of values" (49). But does a careful reading of relevant texts – the short stories about "Europe" – sustain this harsh indictment?

The European stories fall into three distinct phases: a trio of pieces from 1925, infused with romantic optimism; ten stories, mostly about loss and disillusionment, appearing between 1929 and 1932; and two muted, nostalgic narratives written after his final return to the United States. Reading these pieces together, as a complete, virtual sequence rather than as scattered tales interposed (as in Matthew J. Bruccoli's superb collection, *The Short Stories of F. Scott Fitzgerald*) between "Jacob's Ladder," "The Last of the Belles," and the Basil and Josephine stories, we witness the emergence of a larger, composite narrative of displacement and cultural encounter that delineates national identity as it critiques American naiveté and excess. Between the earlier and later European stories we observe a notable shift from exuberant nationalism toward a more tolerant cosmopolitanism, as well as an intensifying awareness of expatriation's irreversible consequences.

Fitzgerald's September 1924 essay, "How to Live on Practically Nothing a Year," provides a benchmark for his changing consciousness. Composed shortly after going abroad – and conceived for a *Saturday Evening Post* audience assumed to share his ethnic and class biases – the article describes in comic terms the author's rocky adjustment to life in France. Acknowledging the economic basis of the expatriate movement, Fitzgerald portrays a couple (implicitly, the Fitzgeralds) going "off to the Riviera to economize" (*AA*, 100–1). Yet the motivation is more complex: the radical difference in living costs, created partly by favorable exchange rates, enabled many displaced Americans to live abroad like "a sort of royalty" (as Charlie

Wales remarks in "Babylon Revisited"), realizing not just a better way of life but often an altogether different class status than they would have known in the United States. Explaining the couple's motives Fitzgerald writes: "We were going to the Old World to find a new rhythm for our lives, with a true conviction that we had left our old selves behind forever – and with a capital of just over seven thousand dollars" (*AA*, 102). For years "the poorest boy in a rich boy's school," Fitzgerald squandered his income on Long Island "extravagance and clamor" and embarked for Europe precisely to join the upper class – a gratification he betrays when describing the couple's "cool clean villa," an estate replete with a gardener who calls the American writer "milord" (113).

This craving for upper-class or aristocratic status manifests itself elsewhere in "How to Live." Fitzgerald condescends to the French, who – whether taxi-drivers or real estate agents – are stereotypically portrayed as conniving, money-hungry types. When a porter bashes a cab driver over the head to settle the question of where the Fitzgeralds will lodge, the writer tosses "several nickels – or rather francs – over the prostrate carbuncular man" (*AA*, 105). The largesse signifies both Fitzgerald's class difference from the driver and his casual attitude toward French money, which he later likens to "gold-colored hat checks" (114). The French language seems likewise meaningless, and Fitzgerald ridicules speakers of French as well as his own inexact *franglais*. In one ludicrous scene he commands a doorman to speak French rather than English, then to repeat the information very slowly in English, before observing to his young daughter: "His French strikes me as very bad" (102). The episode suggests that multiplied wealth and newly elevated class status entitle American expatriates to mock French functionaries openly. This ruling-caste pretension acquires racial connotations when Fitzgerald describes himself and his wife "lounging on a sandy beach in France," burned to a "deep chocolate brown" so dark that they appear to be "of Egyptian origin; but closer inspection showed that their faces had an Aryan cast" (113). These fortunate folk occupy a privileged place on a restricted beach, attended, we are told, by African waiters who deliver drinks and occasionally "chase away the children of the poor" (113). Fitzgerald's glowing image of racial dominance – tanned "Aryan" Americans served by a Senegalese waiter "with an accent from well below the Mason-Dixon line" (114) – speaks volumes about both the assumed readership of the *Post* and the relative lack of racial and ethnic sensitivity marking Fitzgerald's early expatriate writing.

Yet the essay is not devoid of self-critical insight. Fitzgerald denounces other Americans for their avoidance of "French life" while satirizing the Fitzgeralds' own resistance to the foreign. While they munch deviled ham from Illinois and read the *New York Times*, they consider themselves "absolutely French" (113). Giving the issue of cultural contact a further twist, the author insists that the Fitzgeralds have become "cultured Europeans": "The secret is that they had entered fully into the life of the Old World" (114). But they do so by patronizing "quaint" restaurants not in the guidebooks and paying whopping sums for their meals. After a summer on the Riviera, their original seven thousand dollars has disappeared, but the author and his wife have no regrets; insulated from poverty and freed from all labor except writing, the American expatriate can retain a leisure-class status, secure in his superiority to a native population that exists but to serve him.

But "How to Live" also portrays the Riviera as a place of potential unrest. "The whole world has come here to forget or to rejoice," Fitzgerald writes, "to hide its face or have its fling, to build white palaces out of the spoils of oppression or to write the books which sometimes batter those palaces down" (104). Though the observation implies proletarian sympathy, Fitzgerald (as in *Tender is the Night*) betrays his empathy for aristocratic Russian exiles living in France. In marked contrast to middle-class American expatriates, whose elective displacement sometimes enables them to penetrate the upper class, the enforced exile of the Russians reduces them from dukes and czars to domestic workers. Fitzgerald could denounce fugitives from Bolshevism as builders of "white palaces" from "the spoils of oppression"; but he typically did not, instead romanticizing their fall from grandeur and implicitly revealing what Renato Rosaldo calls "imperialist nostalgia" (Kaplan, *Questions of Travel*, 22).

This romanticizing impulse soon produced "Love in the Night" (November 1924), Fitzgerald's earliest effort to adjust his narrative trajectories to the European scene – and his first magazine story after completing *Gatsby*.[3] His young protagonist, Val Rostoff, is the offspring of a Russian Prince and an American woman whose father (Morris Hasylton) helped finance the Chicago World's Fair of 1892. The Rostoffs own one of those "white palaces" – a villa in Cannes purchased with "American gold" – and the narrative hinges on Val's romantic encounter one April evening with a nameless American girl aboard a yacht in the harbor. But the girl goes away, and the heartsick hero falls into the maw of history, returning to Russia just in time for the 1917 revolution. After his parents have been executed "to atone for the blunders of the Romanoffs," the young man quits the Imperial army and returns to Cannes, where he becomes a taxi-driver. After war, revolution, and several years of poverty have "conspired against his expectant heart" (*Short Stories*, 312, 313), Val prepares to flee the city in shame after learning of the return of a certain American yacht. But at the story's turning point, Fitzgerald notes a significant shift. Although Val had, on first meeting the

American girl, insisted adamantly upon his Russian identity (307, 309), the prospect of seeing her again stirs his American instincts:

> The blood of Morris Hasylton began to throb a little in Val's temples and made him remember something he had never before cared to remember – that Morris Hasylton, who had built his daughter a palace in St. Petersburg, had also started from nothing at all.
>   Simultaneously another emotion possessed him, less strange, less dynamic but equally American – the emotion of curiosity. (315)

At the American consulate, his query about the yacht produces a swift reunion with his first love, whom he subsequently marries.

Unique among Fitzgerald's European stories for its narration from the subject position of a European exile, "Love in the Night" nevertheless insists on the dual nationality of Val Rostoff in order to comment on national and ethnic differences. Val's Russian origins enhance his romantic imagination, for among the three nationalities who use the Riviera as an expatriate "pleasure ground," Fitzgerald theorizes that although the English are "too practical" and the Americans have "no tradition of romantic conduct," the Russians are "a people as gallant as the Latins, and rich besides" (303). Val's father, Prince Paul Rostoff, has sumptuous tastes and philandering habits, and his son at seventeen regards Cannes as a "privileged paradise" where because he is "rich and young" with aristocratic blood, he anticipates a "unique and incomparable" encounter with "a lovely unknown girl" (303). Val's mother conversely represents the prim and proper American: she storms "hysterically" at evidence of the Prince's infidelities, refuses to let her son kiss her because he has been "handling money," and always speaks with a "faint irony" when referring to "the land of her nativity" (303–4). As if to deny her humble origins, her early years over a butcher shop in Chicago, she teaches her son to "look down on Americans," but – Fitzgerald notes significantly – "she hadn't succeeded in making him dislike them" (305). Thus Val falls in love with the American girl and five years later responds explicitly *as an American* to the opportunity of seeing her again.

In the closing paragraphs, however, Fitzgerald reinscribes the hero's cultural otherness by invoking the danger of international marriages. According to home-grown wisdom, unions between Americans and foreigners "always turn out badly" (316). But in his early, optimistic phase, Fitzgerald cites this cynical "American tradition" to refute it: at story's end, the Russian *émigré* Val owns a taxi fleet in New York and revisits Cannes each April with his American wife. In this youthful fairytale, affluence presumably resolves cross-cultural differences. While the coda hails an international marriage that has turned out well, the happy ending nevertheless requires us to forget

the marriage of Val's parents, which did not. International romance and marriage, a theme inherited from Henry James, would recur in Fitzgerald's later
European stories as an important test of cultural relations and differences,
with the frequent failure of cross-cultural relationships suggesting (as it does
so often in James) incompatible national sensibilities.

But the psychosocial reality of cultural displacement could also affect li-
aisons between Americans abroad. Like James, Fitzgerald seemed particularly intrigued by encounters between Europeanized Americans and less
sophisticated American travelers, and two stories in 1925 explored that potential pairing. Although the author probably had "Not in the Guidebook"
(February 1925) in mind when in April 1925 he alluded to the "horrible
junk" he had lately written, the story nevertheless depicts an unusual expatriate romance (*Life in Letters*, 101). Heroine Milly Cooley, an American
of Czech and Rumanian descent, travels to France to economize with her
husband Jim, a shell-shocked, decorated war hero. But abandoned by her
dissipated spouse, she arrives in Paris alone, only to be rescued from French
hoodlums by Bill Driscoll, a war veteran and tour guide who has amassed
a "swelling packet of American bonds" (*Price*, 167) living by his wits in
France. Fluent in French and well informed about French culture, he has
for two years operated a tour bus bearing the legend: "WILLIAM DRISCOLL:
He shows you things not in the guidebook" (167). In fact, Driscoll proves
a savvy entrepreneur engaged in the post-war touristic commodification of
France; aboard his "rubberneck wagon," Milly is soon "whirled through fifteen centuries of Paris" (170), entertained by his patter. Yet Driscoll shows
himself to be "unusually level-headed" (169), an admirable fellow who cares
for Milly without exploiting her vulnerability. And he is modest: while es-
corting a group that includes Milly to the battlefield at Château-Thierry, he
recollects the fighting and jokes that he wasn't shot because he was "shak-
ing so much they couldn't aim at [him]" (175). Yet when Milly insists on
contrasting Driscoll's panic with her estranged husband's supposed courage,
Driscoll admits his modest "professional lie" and tells the truth: he had
been wounded the night before the battle, capturing a copy of German orders that a sneak thief later stole from him. Incredibly, Milly recognizes
in these very details the story of her husband's spurious valor and instantly
discerns the true hero from the false one. The following spring, after Driscoll
and Milly are married, they embark on their honeymoon in the tour bus,
filling its vacant seats with pedestrians picked up along the "poplar-lined
roads of France" (176) – a charming image of their acculturation. In a
story marred by shifts in point of view and by the colossal coincidence of
the intercepted German orders, Fitzgerald portrays a resourceful expatriate thriving in France because he knows things not in the guidebook – and

because he invests his income in American bonds and his love in an American woman.

Likewise marred by plot contrivances, "A Penny Spent" (July 1925) focuses on the relationship between a rich American girl and a profligate American expatriate, Corcoran, who was born and raised at the Brix Grill (identified in manuscript as the Paris Ritz).[4] Having wasted a half-million dollars because "a childhood and youth in Europe with a wildly indulgent mother had somehow robbed him of all sense of value or proportion" (*Bits*, 117), Corcoran takes a position as *cicerone* to Hallie Bushmill, the daughter of an American millionaire. The young man's cultural competence includes the ability to "speak most languages" (115), to correct the historical slips of a Belgian guide (118), and to orchestrate dazzling social events that bring Hallie in contact with titled Europeans. In giving Corcoran his delicate assignment, Mr. Bushmill has set strict fiscal limits to help him recover a commonsense American regard for money and value, and for a time Corcoran practices a Franklinesque frugality as he arranges visits to Brussels and Waterloo aboard a tour bus. Fitzgerald distinguishes here between the long-term expatriate and the tourist: a European native who has never done vulgar "sight-seeing," Corcoran must study histories and guidebooks so that he can regale Hallie and her mother with touristic information. Although he already knows Europe "like a book" (116), as the place of his birth and residence, he has no sense of its otherness as a cultural commodity to be approached in a "rubber-neck wagon" (118). But when Hallie becomes bored with monuments and battlefields, he demonstrates his European connections by arranging a country-club luncheon with "Prince Abrisini, Countess Perimont and Major Sir Reynolds Fitz-Hugh, the British attaché" (122). Abandoning his guidebooks, Corcoran rents a lodge and introduces Hallie to more European aristocrats, reverting to his free-spending ways to entertain the girl and expand her cultural horizons.

His eagerness to help Hallie spread her wings in Europe contrasts with the paternalism of Claude Nosby, the obnoxious American to whom Hallie is "practically engaged" (120). Upon his arrival in Europe, Nosby finds Hallie "less docile and less responsive" than before and worries that Corcoran has infected her with "nonsense" that will make it harder to take her back to the factory town and "the little circle where she had grown up" (129). Hallie responds eagerly to the expansive cosmopolitan life that Corcoran represents, and on the Isle of Capri (where the Fitzgeralds stayed in February 1925), she finally escapes Nosby's presence long enough to profess her love for Corcoran, who redeems his spendthrift reputation in Italy when he saves Hallie from a gang of criminals bent on robbery and kidnaping. Conscious of threats posed by the Mafia and the Black Hand, Corcoran spots a car full of pursuing *banditti* and confounds them by throwing money away – literally, by scattering English banknotes across the landscape. Having recorded the serial numbers to prevent the bills from being exchanged for *lire*, the clever Corcoran saves Mr. Bushmill's capital as well as his daughter. The young hero succeeds both by using his knowledge of Europe and by casting off the expatriate *insouciance* that deprived him of "all sense of value or proportion." He negotiates cultural difference in a way that affirms both American values and Continental sophistication. As in the two earlier stories, Fitzgerald portrays Europe as a scene of romance; a touristic exploration of cultural differences helps to cement the attachment between the cosmopolitan male and a less worldly American female. At this early juncture, despite domestic tension after Zelda's 1924 dalliance with Jozan, the author still idealized life abroad as a glittering transcultural adventure that led inevitably to a romantic ending.

During those years the Fitzgeralds lived principally in Paris, near the Arc de Triomphe, and on the Riviera, within the social orbit of the Murphys; they spent one winter in Rome and part of another in the Pyrenees, where Zelda received treatment for colitis. Upon their return to the United States in late 1926, though, Fitzgerald abandoned the international theme in his short fiction for almost four years, mainly because the American scene recaptured his attention and because he was channeling expatriate story lines into a novel set in France. During this era he worked in Hollywood and published "The Rich Boy" as well as a series of slick coming-of-age stories about a young midwesterner named Basil Duke Lee. Income from the Basil stories in fact financed Fitzgerald's third trip abroad, a five-month visit to France in 1928 that he undertook to complete his novel-in-progress about a glamorous expatriate couple. The Fitzgeralds rented an apartment on the rue de Vaugirard opposite the Jardin du Luxembourg, and Zelda plunged maniacally into ballet lessons with Madame Egorova. If Fitzgerald made little headway that summer in his major project, he did meet James Joyce at a dinner party (and offered to leap from a window in homage); but the visit yielded no new stories featuring foreign themes or transatlantic contrasts. When he returned the following spring, however, for what would be his last, harrowing sojourn in Europe, he began almost immediately to mine the related subjects of international relationships and expatriate social life. Between May 1929 and April 1931 he wrote ten new stories about Americans abroad, and although the earliest follows the romantic scripting of the 1925 stories, the narratives composed thereafter focus more typically on the complications of European courtships and marriages and often expose the decadent, self-indulgent behavior of the American leisure class. Especially in the seven stories written after Zelda's 1930 breakdown, Fitzgerald appears increasingly mindful of the boorishness and blindness that accompanied inflated expatriate wealth.

Following a transitional piece ("The Rough Crossing") about jealousy and marital conflict aboard a ship bound for Europe, "Majesty" (May 1929) offers another romanticized treatment of international courtship and marriage. As her family name portends, the American beauty Emily Castleton longs for aristocratic connections, and after leaving her fiancé, Brevoort Blair, at the altar, she returns to Europe (where she had earlier led an "artistic" life) and drops out of sight. Her name soon appears, however, in a newspaper account linking her with a "dissipated ne'er-do-well" (*Short Stories*, 473) of "obscure nationality" (474) named "Tutu" Petrocobesco. Although he calls himself a prince, Petrocobesco has been expelled from Paris by the French police, and believing Emily to be "mixed up with a deported adventurer in disgraceful scandal" (474), her father asks Brevoort (now married to Emily's cousin Olive) to rescue her from ruin. In a plot transparently lifted from James's *The Ambassadors*, Brevoort and Olive track Emily to Hungary and thence to "Tutu's native country" (478), a tiny, run-down province called Czjeck-Hansa, where the "peasant party" controlling the new republic agrees to let Petrocobesco claim the title of king if he will become ceremonial head of state. Emily has consented to marry Tutu, we learn, on condition that he "insisted on being king instead of prince" (479) – for she yearns to be a queen. Initially appalled by the "crazy life" (478) Emily is leading abroad, Olive watches at the end in rapt admiration as her cousin rides through the streets of London in a royal carriage: "There was about the scene the glamour shed always by the old empire of half the world, by her ships and ceremonies, her pomps and symbols" (480). This is "imperialist nostalgia" with a vengeance; Emily fulfills her notion of the American Dream by marrying European nobility, thereby escaping the ambiguities of the American social classes and securing regal status. Although Fitzgerald elsewhere manifests ethnic derision of non-Anglo Europeans (as witness the West Egg guests in *The Great Gatsby*) and here portrays Czjeck-Hansa as a place of "filthy streets" and "tumble-down" houses (475), Emily nevertheless weds "a fat little fellow with an attractive leer and a quenchless thirst" (474) precisely to insert herself into the scene of "glamour." Although Brevoort remarks that "it's all so silly," Olive's final, "helpless adoration" (480) of the London spectacle seems to validate Emily's quest while ignoring questions about the heroine's anti-democratic craving for nobility.[5]

A more richly nuanced exploration of cultural difference figures in "The Swimmers" (July–August 1929), which develops an ambiguous theory of American identity in the context of an expatriate's struggle to contend with an unfaithful French wife and to reaffirm his own threatened manhood. The story begins in Paris, where for eight years American Henry Clay Marston has been living because "the questions which [his] life propounded could be answered only in France" (*Short Stories*, 496), and it ends with Marston sailing from America back to Europe (presumably to France).[6] Fitzgerald never fully clarifies the "questions" that attach the hero so obstinately to France, though he notes that Marston's apartment on the rue Monsieur was "the sort of thing [he] could not have afforded in America" (496). Elsewhere he suggests that Marston had adapted himself to life abroad by "substituting for the moral confusion of his own country, the tradition, the wisdom, the sophistication of France" (502). Marston's curious need for France is in fact deeper than his attachment to his wife Choupette, whom he discovers *in flagrante delicto* with another man at the beginning of the story. He subsequently brings her to Virginia, presumably to deliver her from temptation and to restore his masculinity by taking a lucrative reassignment, for (as he tells his wife) "American men are incomplete without money" (501). Indeed, several comments in "The Swimmers" comprise a virtual critique of American culture: when first offered the opportunity to return to Richmond at double his Paris salary, the unenthusiastic Marston can barely refrain from "stating his frank opinion upon existence at home" (496), and he later is said to believe that "America is superficial and full of silly fads" (502). Choupette calls the droves of American tourists in France "parasites such as Europe has not known in a hundred years" (499), and Marston himself regards Americans as "restless and with shallow roots," a people eager to forget "history and the past" (506). Mr. Wiese, the millionaire with whom Choupette becomes involved in Virginia, declares about the United States, "Money made this country, built its great and glorious cities" (508), thus producing a vulgar conflation of patriotism and materialism.

Yet playing to a *Saturday Evening Post* audience possibly dubious about the expatriate author's own loyalties, Fitzgerald delivers in closing a resonant nationalistic pronouncement:[7]

> The best of America was the best of the world . . . France was a land, England was a people, but America, having about it still that quality of the idea, was harder to utter – it was the graves at Shiloh and the tired, drawn, nervous faces of its great men, and the country boys dying in the Argonne for a phrase that was empty before their bodies withered. It was a willingness of the heart. (512)

Watching from the deck of the *Majestic* as the American landscape recedes in the distance, the now-divorced Marston repents his earlier unpatriotic views: "All his old feeling that America was a bizarre accident, a sort of historical sport, had gone forever" (512). Not by accident he is reunited aboard ship with a comely young Virginian, "that perfect type of American girl" (499) who four years earlier in France had taught him how to swim and thus restored his masculine self-assurance. But the romantic ending obscures an unsettling question: why, after this change of heart, after coming to regard America as a "generous mother" (511), is Marston nevertheless returning to Europe and an expatriate existence? As a Virginian of the sort "prouder of being Virginians than Americans" (498), why is he leaving Richmond – presumably – to resume his life in a city associated, in the story's first two paragraphs, with gasoline exhaust and death: "black horror" (495)? In the final analysis Marston's resumption of displacement implies an inability to go home again, to readjust to American culture.[8] Such is the risk of living long years abroad, for as sculptor William Wetmore Story once observed, "a man always pays, in one way or another, for expatriation, for detachment from his plain primary heritage."[9] By 1929 Fitzgerald recognized the force of that truth, and "The Swimmers" marks an effort to grapple with its unsettling implications.

But the converse dilemma lies in the difficulty of adapting fully to an alien culture. In his first story completed after the stock market crash, Fitzgerald fashioned a study of dissolution titled "Two Wrongs" (October–November 1929) that in one section depicts expatriate recklessness provoked by cultural difference. It was the first of several narratives written over a two-year period that worked variations on the motif of expatriate debauchery in Europe, often associated with marital strife and what Fitzgerald elsewhere called "emotional bankruptcy."[10] The story follows the troubled romance of Emmy Pinker, an aspiring actress from South Carolina, and Bill McChesney, a hard-drinking New York stage producer with a nasty temper. Emmy's sympathy for Bill when he brawls with an actor precipitates their marriage; yet after two flops on Broadway, when Bill goes to London with the pregnant Emmy to reestablish his theatrical prowess, he succumbs there to the lure of drink and the seductive appeal of European nobility. Socializing with "a lot of dukes and ladies" he proclaims at a bar that he would like to become "the Marquis of McChesney" (*Short Stories*, 520). Despite Emmy's reminder that he is imbibing too much, Bill seems driven by an inchoate (and unexamined) Irish-American need to force his way into English high society, and when Lady Sybil Combrinck, his patroness, excludes him from her guest list, Bill crashes the event – despite his lack of evening wear – to claim a place among the social elite. Promptly ejected, the producer seeks solace at a cabaret and returns home sodden, only to learn that his wife has just delivered a still-born child – an emblem of their doomed marriage. "I'm done with you," she tells her foul-smelling husband at the hospital (525). Upon their return to the United States, Emmy (like Zelda) takes up ballet and becomes self-reliant, while the suddenly dependent, chain-smoking Bill develops tuberculosis. The story's conclusion finds Emmy accepting an offer to dance with a New York ballet company rather than accompany her spouse to a Colorado sanitarium.[11] She flourishes ostensibly because she has American "character," while the reprobate Bill heads West "for a definite finish" (530), having been ruined less by lung disease than by a costly London debauch.[12]

The riotous living of monied expatriates receives lighter treatment in "The Bridal Party" (May 1930), the first work Fitzgerald completed after Zelda's nervous breakdown in April 1930. Set entirely in Paris, the story depicts precious little cultural interaction in this expatriate "contact zone," to borrow Mary Louise Pratt's term.[13] Fitzgerald includes several references to Right Bank locales and even a prophetic image of the German Graf Zeppelin, "shining and glorious, [a] symbol of escape and destruction" (*Short Stories*, 562), gliding over the rue de Castiglione. But his all-American plot turns rather on Michael Curly's struggle to accept the Paris marriage of his former sweetheart, Caroline Dandy, to a go-getter named Hamilton Rutherford. Fitzgerald brackets the wedding, captured by "motion-picture machines" (573), between spectacles of expatriate ostentation: festivities include a prenuptial champagne dinner at Chez Victor, a bachelor dinner at the Ritz bar, and a wedding reception and breakfast at the Hôtel George-Cinq. Apart from brief dealings with functionaries, however, the invitees seem oblivious to France or the French; they are too preoccupied with self-indulgent social rituals. Money and investment form the conversational leitmotif, and we learn that Rutherford has made a fortune selling his seat on the stock exchange just prior to the crash.

A bit like Fitzgerald before his literary success, the Irish-American Curly has never had money, and when he arrives at Chez Victor wearing an old dinner coat he encounters people who were "rich and at home in their richness with one another." In his alienation, he sees them as "too weary to be exhilarated by any ordinary stimulant," because for weeks (since the crash) they have been quaffing cocktails, wines, brandies, beer, and whiskey "like some gigantic cocktail in a nightmare" (565). Curly seems on the surface an appealing figure: he retains fond memories of American places where he has romanced Caroline, and he mocks the blatant male chauvinism of Rutherford. Yet when a concierge, delivering news of his grandfather's death, consoles Curly by murmuring "Too bad – too bad," the young protagonist crassly retorts, "Not too bad...It means that I come into a quarter of a million dollars" (563). The wealth enables him to buy new social attire, and in a transformation straight out of Gogol's "The Overcoat," the hero takes on a different attitude: "Michael was surprised to find what a difference his new dinner coat, his new silk hat, his new, proud linen made in his estimate of himself; he felt less resentment toward all these people for being so rich and assured. For the first time since he had left college he felt rich and assured himself" (569). Here as elsewhere Fitzgerald draws a fine line between envy of and contempt for wealth. Curly's sudden affluence fires the dream of winning back Caroline's love, but when she reaffirms her desire to marry Rutherford – after learning that he has lost "almost every cent" (572) in bad investments – Fitzgerald undercuts the assumption that money is her motive. We see Curly suffering through the nuptials and anaesthetizing himself later with champagne and then "much more champagne" (575) before realizing that he is "cured" (576) of his yearning for Rutherford's bride. Whether Fitzgerald wants us to regard Curly finally as a sympathetic romantic hero or, more likely, a silly, shallow fellow (last seen at the reception "trying to remember which one of the bridesmaids he had made a date to dine with" [576]) seems the interpretive crux of this ambiguous treatment of expatriate social life.[14]

In two better-known stories of European self-ruin, Fitzgerald sharpened his critique to suggest that American expatriates, released from the ethical constraints of their own culture and possessed of wealth multiplied by foreign exchange, inhabited an unreal cultural space conducive to exploitation and personal dissolution. Yet he refused to ascribe the undoing of his Americans abroad to some corrupting influence in European life; indeed, his protagonists often seem dismissive of foreign culture, oblivious to the reality that they are guests, transients in a place not their own. By virtue of their economic clout, his expatriates occupy a fantastic sphere that is (like the international pier in "The Rough Crossing") neither *here* nor *there*. In this space they assume a privileged status, narcissistically pursuing pleasure while regarding Europeans as inferiors to be commanded and European places as touristic sites to be exhausted and abandoned. Fitzgerald personifies this mentality in "One Trip Abroad" (August 1930) through Mr. and Mrs. Miles, the older American couple whom Nelson and Nicole Kelly first meet aboard a tourist bus in Algeria. Mrs. Miles glibly opines: "Every place is the same... The only thing that matters is who's there. New scenery is fine for half an hour, but after that you want your own kind to see. That's why some places have a certain vogue and then... the people move on somewhere else. The place itself never really matters" (*Short Stories*, 580). Unable to comprehend cultural meanings attached to localities, Mrs. Miles regards "scenery" as an irrelevant backdrop to the essential rituals of expatriate social life. "Bored with themselves" and "somewhat worn away inside by fifteen years of a particular set in Paris" (578), the Mileses entertain the illusion that they are pursuing "the real customs and manners of the country" (581) as they wait for a troupe of pubescent Arab girls called the "Ouled Naïls" to dance naked before affluent tourists. The spectacle implicitly reifies the social and economic disparity between the ungarbed girls (dancing to raise dowries) and the well-attired, well-heeled Anglo-American audience. With characteristic snobbery, the Mileses refuse to regard their Algerian excursion as touristic; Mr. Miles declares, "I don't consider myself a tourist. A tourist is someone who gets up early and goes to cathedrals and talks about scenery" (579). In their boredom, class and ethnic elitism, and indifference to their exploitation of native people, the Mileses typify the mindless decadence Fitzgerald had by this time come to associate with the American expatriate colony.

The implied corruption of the Mileses anticipates the dramatic disintegration of the Kellys, who figure as working sketches for Dick and Nicole Diver. As John Kuehl has pointed out, "One Trip Abroad" unites many key motifs scattered among the so-called *Tender is the Night* "cluster stories."[15] But while the story's relationship to the novel has been capably elucidated by Kuehl and others, its representation of cultural difference and expatriate profligacy warrants closer attention. The experience of the Kellys epitomizes the process of European self-ruin, and as Fitzgerald takes pains to note in the final section of the story, their travels define a course that is both moral and geographical. Drifting from North Africa to Italy to the Riviera and thence to Paris before fleeing to Switzerland, "a country where very few things begin, but many things end" (594), the Kellys complete a journey that strips them of youth, health, and hope. We see them initially as a dazzling young couple, virtual honeymooners, who have decided to go abroad after Nelson has inherited a half-million dollars. Yet in each of the places where they mix with the expatriate crowd – now and again spotting another couple who seem their exact counterparts – they become involved in conflicts that mark stages of deterioration. These conflicts all involve reactions to cultural difference: they quarrel in Algeria over the propriety of watching the Ouled Naïls; they become bibulous, irritable, and bored in Sorrento, where Nelson gets into an outrageous clash with a reserved British couple; Nelson's affair in Monte Carlo with "an exquisite young French woman" (586) provokes an insane outburst from Nicole (to which her spouse retaliates abusively); in Paris the Kellys befriend Austrian Count Chiki Sarolai to gain access to "the ancient noblesse" (592) but find themselves robbed of jewels and ruined financially by a European confidence man.

Early in the story a self-confessed "sponger" named Oscar Dane had warned Nicole about the corrupt, international set with whom they have been socializing: "Do you call that crowd of drunks you run with amusing people? Why, they're not even very swell. They're so hard that they've shifted down through Europe like nails in a sack of wheat, till they stick out of it a little into the Mediterranean Sea"(585). Repeatedly the Kellys vow to avoid the moneyed expatriate group, but in a foreign place the need for social connection proves irresistible: "The first crowd they had known was largely American, salted with Europeans; the second was largely European, peppered with Americans." In Paris, where they yearn to penetrate some "ultimate *milieu*" (590) defined by status, wealth, genius, and power, the Kellys fall victim to their own social striving. The seemingly romantic image of the canal-boat party – which they have unwittingly financed – captures the utter unreality of the cultural sphere inhabited by the expatriate set: "The boat was hung with fragile lanterns, which blended with the pastels of the bridges and the reflected stars in the dark Seine, like a child's dream out of the Arabian Nights" (592). Occupying a space that is neither American nor French, the artificial paradise of "those who sought pleasure over the face of Europe" (594), the Kellys at last become alienated from themselves – a point Fitzgerald dramatizes in the shocking final encounter with their unnamed doubles. In Switzerland (where the author would keep vigil near his hospitalized wife) Nicole asks Nelson the overwhelming question, "Why did we lose peace and love and health, one after the other?" (596). Their effort to elide cultural difference by exploiting economic advantage – to spend their way into international high society – appears to explain much of their self-inflicted misery.

Fitzgerald articulates the unreality of expatriate experience most brilliantly, of course, in "Babylon Revisited" (December 1930), his often-anthologized story of European self-ruin. The author was then living in a Lausanne hotel, monitoring Zelda's condition and visiting daughter Scottie (under the care of a French nanny in Paris), while resisting suggestions by his sister-in-law Rosalind that Scottie live with her in Brussels. When Fitzgerald's hero, Charlie Wales, returns to Paris seeking custody of his daughter Honoria, he necessarily confronts the memory of the "crazy years" (*Short Stories*, 629) when sudden, unearned wealth – the result of getting "lucky in the market" (626) – allowed Americans to behave as if they ruled the city. Charlie's remembrance of that fantastic boom period alternately evokes nostalgia and disgust: "We were a sort of royalty, almost infallible, with a sort of magic around us," he recollects (619). At his first stop, the Ritz bar, he comes to the jolting realization, however, that "it was not an American bar any more – he felt polite in it, and not as if he owned it." With the stock market crash, the onset of hard times in the United States, and the decline of European tourism, the Ritz (like other expatriate haunts) has "gone back into France," resuming its place in indigenous culture (616). When he revisits Montmartre, the scene of so much expatriate revelry, Charlie similarly finds a "local, colloquial French crowd" in the rue Blanche. With clearer eyes he now sees the insidious function of Zelli's and other night spots – that of consuming the expatriate consumer: "The Café of Hell still yawned – even devoured, as he watched, the meager contents of a tourist bus." Buoyed by economic good fortune, Charlie and other expatriates of the twenties failed to recognize the consequences of their wastefulness. For them, the unreality of money created a fantastic sphere of European profligacy; Charlie recalls the reckless spending of French cash, converted (by the mid-twenties) at twenty-five francs to the dollar: "thousand-franc notes [were] given to an orchestra for playing a single number, hundred franc notes tossed to a door-man for calling a cab" (620). In its ultimate fantastic deployment, American expatriate wealth denied not just the fact of cultural difference but the real-ity of the natural order: "The snow of twenty-nine wasn't real snow. If you didn't want it to be snow, you just paid some money" (633).

Upon his return to Paris, Charlie feels strangely alienated from the city, as if losing the sense of ownership has somehow exposed just how little he understands about it. With chagrin he realizes that "he had never eaten at a really cheap restaurant in Paris . . . For some odd reason he wished that he had" (618). He knows the gathering spots of the expatriate crowd but not the places important to the French; when he visits his sister-in-law and her husband, he never mentions the Eglise St. Sulpice, which looms before all res-idences on the rue Palatine. He speaks (English) to waiters and taxi-drivers but seems otherwise oblivious to the French denizens of Paris. Summing up the result of his heedlessness Charlie observes poignantly, "I spoiled this city for myself." By inhabiting the unreal space of expatriate self-indulgence, he has in effect missed the city and French culture altogether, losing in the pro-cess not simply the rich experience of cultural and linguistic otherness but (more to the point) his wife, his marriage, and his daughter: "Everything was gone and I was gone" (618). While he was commanding, ordering, con-suming – "throwing away money" (626) to sustain a sense of magical domi-nance over a city that existed (it seemed) only to entertain him and gratify his needs – Charlie in fact corrupted himself, and his recurrent attraction to the Ritz bar places in question the completeness of his rehabilitation. Whether he can recover from self-ruin and reclaim his daughter (and the honor she represents) remains an open question in "Babylon Revisited," for the intru-sion of two drunken friends, "sudden ghosts out of the past" (622), just when he seems about to regain custody of Honoria, spoils Charlie's bid for respectability. He must live with his remorse a while longer, pondering the "nightmare" of "utter irresponsibility" (629) that in retrospect accurately defines the expatriate dream world.[16]

Fitzgerald's darkest treatment of European excess unfolds, however, in "A New Leaf" (April 1931), which depicts the infatuation of American tourist Julia Ross with Dick Ragland, a longtime expatriate with "the worst reputation of any American in Paris" (*Short Stories*, 635). Julia's admirer, Phil Hoffman, warns her about Ragland's drunken pranks, but Julia succumbs to his charm and remarkably handsome visage. To explain why he drinks so much, Ragland recalls his service in the Great War and subsequent boredom; when he went abroad to study at the Ecole des Beaux Arts, we learn, "something happened to him" (637) – he drank excessively, quarreled with friends, and became involved in a case of vehicular homicide. Fitzgerald suggests that away from the restraining influences of American life (family, community, ethics), Ragland has become a pitiful alcoholic, morally adrift. When he arrives for a lunch date looking unkempt, his face fixed in a disgusting sneer, Julia writes him off, at least temporarily. She falls for him again, however, on the ocean liner bound for the United States, and back in New York his "misdemeanors" in Paris assume "a far-off unreality" (643). But Ragland at last proves disloyal to Julia, and en route to London he shockingly commits suicide at sea. Ruined by expatriate dissolution, Ragland (another Dick Diver prototype) proves incapable of returning to his native land and adjusting to workaday, middle-class life. By casting himself into the Atlantic, he acknowledges his inability to respond to Julia's last plea: "Change, change, Dick – change" (646). The story marks one of Fitzgerald's most searing (and patently self-critical) treatments of the irreversible effects of prolonged exile.

About another tale of European debauchery, the inferior "Flight and Pursuit" (April 1931), less needs to be said. In this rewriting of the girl-that-got-away plot, millionaire Sidney Lahaye makes amends to Caroline Corcoran (whom he once jilted), by secretly arranging for her to travel around Europe as the companion of Helen O'Connor, a worldly expatriate. Caroline's holiday lasts three dizzying years: "Its most enduring impression was a phantasmagoria of the names of places and people – of Biarritz, of Mme de Colmar, of Deauville, of the Comte de Berme, of Cannes, of the Derehiemers, of Paris and the Château de Madrid. They lived the life of casinos and hotels so assiduously reported in the Paris American papers" (*Price*, 315). The project to cheer up Caroline goes awry, though, when she becomes dissipated, "directionless," and "increasingly restless"; for her "no potion was too strong or any evening too late" (315). She threatens suicide (recalling the fate of Ragland) and in Locarno coughs up blood, revealing that she has (like Bill McChesney) contracted tuberculosis. A remorseful Sidney places Caroline in a sanitarium at Montana Vermala – where the younger son of Gerald and Sara Murphy was then being treated – and though the heroine recovers her health, she still mistrusts men. But news that Sidney has survived a plane crash in the Black Sea arouses her tenderness and inspires a passionate telegram. Marred by plot contrivances, the story portrays the experience of expatriate self-ruin from a female perspective but adds little to our understanding of cosmopolitan social relations or cultural difference.

In two other stories from his last trip abroad, however, Fitzgerald showed keener insight into the operation of national, class, and ethnic prejudices in international expatriate circles. To be sure, he still retained certain prejudices, and in "Echoes of the Jazz Age" (1931), his retrospective essay on the Roaring Twenties, he caricatures an Italian-American bound for Europe and a "fat Jewess, inlaid with diamonds," associating them with the "fantastic neanderthals . . . traveling in luxury in 1928 and 1929, who, in the distortion of their new condition, had the human value of Pekinese, bivalves, cretins, goats" (*Crack-Up*, 20–1). But despite this reflexive ethnic innuendo (and one might psychoanalyze the Irish-American Fitzgerald's chronic need to identify himself as "white" by dishing up such remarks), there is evidence elsewhere that by the early thirties the author was developing greater sensitivity to bigotry. In "The Hotel Child" (November 1930), for example, he develops a scathing treatment of the decadence and snobbery associated with members of the European nobility ensconced in a Swiss hotel. The story is all the more intriguing because Fitzgerald's heroine, Fifi Schwartz, is a ravishing Jewess who shows maturity beyond her eighteen years in dealing with an aristocratic masher (Marquis Bopes Kinkallow), a suave thief (Count Borowki), and a condescending inebriate (Lady Capps-Karr), all the while supervising her sottish brother and comforting her worried mother. As Barry Gross and Eric Fretz point out, Fitzgerald's representation – during an era of mounting anti-Semitism – of "an 'other' who resists the dominant order" marks a noteworthy move.[17] Although Fifi is initially enthralled (like Emily Castleton of "Majesty") with the idea of marrying a European nobleman in order to live "fully and adventurously" (*Short Stories*, 610), and although the Count pursues his wealthy "American dream girl" (601), the heroine finally recognizes Borowki as a scheming parasite and exposes his larceny.

But a more interesting problem inheres in Fifi's relationship to her own ethnicity. Gross and Fretz aptly comment that Fifi strives at the outset to make herself a fully assimilated member of an international social scene. Fitzgerald depicts her at her birthday party walking sensuously across a room, "followed by a whole platoon of young men of all possible nationalities and crosses" (600), and he later remarks that she felt no "insufficiency" (604) within the expatriate community. Even though Fifi prefers Europe to the United States, where "everybody is so bigoted" (605), a tacit anti-Semitism nevertheless pervades the Swiss hotel. Long inured to bigotry, Mrs. Schwartz ignores the whispering: "It was a matter of effortless indifference to her what was said by the groups around the room" (599). Fifi's rival and Anglo-American counterpart, Miss Howard, is said to have "taken pains not to make Miss Schwartz's acquaintance." Heading to London for the social season, Miss Howard and the Taylors (who will present her) are "very Europeanized Americans" who "could hardly be said to belong to any nation at all," but they nonetheless consider that "Fifi was as much of a gratuitous outrage as a new stripe in the flag" (600). Fitzgerald here alludes to the bigotry, fueled by the great Eastern European ethnic influx into the US after 1880, and the "Anglo-Saxon panic" that, as Alex Zwerdling has shown, inspired the 1921 Johnson Bill and other legislation to put new restrictions on immigration (*Improvised Europeans*, 54–5). Perhaps the most ominous practitioner of covert bigotry is the German-named assistant hotel manager, Mr. Weicker, who wants to appease his aristocratic clientele by expelling the Schwartzes. His hostility toward Fifi and his determination to cast her as a scapegoat produce the late comic scene in which he refuses to believe that Borowki's companion (and apparent accomplice) is Miss Howard: "A wave of horror swept over Mr. Weicker. Again he craned his head forward, as if by the intensity of his astonishment he could convert her into Fifi" (*Short Stories*, 613–14). Whether he dislikes the Schwartzes because they are American, or Jewish, or because Fifi provokes sexual excitement is a nice question, and Fitzgerald eschews analysis while hinting unmistakably at Weicker's prejudice. Here an emerging political consciousness foregrounds class and ethnic tensions in a cosmopolitan expatriate milieu; tacitly Fitzgerald shows sympathy for the outsider and valorizes respect for cultural difference.

Even more stunning in its critique of benighted attitudes, "Indecision" (January–February 1931) prefigures the stereotype of the "Ugly American." Although Ruth Prigozy consigns this piece to a handful of Depression-era stories "so trivial as to demand nothing but wonder that they managed to find their way into print," "Indecision" nevertheless figures importantly in a reconsideration of cultural difference in Fitzgerald, because despite its palpable silliness, it presents with unusual candor the racist and sexist arrogance of a white American male who patently features himself God's gift to women.[18] The multicultural setting – a Swiss ski resort teeming with international types – gives the protagonist, Tommy McLane, ample opportunity to flaunt his contempt for different ethnicities. A native (like Fitzgerald) of Minnesota, McLane has dropped down from Paris – where he is assistant manager at an American bank – to cruise "one of the gayest places in Switzerland with the idea that if he had nothing else to think of for ten days he might fall in love" (*Price*, 293). Fancying himself "analytical and cagy" (293), McLane instead proves confused, fearful, and dim-witted: fatuously he narrows down his romantic prospects from a dozen "girls and women" to a half-dozen to two: "He had actually written all this down on a blotter as if he were in his office in the Place Vendôme, added and subtracted them, listed points" (294). Parodically prefiguring the dilemma of Dick Diver, McLane finds himself caught between a twenty-five-year-old divorcée, Emily, and an eighteen-year-old Southern innocent, Rosemary.

Torn between two lovers but unable to recognize himself as a fool, McLane vacillates throughout the story, invariably fantasizing about the one woman while he is with the other. Along the way he becomes especially jealous of attentions to his white "angel," Rosemary, by certain darker-skinned rivals. After she dances with a Greek, "a young Levantine whom he disliked," he advises her: "Tell that Spic to go count his piasters and I'll talk turkey with you" (294). He chides her for dancing with "gigolo numbers from Cairo" and urges her to address the Greek as "greasy" rather than "honey" (294). When McLane likens his rival's dancing style to "stilling the waves," he adds an incongruous anti-Semitic inflection to a rant that conflates several ethnicities. Suspecting that Rosemary's Louisiana origins dispose her to dark-skinned men, he inquires: "I suppose the boys are all Spics down in New Orleans?" (295). Later he becomes indignant at Rosemary's socializing with a guitar-playing Spaniard, Count de Caros Moros; when he sees the Andalusian slip his arm around Rosemary during a winter ride, the sight is "horrible," and McLane briefly wants to "jerk Caros Moros to his feet and pull him from the sleigh" (299). The next day McLane telephones Rosemary, apparently to chastise her for being ethnically indiscriminate, for his unfinished taunt implicitly accuses her of acting "black" : "'Are you sorry you were so terrible to me last night, baby?' he demanded. 'No real pickaninny would –'" (301). The nadir of McLane's racism and sexism comes, however, during a moment of insecurity in which he wonders about his attractiveness to Rosemary and Emily:

> Yesterday he had been sure of these two, holding them in the hollow of his hand. As he dressed for dinner he realized that he wanted them both. It was an outrage that he couldn't have them both. Wouldn't a girl rather have half of him than all of Harry Whitby, or a whole Spic with a jar of pomade thrown in? Life was so badly arranged – better no women at all than only one woman. (300)

This interior monologue makes plain the pathetic immaturity and ultimate fear of emotional commitment that generate McLane's romantic "indecision," as well as suggesting that his virulent racism operates, like his blatant sexism, to prop up a fragile ego haunted by justifiable worries about his own vacuity. As an expatriate banker and bon vivant, McLane epitomizes a crass, American insensitivity to cultural and ethnic otherness; from the moment he arrives among the "alien mountains" at the "Dent de Something," attired in a "convictlike uniform" and confused by words uttered "in some strange language," we see him as a prisoner of his own ignorance and narcissism (292–3). Among the thoughtless Americans who flaunt their wealth, bigotry, and insouciance in Fitzgerald's short fiction, Tommy McLane is in a class by himself. As one of the last stories written before the Fitzgeralds' somber return from Europe in September 1931, "Indecision" reveals, in its ironic treatment of the protagonist, the author's development of a critical perspective on the politics and ethics of transculturation. Juxtaposed against the crudities of "How to Live on Practically Nothing a Year," the story reveals just how much Fitzgerald had matured as a cultural observer since 1924.

Two late expatriate pieces, composed in the United States long after the author's return, add little to the critique of cultural difference but place his years abroad in a poignant personal perspective. Already estranged by mental illness, the Fitzgeralds had lived apart in 1930–1 while Zelda's protracted hospitalization at Nyon and Scott's rootless existence in Swiss hotels enforced a physical separation. Matthew J. Bruccoli notes that during this epoch Fitzgerald "began sleeping with other women," possibly to refute Zelda's imputation of homosexuality (Bruccoli, *Some Sort of Epic Grandeur*, 311). When the couple returned to the United States, they tried to resume a semblance of marriage while both translated their wild, ultimately woeful expatriate years into novels. During her second collapse, Zelda completed *Save Me the Waltz* in early 1932 at the Henry Phipps Psychiatric Clinic of the Johns Hopkins University, and Fitzgerald – complaining of stolen material and indiscreet disclosures – warily supervised her revisions as he toiled to complete *Tender is the Night*. Yet after a precarious reconciliation, they drifted further apart, Zelda into suicidal derangement (and hospitalization at the Sheppard and Enoch Pratt Hospital) and Scott into alcoholic escapism.

By the time he wrote "The Intimate Strangers" (February-March 1935), Fitzgerald was rusticating in North Carolina, seeking a respite from symptoms of tuberculosis. Based ostensibly on the unconventional marriage of his friends Nora and Lefty Flynn, the story nevertheless incorporates thematic vestiges of Fitzgerald's years in Europe. In the details of Sara's marriage to the Marquis de la Guillet de la Guimpé, we discover again the American social desire for European, aristocratic status. But unlike the plot of "Majesty," Sara's dream of glamor on the rue du Bac culminates in the despair that impels her early, one-week fling with Killian, the exuberant American to whom she later confesses that she has never loved the Marquis. Even after the death of her husband (a veteran of the Great War), she finds herself pressured to sustain a French sense of family honor by rejecting the "wild man from nowhere" (*Price*, 622) with whom she wants to return to her native land. If this story is the "poorest" of Fitzgerald's Depression-era narratives, as Prigozy maintains, "The Intimate Strangers" still evokes the chaotic war era and its aftermath and suggests that despite their passion, Sara and Killian will remain "strangers" scarred by previous relationships (Bryer, *Short Stories: New Approaches*, 115). Revealing that Killian still mourns his first wife, Fitzgerald perhaps acknowledges his own marital bereavement, and by naming Sara's first husband "Eduard" he implicitly attributes the Fitzgeralds' domestic discord to Zelda's infatuation a decade earlier with Edouard Jozan. In a narrative about finding, losing, and recapturing love, Fitzgerald apparently sought to bury a tormenting expatriate episode by reexcavating it, but the effort did not succeed.

Six months later, the memory of Zelda's *amour* patently inspired "Image on the Heart" (September 1935). Set entirely in France, the story limns the romantic dilemma of Tudy, a nineteen-year-old American widow whose year in Provence has been financed by Tom, a family friend who first pities her, then proposes marriage. When he arrives in France to make Tudy his bride, Tom discovers that she has been spending time with Lt. Riccard, an "impetuous and fiery" (*Price*, 667) naval aviator. After Riccard displays his ardor with an aerial daredevil stunt, Tom sends Tudy away until their nuptials. From Paris she writes revealingly about Franco-American differences: "They [the French] have a life they never take us into. They plan their lives so differently. But our American lives are so strange that we can never figure things out ahead" (671). Whatever Tudy may be intimating about her ambivalence, Fitzgerald's allusion to an inscrutable French privacy seems to acknowledge his obsession with Zelda's affair and its ultimate role in the unraveling of the Fitzgeralds' marriage. Surely the publication of *Save Me the Waltz*, with its luminous portrayal of "Lieutenant Jacques Chevre-Feuille of the French Aviation," had helped to excite his retrospective jealousy. There Zelda had boldly depicted Alabama Knight's sexual attraction to the Frenchman, as well as her disregard for her husband's feelings: "He [Jacques] was bronze and smelled of the sand and sun; she felt him naked underneath the starched linen. She didn't think of David. She hoped he hadn't seen; she didn't care. She felt as if she would like to be kissing Jacques Chevre-Feuille on the top of the Arc de Triomphe" (Zelda Fitzgerald, *Collected Writings*, 86). Fitzgerald's rewriting of the romance in *Tender is the Night* indeed has the French mercenary Tommy Barban finally winning Nicole Diver away from her American husband, but in "Image on the Heart," Tom and Tudy exchange wedding vows despite the bride's "air of confusion" (*Price*, 675). As Tom later learns, Tudy had on the eve of her marriage spent several intimate hours with Riccard on the train from Paris. Faced with Tudy's reluctant offer of annulment, Tom must make a hard choice: "He had to decide now not upon what was the truth, for that he would never know for certain, but upon the question as to whether he could now and forever put the matter out of his mind, or whether it would haunt their marriage like a ghost" (677). In the story's happy ending, Tom vows not to give up Tudy and never to reproach her, even though he will also never know the "unfathomable" (678) thought in the depths of her heart. Yet the story bears witness to a contrary reality: Fitzgerald's inability to put the Jozan affair out of his mind or to resist the implicit reproach of his fictional reenactments (from *Gatsby* onward) of female inconstancy. Precisely because the Riviera episode "haunt[ed] their marriage like a ghost," the author recurrently projected in his fiction scenes of romantic rivalry and domestic mistrust.

Fitzgerald returned to the subject of expatriate life on two occasions in 1940: in a never-completed story called "News of Paris – Fifteen Years Ago" and in a filmscript based on "Babylon Revisited." In both works the foreign scene figures as little more than a superficial backdrop; with the world at war, half of France under German occupation, and Fitzgerald living in Hollywood, the Paris of the twenties seemed remote and nearly unimaginable. Yet in April 1940 he wrote to Zelda, "I have grown to hate California and would give my life for three years in France" (*Life in Letters,* 442). Badly in need of health and replenishment, already writing about his career in the past tense, Fitzgerald shared Archibald MacLeish's nostalgia: "I am sick for home for the red roofs and the olives,/ And the foreign words and the smell of the sea fall." In his nearly six years in Europe, Fitzgerald had despite adversity produced a body of short fiction that relentlessly exposes the revealing conflicts and practices of Americans abroad. Beyond timeworn clichés about the "Lost Generation," Fitzgerald's stories about Americans abroad focus persistently on the encounter with difference that defined expatriation. They explore such problems as the nationalist ethos of Americans in Europe, their class-conscious relations with other displaced Americans, their contact *as foreigners* with "foreign" peoples and languages, and their adaptation (or lack thereof) to different cultures. From our present-day vantage point, they also challenge preconceptions about Fitzgerald's abilities as a political observer and reveal a changing social consciousness. Far from indifferent to "socioeconomic realities," Fitzgerald in fact produced a literature often sharply critical of reckless, moneyed expatriates and their disdain for foreign peoples and practices. In such stories as "One Trip Abroad" and "Indecision," he openly satirized the delusions of Americans embodying a "repressive hierarchy of values" (to recall Kaplan's charge) and thereby deconstructed the assumed superiority of the Baedeker-wielding expatriate to deliver transcultural insights not to be found in any guidebook.

NOTES

1 This list does not include two additional stories, "The Rough Crossing" and "The Rubber Check," both of which contain very brief European scenes.

2 See Malcolm Cowley, *Exile's Return: A Literary Odyssey of the 1920s*; George Wickes, *Americans in Paris*; Humphrey Carpenter, *Geniuses Together: American Writers in Paris in the 1920s*; J. Gerald Kennedy, *Imagining Paris: Exile, Writing, and American Identity*; Donald Pizer, *American Expatriate Writing and the Paris Moment: Modernism and Place*.

3 I list parenthetically the date of each story's composition as established by Jackson R. Bryer in his edited volume, *The Short Stories of F. Scott Fitzgerald: New Approaches in Criticism*, pp. 348–77.

4 See *F. Scott Fitzgerald: Manuscripts* VI: *"The Vegetable," Stories and Articles*, Part 1, ed. Matthew J. Bruccoli, 131.

5 Alice Hall Petry nevertheless insists: "The element of open mockery in the jaded-but-plucky Emily and her king, the pudgy milquetoast ruler of a vest-pocket Balkan principality, hardly sound like a heartfelt toast to the American girl." See *Fitzgerald's Craft of Short Fiction: The Collected Stories 1920–1935*, 186.

6 Robert Roulston briefly notes "a contrast between continents" underlying "The Swimmers." See "'The Swimmers': Strokes Against the Current," in *New Essays on F. Scott Fitzgerald's Neglected Stories*, ed. Jackson R. Bryer, 161.

7 The patriotic coda was quite possibly inspired by Archibald MacLeish's 1929 poem "American Letter" to Fitzgerald's expatriate friend, Gerald Murphy, which suggests that America is an "idea" rather than a place: "America is neither a land nor a people,/A word's shape it is, a wind's sweep." See Archibald MacLeish, *Collected Poems, 1917–52*, p. 64.

8 Melvin J. Friedman has commented that Marston's "systematic attempts at recovering his 'roots' prove both futile and frustrating." See "'The Swimmers': Paris and Virginia Reconciled," in *Short Stories: New Approaches*, ed. Bryer, 256.

9 In an indispensable recent study, Alex Zwerdling thus cites Henry James's *William Wetmore Story and His Friends* (1903). See *Improvised Europeans: American Literary Expatriates and the Siege of London*, 202.

10 Fitzgerald used the phrase as the title of his 1931 story about Josephine Perry, the rich girl based upon his own collegiate sweetheart, Ginevra King.

11 Scott Donaldson notes that "Two Wrongs" illustrates the "transference of vitality" seen in *Tender is the Night* but rightly exposes the unbelievability of Bill's late saintliness in "'Two Wrongs,' or One Wrong Too Many," in *New Essays on F. Scott Fitzgerald's Neglected Stories*, ed. Bryer, 167, 173.

12 Casting the abusive, self-destructive McChesney finally as a victim of his wife's ambition, Fitzgerald was of course rewriting the story of his own careerism and Zelda's decision two months earlier to decline a position in the San Carlo Opera Ballet Company of Naples. He portrays McChesney's craving for aristocratic connections as a debasing impulse – thus countering the fantasy of "Majesty" – yet couches the story's main conflict more in domestic than cultural terms, for he

then faced the complications of his own alcoholism and Zelda's frenzied competitiveness.

13 See Pratt, *Imperial Eyes: Travel Writing and Transculturation*, pp. 6–7.

14 James J. Martine contrasts the romantic Curly with the pragmatic Rutherford in "Rich Boys and Rich Men: 'The Bridal Party,'" in *The Short Stories of F. Scott Fitzgerald: New Approaches in Criticism*, ed. Bryer.

15 John Kuehl, "Flakes of Black Snow: 'One Trip Abroad' Reconsidered," in *New Essays on F. Scott Fitzgerald's Neglected Stories*, ed. Bryer, 179.

16 Kuehl traces Charlie's "self-destructive circular journey" but concludes that he will escape a "death-in-life paralysis" because he possesses "character." See *F. Scott Fitzgerald: A Study of the Short Fiction*, 85, 86. My own reading is less sanguine; see J. Gerald Kennedy, "Figuring the Damage: Fitzgerald's 'Babylon Revisited' and Hemingway's 'The Snows of Kilimanjaro,'" in *French Connections: Hemingway and Fitzgerald Abroad*, ed. J. Gerald Kennedy and Jackson R. Bryer, 318–27.

17 Barry Gross and Eric Fretz, "What Fitzgerald Thought of the Jews: Resisting Type in 'The Hotel Child,'" in *New Essays on F. Scott Fitzgerald's Neglected Stories*, ed. Bryer, 190.

18 Ruth Prigozy, "Fitzgerald's Short Stories and the Depression: An Artistic Crisis," in *Short Stories: New Approaches*, ed. Bryer, 112–13.

8

RENA SANDERSON

Women in Fitzgerald's fiction

F. Scott Fitzgerald is best known as a chronicler of the 1920s and as the writer who, more than any other, identified, delineated, and popularized the female representative of that era, the flapper. Though it is an overstatement to say that Fitzgerald created the flapper, he did, with considerable assistance from his wife Zelda, offer the public an image of a modern young woman who was spoiled, sexually liberated, self-centered, fun-loving, and magnetic. In Fitzgerald's mind, this young woman represented a new philosophy of romantic individualism, rebellion, and liberation, and his earliest writings enthusiastically present her as an embodiment of these new values. Although she is often seen now as a mere fashion of the bygone Jazz Age, the flapper should be regarded as one of the great authentic characters in American history. A virtual emblem of American modernity, she and all she stood for were envied, desired, feared, and emulated throughout much of the Western world, and it was Fitzgerald's particular version of the flapper that "women imitated for more than four decades" (Solomon, *Ain't We Got Fun?*, 22).

Fitzgerald's early and widely publicized association with the flapper, however, has led many readers to misconstrue and to oversimplify the author's portraits of women and of relations between the sexes. It is important to understand that, almost from the start, Fitzgerald was ambivalent toward his "creation," fearing that the flapper embodied not freedom but moral anarchy and lack of direction. Increasingly he used her as a symbol not only of a new order, but also of social disorder and conflict. As he wrote to Edmund Wilson in May 1925, "If I had anything to do with creating the manners of the contemporary American girl I certainly made a botch of the job" (*Life in Letters*, 110). But the public mistakenly assumed that Fitzgerald, whose early success was tied to the flapper, necessarily endorsed her. In fact, Fitzgerald became the victim of that success. His artistic ambitions were thwarted by the public's desire for more flapper stories, and his association with that one female type prevented readers from appreciating the full range and complexity of his interest in modern women.

In a posthumous tribute to her husband in 1941, Zelda said that he had "seized, from the nebulous necessities of an incubating civilization, the essence of a girl able to survive the new, and less forbearing, dramas . . . [of] that troubled and turbulent epoch between world wars" (Zelda Fitzgerald, *Collected Writings*, 709). In her inimitable style, Zelda identified the subtle nuances of Fitzgerald's accomplishment, his recognition of the modern young woman as a product of the social flux and of the particular pressures on women during that "turbulent epoch." He was, in other words, a major male author who had particular insight into female psychology and the social evolution of the American woman.

Not surprisingly, from the very start of Fitzgerald's career, literary critics have paid special attention to his women characters and have sought to decipher his attitude toward them. While some see him as a sympathetic spokesman for modern women,[1] a large majority read the author's works as outright condemnations of women for their failure to live up to the male hero's romantic dreams.[2] Both views, however, depend on one-sided and polemical interpretations of the evidence. The truth is that Fitzgerald was ambivalent, both fascinated and disturbed by women and by the changing distribution of power between the sexes. Indeed, the often-noted split in Fitzgerald – between a romantic side and a pragmatic/judgmental side – may be regarded as both cause and effect of his ambivalence about women. Perhaps the divided self that readers have often detected needs to be recognized more positively as the expression of an androgynous creativity. Fitzgerald himself, attempting to explain his creative impulses, reportedly declared, "I don't know why I can write stories. I don't know what it is in me or that comes to me when I start to write. I am half feminine – at least my mind is" (quoted in Turnbull, *Scott Fitzgerald*, 259).

As we shall see, Fitzgerald's exploration of "the New Woman" was inseparable from his attempts to formulate the appropriate male response. This study proposes to describe Fitzgerald's changing views of women by examining his major works in their most revealing contexts, both cultural and personal. Before we turn to those individual works, however, it will be helpful to have a sketch of women's history up to and during the time that Fitzgerald began mapping and even shaping the roles of both women and men. The brief remarks that follow, which are of necessity overly simple and overly general, are meant to provide such a sketch.

It is a commonplace that life in the Victorian era was divided into two spheres, the public, economic sphere run by men, and the private, domestic sphere run by women. Charged with maintaining the home as a safe haven for their husbands and children, women were expected to embody the qualities of piety, purity, domesticity, and submissiveness. Not surprisingly, when these "angels of the house" began to get more involved in the cultural and political life of the nation, they did so by applying the "higher morality" that men expected of them, promoting "domestic" values in a variety of reform movements, notably abolitionism, temperance, and women's rights. The troubles of the 1890s – economic depression, labor violence, the spread of poverty, slums, and disease – brought forth an unprecedented rise in women's public activity. In the early twentieth century, women's organizations, with a combined membership in the millions, engaged in self-described "progressive" reforms of American life, especially in such areas as education, health, social services, the arts, race relations, family relations, and women's roles (Riley, *Inventing the American Woman*, 153). In short, from the 1890s into the 1920s, there was a rise in women's public power – a feminization of American culture.

As women entered the public sphere in the late nineteenth century, as American culture became feminized, there was a variety of male reactions. By 1900, in response to a perceived overcivilizing of the country by women, there was a popular cult of virility, whose supporters celebrated masculine primitivism, physical strength, outdoorsmanship, and such sports as boxing, football, and bicycling (Lears, *No Place*, 107–8).

Internationally, various male thinkers, such as Oswald Spengler, D. H. Lawrence, and Wyndham Lewis, declared that women who abandoned their traditional submissive gender roles were causing "the decline of the West" (Carey, *Intellectuals and the Masses*, 182–208). In America, H. L. Mencken, Harold Stearns, and Harvard psychologist Hugo Münsterberg, among others, denigrated women's cultural activity as sentimental, overly emotional, and intellectually inferior. The nation's social and cultural problems, it was claimed, could best be solved not by the sympathies of women amateurs but by the application of new expertise in education, natural science, technology, and social science (including psychology and psychoanalysis) – expertise in the hands of men.

These developments were inseparable from the emergence of what we now call modernity. As the economy improved, mass production of affordable goods, new technologies (automobiles, movies, telephones), unprecedented class mobility, urbanization, the rise of consumerism, advertising, and mass culture all worked to transform American values. Starting before World War I, and then accentuated by the war and by post-war prosperity, this revolutionary change "in manners and morals" downplayed the importance of self-denial and social justice and glorified "individual gratification" (Friedman, *Our American Sisters*, 417).[3]

An early manifestation of this emphasis on the self was the Gibson Girl, the most immediate historical precursor of the flapper. Created in 1896 by

Charles Dana Gibson, an illustrator for *Life* magazine, the Gibson Girl was a beautiful young woman, tanned and fit, whose short skirt allowed her to be athletic – wholesome rather than sexual, self-fulfilling rather than dependent on male desires (Brown, *Setting a Course*, 30). While the Gibson Girl was shortly supplanted in the public imagination by the more sexualized flapper, who aimed at attracting men, both female types shared a refusal to play the selfless angel whether of the house or of the nation. In fact, they defined themselves by rejecting the established ideal of woman's nurturing, maternal "nature." Noting this shift in moral authority from the family and the community to the individual, some historians have dated the appearance of the flapper not in the 1920s but well before World War I (McGovern, "American Woman's Pre-World War I Freedom," 428–9).

F. Scott Fitzgerald was a keen observer of these changes in women's mores and behavior. Throughout many of his earliest stories – read by thousands of women – many golden girls, popular daughters, and debutantes adopt the deportment, fashions, and attitudes of the flapper and sprinkle the magic dust of their high spirits. In spreading these images, Fitzgerald helped to guide women's modernization. In his own stated view, the significance of his early flappers was that they "were not a type – they were a generation. Free spirits evolved thru the war chaos and a final inevitable escape from restraint and inhibitions" (Bruccoli and Bryer, *In His Own Time*, 279). He traced the American flapper to several influences, especially the rise of a new moneyed class in the American Midwest "without background, tradition, or manners," and the popularization of Sigmund Freud, whose ideas "at third-hand" convinced "wealthy young girls" that "they were all victims of repressed desires" and that they should "cut loose" (Bruccoli and Bryer, *In His Own Time*, 264–5).

While these new attitudes represented new freedom for some women, they also undermined important features of gender politics that had thrived in the nineteenth century: women's solidarity, the cultivation of female friendship, and women's "maternal" leadership in social reform. Throughout the prosperous twenties, various discourses of mass culture co-opted the rhetoric of feminism and resulted in a shift from activist feminism to lifestyle feminism.[4] The promotion of mass-produced clothing and cosmetics through mass advertising, movies, and beauty pageants encouraged a new, ostensibly freer, female ideal. Embracing the values of individual self-creation (and female rivalry), women sought to keep up with the new fashions in dress, attitude, and behavior.

Soon, what had seemed like liberation became prescription. Women were not just free to be modern – they were expected to be modern. By 1922, in her "Eulogy on the Flapper," Zelda was announcing the flapper's demise:

"Flapperdom has become a game; it is no longer a philosophy" (*Collected Writings*, 392). As "philosophy," flapperdom stood for individual rebellion against the old pieties and restraints. As fashion, it stood for the opposite, conformity to convention. Contemporary women writers Dorothy Parker, in "The Waltz," and Edna St. Vincent Millay, in the following sonnet lines, described the dishonesty of the roles modern women felt compelled to play:

> Come, I will show you now my newest hat,
> And you may watch me purse my mouth and prink!
> Oh, I shall love you still, and all of that.
> I never again shall tell you what I think.
> I shall be sweet and crafty, soft and sly:
> You will not catch me reading any more;
> I shall be called a wife to pattern by.... (Millay, *Collected Sonnets*, 31)

To the many commentaries on this popular topic Fitzgerald added his male perspective of puzzled ambivalence. Fascinated with femininity as the product of self-fashioning – an alluring yet deceptive theatrical pose – he provided in his fiction both manuals on the construction of that pose and sermons condemning its duplicity.

Fitzgerald early came to think of women in terms of social approval and male validation. Biographers agree that Fitzgerald was embarrassed by his mother Mollie McQuillan who represented the moneyed side of the family but lacked social distinction and social grace. Rather dowdy and unkempt in appearance, she was outspoken and enjoyed a reputation as an eccentric. She spoiled her son, but he preferred his father Edward Fitzgerald (a romantic figure of impoverished gentility) and resented it that his mother overshadowed her husband.

Although Fitzgerald in his youth gained valuable mentors and friends – such as Father Sigourney Webster Fay, John Peale Bishop, and Edmund Wilson – he was haunted by his social inferiority and feared rejection. He turned to women for approval. As biographer Scott Donaldson suggests, "If he could win the heart of the girl – especially the golden girl over whom hung an aura of money, beauty, and social position – surely that meant that he had arrived, that he belonged" (*Fool For Love*, 43).

According to Sheilah Graham, his lover late in life, Fitzgerald prepared "lists of his 'fixations,' from Marie (Hersey) (1911) to S. (Graham) (1937–40). His total of feminine fixations from the age of fourteen: sixteen persons" (*College of One*, 60). Especially memorable for Fitzgerald, and the model for many popular daughters in his fiction, was the beautiful, wealthy, and popular Ginevra King, whom he courted during his college days in 1915–16. She was his first love and, as he later wrote, she dropped him "with the most supreme boredom and indifference" (*Letters*, 19). She "was the golden girl that Fitzgerald, like his male protagonists, could not have" (Donaldson, *Fool For Love*, 51).

At Princeton, an all-male university, the Triangle Club used a photo of Fitzgerald dressed as a show girl to publicize its play *The Evil Eye* – but we should not make too much of this fact since male undergraduates always played female roles in such performances. Nevertheless, his college writings, such as the one-act play *The Debutante*, do reflect his early interest in exploring the female point of view. By this time, his views of womanly and manly behavior were also at least partly informed by his reading, which included large doses of British Romantic poetry.

By the time Fitzgerald met Zelda Sayre at the Montgomery Country Club in July 1918, he had joined the U.S. Army and started writing his first novel. Eighteen-year-old Zelda (born July 24, 1900, in Montgomery, Alabama) was the lovely, spoiled, and popular daughter of an established genteel Southern family headed by Judge Anthony Sayre. She had studied ballet from ages nine to seventeen and loved to swim; she was fearless, pretty, and outspoken; and she was voted "The Prettiest and The Most Attractive Girl" in her senior class (Milford, *Zelda*, 22).

While Zelda enjoyed perhaps one of her most carefree periods, Fitzgerald struggled to establish himself. In 1918, Scribners twice rejected his novel and later that fall rejected a second version. After being discharged from the army, Fitzgerald started working for Barron Collier Advertising Agency in New York City. Also that spring, Zelda and Scott became engaged, but in June 1919, Zelda broke off their engagement.

And then, suddenly, Fitzgerald was a great success. In fall 1919, after Scribners editor Maxwell Perkins accepted *This Side of Paradise* for publication, Zelda and Scott renewed their engagement; in February 1920, the *Saturday Evening Post* for the first time published one of his stories; in March 1920, Scribner's published *This Side of Paradise*; and on April 3, 1920, Zelda and Scott were married. Thus, by the age of twenty-four, he had gained literary fame, financial success, and the woman he loved.

Central to Fitzgerald's writing was the modern and exciting kind of girl that Zelda herself epitomized. "Indeed," he said in an interview in 1921, "I married the heroine of my stories. I would not be interested in any other sort of woman" (Milford, *Zelda*, 77). He preferred the "young woman of 1920 [who was] flirting, kissing, viewing life lightly, saying damn without a blush, playing along the danger line in an immature way – a sort of mental baby vamp" (Bruccoli and Bryer, *In His Own Time*, 244–5).

Zelda, as his artistic model or prototype, participated fully in various promotional strategies – photos, writings, and interviews – that established

Fitzgerald as "creator" of the flapper. In the early 1920s Zelda wrote two articles on the flapper. The first of these, "Eulogy on the Flapper" (*Metropolitan Magazine*, June 1922), featured a realistic drawing of Zelda's profile and a caption that stressed that Fitzgerald put Zelda in his first two novels.[5] Such illustrations or photos of the couple or of Zelda alone routinely accompanied both Scott's and Zelda's early writings as well as interviews.

The interviews typically also stressed that Zelda's fictional counterpart could be found in her husband's writings. In an interview of 1923, for example, Zelda told a newspaper reporter that she preferred those of Fitzgerald's fictional heroines that were like her: "That's why I love Rosalind in *This Side of Paradise*... Rosalind was the original American flapper" (Bruccoli and Bryer, *In His Own Time*, 259). A framed insert with the heading "Is She His Model?" listed for the hurried reader the key characteristics of Zelda, the "living prototype... of the American flapper" (Bruccoli *et al.*, *Romantic Egoists*, 112).

Fitzgerald himself described his first book, *This Side of Paradise*, as "a novel about flappers written for Philosophers" (*Correspondence*, 55). Strongly autobiographical, the novel details Amory Blaine's quest for self-knowledge from childhood through college. His encounters with women are an important part of Amory's initiation into adulthood. In other words, the book explores both the flapper and the male response to the flapper. As Fitzgerald said in an early preface, the protagonist "loved many women and gazed at himself in many mirrors – in fact, women and mirrors were preponderant in all the important scenes" (Preface, *TSOP*, 393).

The girls Amory finds most interesting – Isabelle, Rosalind, Eleanor – are "popular daughters": they are white, wealthy, lovely, bright, athletic, confident, spoiled, outspoken, and young flirtatious debutantes. Each of the three girls introduces a particular trait that Fitzgerald explored more fully in his subsequent writings.

Isabelle Borgé represents a topic of particular fascination to Fitzgerald: the popular young girl's theatricality. A letter which Fitzgerald wrote to his fifteen-year-old sister Annabel when he was about nineteen (*c.* 1915) shows that the author believed that popularity was, in fact, the inevitable reward for a carefully constructed persona. The letter offers detailed tips on "The General Subject of Conversation," "Poise: Carriage: Dancing: Expression," and "Dress and Personality." Especially revealing is Fitzgerald's advice, "always affect a complete frankness but really be only as frank as you wish to be" (*Correspondence*, 15). Fitzgerald apparently believed that being "natural is simply a pose," as one character asserts in Oscar Wilde's *The Picture of Dorian Gray*, the work which Fitzgerald said "largely flavored" his first novel (Preface, *TSOP*, 393).

In his novel, the modern young girl's self-dramatization defies traditional ideals of female self-effacement. While a lady stayed out of public view, the flapper puts herself in the spotlight and flaunts her outrageously modern self. She invites the public gaze and grooms herself accordingly.

Only sixteen years old, Isabelle Borgé knows how to put on a show. When first introduced, she is compared to a leading lady on stage or to an athlete performing for a crowd (*TSOP*, 67). Amory and Isabelle both know that they are acting, and they respect each other's right to a cultivated pose: "He waited for the mask to drop off, but at the same time he did not question her right to wear it. She, on her part, was not impressed by his studied air of blasé sophistication... But she accepted his pose" (72).

Courtship patterns are also shown to have changed. Amory early becomes familiar with "that great American phenomenon, the 'petting party'" (64), and he finds it "rather fascinating to feel that any popular girl he met before eight he might quite possibly kiss before twelve" (66) – a risqué passage which reviewers loved to quote.

Nineteen-year-old Rosalind Connage illustrates the tendency of Fitzgerald's females to be more practical than their starry-eyed admirers. Although she exhibits admirable traits, such as "her endless faith in the inexhaustibility of romance, her courage and fundamental honesty," and although she loves Amory, she does not want to marry him and share his poverty (175).

As Fitzgerald had advised his sister Annabel, a girl must "learn to be worldly. Remember in all society nine girls out of ten marry for money and nine men out of ten are fools" (*Correspondence*, 16). His flappers, generally spoiled daughters from wealthy or once-wealthy families, expect material comforts and yet are economically dependent on male providers. Young men must prove themselves financially before they can gain a rich girl's hand – a recurrent pattern in the fiction that may derive from Fitzgerald's experiences with Ginevra and with Zelda. Though Fitzgerald's early works depicted girls such as Rosalind still with some sympathy, he later "gradually de-romanticized the girl and de-emphasized the glory of the quest" (Donaldson, *Fool For Love*, 102–3).

Eighteen-year-old Eleanor Ramilly Savage illustrates the dangerous side of women who lack identity or purpose (such as Gloria Patch, Daisy Buchanan, and Nicole Diver in the later novels). Somewhat like Jo March of Louisa May Alcott's *Little Women* (which Amory Blaine read *twice* as a youngster), Eleanor asks, "oh, *why* am I a girl?... here I am with the brains to do everything, yet tied to the sinking ship of future matrimony." Although she is "hipped on Freud," she nevertheless is expected "to marry into a dinner-coat" (*TSOP*, 240) and chafes against the role of uselessness. When she almost plunges off a cliff in an incident that kills her horse, Amory stops loving her: "But as Amory had loved himself in Eleanor so now what he hated was only a mirror" (242). Precisely because they think alike and share a passion for poetry and rebellion, he recognizes in her the dangerous potential of his romantic self.

In addition, the novel introduces two rather stereotypical women representing opposite extremes. Axia Marlow, a chorus girl from the Summer Garden Show, is an early example of the vulgar working-class women that appear in Fitzgerald's fiction and indicate his sexual prudishness. The opposite of Axia is Clara, whom Amory idealizes: "She was immemorial . . . Amory wasn't good enough for Clara, Clara of ripply golden hair, but then no man was" (141). Clara – lovely, strong, and devout – resembles the lady of the medieval courtly love tradition by which, some have argued, Fitzgerald "judges the relationships that develop during the decline of modern civilization" (Moreland, *The Medievalist Impulse*, 136). As stereotypes representing the extremes of bad and good, Axia and Clara are early indicators of Fitzgerald's lifelong fascination with the symbolic uses of women.

Although in the end, Amory ends up alone, he congratulates himself on his sexual choices: "Own taste the best; Isabelle, Clara, Rosalind, Eleanor, were all-American. Eleanor would pitch, probably southpaw. Rosalind was outfield, wonderful hitter, Clara first base, maybe" (*TSOP*, 262). Interestingly, Amory makes the women into active players in a man's game. The girls he encounters help him to discover himself, and Fitzgerald presents them, in all their flaws, with respect and at times even enthusiasm.

The short story "Bernice Bobs Her Hair" (1920), however, suggests that Fitzgerald was already feeling ambivalent about his "creation." Based, by his own account, on his letter (*c.* 1915) to his sister Annabel, the story itself is "virtually a handbook of advice on how to become a successful flapper" (Solomon, *Ain't We Got Fun?*, 21). Through literary allusions to Louisa May Alcott's *Little Women*, Fitzgerald makes it clear that the construction of the flapper implies the dismantling of outdated ideals of femininity. Indeed, Fitzgerald "borrowed his major plot elements and themes from *Little Women*" and turned them "upside down in a Jazz Age revision."[6]

A pair of contrasting characters, fair Marjorie Harvey and her dark cousin Bernice, represent contrasting modern and Victorian ideals of femininity. When old-fashioned, provincial Bernice allows herself to be remodeled for popularity's sake, Marjorie provides concrete suggestions for improving Bernice's conversation, appearance, and manners. The change is more than superficial since Bernice's new exterior signals a change in philosophy, but for Fitzgerald this new philosophy calls all in doubt. By the end of the story, it seems that the modern young woman's liberation amounts to little more than license to run wild.

Bernice's reconstruction also includes a changed attitude toward women, a mark of the historic shift from female nurturance and solidarity to female self-fashioning and rivalry. Her model Marjorie (like her literary predecessor Rosalind and like Zelda) has "no female intimates – she considered girls stupid. Bernice on the contrary . . . had rather longed to exchange those confidences flavored with giggles and tears" (*Short Stories*, 29). In effect, the modernization of Bernice means that she becomes catty and nasty, a foe rather than a friend.

In capturing Fitzgerald's concern over the flapper's moral dissoluteness, the story anticipates the emphasis of his next novel, *The Beautiful and Damned* (serialized 1921–2; and published as a book in 1922). Since he wrote it during the first months of his marriage, readers may have expected privileged glimpses into the Fitzgerald household. The media encouraged that expectation. Newspapers and magazines featured photos of the happy young parents and their baby daughter Frances "Scottie" (born October 26, 1921), and interviews explored the effects of the flapper's philosophy on family life. Indeed, Fitzgerald did draw extensively on his early married life. His fictional use of Zelda's diary and letters prompted her to comment, in her 1922 review of the novel, that "plagiarism begins at home" (Zelda Fitzgerald, *Collected Writings*, 388).

Readers expecting an entertaining family romance may have been disappointed that the novel showed instead, according to the author, how the Fitzgeralds' fictional counterparts Anthony Patch and "his beautiful young wife [Gloria] are wrecked on the shoals of dissipation" (*Life in Letters*, 41). As one biographer has observed, the novel repudiates "the Younger Generation thesis" that had made Fitzgerald famous: "Gloria and Anthony Patch – young, glamorous, emancipated – live selfishly and hedonistically after the mode of rebellious youth and end up desperate and degraded" (Turnbull, *Scott Fitzgerald*, 131).

In a 1922 interview, Fitzgerald blamed Gloria for the "damnation" described in the novel. He asserted: "Our American women are leeches. They're an utterly useless fourth generation trading on the accomplishments of their pioneer great-grandmothers. They simply dominate the American men" (Bruccoli and Bryer, *In His Own Time*, 256). In subsequent years, in his private correspondence as well as in his fiction, he continued to explore those two particular flaws in modern women – their uselessness and their dominance over men. Unfortunately, his comments may have encouraged reductionist interpretations that read the novel primarily as an indictment of Gloria (read Zelda) and of women generally.[7] *The Beautiful and Damned* is, however, certainly much more than a fictional attack on Zelda.

Gloria Gilbert is beautiful, spoiled, and modern enough to insist on a woman's right "to kiss a man beautifully and romantically without any desire to be either his wife or his mistress" (*B&D*, 113). She revolts at the prospect of a colorless, humiliating marriage like her mother's, and she rejects the woman's traditional role of maternal self-effacement. She wants a marriage that will be a "live, lovely, glamorous performance" (147). According to one critic, Gloria is Fitzgerald's depiction of "the young American bitch" who "rejects domesticity not out of any libertarian principle or career aspiration but out of sheer theatrical hedonism" (Tuttleton, "Combat," 280).

More recently, critics have shown more sympathy for Gloria. She demonstrates a "moral strength" (*B&D*, 371) her husband does not possess and unlike him wants to find meaningful work (Fryer, *Fitzgerald's New Women*, 30). When she decides to become an actress, she discovers, however, that she is by the age of twenty-nine too old to play the role of a flapper. In a suggestive mirror scene, Gloria collapses and lies sobbing at the image of her "aging" face (*B&D*, 404). It is a vivid reminder that the identity she has created for herself (or that has been created for her) is inadequate. In short, Fitzgerald depicts Gloria sympathetically.

While it is true that Fitzgerald "couldn't help recognizing in the New Woman what she so often recognized in herself – boredom, insincerity, triviality, and hedonistic irresponsibility" (Tuttleton, "Combat," 280), the weaknesses of the New Woman also reflect and magnify the weaknesses of the New Man. Anthony himself is as useless, lazy, self-indulgent, irresponsible, and hedonistic as any woman in Fitzgerald. Indeed, the novel shows that shifting definitions of womanhood posed a major challenge to men, who had to redefine their own concepts of manhood, social responsibility, and power.

Unlike Joseph Bloeckman (a self-made man of the world and an embodiment of Franklinesque success), Anthony Patch is a man divided between his romantic fantasies and a reality he regards as vulgar. His adulterous affair with Dorothy Raycroft, "a girl of a lower class," is part of the vulgar reality he wants to deny (*B&D*, 323). Although Dot at nineteen already has an "unsavory reputation" and is pathetically passive and masochistic, she is depicted sympathetically as a victim of her circumstances, including her betrayal by Anthony.

There are also, however, several less sympathetic depictions of women, some from the working class (69–79) and some, including Gloria's friends, from the rising middle class. Muriel Kane, a would-be vamp, is a travesty of everything Fitzgerald advised his sister to cultivate – from the "timely" expressions in her conversation to her excessive make-up and dress (84); and then there is Rachael Jerryl, "an exquisitely dressed Jewess," whose adultery Gloria condemns as "utterly common" (83–4; 368).

Despite Gloria's insistence to the contrary, Anthony asserts that she is superior to ordinary women, whom he dismisses as "breeders and bearers" (104). He needs her as his inspiration – an uncontaminated embodiment of his romantic ideals of "beauty and all illusion" (72–3). In his presentation of Gloria, we can see Fitzgerald examining how men, acting from their own needs, tend to see women symbolically, as representations of virtue or of worldly taint – examining, in other words, the essential importance of perspective.

The Beautiful and Damned may thus be regarded as an apprentice work anticipating *The Great Gatsby* (1925). In the later novel Fitzgerald fully explores the modern woman's symbolic significance in an era of disintegration. Demonstrating that in the modern world "personal identity resides in the perception of others" (Prigozy, "Introduction," *The Great Gatsby*, xxxiii), the book suggests that a woman has no identity except in the eyes of her beholder.

One reviewer did not think that *The Great Gatsby* was "a book to be read by the reader who believes the American girl to be the ideal girl of the twentieth century. We wonder if the author is as cynical as he paints his characters" (Bryer, *Critical Reception*, 195). And according to Fitzgerald himself, he "dragged" the book "out of the pit of [his] stomach in a time of misery." As he reminded Zelda, when he wrote the novel in 1924 there was "no one believing in me and no one to see except you + before the end your heart betraying me and then I was really alone with no one I liked" (*Correspondence*, 239). In June 1924, Zelda had met French aviator Edouard Jozan at the beach on the Riviera, and though the exact nature of their relationship remains unclear, Fitzgerald entered in his ledger a "Big Crisis – 13th of July" (*Ledger*, 178). By August he recorded that he and Zelda were "close together" (*Ledger*, 179), but Zelda reportedly took an overdose of sleeping pills in late summer (Milford, *Zelda*, 111). As Fitzgerald would later recall, "That September 1924 I knew something had happened that could never be repaired" (*Notebooks*, 113).

Although Fitzgerald himself thought that "the book contains no important woman character" (*Life in Letters*, 107), his central heroine Daisy Buchanan occupies a prominent place within the American literary tradition that features females of questionable morality – from Henry James's Daisy Miller to Willa Cather's Marian Forrester (*Life in Letters*, 100–1). Like James and Cather, Fitzgerald experiments with narrative point of view and presents the female characters through a central male consciousness.

Readers familiar with Fitzgerald's earlier fiction will immediately recognize Daisy as Fitzgerald's golden girl and Myrtle Wilson as the lower-class sexualized woman. New in the female cast is Jordan Baker, a champion golfer with a slim, boyish body and "an erect carriage" which she shows off "like a young cadet" – an indication of her androgynous tendencies (*GG*, 12).

It is through the eyes of Nick Carraway that we get our first glimpse of Daisy and Jordan. Set off by an elegant decor and airy nature images, the two women impress Nick as incarnations of female loveliness associated with a suggestive mix of purity, ethereal weightlessness, adventure, and maybe even witchcraft: "They were both in white, and their dresses were rippling and fluttering as if they had just been blown back in after a short flight around the house" (10).

From the beginning, however, Nick suspects that the two women are hiding their true selves behind cultivated public fronts. He glimpses in Daisy's sophisticated cynicism a "basic insincerity . . . a trick of some sort" (17). The theatrical tendency he questions may reflect the formative influence of popular culture, especially Hollywood, on women's roles. According to Ronald Berman, all the book's characters except Nick act as if they had "scripts in mind" (Berman, *"The Great Gatsby" and Modern Times*, 113). For example, Daisy in the novel identifies a woman's ideal identity as that of "a beautiful little fool" (*GG*, 17), and she seems to adopt the disguise of "agreeable female stupidity" promoted by a flood of popular movies starring dumb blondes (Berman, *"The Great Gatsby" and Modern Times*, 127).

Jordan's identity, too, seems to be a product of the popular media. Nick first recognizes her face because he has seen her photo, and during their last meeting she still reminds him of "a good illustration" (*GG*, 141). Noting that this sports celebrity is surrounded by sensationalist rumors, Nick decides that the "bored haughty face that she turned to the world" conceals an incurable dishonesty born of her unwillingness to be at a disadvantage (47–8).

For Nick, Myrtle is simply a less successful and more blatant fraud who puts on an air of "impressive hauteur" (26) which she associates with high society – as she has come to know it through tabloids and movies. Surrounded by vulgar mass-produced decor, she is a mockery of everything she aspires to imitate. In this respect, she resembles Jay Gatsby, whose self-invention parodies Benjamin Franklin's success story of hard work and moral self-improvement. Nick concludes, with grim resignation, that "Dishonesty in a woman is a thing you never blame deeply" (48).

In contrast to Nick, who perceives all three women as impostors, Gatsby idealizes Daisy. As unappreciated outsider/dreamer/host, Gatsby recalls Joseph Bloeckman and anticipates Dick Diver (and of course resembles Fitzgerald). With his "white flannel suit, silver shirt, and gold-colored tie," he is the knight who idealizes Daisy according to the courtly love tradition (67), and although this worship is misplaced, "Gatsby's ability to wonder, to dream, and to quest is presented as admirable" (Moreland, *Medievalist Impulse*, 143).

Nick admires Gatsby's commitment to an "incorruptible dream" (*GG*, 123) – "his heroic though misguided romanticization of Daisy" (Fetterley, *Resisting Reader*, 95–6). Daisy's corruption – her irresponsibility and betrayal of Gatsby – may kill Gatsby, but in the judgment of Nick her corruption only proves the superiority of Gatsby and his dream. In a deceptive, fraudulent world, Daisy still retains her value as a symbol. She represents illusion itself, the illusion of everything admirable, authentic, desirable, and unattainable.

The Great Gatsby thus defends the importance of inspirational symbols and the male tendency to see women as such symbols, perhaps especially during a time of personal, sexual, familial, and national disintegration. This book contends that we need "something commensurate" with our human "capacity for wonder" (*GG*, 143).

After *The Great Gatsby*, Fitzgerald's literary depiction of women reflects a difficult period in his life and career. Among the troubles that may have influenced his views of women were his disappointments in Hollywood, changes in his marriage, Zelda's mental deterioration and institutionalization, and his increasing self-consciousness and sense of failure as an artist.

Although Fitzgerald was pleased with his success following *The Great Gatsby* (*Correspondence*, 239), by early 1927 he encountered professional frustrations while working in Hollywood on a flapper screenplay, "Lipstick" (which was never produced). At this time, he also fell in love with the seventeen-year-old actress Lois Moran. He later described the affair as revenge for Zelda's earlier involvement with Edouard Jozan (*Life in Letters*, 211). After the Fitzgeralds returned to Paris in 1928 and Zelda took ballet lessons from Madame Lubov Egorova, marital relations were further strained when Zelda became infatuated with her teacher (*Correspondence*, 248); in addition, she questioned Fitzgerald's manhood and, according to Fitzgerald, dragged him "into her homosexual obsession" by charging that he "was a fairy" (*Correspondence*, 243, 241, 244). Fitzgerald, who later had several affairs with other women, continued to explore adultery in his writings, and in his next novel, *Tender is the Night*, he also examined the issue of homosexuality.

While Fitzgerald, drinking more heavily, struggled to complete this next novel, Zelda experienced a creative awakening. Not only was she taking ballet lessons and practicing at least eight hours a day in hopes of becoming a professional dancer, but she also resumed her writing. Between 1925 and

1934, she wrote more than a dozen articles and stories, including six stories about different types of girls for *College Humor*, most of which appeared in print under the joint byline "F. Scott and Zelda Fitzgerald" (Bruccoli, *Descriptive Bibliography*, 306–9).

Even when her emotional health declined and she was hospitalized, Zelda continued to write and paint. In April 1930, she had her first breakdown in Paris and was admitted to Malmaison Clinic. In early March 1932, just a few weeks after her second breakdown and admission into Phipps Clinic, she completed her novel *Save Me the Waltz*. Fitzgerald, who had been mostly supportive of Zelda's writings up to that point, felt betrayed. As he saw it, Zelda, for whom he had done so much, had incorporated into her book "one whole section" of the novel on which he had worked "intermittently for four years" and which he had been unable to complete "*because* of the necessity of keeping Zelda in sanitariums" (*Life in Letters*, 209). He resented having become her "work horse," paying to support her treatment and artistic pretensions with his "damn *Post* story writing" (*Life in Letters*, 220). Indeed, the couple's artistic rivalry, considered a central issue in discussions of Zelda's development, also contributed to Fitzgerald's changing view of himself and his craft.[8]

Throughout the early 1930s, in the short stories, essays, and drafts leading up to his novel, Fitzgerald explored his emotional and artistic crisis as a writer and developed the literary methods that found full expression in *Tender is the Night*.[9] As always, his views of women were central to this process.

One of his concerns was female competition. "What a Handsome Pair!" (August 1932) shows that there is nothing quite as bad as being married to a competitive and more successful wife. The artist protagonist, however, transforms his disappointments into music just as Fitzgerald transformed his competition with Zelda into this marketable story and developed artistic rivalry into a theme in *Tender is the Night*.[10]

Another recurrent concern in stories of the later 1920s, such as "Jacob's Ladder" (August 1927) and "At Your Age" (August 1929), as well as in *Tender is the Night*, is the inappropriateness of a middle-aged man's infatuation for a young girl. Although these writings may express Fitzgerald's response to Lois Moran, they also suggest his larger need to reevaluate his situation as an aging writer with an outdated topic in a changing market.

As early as 1920, Fitzgerald had apparently felt typecast and complained, "I'll go mad if I have to do another debutante, which is what they want" (*Letters*, 145). Nevertheless, encouraged by the success of the eight Basil Duke Lee stories (1928–9) which provided an autobiographical exploration of male adolescence and earned him $31,000, Fitzgerald wrote the five

Josephine Perry stories that recreated Ginevra King and that appeared in the *Saturday Evening Post* in 1930 and 1931.

"Emotional Bankruptcy" (August 1931), the last of the Josephine Perry stories, may be read as Fitzgerald's self-conscious tale about his bankruptcy as a writer. The first sentence draws attention to the perspective of the "male gaze": "There's that nut with the spy glass again," says Josephine. The voyeur spies on the adolescent girls of Miss Truby's finishing school. His perverse interest in the girls is matched by the exhibitionism of the girls, who respond with "indifference" to being watched. In fact, Josephine believes that his interest is quite normal. "They're all the same," she suggests. "I bet almost every man would do the same thing, if he had a telescope" (*Short Stories*, 546). As a writer in his thirties, still creating stories about spoiled young girls, Fitzgerald may indeed have regarded his lifelong investigation of female adolescence as inappropriate voyeurism; furthermore, the story anticipates his next novel's experimentation with narrative perspective and its fuller treatment of America's obsession, especially in popular film, with an erotically charged girl culture.

In "Babylon Revisited" (February 1931), Fitzgerald sought to redeem the image of the young girl by making the girl younger, purer, a symbol of regained honor. But he later explained that this, like his other last *Post* stories, "announced pretty much the death" of his young illusions (*Letters*, 588).

Although Fitzgerald called *Tender is the Night* (1934) "a woman's book" (*Letters*, 247), Judith Fetterley correctly suggests that the novel is an indictment of "the feminization of American culture." Nevertheless, it is an oversimplification to say that the "enemy in the text is the American woman and the text does a job on her" (Fetterley, "Who Killed," 114), for the text also "does a job" on the American man and his role in that feminization.

The book's leading lady is Nicole Diver, who loosely resembles Zelda and is married to the psychiatrist Dick Diver. Her foil is the younger Rosemary Hoyt, a movie star and the fictional counterpart of Lois Moran. In an experimental move, Fitzgerald framed the book by presenting the perspectives of those two female characters in two separate beach scenes, one in the opening and the other in the conclusion. In the opening scene the reader shares Rosemary's first glimpses of the "self-sufficient little group" that centers around Dick and Nicole Diver (*TITN*, 16). There is a momentary suggestive exchange between Rosemary and Dick. Rosemary, the naive outsider, finds Dick "kind and charming" and hears a promise in his voice "that he would take care of her ... open up whole new worlds for her" (16). By the end of the book, five years later and on the same beach, after watching with growing contempt Dick's efforts to show off to Rosemary, Nicole finally decides to leave him and the beach "where she had played planet to Dick's sun" (289).

One of the book's central concerns, in other words, is male performance, especially as seen and judged by women.

In a brilliant move, Fitzgerald made Dick a psychoanalyst (modernity's version of the priest) and a writer of mediocre publications. Fitzgerald, who exchanged with Zelda's psychiatrists lengthy letters diagnosing her case, saw himself as "somewhat of an amateur expert on the subject" of mental illness (*Life in Letters*, 217). Indeed, Sarah Beebe Fryer praises his characterization of Nicole for its "evident grasp of the vulnerabilities of an incest victim." Other critics, Fryer suggests, often exaggerate Nicole's "madness" and blame her for all of Dick's problems when her condition should be recognized as symptomatic of her trauma (*Fitzgerald's New Woman*, 72). In addition, Nicole is doubly victimized since she is betrayed by *two* men, first her father and then Dick, who were supposed to protect her but instead, in the name of love, abuse her.

As a psychiatrist, Dick assumes a fatherly role of trust; however, when he becomes Nicole's lover and husband, he violates professional ethics, responding to his patient's love transference not with objectivity but with "countertransference," a transgressive move like the incest committed by Nicole's actual father.[11] As Richard Lehan notes, Dick's "symbolic incest with Rosemary, an act which [further] leagues him with Devereux Warren, reveals Dick's failure to become a responsible 'father.' " The death of Dick's own father just before Dick consummates his affair with Rosemary "symbolically parallels his [Dick's] own loss of authority and self-discipline."[12] Dick's fall signifies the failure of patriarchal leadership.

Dick writes pop-psychology for a lay audience rather than serious scientific studies for experts (and is thus an image of Fitzgerald's own squandered talents). He has grown professionally "soft," and by taking the easy way he teaches Nicole to do the same. Although she initially asks him to find meaningful work (*TITN*, 123), she instead turns to hedonism and defends her choice as therapy. She shops for pleasure and initiates an affair. Rejecting Victorian repression, she would rather be "a sane crook than a mad puritan" (293). In an ultimate display of her regression into a primitive stage of self-indulgence, she prefers the warrior Tommy Barban, the epitome of martial masculinity, to the sensitive but weak father-psychiatrist who "created" her.

Without acquitting Dick Diver of his responsibility, we need to recognize that Dick first meets Rosemary and Nicole when they are both young girls who wear deceptive masks of innocence and yet take the initiative in seducing him. Rosemary Hoyt's film *Daddy's Girl* with its theme of incestuous father/daughter relationships provides a central metaphor, as Ruth Prigozy demonstrates, for "the decline of a civilization which, after a bloody, disillusioning war, sought sanctuary in the nursery, free of the claims of adulthood – morality, rationality, responsibility for others."[13] *Daddy's Girl* signals the ascendancy of a popular culture idealizing youth and hedonism and the decline of parental and other traditional authority.

Father figures are not the only ones held responsible for the young generation's moral confusion. Although Rosemary regards her mother, Mrs. Elsie Speers, as "her best friend" who displays "a cheerful stoicism," some of the mother's guidance seems questionable and reflects the kind of aggressive male competition which her phallic name implies. Judging by Fitzgerald's similar advice to his daughter Scottie in many of his letters, he probably thought it was good that Rosemary was "brought up to work – not especially to marry" and that she was, according to her mother, "economically... a boy, not a girl" (*TITN*, 40). But surely we are meant to question why her mother would allow her to catch pneumonia for the sake of a difficult shoot and especially why her mother would encourage her to pursue a married man (40). In fact, in the novel's first draft, the figure corresponding to Rosemary was an angry young man, Francis Melarky, who was going to kill his mother. Fetterley argues that "matricidal intent" still exists in the final novel (Fetterley, "Who Killed," 114), but it could also be argued that the book presents a eulogy on the extinction of true mothering as much as it eulogizes the passing of the father's law.

Ultimately, both male failure and social disorder are blamed on unruly female power – in the form of either seductive child-women or mannish women. One of several assertive women in the book is Nicole's sister Beth Evan "Baby" Warren who controls the family money which corrupts and emasculates Dick. Described as a frigid spinster, Baby is identified as the force behind America's feminization. She is "the American Woman... the clean-sweeping irrational temper that had broken the moral back of a race and made a nursery out of a continent," a person who wins her battles (*TITN*, 232).

Also embattled is Dick's favorite patient, who imagines she is "sharing the fate of the women of my time who challenged men to battle" (184). A thirty-year-old American painter, she suffers, as Zelda did, from eczema, and sees herself as "a symbol of something" (185). Dick effectively restrains her threatening assertiveness by telling her that she is too "sick" and fragile to be an artist (183–5).

Early in the book, Nicole, Rosemary, and Mary North are presented as a "trio of women" who unlike "so many American women... were all happy to exist in a man's world – they preserved their individuality through men and not by opposition to them" (53). Nevertheless, Mary North Minghetti and the lesbian Lady Caroline Sibly-Biers are eventually arrested for crossdressing and for trying to pick up girls (303). Perhaps to stress the danger of lost gender distinctions, Fitzgerald added two pages about a Chilean male homosexual in his revision of the serialized version for book publication (Bruccoli, *Composition*, 205). In an endorsement of contemporary popular views, promoted by sexologists such as Havelock Ellis, homosexuality is presented as an unnatural inversion.

In *Tender is the Night*, Fitzgerald expressed his uneasiness at the feminization of American culture and at the threat of emasculation posed by seductive girls as much as by masculine women. Like Carl Jung, D. H. Lawrence, and Oswald Spengler, whose theories he admired, Fitzgerald believed that men and women had complementary natures and feared that a loosening of binary gender distinctions simply encouraged each side to adopt the worst characteristics of the opposite sex (Gibbens, *The Baby Vamp*, 35). In his writings, "the breakdown of sexual identities is a sign of the breakdown of moral certainties" (Stern, *"Tender is the Night": The Broken Universe*, 41). Thus, his works express his period's fear that cultural feminization was a symptom of a larger disorder – the decline of the West.

Tender is the Night also reveals the inadequacy of some of the male responses to cultural feminization that were most prominent during Fitzgerald's time. Neither the cult of masculinity (Tommy Barban) nor male expertise (Dick Diver) is depicted as an effective solution. Nevertheless, Fitzgerald's novel reminds us that psychiatry, one new field of male expertise, had an instrumental role in the sweeping backlash that questioned women's emancipation and reinscribed the "natural" differences between men and women which modern tendencies threatened to erase.

As a writer, Fitzgerald resented it that "women control[led] the fiction market" (*Life in Letters*, 107). Like other Modernist writers, he disdained the inferior literary products of this mass market. From "Head and Shoulders," his first story in the *Saturday Evening Post*, to *Tender is the Night*, he consistently expressed his fear of being tricked into wasting his male genius in writing trash for popular magazines. It was a prostitution of his talent: "the *Post* now pay [*sic*] the old whore $4000. a screw" (*Life in Letters*, 169). His views on this point thus seem to confirm those literary theories which suggest that the aesthetics of High Modernism, embodying "male" values, took shape as a reaction to the aesthetics of mass culture, associated with "female" sentimentality and superficiality.[14]

Nevertheless, Fitzgerald's continued popularity may be due precisely to the presence of both "female" and "male" tendencies in his works. His writings contained elements typically associated with female-dominated popular literature – romance, sentimentality, melodrama, sensationalism. Yet his works also displayed the marks of masculine Modernist art – experimental form, narrative complexity, irony, and unresolved ambiguity. In other words, his writings are strongly androgynous.

Great writers, such as William Shakespeare, often are recognized for their androgynous complexity and richness. As Carolyn G. Heilbrun explains, androgyny suggests "a full range of experience open to individuals who may, as women, be aggressive, as men, tender . . . without regard to propriety or custom" (Heilbrun, *Toward a Recognition*, x–xi). It was Fitzgerald's American young girl with her "boyish" characteristics that helped to dismantle established concepts of male and female nature. True, the same Fitzgerald who introduced to the world this spunky young woman in defiance of old codes of morality (and created several delightfully sensitive and unconventional men) mourned the loss of those old codes, the passing of the father's law and the consequent drifting of a feminized, emasculated world. He adhered to old values and did not acknowledge his own androgynous tendencies. Nevertheless, those very tendencies may have been the driving force that sustained his fascination with women, inspired his characterization of exceptional men and women, and allows his work to transcend its own historical contingency. As Ben Jonson said of Shakespeare, and as might be said of all great writers, Fitzgerald was the "Soul of the age" and yet "not of an age, but for all time."[15]

NOTES

Quotations in this chapter are from the 1995 edition of *The Beautiful and Damned*, the 1998 edition of *The Great Gatsby*, the 1995 edition of *Tender is the Night*, the 1995 Scribner edition of *This Side of Paradise*, and the Preface to the 1995 Cambridge University Press edition of *This Side of Paradise*. See Bibliography for details.

1 See Sarah Beebe Fryer, *Fitzgerald's New Women: Harbingers of Change* and Mary A. McCay, "Fitzgerald's Women: Beyond Winter Dreams," 310–24.

2 See David Fedo, "Women in the Fiction of F. Scott Fitzgerald"; James W. Tuttleton, " 'Combat in the Erogenous Zone': Women in the American Novel Between the Two World Wars"; Judith Fetterley, *The Resisting Reader: A Feminist Appproach to American Fiction*.

3 See also T. J. Jackson Lears, "From Salvation to Self-Realization: Advertising and the Therapeutic Roots of the Consumer Culture, 1880–1930."

4 See Rayna Rapp and Ellen Ross, "The 1920s Feminism, Consumerism, and Political Backlash in the United States," 52–61.

5 The essay is reprinted without the illustration in Zelda Fitzgerald: *The Collected Writings*, 391–3.

6 See Susan Beegel, " 'Bernice Bobs Her Hair': Fitzgerald's Elegy for *Little Women*," in *New Essays on F. Scott Fitzgerald's Neglected Stories*, ed. Jackson R. Bryer, 58.

7 See Tuttleton, " 'Combat in the Erogenous Zone' "; Fedo, "Women in the Fiction of F. Scott Fitzgerald."

8 See Alice Hall Petry's "Women's Work: The Case of Zelda Fitzgerald," and Anna Valdine Clemens, "Zelda Fitzgerald: An Unromantic Revision."

9 See Ruth Prigozy, "Fitzgerald's Short Stories and the Depression: An Artistic Crisis," in *The Short Stories of F. Scott Fitzgerald: New Approaches in Criticism*, ed. Jackson R. Bryer, 111–26.

10 See James L. W. West III, " 'What A Handsome Pair!' and the Institution of Marriage," in *New Essays on F. Scott Fitzgerald's Neglected Stories*, ed. Jackson R. Bryer, 219–31.

11 See Jeffrey Berman, "*Tender is the Night*: Fitzgerald's *A Psychology for Psychiatrists*," in *The Talking Cure: Literary Representations of Psychoanalysis*, 60–86.

12 Richard Lehan, "*Tender is the Night*," in *"Tender is the Night": Essays in Criticism*, ed. Marvin J. LaHood, 68.

13 Ruth Prigozy, "From Griffith's Girls to *Daddy's Girl*: The Masks of Innocence in *Tender is the Night*," 190.

14 For further discussion of these theories, see Andreas Huyssen, "Mass Culture as Woman: Modernism's Other," in *After the Great Divide*, 44–62; Marianne DeKoven, *Rich and Strange: Gender, History, Modernism*; Elaine Showalter, "The Other Lost Generation," in *Sister's Choice: Tradition and Change in American Women's Writing*, 104–26; Suzanne Clark, *Sentimental Modernism: Women Writers and the Revolution of the Word*; Deborah F. Jacobs, "Feminist Criticism/Cultural Stuides/Modernist Texts: A Manifesto for the '90s"; David Minter, "The Fear of Feminization and the Logic of Modest Ambition," in *A Cultural History of the American Novel: Henry James to William Faulkner*, 117–24; Rita Felski, *The Gendering of Modernity*; Guy Reynolds, *Willa Cather in Context: Progress, Race, Empire*; Frances Kerr, "Feeling 'Half Feminine': Modernism and the Politics of Emotion in *The Great Gatsby*"; Michael Nowlin, " 'The World's Rarest Work': Modernism and Masculinity in Fitzgerald's *Tender is the Night*."

15 From Ben Jonson, "To the Memory of My Beloved, The Author, Mr. William Shakespeare, And What He Hath Left Us", in *Poems*, ed. Ian Donaldson, 308, line 17; 309, line 43.

9

SCOTT DONALDSON

Fitzgerald's nonfiction

F. Scott Fitzgerald will be remembered primarily for his novels and stories, but during his twenty years as a professional writer, he also produced an important and revealing body of work in the form of articles and essays and correspondence. The very best of these – the autobiographical pieces written in the 1930s – command the lyrical magic and emotional power of his most lasting fiction. And even at their least meritorious, in the advertisements for himself Fitzgerald composed as a beginning author, these articles reveal a great deal about the way he wanted to present himself to his readers. Read chronologically, they trace the rise and fall of his career from the publication of *This Side of Paradise* in March 1920 to his final years in Hollywood.[1]

In accepting *This Side of Paradise* for publication, editor Maxwell Perkins at Scribners asked Fitzgerald for a photograph and some publicity material. "You have been in the advertising game long enough to know the sort of thing,"Perkins added (*Dear Scott/Dear Max*, 21). In fact, Fitzgerald had worked only four months for the Barron Collier agency in New York, from March to July 1919, but he did understand how promotion could help sell books and was eager to cooperate in the enterprise. In a letter presented at the American Booksellers' Convention and included on a leaf added to several hundred copies of the novel, he began to establish a public personality designed at once to shock and attract his audience.

Fitzgerald had been struggling to complete *This Side of Paradise* for two years – longer, if one considers how much of the book is borrowed from his undergraduate writing at Princeton – and it had gone through two substantial revisions before Scribners accepted it. But to the booksellers, Fitzgerald acknowledged none of these difficulties: "to write it . . . took three months; to conceive it, three minutes; to collect all the data in it, all my life." The idea for the novel had first come to him the previous July, he lied, and he regarded the process of composition as "a substitute form of dissipation." As an author, he was writing "for the youth of his own generation, the critics of the next, and the schoolmasters of ever afterward." In signing off,

Fitzgerald reverted to the dissipation motif. "So, gentlemen, consider all the cocktails mentioned in this book drunk by me as a toast to the Booksellers' Convention" (*Letters*, 477–8). Fitzgerald was so pleased with this letter that he retailed its best lines to the wider audience of the *New York Tribune* on May 7, 1920, in a feature article demonstrating that he did indeed know his way around in the world of publicity. The supposed occasion for the article was an interview with Fitzgerald conducted by Carleton R. Davies. But Davies was fictitious: both questions and answers were written by Fitzgerald himself. The idea for this mock interview came from him as well, in a proposal to the advertising manager at Scribners (Bruccoli and Bryer, *In His Own Time*, 162).

The image that emerges from Fitzgerald's flippant remarks to the booksellers is that of a brash young genius who has tossed off a novel as cavalierly as the characters in his novel toss back a drink. His appeal is to a youthful audience who will presumably be delighted to join him in repudiating the outmoded mores of the past. Read the book, he seems to be saying, for our mutual profit. At the same time, the author wants more than immediate reward. One eye is cocked on the sales figures, the other looks for approval from the critics and even from posterity.

By any standard, the sales of *This Side of Paradise* were remarkable. Its portrayal of the younger generation, and particularly of the flapper and her liberated ways, made the twenty-three-year-old author famous overnight. Buoyed on the first wave of success, he reviewed his brief career in "Who's Who – and Why," in the *Saturday Evening Post* for September 18, 1920. "The history of my life," Fitzgerald began, "is the history of the struggle between an overwhelming urge to write and a combination of circumstances bent on keeping me from it." The essay reviewed the various literary ventures of the author-in-the-making, from musical comedy to poetry to short stories and a novel. The tone throughout is lighthearted and confident, even when Fitzgerald is making fun of himself. According to his account, for instance, he produced the first draft of his novel while in infantry training at Fort Leavenworth, hurrying to the officers' club every Saturday afternoon to work at breakneck speed through Sunday evening. Over the weekends of three months, Fitzgerald maintains, he set down a novel of 120,000 words. Only then could he allow himself to concentrate on *Small Problems for Infantry* and the rest of his military training: "I went to my regiment happy. I had written a novel. The war could go on" (*AA*, 84–5).

As in the letter to the booksellers and the mock interview, Fitzgerald characterized himself as a youth blessed with talent far beyond his years. The pose exasperated some commentators, who thought it hopelessly sophomoric.

The journalist Heywood Broun labeled Fitzgerald a "Princeton Daisy Ashford," comparing his novel (which was littered with "mistakes in spelling, grammar, chronology, and fact") to *The Young Visiters* [*sic*], a mystery story by the nine-year-old Miss Ashford published the previous year, with its childish errors intentionally left intact for reasons of authenticity (*TSOP*, ed. West, xxxv–xxxvi, 105). Others were merely amused by the author's presentation of himself as a youth afflicted with genius. His friend Ring Lardner effectively reduced the image to absurdity: "Mr. Fitzgerald sprang into fame with his novel *This Side of Paradise* when only three years old and wrote the entire book with only one hand" (quoted in Woodward, *F. Scott Fitzgerald: The Artist As Public Figure*, 15).

In the early years of his career, handsome Scott Fitzgerald and his beautiful wife Zelda cooperated fully with the media effort to portray them as exemplars of flaming youth. During much of the time between 1920 to 1924 they lived in Connecticut and Long Island, suburban extensions of New York City, the publicity capital of the nation. For both of them, as Fitzgerald wrote in "My Lost City," Manhattan "was inevitably linked up with Bacchic diversions, mild or fantastic" (*Crack-Up*, 29). Newspaper columnists eagerly recorded these diversions, from a table-side interview at a night club to their midnight dive into the Pulitzer fountain (Woodward, *The Artist as Public Figure*, 53). Even to his literary friends, Fitzgerald was dwindling into a celebrity instead of a writer, and as Robert Sklar put it, "not a celebrity to whom particular deference need be paid" (Sklar, *F. Scott Fitzgerald*, 121). In the public mind, he was indelibly associated with a younger generation determined to defy its elders. It did not help that he titled his first two collections of short stories *Flappers and Philosophers* (1920) and, over the objections of Perkins, *Tales of the Jazz Age* (1922). Flappers and sheiks drawn by John Held, Jr. danced frantically on the jacket of the second volume, and Fitzgerald contributed jaunty vignettes to introduce each of the stories. "'The Camel's Back'," he revealed, "was written during one day in the city of New Orleans, with the express purpose of buying a platinum and diamond wrist watch which cost six hundred dollars. I began it at seven in the morning and finished it at two o'clock the same night." Published originally in the *Saturday Evening Post*, this amusing yarn about a drunken evening at a Midwestern party was chosen as an O'Henry prize story for 1920. Despite this honor, Fitzgerald said he "liked it least" of all the stories in *Tales of the Jazz Age*.

These comments, and those that introduced other stories in the book, dramatized the author as someone who could turn out fiction with disarming ease and gain expensive rewards therefrom. Writing, for him, seemed a casual occupation that in no way inhibited the pursuit of a pleasurable and carefree life (Woodward, *The Artist as Public Figure*, 65). But if he refused to take himself seriously as an artist, he could hardly expect others to do so – a problem that came to the fore with the reception of his second novel, *The Beautiful and Damned*, published in March 1922.

Written under the influence of H. L. Mencken, *The Beautiful and Damned* is a dark and serious novel that portrays the decline and fall of Anthony and Gloria Patch, a hedonistic young couple obviously modeled on the Fitzgeralds themselves. A number of critics, expecting less weighty fare, chose to ignore its pessimistic message. "With what gusto, what exuberance of youth, what vitality Fitzgerald writes," one commented. "He has romance and imagination and gaiety," observed another. "Perhaps when he is a little older he will be less larky and unsteady" (quoted in Woodward, *The Artist as Public Figure*, 90). Fitzgerald encouraged this larky, unsteady view of himself in a lighthearted piece on "How I Would Sell My Book If I Were a Bookseller" (January 1923). In a defensive opening, Fitzgerald claimed that he had not known *This Side of Paradise* was "a flapper book" until George Jean Nathan told him it was. His heroines were complicated and individual women, he insisted, not stereotypical and rather dull flappers. But, getting down to business, he admitted that the best way to sell *The Beautiful and Damned* would be to cash in on the public perception of his work. "This is a novel by Fitzgerald," booksellers might say to customers, "the fella that started all that business about flappers. I understand that his new one is terribly sensational (the word 'damn' is in the title). Let me put you down for one" (Bruccoli and Bryer, *In His Own Time*, 167–8).

In "What I Think and Feel at Twenty-Five" (September 1922), Fitzgerald obliquely addressed the issue of his reputation. The article opens with an old family friend objecting to the gloominess of Fitzgerald's new novel. He was young and healthy and successful and happily married: why did he have to write such unpleasant books? Next a newspaper interviewer comes to call. Was the rumor true that he and Mrs. Fitzgerald were going to commit suicide at thirty because they dreaded middle age? And would their suicide be "largely on account of past petting-parties?" Fitzgerald's answer to them both was that as he grew older he did indeed feel more vulnerable. Once only *he* could be hurt, he pointed out, but now – at twenty-five – he could be wounded through his family. "Attack him through his wife!" "Kidnap his child!" "Tie a tin can to his dog's tail!" Fitzgerald writes in humorous fashion, but the basic point was serious enough. In another article written eighteen months later, he cited "that ghastly moment once a week when you realize that it all depends on you – wife, babies, house, servant, yard and dog. That if it wasn't for you, it'd all fall to pieces" (Bruccoli and Bryer, *In His Own Time*, 213–16, 184–6).

Fitzgerald was no longer so careless of consequences as he had been two years before. His image as a representative of the unbridled younger generation was proving difficult to get rid of. Sometimes it seemed that as a legendary figure associated with that generation he was to be held responsible for any and all of its excesses. In May 1922, for example, Burton Rascoe reported in his *New York Tribune* column that Fitzgerald, in the course of a conversation with Robert Bridges, the editor of *Scribner's Magazine*, had leaned over and plucked six gray hairs from Bridges's beard. The anecdote was entirely apocryphal, and Fitzgerald was obliged to write a letter of protest to Rascoe and one of apology to Bridges. It was time to shake off the role of the playboy genius and assume the responsibilities of the dedicated artist.

An unfortunate component of Fitzgerald's public persona was his reputation as a spendthrift, and in this case the reputation was well earned. Fitzgerald careened around New York with large bills protruding from his pockets. He lectured his mother to the effect that all great men spent freely. He and Zelda certainly did so, whether they could afford to or not. Edmund Wilson focused on his precarious financial condition in "The Delegate from Great Neck," his April 30, 1924, *New Republic* essay, in the form of an imaginary dialogue between Fitzgerald, as representative of the younger generation of writers, and the distinguished literary historian Van Wyck Brooks. In conversation, Fitzgerald laments that he cannot live at Great Neck (Long Island) for less than thirty-six thousand a year, and that to support himself he has "to write a lot of rotten stuff that bores me and makes me depressed." Brooks gently chides the young author. His heavy expenses laid him open to exploitation by the popular magazines, and Fitzgerald himself seemed (1) to have descended to the language of advertising in expressing himself, and (2) to have fallen into the trap of regarding his writing more as a commercial than an artistic product (Wilson, "The Delegate from Great Neck," 151).

Here Wilson was obviously hectoring his Princeton friend Fitzgerald, whom he considered his intellectual and moral inferior. The $36,000 figure was drawn directly from "How to Live on $36,000 a Year," Fitzgerald's piece for the *Saturday Evening Post* of April 5, 1924. In this article, Fitzgerald details his financial results for 1923. He and his wife had begun the year determined to save some money. Family living expenses they estimated at about $1,500 a month, and income from writing at $2,000: presto, an annual saving of $6,000. But expenses ran higher and income lower than anticipated, especially after Fitzgerald's play *The Vegetable* bombed in out-of-town tryouts. As the year neared its end, he found that they had spent $36,000, or twice as much as they had budgeted, and were $5,000 in debt. There was only one solution.

"Over our garage," he wrote, "is a large bare room whither I now retired with pencil, paper, and the oil stove, emerging the next afternoon at five o'clock with a 7,000-word story." That averted the immediate crisis, but "[i]t took twelve hours a day for five weeks to rise from abject poverty back into the middle class." This was not an exaggeration, or not much of one. Between November 1923 and April 1924 Fitzgerald produced eleven short stories, several magazine articles, and earned nearly $20,000. Such a lavish expenditure of energy could not go on indefinitely, Fitzgerald realized, and he was curious about where all the money had gone. To find out, he and Zelda assembled their account books and household records, and worked out the figures. With everything they could think of accounted for, their monthly expenditures came to only $2,000, or $1,000 less than they had actually spent. A thousand dollars had vanished each month, it seemed, without buying anything at all (AA, 87–99).

Fitzgerald's bewilderment at this discovery had its comic side: "Good heavens! . . . We've just lost $12,000!" And he worked the same vein in "How to Live on Practically Nothing a Year," a September 20, 1924 sequel. This article told of the Fitzgeralds' decision to escape "from extravagance and clamor" and "to find a new rhythm" for their lives in the Old World. In the spring of that year, they set out for the Riviera, armed with capital of $7,000 and a determination to live for the summer on "practically nothing." But the change of location did not solve their financial problems. The Riviera was supposed to be a winter resort, and much cheaper in the summer, but the French saw them coming and immediately jacked up their prices. At the end of the summer, the seven thousand dollars was gone. And in the south of France as on Long Island, the Fitzgeralds were unable to figure out exactly *where* it had gone, except that they were sure that they had been victimized by the real estate agent, the maid and the cook, the butcher and the grocer (AA, 102, 113–15). The humor in these articles depended on reader willingness to identify with the plight of the Fitzgeralds as a newly rich bourgeois family unable to cope with their circumstances. In other articles of this period, like "The Cruise of the Rolling Junk" (February–March–April 1924) and "My Old New England House on the Erie" (August 1925), Fitzgerald again played the role of the bumbling incompetent, easily hoodwinked by those who knew far more than he about houses and automobiles.

In actuality, of course, there was nothing particularly funny about Fitzgerald's lifelong inability to make ends meet. No matter how much money he made, at every stage of his career he was in debt to his publisher and agent. His letters to Perkins and to Ober, reprinted in *F. Scott Fitzgerald: A Life in Letters*, vividly tell the unhappy story. "I hoped that at last [!] being square with Scribners I could remain so," he wrote Perkins in some desperation on

December 31, 1920, with his career barely begun. But he was at his wits' end, and so worried that he was "utterly unable to write." Couldn't Perkins send him the $1,600 he needed as an advance on his next novel, or as a loan at the same interest it cost them to borrow, or as a month's loan with his "next ten books as security?" (*Life in Letters*, 44).

Perkins responded to this appeal, as he responded to almost all such appeals for the next decade and a half. So did Ober, who – to take one extreme example – during the three months between September and December 1927 was bombarded by no fewer than nine telegraphed requests from Fitzgerald for funds as an advance on a "two-part sophisticated football story" aimed at the *Saturday Evening Post*. "Can you deposit five hundred?" Fitzgerald's first wire inquired, and the succeeding ones asked for 500, 500 more, 300, 100, 100, 400, 200, and 250, with repeated promises in these telegrams that the story was almost completed, and/or that he would be coming in to deliver it no later than "tomorrow morning" (*Life in Letters*, 150–3). In the mid-1930s, Fitzgerald signed over part of his life insurance to secure his debts to Perkins and Ober so that in the end the accounts were squared, but the fact was that Fitzgerald was forever engaged in a struggle to live within his income.

Nonfiction articles provided one way of supporting himself, and a relatively important one, during the mid-1920s. The initial self-promoting pieces brought in nothing at all, but in 1922, when his highest story price was $1,000, he was paid $800 for his reflections on what he thought and felt at twenty-five. In 1924, his two essays on how to live on a great deal of money and how to live on not much sold for $1,000 and $1,200, respectively (*Ledger*). In most of the articles from this period, Fitzgerald – and on occasion his wife – held forth as experts on such matters as courtship and marriage, child-rearing, the rich, and the war between the sexes. The magazines and newspaper syndicates that commissioned these pieces wanted the Fitzgerald byline, for he had been firmly established in the public mind as a spokesman for the younger generation. Who else knew more about what was happening to these rebellious young people? The very celebrity that undercut his artistic reputation made it possible for him to earn easy money as a putative expert, and he was no more able to resist this opportunity than he was to stop churning out formulaic stories for the popular magazines.

In an April 1922 example of his expertise on the younger generation, Fitzgerald was depicted as a debonair professor lecturing with the aid of a map of the United States. He was described as the "young St. Paul authority on the flapper," and the subject under discussion was the difference between the girls of the South, the East, and the Midwest. In this competition, the Midwestern flapper – "unattractive, selfish, snobbish, egotistical, utterly graceless" – finished a distant third. Next came the rather sophisticated Eastern girl, with the Southern girl a clear winner for, among other things, "retain[ing] and develop[ing] her ability to entertain men." Of course, Fitzgerald admitted, he was somewhat prejudiced on the subject, having married a Southern girl[2] (Woodward, *The Artist As Public Figure*, 59–61).

Three separate articles in the spring of 1924 dealt with the difficulties young couples faced after marriage. The most interesting of these, "Why Blame It on the Poor Kiss if the Girl Veteran of Many Petting Parties Is Prone to Affairs after Marriage?" was syndicated by Metropolitan Newspaper Service to its subscribing papers under the alternate title of "Making Monogamy Work." Making it work, Fitzgerald asserted, was not easy, for in his view monogamy was "not (not yet at least) the simple natural way of human life." On balance he regarded marriage favorably, for it kept people out of messes and required less time and money than supporting a chorus girl. But opportunities to stray abounded, and were becoming more pervasive. As an example he cited the case of Harry and Georgianna (hypothetical clones of Scott and Zelda), "two highly strung and extremely attractive young people" who had married with the understanding that when the first flush was over, they were to be "free to ramble." Four years later, living in the highly permissive atmosphere of New York City, they began to seek illicit companions, and straightaway drove each other mad with jealousy. The only sensible course, they decided, "was to remain always together. Harry never goes to see a woman alone nor does Georgianna ever receive a man when Harry is not there." As a result, theirs was one of the extremely rare, truly happy marriages.

What of the girl who engaged in so many premarital petting parties? If anything, Fitzgerald suggests, those parties "tend[ed] to lessen a roving tendency." A girl who discovered before she married that there was more than one man in the world was, he reasoned, "less liable to cruise" later on in order to find that out. In conclusion, Fitzgerald acknowledged that he could provide no sure solution to the problem of making monogamy work. On the constructive side, though, he believed in "early marriage, easy divorce and several children" (Woodward, *The Artist As Public Figure*, 128–9; Bruccoli and Bryer, *In His Own Time*, 179–84).

As it happened, he and Zelda were destined to have no more than one child – their daughter Scottie, born in October 1921. Despite his limited experience as one-time father, Fitzgerald wrote two magazine articles for the women's magazines on how to bring up children. In "Imagination and a Few Mothers" (June 1923, *Ladies' Home Journal*), he concocts two very different women. Mrs. Judkins is a hopeless worrier, whose every moment is tortured by fears that her joyously blooming daughter is on the verge of a nervous breakdown and that her vigorously active son is not getting enough rest. As a result she overprotects her children and denies them the right to full self-realization. To contrast with Mrs. Judkins (who bears a family resemblance to Fitzgerald's mother), he invents the enlightened Mrs. Paxton. Because she understands that "the inevitable growth of a healthy child is a drifting away from the home," Mrs. Paxton stays out of her children's way and lets them grow up on their own. Generalizing on the grounds of these manufactured cases, Fitzgerald deplores those mothers who abandon themselves to their children. Where influence on the child is the issue, "[a] woman happy with her husband is worth a dozen child-worshippers" ("Imagination," 21, 80–1).

In "'Wait Till You Have Children of Your Own!" for the July 1924 *Woman's Home Companion*, Fitzgerald elaborates on this doctrine of permissiveness. The article is noteworthy for the initial appearance in print of Zelda's (and Daisy Buchanan's) childbirth remark that she hopes her baby daughter will be "a beautiful little fool." But this is hardly the message Fitzgerald wants to convey. The previous generation, in his judgment a dull and worthless one, had attempted to guide its young according to outmoded values. This was a mistake, and he will force no standards on his children, Fitzgerald insists, for nothing that they are told will be of any value compared to what they find out for themselves. In a closing peroration, he advances his ideal child-rearing program. "We shall give" our children

> a free start, not loading them up with our own ideas and experiences... We will not even inflict our cynicism on them as the sentimentality of our fathers was inflicted on us... We shall not ask much of them – love if it comes freely, a little politeness, that is all. They are free, they are little people already, and who are we to stand in their light? (Bruccoli and Bryer, *In His Own Time*, 193–4, 197, 201)

According to Fitzgerald, rich boys were especially likely to grow up without developing self-reliance. In "What Kind of Husbands Do 'Jimmies' Make?" (March 1924) Fitzgerald presents – irony intended – "that peerless aristocrat, that fine flower of American civilization, young Mr. Jimmy Worthington." Jimmy learns early that his father's money will pay for his sins, that "if he has the bad luck to run over someone when he's drunk, his father will buy off the family and keep him out of jail." Nor is Jimmy encouraged like the young English aristocrat to pursue a life of service by going into politics and running the government. Instead he joins the American leisure class – "the most shallow, most hollow, most pernicious leisure class in the world" – and lives a life of privilege without ever grasping the idea that privilege implies responsibility. In the United States, Fitzgerald maintains, the greatest Americans have "almost invariably come from the very poor class – Lincoln, Edison, Whitman, Ford, Mark Twain." These men formed their character in the forge of experience, while the young rich boys of the 1920s – insulated from that fire – were shaped into complete parasites: healthy, good-looking, and perfectly useless (Bruccoli and Bryer, *In His Own Time*, 186–7, 191).

This analysis of the rich came from a writer who was himself unable to get along on the princely income of $36,000 a year. Characteristically, Fitzgerald situated himself both within and without the world of the wealthy. It was as if while dancing among the favored few inside the ballroom, he simultaneously was outside gazing through the window at the brilliant party within. This was very much the position of Nick Carraway in *The Great Gatsby*, and of the narrator in "The Rich Boy," to cite two stunning fictional accomplishments that put his reaction to the rich – which seemed basically pedestrian in his magazine articles – into lasting form.

The same point could be made about Fitzgerald's changing attitudes toward women. The spate of essays that he produced in 1924 to help pay off debts subsided, not to be resumed until the country turned the corner into the 1930s and he was inspired to trace his own rise and fall against the background of the nation's economic debacle. But in his final venture into the genre of the expert, Fitzgerald announced the arrival of the independent woman. As the title "Girls Believe in Girls" (February 1930) suggested, this woman no longer believed that she had anything to learn from men. The era of the flapper had passed, and she was replaced by "the contemporary girl" who possessed beauty, charm, and courage, and radiated poise and self-confidence. She had also, in a somewhat frightening development, become sexually liberated. "[T]he identification of virtue with chastity no longer exists among girls over twenty," Fitzgerald wrote, although his readers were welcome to pretend that it did if it gave them any comfort. He expected wonders from this independent girl. It was "the poor young man" he was worried about (Bruccoli and Bryer, *In His Own Time*, 210–11). Just as his mundane pronouncements about the rich were reinvigorated in fiction, so the confident New Woman of this article was to engage the young man he worried about in a dramatic fictional struggle between the sexes – and to emerge victorious, like Nicole Diver at the end of *Tender is the Night*.

The Fitzgeralds' own history, as he was well aware, paralleled that of the nation. As the post-war boom began in 1920, Scott had his private triumph with the publication of *This Side of Paradise* and his marriage to Zelda. A decade later, the stock market crash of October 29, 1929, mirrored their declining fortunes and was closely followed by Zelda's mental collapse in April 1930. The passing of the decade marked a watershed for the

Fitzgeralds, and for his writing career. In his essays thereafter he dropped the pose of the expert, and was moved to reminisce about the not entirely golden past.

Drinking lay at the heart of Fitzgerald's problems, as close readers of his fiction might have intuited. Yet however compulsively his characters may have consumed liquor, Fitzgerald was not ready in assessing his own life to draw the connection between excessive drinking and physical or emotional breakdown. He treats the issue with levity in "A Short Autobiography," which appeared in the May 25, 1929 *New Yorker*. This fragmentary piece purports to tell the story of the author's life in the form of diary entries about his liquor intake through the years. It begins with "1913: The four defiant Canadian Club whiskeys at the Susquehanna in Hackensack" and concludes, unapologetically, with "1929: A feeling that all liquor has been drunk and all it can do for one has been experienced, and yet – *Garçon, un Chablis-Mouton 1902, et pour commencer, une petite carafe de vin rosé. C'est ça – merci*" (Bruccoli and Bryer, *In His Own Time*, 223–5).

In "My Lost City" (July 1932), Fitzgerald writes that in the latter years of the boom "[m]any people who were not alcoholics were lit up four days out of seven... and the hangover became a part of the day as well allowed-for as the Spanish siesta." But he immediately distances himself from this pattern. "Most of my friends drank too much – the more they were in tune to the times the more they drank." Only when he came to New York City to visit those friends – as in 1927, for example – was he caught up in a frenzy that "deposited" him a few days later "in a somewhat exhausted state on the train to Delaware." In his view liquor was a symptom of what had gone wrong, and not a cause. More at fault were those who had made fortunes overnight and did not bother with manners. In the speakeasies, "there was nothing left of joviality but only a brutishness that corrupted the new day." Everywhere, morals were looser (*Crack-Up*, 30–1).

In his articles about marriage and child-rearing of the mid-1920s, Fitzgerald consistently criticized the social conventions of the time for limiting the experiences available to the young and thereby stunting their growth. By the 1930s, however, he looked back on a decade of recklessness and waste and decided that *too much* freedom was at fault. If anything, he observed in a September 1933 *New York Times* interview, the older generation had failed to pass along a proper sense of the "eternally necessary human values." As a result, he commented, his contemporaries lacked "religious and moral convictions" and were rendered "incompetent to train their children" (Woodward, *The Artist As Public Figure*, 254–5, 264). In his notebooks, also, he regarded the permissive policies he had once advocated with a jaundiced eye. To think, he wrote in some wonderment, that "Imagination and a Few Mothers" may have "influenced Mrs. [Rita] Swann's whole life" (*Crack-Up*, 179).

Fitzgerald announced the death of the Jazz Age in his November 1931 "Echoes of the Jazz Age," a reminiscential article that is not overtly autobiographical. The age, he wrote, had lasted only ten years. It had been born about the time of the May Day riots in 1919 and had "leaped to a spectacular death in October, 1929," much as one of his classmates tumbled "accidentally" from a skyscraper in Philadelphia and another purposely from a skyscraper in New York. The word "jazz" itself had progressed toward respectability: originally it meant sex, then dancing, then music. But the generation it spawned was the wildest ever – "a whole race going hedonistic, deciding on pleasure." The most hedonistic migrated to the winter resorts at Palm Beach and Deauville, or alternatively to the summer Riviera where you "could get away with more." Fitzgerald was ambivalent about those wasted years. Like Charlie Wales in his "Babylon Revisited" (February 1931), the boom years had taught him the true meaning of the word "'dissipate' – to dissipate into thin air; to make nothing out of something" (*Short Stories*, 620). But also like Wales, he could not entirely forget how "rosy and romantic" it had all seemed when he was young and could still feel everything with great intensity (*Crack-Up*, 13, 15–16, 19, 22).

In fact, the greatest loss Fitzgerald had suffered, it became clear in his several autobiographical essays of the mid-1930s, was the capacity to feel as deeply as he once had. He had succumbed to "emotional bankruptcy," in the phrase he used to title a story of August 1931, and so had very nearly lost all reason to write. In "One Hundred False Starts" (March 1933), he directly confronted this dilemma. His output as a professional writer was slacking off, for he could find so little that he really cared about to convert to fiction. There was no shortage of serviceable plots; he could find a thousand of them in criminal law libraries and the personal revelations of friends and acquaintances. But these would not work. As he observed in a much-quoted passage,

> Mostly, we authors must repeat ourselves – that's the truth. We have two or three great and moving experiences in our lives – experiences so great and moving that it doesn't seem at the time that anyone else has been so caught up and pounded and dazzled and astonished and beaten and broken and rescued and illuminated and rewarded and humbled in just that way ever before.
>
> Then we learn our trade, well or less well, and we tell our two or three stories – each time in a new disguise – maybe ten times, maybe a hundred, as long as people will listen.

The fanciful and fantastic would not serve. As a professional writer, he had to start out with an emotion – one that was close to him and that he could understand (*AA*, 132).

This essential part of his creed he underlined in a rather harsh commentary on a story that young Frances Turnbull sent him in November 1938. She had not invested enough of her own emotional capital in the story, Fitzgerald told her. He was afraid that "the price for doing professional work" was a good deal higher than she was prepared to pay: "You've got to sell your heart, your strongest reactions, not the little minor things that only touch you lightly..." The only thing writers had to sell – especially young writers – was their emotions. This was as true of Dickens in *Oliver Twist*, he pointed out, as it was of Hemingway in *In Our Time* or of himself in *This Side of Paradise*, when he was writing about a love affair "still bleeding as fresh as the skin wound on a haemophile" (*Life in Letters*, 368).

The discouragement of many false starts, Fitzgerald observed in his essay, had made him almost ready to quit. But in his troubled state he went to an old Alabama Negro for advice.

"'Uncle Bob, when things get so bad that there isn't any way out, what do you do then?'

'Mr. Fitzgerald,' he said, 'when things get that-away I wuks.'"

It was good advice, he decided, for work "was almost everything" (*AA*, 135). He insisted on this point time and again in letters from Hollywood to his daughter Scottie at Vassar. The strongest statement came in a July 7, 1938 letter that he implored Scottie to read twice, bitter though it might seem. The basic message was that Scottie's mother had ruined her life because she was brought up spoiled. Zelda "realized too late that work was dignity, and the only dignity, and tried to atone for it by working herself, but it was too late and she broke and is broken forever" (*Letters*, 46–7). Never again, he added, did he want to see women raised to be idlers. This interpretation undoubtedly laid too much emphasis on Zelda's highly permissive upbringing – she was the baby of the family – as the cause of her mental breakdown. In this letter, Fitzgerald obviously wanted to frighten Scottie into working hard at college. But he was also expressing his own convictions. When he called work "the only dignity," he meant it.

In "Ring" (October 1933), a memorial essay on Ring Lardner, Fitzgerald wrote about a friend and fellow writer who had failed to pour enough of himself into his craft. Lardner had been the most amiable of drinking companions during Fitzgerald's time in Great Neck. "Many the night," he reports, "we talked over a case of Canadian ale until bright dawn," but no link is suggested between Lardner's drinking and the "impenetrable despair" that dogged him for a dozen years before his death. The saddest part of the story, as Fitzgerald related it, was that Ring had not lived up to his promise as an artist. The causes were several. Lardner spent too much time helping others. He did not aim high enough. He adopted a cynical attitude toward his work. And above all, he did not express his innermost thoughts and feelings. Once Fitzgerald suggested to him that he should write something "deeply personal," but Lardner refused: by his lights, "telling all" simply wasn't done. "So one is haunted," Fitzgerald observes in his elegy, "not only by a sense of personal loss but by a conviction that Ring got less percentage of himself on paper than any other American of the first flight" (*Crack-Up*, 35, 37–8).

Fitzgerald's memorial essay reads very much like a cautionary tale directed at himself. Confession was good for art as well as the soul, and Lardner's mistake served to warn him against concealing the contents of his own mind and heart. At the time, Fitzgerald was profoundly concerned with his own literary reputation. In the month of Lardner's passing, he wrote Perkins suggesting an "advertising approach" for *Tender is the Night*. Scribners, he proposed, should put out a statement along these lines:

> For several years the impression has prevailed that Scott Fitzgerald had abandoned the writing of novels and in the future would continue to write only popular short stories. His publishers knew different and they are very glad now to be able to present a book which is in line with his three other highly successful and highly esteemed novels, thus demonstrating that Scott Fitzgerald is anything but through as a serious novelist.

In retrospect, this copy seems almost pathetic. Its mixture of verb tenses, shaky grammar ("knew different") and unfortunate repetitions ("Scott Fitzgerald," "highly successful and highly esteemed") make it sound as if Fitzgerald were trying to reassure *himself* that he was "anything but through" (*Life in Letters*, 241). The nine-year lapse between his two greatest novels shook his confidence, and he never stopped excoriating himself for letting it happen. As he wrote Scottie in June 1940, "I wish now I'd *never* relaxed or looked back – but said at the end of *The Great Gatsby*: 'I've found my line – from now on this comes first'" (*Life in Letters*, 451).

Fitzgerald's "Sleeping and Waking" (December 1934) further revealed a man seriously at unease with himself. A victim of insomnia, he lay awake in the early hours beset by thoughts of "Horror and waste – Waste and horror – what I might have been and done that is lost, spent, gone, dissipated, unrecapturable" (*Crack-Up*, 67). He could neither relive the past nor summon the emotional intensity that had once brought his fiction to life. Desperately searching for material, he tried a series about a father and daughter, the Gwen stories, and another about the medieval Count of

Darkness, but these ranked among the worst of his stories. His well was running dry. As he observed in his notebooks, there seemed less weather than in his youth, and "practically no men and women at all" (*Crack-Up*, 128).

So in November 1935 he tried something different. He holed up in the mountains of western North Carolina, at the Skylands Hotel in Hendersonville. Arnold Gingrich, editor of *Esquire*, armed him with a mantra to break his writer's block. Fitzgerald was to repeat, "I can't write stories of young love for the *Saturday Evening Post* because I can't write stories of young love for the *Saturday Evening Post* because," and so on. Strapped for funds and living on tinned meat and Uneeda biscuits, he wrote his *Crack-Up* articles instead – articles that in their exploration of his "dark night of the soul" amply demonstrated *why* "he couldn't go on writing stories of young love for *The Saturday Evening Post*" (quoted in Potts, *The Price of Paradise*, 88–9).

The three *Crack-Up* articles ran in *Esquire* during February, March, and April 1936, and elicited an extraordinary reaction. "I get letters from all over," Fitzgerald wrote Gingrich. Old friends counseled him to cheer up, and fans begged him to keep writing. But those in his immediate literary circle were, generally, appalled at Fitzgerald's admission of emotional exhaustion and personal collapse. "Christ, man," John Dos Passos objected, "how do you find time in the middle of the general conflagration to worry about all that stuff?" Fitzgerald had become the "Maxie Baer" of writers, Ernest Hemingway wrote Perkins, associating him with the heavyweight fighter Hemingway thought had been cowardly in his bout with Joe Louis. Perkins himself considered the essays an "indecent invasion of [Fitzgerald's] privacy." Ober feared that they would compromise his client's chances of securing a contract in Hollywood (Donaldson, "The Crisis of Fitzgerald's 'Crack-Up'," 171–3).

Subsequent critics have been divided as to the honesty of these essays. Glenway Wescott, in a memorial essay of 1941, called them "wonderful" for their "candor; verbal courage; simplicity," and Sergio Perosa admired Fitzgerald for examining himself with detachment and without pity or sentimentality. Milton Hindus, on the other hand, thought the author had not presented "enough close-ups of actual experience," and Alfred Kazin felt, on reading the essays, that "something is being persistently withheld, that the author is somehow offering us certain facts in exchange for the right to keep others to himself" (*Crack-Up*, 323–4; Potts, *The Price of Paradise*, 90; Donaldson, "The Crisis," 178). In fact, important things *are* withheld. The essays do not even mention Zelda's illness and its effects. In addition, they bring up drinking only in order to rule it out as a cause of Fitzgerald's difficulties. This was not an intentional violation of the two rules he set for himself as an intellectual and a man of honor – "that *I do not tell myself lies that will be of value to myself*, and secondly, *I do not lie to myself*" (*Crack-Up*, 197). Fitzgerald was simply unable to admit to his alcoholism. Denial was part of the disease.

By the standards of Robert Lowell's *Life Studies* (1959) and the flurry of confessional novels, poems, and memoirs that have followed that ground-breaking work, Fitzgerald's account of his breakdown seems peculiarly reticent. A creative writing instructor of the 1990s, reading these essays in manuscript form, would be likely to scribble "More Specificity!" in the margins. There is surprisingly little detail, and even less of the scene-and-picture that enlivens Fitzgerald's fiction. And there is really only one character involved: the distressingly enervated and somewhat cynical persona of F. Scott Fitzgerald, at the end of his rope. Other names, with the notable exception of Edmund Wilson, are conspicuously withheld.

Yet the *Crack-Up* articles clearly struck a nerve at the time of publication, and they continue to fascinate readers over sixty-five years later. Vague in the lack of concrete detail, the essays still generate emotional power. What are the sources of that power? Above all, and despite their evasions, one is never in doubt in reading them that they come from the heart, that they convey the very real depths of the author's depression. In one sense, the "tension between concealment and revelation" (Dolan, *Modern Lives*, 142) – Fitzgerald's obvious reluctance to tell too much – is symptomatic of his troubles. He cannot articulate what he cannot admit to himself. Besides, if important matters are withheld, that is in part a consequence of the brevity of these essays: they occupy only sixteen pages in book form. Fitzgerald undoubtedly kept them short to satisfy the requirements of *Esquire* magazine, but he understood too the authority of the thing left out.

The essays gain further intensity from the clear division between "the cool, detached observer" whose voice dominates the narration and the desperately suffering figure whose story he is relating (*AA*, 11). And of course it matters that the downfall under analysis involves one of the century's most accomplished writers. Furthermore, the chronicle of Fitzgerald's personal journey from boom to bust resonates in the wider culture as well. Particularly in "Handle with Care," the last of the three essays, he is also lamenting what has gone wrong in American society, as of 1936: materialism running roughshod over love, friendship, honor – all the lovely abstractions he once believed in.

Fitzgerald writes about his deepest feelings in the *Crack-Up* articles with the aid of almost no plot at all. Instead he adopts the indirection of poetry and seeks to communicate how he felt through metaphor. It is extraordinary how often Fitzgerald compares himself in these essays: to other human beings, to animals, to inanimate objects. These comparisons are crucial to the artistic success of the whole, for they tell his unhappy tale without undue pointing or breast-beating.

Aging is the basic theme of "The Crack-Up" (February 1936), the first of the three essays. "Of course," it somberly begins, "all life is a process of breaking down." But Fitzgerald immediately segues back to the optimism of his youth when he was capable of believing that "[l]ife was something you dominated if you were any good." As Morris Dickstein has observed, "this project of mastering life was very much in the American grain" ("The Authority of Failure," 559). For a long time, Fitzgerald had clung to that sunny prospect, only reluctantly reducing his two "juvenile regrets" – not playing football in college, not getting overseas during the war – into "childish waking dreams," and still possessed of a romantic notion that with fame as the spur almost anything was possible. But after hearing "a grave sentence" from a "great doctor" (an exaggeration of his bouts of tuberculosis, probably) his outlook darkened. He stopped caring about others and went away to where he did not know many people. He found that he was "good-and-tired" and spent his time dozing or making lists. Suddenly he got better, and then "he cracked like an old plate," in the homely simile that structures this essay and leads on to the next.

In the paragraph after the cracked plate metaphor, Fitzgerald introduces a financial one: "I began to realize that for two years my life had been a drawing on resources that I did not possess, that I had been mortgaging myself physically and spiritually up to the hilt." This banking motif was to recur in the second *Crack-Up* essay, and he also used it in warning Scottie against reckless expenditure of her energy. "Our danger is imagining that we have resources – material and moral – which we haven't got," he wrote her on April 5, 1939. Every few years, he found himself "climbing uphill to recover from some bankruptcy." Scottie should understand exactly what bankruptcy meant: "drawing on resources which one does not possess" *(Letters,* 70).

Then, in the paragraph after that in "The Crack-Up," he reverted to the growing-up process with the comment that he "had *weaned* [my emphasis] [himself] from all the things [he] used to love" and was left with almost no fellow feeling for other people. He liked only doctors and girls short of puberty and boys eight and over and old men. There was a substantial category of those he could not stand the sight of: "Celts, English, Politicians, Strangers, Virginians, Negroes (light or dark), Hunting People, or retail clerks, and middlemen in general, all writers... and all the classes as classes and most of them as members of their class." With a measure of cynicism, he puts a question to his readers: "All rather inhuman and undernourished, isn't it? Well, that, children, is the true sign of cracking up."

This first essay concludes with the only extended anecdote of the entire series. Fitzgerald recounts the attempt of an unnamed woman – Nora Flynn, almost certainly – to act as "Job's comforter" in ameliorating his distress. "Suppose this wasn't a crack in you," she says, adopting his metaphor, "suppose it was a crack in the Grand Canyon." She asks him, in effect, to stop feeling sorry for himself and start considering the wider world. And she tells him of her private woes, and how she had overcome them.

Fitzgerald felt the logic of what she said. He might even have fought free of his depression, if he had been able to muster the vitality she possessed in such abundance. But vitality was a natural force that could not be passed on, not even if he waited "for a thousand hours with the tin cup of self-pity." There was no use in playing the beggar outside Nora's door. All he could do was walk away, "holding himself very carefully like cracked crockery" (*Crack-Up*, 69–74).

"Pasting It Together" (March 1936), the second *Crack-Up* essay, picks up the cracked-plate and bankruptcy metaphors, and adds several new ones designed to communicate the violent nature of his collapse. To begin with, Fitzgerald elaborates on the condition of the plate which despite its crack still has to be kept in service. It will not be brought out for company, he acknowledges, but will do to "hold crackers late at night or to go into the ice box under left-overs." But night brings on insomnia and sorrow and despair. At three o'clock in the morning, the hour of "the real dark night of the soul," he feels like "an unwilling witness of an execution," the disintegration or "shear[ing] away" of his own personality.

In his present crisis Fitzgerald is distressed by recollections of what he has twice lost in the past, and military images invade his thoughts. The first great crisis came at Princeton, where his departure in junior year (in Fitzgerald's not entirely forthcoming version, for medical reasons alone and not because of failing grades) had cost him the "badges" and "medals" he had rightfully earned, and so ended his "career as a leader of men." The second loss involved "one of those tragic loves doomed for lack of money." The blow fell when "the girl" (Zelda) turned him down because of his dim financial prospects, and though eventually it came out all right, he never got over an animosity – "not the conviction of a revolutionist but the smoldering hatred of the peasant" – toward the leisure class. While trying to emulate the rich, his horse had been "shot out from under" him. That defeat, like the one at Princeton, had resulted from "over-extend[ing]" his flank.

This last martial expression is repeated as Fitzgerald summarizes the family resemblance among the three periods of darkness in his life. Each had been the result of "an over-extension of the flank, a burning of the candle at both ends; a call upon physical resources that I did not command, like a man over-drawing at a bank": the triplet of metaphors substituting for what he could not or would not state explicitly. His most recent crack-up was more violent than the others, but in all three cases he felt as if he were "standing at twilight on a deserted range, with an empty rifle in my hands and the targets down" – only apparently armed, and powerless to alter his fate.

The essay goes on to illustrate how Fitzgerald had been so unmanned. With the advent of motion pictures, he observes, the power of the written word had become subordinate to the "grosser power" of the image on the screen. The effect threatened to render him obsolescent, just as "the chain stores have crippled the small merchant, an exterior force, unbeatable," an analogy that applies forcefully at the start of a new century. In part, though, Fitzgerald was complicit in the "disintegration" of his personality, since he had done so little to construct it himself. Instead he had borrowed his intellectual conscience from Edmund Wilson (the only contributor named in the essay), his sense of the good life from Sap Donahoe (a friend going back to his days at Newman School), his artistic conscience from Ernest Hemingway, his concept of how to conduct his relations with other people from Gerald Murphy, and his political conscience from a "man much younger than myself," possibly V. F. Calverton. Because he was made up of parts of other people, there was no intrinsic self, no basis (as Fitzgerald put it) on which to organize his self-respect. In a closing comparison he reduced the soldier alone on the range at night to a still more pitiable figure: "It was strange to have no self – to be like a little boy left alone in a big house," knowing that he could do anything he wanted to, but finding there was nothing that he wanted to do (Crack-Up, 75–80).

In the first two essays of the Crack-Up series, Fitzgerald appealed to his readers' compassion by ending with sentimental glimpses of himself in extremity: a beggar with a tin cup, a little boy left alone. He adopts a far more aggressively cynical tone in the final essay, "Handle with Care" (April 1936). In this profoundly bitter article, he excoriates American society and repeatedly diminishes himself by comparison to the least admirable people and things around him. The cracked plate, fashioned to arouse at least a modicum of pity, stays in the cupboard this time. Instead Fitzgerald writes of floundering in a "morass," of springing a "leak" through which his "enthusiasm and vitality" prematurely trickles away, of "self-immolation," of slaying "the empty shell" he has let himself become.

In order to recover, Fitzgerald decides that there will be no more "giving of [him]self." He is off "the dispensing end of the relief roll forever." "The conjurer's hat [is] empty." In the foolishness of youth, as he wrote Scottie, he had imagined he was "a sort of magician with words" without any effort on his part. Later he came to realize that what seemed to be magic was really the result of unremitting effort (Epstein, "F. Scott Fitzgerald's Third Act," 56). And there was only so much energy to go around. As with Dick Diver in *Tender is the Night* – a character who started out modeled on Gerald Murphy but later became closely identified with his creator – Fitzgerald found himself drained of almost all vitality. Diver's charm, his compulsion to use his "fatal pleasingness," had worn him down: it led directly to his downfall. So in 1936, the same year that Dale Carnegie's immensely popular *How to Win Friends and Influence People* advocated success through glad-handing, Fitzgerald resolved to stop bestowing carnivals of affection on others and to save himself by becoming at last "a writer only" (Dickstein, "Fitzgerald's Second Act," 574).

"Handle with Care" also delivers a satirical attack on the materialism rampant in American culture. This attack becomes most vivid in Fitzgerald's sardonic description of how he plans to conduct himself in the future. He will no longer expend any of his time and energy on other people – unless he stands to profit by doing so. In order to get through unavoidable human encounters he will cultivate a false smile and develop a new voice. The practiced smile, Fitzgerald writes, will "combine the best qualities of a hotel manager, an experienced old social weasel, a headmaster on visitors' day," and so on through a catalogue of artificial smilers finishing with "all those from Washington to Beverly Hills [again, how up-to-date Fitzgerald's satire seems] who must exist by virtue of the contorted pan." A lawyer is working with him on the voice, which will be designed to elicit the word "yes" from some but toward others will be notable for its "polite acerbity that makes [them] feel that far from being welcome they are not even tolerated."

The *Crack-Up* essays end with a series of demeaning self-characterizations expressed in similes or metaphors. In his youth Fitzgerald had aspired to be "an entire man" – athlete, scholar, artist, warrior, man of affairs, man of the world. Now, however, he has "cut... loose" that idealistic goal "with as little compulsion as a Negro lady cuts loose a rival on Saturday night." That ambition has been relegated to "the junk heap of the shoulder pads worn for one day on the Princeton freshman football field and the overseas cap never worn overseas." The most degrading metaphor comes at the very end. He no longer will allow himself to like anyone, Fitzgerald admits, and he has hung a sign, *Cave Canem*, above his door. "I will try to be a correct animal though, and if you throw me a bone with enough meat on it I may even lick your hand."

In his extremity, Fitzgerald compares himself to a dog who will alternately snarl or fawn, depending on how he is treated. It is not much of a role for a forty-year-old man to play, but he suggests that it is the only way he can adapt to a society populated by "grasping, amoral, beady-eyed, smooth articles"

(Grenberg, "Fitzgerald's 'Figured Curtain'," 18). His mood of dejection, as he points out in the penultimate paragraph of "Handle with Care," parallels "the wave of despair" that swept the nation in the aftermath of the boom. In the days before boom turned to bust, Fitzgerald had been capable of a happiness so intense that he had to go off by himself to walk the ecstasy away. But that apparent happiness, he reflects, may have been no more than "a talent for self-delusion." Certainly it was an exception to what he has come to believe: "that the natural state of the sentient adult is a qualified unhappiness" (*Crack-Up*, 80–4).

What chiefly makes Fitzgerald's writing last, Joseph Epstein has suggested, is his great theme of loss ("F. Scott Fitzgerald's Third Act," 57). The worst loss of all, in his stories and novels, is the loss of illusion that overcomes Dexter Green at the end of "Winter Dreams" and that Jay Gatsby struggles against on the last day of his life. The *Crack-Up* essays, like nothing else he wrote, testify that Fitzgerald had cast his private illusions aside, and must soldier on deprived of their emotional support. Gone, too, was most of the fund of energy that drove him to accomplish so much in the first fifteen years of his career, and that he still desperately needed for his work. "Vitality shows in not only the ability to persist but the ability to start over," as he reminded himself in his notebooks (*Crack-Up*, 126). The theme of loss, in short, is pervasive throughout these essays that, despite their silences and evasions, take us to the core of a man in the throes of despondency.

Fitzgerald continued to work an autobiographical vein in the pieces for *Esquire* – some fact, some fiction, but in either case drawn from experience – that followed the account of his crack-up. In the summer of 1936, for example, he composed an "author" trilogy for the magazine: "Author's House," "Afternoon of an Author," and "An Author's Mother." Despite using the camouflage of fiction more than the *Crack-Up* essays had, this group of three cuts close to the bone in revealing intimate details of Fitzgerald's life.

"Author's House" (July 1936) takes the form of a tour of the writer's home, from the damp unfinished cellar to the isolated cupola on top. One dark corner of the cellar, Fitzgerald as guide tells a visitor, conceals the crucial moment – three months before he was born – when his mother lost her other two children. "I think I started then to be a writer," he observes. Beneath a mound of dirt in another corner is buried his childhood self-love that enabled him to think that he "wasn't the son of [his] parents but a son of a king ... who ruled the whole world." Outside the living room the two men see a group of children playing football. Fitzgerald is taken back in memory to the time in prep school when he was accused of shying away from a tackle because of physical cowardice. It was not that way at all, he maintains, in a probable distortion of the facts. Another fiction develops as they progress upstairs. Fitzgerald invents a correspondence in which he has played a cruel hoax on an illiterate woman whose brother is in jail. The tale prompts him to regret that in his own writing he has necessarily meddled with other people's emotions, done "things he can never repair." The attic, pleasant enough for a short visit, is full of the school books and ballet programs and old magazines and maps that comprise "the library of a life." Finally they mount to the cupola as the wind whistles past. He had lived there once in his youth, Fitzgerald says, probably referring to the summer of 1919, when he shut himself in the topmost room of his parents' row house in St. Paul to finish *This Side of Paradise*. But he could not do it again even if he wanted to (*AA*, 183–9).

The "emotional exhaustion" Fitzgerald refers to in the *Crack-Up* essays is poignantly demonstrated in "Afternoon of an Author" (August 1936). Unlike his previous autobiographical essays, Fitzgerald uses the third person here, but if anything the article gains authority through such distancing. The essay purports to describe an actual day in the author's life. He wakes in his Baltimore apartment feeling better than he has in weeks, yet after breakfast lies down for fifteen minutes before starting work on a story that has "become so thin in the middle that it was about to blow away." He gives up this project, and after shaving rests for five minutes "as a precaution" before getting dressed. He'd like to get away for a while, but lacks the time and energy to drive down the Shenandoah valley or ride the boat to Norfolk. Instead he goes downtown on the bus to see his barber. In the business section he suddenly sees "brightly dressed girls, all very beautiful," and the sight restores his spirits so that "he love[s] life terribly for a minute, not wanting to give it up at all."

After alighting from the bus, however, he must hold "carefully to all the railings" as he walks the block to the hotel barbershop. After his haircut and shampoo, he hears an orchestra playing across the way, and is reminded of the review of his last book that declared that he was fond of night clubs and that he was "indefatigable." The mere word brings tears to his eyes. It was like the early days of his career, when despite laboring hard over every sentence Fitzgerald had been accused of a "fatal facility." At any rate, on this afternoon he is as easily fatigued as a man twice his forty years. He has some trouble mounting the steps of the bus that takes him home, then is revived by the sight of a couple of high school kids perched atop the Lafayette statue. As for himself, he "needed reforestation and . . . hoped the soil would stand one more growth." Back in his apartment, he drinks a glass of milk, and decides to lie down for ten minutes before trying to get started on an idea for a new story (*AA*, 177–82).

The slightest of the three "author" essays is "An Author's Mother" (September 1936). Presented in the guise of fiction, it chronicles the last day in the life of "Mrs. Johnston," a halting old lady who is patently modeled on Fitzgerald's mother. The piece was written after Mollie McQuillan Fitzgerald had fallen fatally ill, and appeared in print shortly before her death on September 2, 1936. Mrs. Johnston, her fictional counterpart, is not particularly pleased that her son Hamilton has become an author. She had wanted him to become an army officer or go into business. Authors were regarded as "freak[s]" in the Midwestern city (St. Paul) she came from, and she thought the profession was "risky and eccentric." It would have been different if he were a popular author along the lines of Longfellow or Alice and Phoebe Cary, nineteenth-century sentimental poets she admires. Mrs. Johnston suffers a fall as she is leaving a bookstore where she has been unable to purchase a copy of the Carys' poems. Taken to a hospital, she rouses herself and in her delirium "announce[s] astonishingly" that her son Hamilton was the author of "The Poems of Alice and Phoebe Cary." As an obituary for Fitzgerald's own mother, this brief story is touching in its gentle account of her weakness and confusion. Yet there is more than a trace of resentment, too, in her lack of respect for her son as a serious man of letters ("An Author's Mother," 36).

In a number of stories published in *Esquire* during the next two years, Fitzgerald introduced material from his own life that he had ignored or barely touched on in the *Crack-Up* essays. "'I Didn't Get Over'" (October 1936), for example, combines his regret at not getting overseas in the war with his persistent sense of social insecurity. Fitzgerald used to keep lists of those who had snubbed him, as he mentions in "The Crack-Up" (*Crack-Up*, 72). Like his admirer John O'Hara (who has been characterized as master of the imagined slight), he was tremendously sensitive to real or apparent putdowns. The story itself, rather convoluted in form and dependent on a surprise ending, illustrates the sometimes deadly consequences of one such social snub (*AA*, 169–76). "An Alcoholic Case" (February 1937) is based on the bouts of alcoholism that on several occasions placed Fitzgerald under the care of a trained nurse, and so comes to grips with the disease he had explicitly denied in "The Crack-Up" (70–1). The nurse in the story is taking care of a cartoonist whose indomitable will to die defeats her every attempt to make him better. She hates the idea of handling alcoholic cases. "It's just that you can't really help them and it's so discouraging"(*Short Stories*, 436–42).

"The Long Way Out" (September 1937) plays a variation on Zelda Fitzgerald's mental illness and hospitalization. The schizophrenic woman in the story has been promised a five-day trip with her husband away from the clinic. She joyfully prepares herself on the morning of their scheduled departure, and is happily waiting when word comes to the doctors that her husband has been killed in an automobile accident. No one dares tell her what has happened; her husband has been delayed, they say, and will pick her up tomorrow. So she goes on each day for years, readying herself each morning for her holiday. After waiting so long, as she daily reassures herself, one more day hardly matters. Perhaps this story derives in part from Fitzgerald's feelings of guilt. Zelda often implored him in her letters to take her on trips away from the hospital. Occasionally he did so, as on a four-day journey to Charleston and Myrtle Beach in the same month that this story appeared in print. Almost always these trips had disastrous consequences for both of them[3] (*Short Stories*, 443–7).

"Financing Finnegan" (January 1938), a fourth story dealing with what was left out of the *Crack-Up* essays, addresses the subject of Fitzgerald's financial unreliability. The story is written with wry self-deprecating humor. The tone is implicit in the very name of the protagonist, which is more suggestive of the stereotypical barroom Irishman than the distinguished-sounding "Fitzgerald." Like Fitzgerald, Finnegan borrows repeatedly from his agent and editor against the promise of work as yet undone. Like Fitzgerald, he signs over his life insurance to them. Like Fitzgerald, he has recently broken his shoulder during a dive from the high board. With so much invested in his cause, agent and editor become cheerleaders for Finnegan. The book he has promised may not have materialized, they acknowledge, but when it does it is bound to be wonderful. Yet after having dispensed so much to Finnegan, even they become desperate for funds. At the end of the story, the editor is reduced to putting the touch on another of his authors (*Short Stories*, 448–55).

Fitzgerald returns to the beginning of his literary career in the autobiographical article "Early Success" (October 1937). Here he recalls the "first wild wind of success" that had sprung up with the letter from Scribners accepting *This Side of Paradise* in the fall of 1919. "[T]hat week," he writes, "the postman rang and rang, and I paid off my terrible small debts, bought a suit, and woke up every morning with a world of ineffable toploftiness and promise." That early realized dream created the illusion that the gods were on his side, that life was a romantic matter. Yet from the beginning Fitzgerald understood that his time of ecstasy, like the "great gaudy spree" the nation was about to embark upon, could not last. All the stories that came into his head "had a touch of disaster in them." By 1937, he has taken on a protective shell to harden himself against the disappointments of his personal and professional life. But he will not dismiss from memory the intense excitement that had once enraptured him. There are still times, he concludes, when he can go back into the mind of the youth who had walked the streets with cardboard soles – "times when I creep up on him, surprise him on an autumn morning in New York or a spring night in Carolina when it is so quiet that you can hear a dog barking in the next county" (*Crack-Up*, 85–90).

In the prose of this poetically evocative essay, the last important piece of nonfiction writing Fitzgerald published, he takes us back into the realm of what has been sadly, irretrievably lost. The early success of his youth had made him foolishly over-confident, even arrogant, and in that mood he had capered and gamboled for the sheer pleasure of taunting his sober elders. In one sense, Fitzgerald must have rued that heedless exuberance, for it stamped him in the public mind as "larky" and unserious. Yet he will not and cannot repudiate that brief wonderful time when the young man with cardboard soles and the professional author in the making "were one person, when the fulfilled future and the wistful past were mingled in a single gorgeous moment – when life was literally a dream"(*Crack-Up*, 90). At the conclusion of "Early Success," Fitzgerald summoned all of his lyrical power in a statement of overpowering regret for what was forever lost to him – as it has been or will be to those of us who read his prose and are unaccountably moved by it.

NOTES

1 For his invaluable research in the newspapers and magazines of the time, I am indebted to the doctoral dissertation (University of Pennsylvania, 1992) of Jeffrey Harris Woodward, *F. Scott Fitzgerald: The Artist as Public Figure, 1920–1940.*

2 Here as elsewhere, I am following Fitzgerald's customary usage of "girl" for "young woman."

3 It is curious that the woman in the story is called "Mrs. King" and the principal doctor "Dr. Pirie." Ginevra King, the love of Fitzgerald's young life, was eventually to marry John Pirie, but at the time this story was published, she had recently been divorced from William H. Mitchell III. She and Fitzgerald saw each other in Santa Barbara in the fall of 1937, following publication of this story.

10

ALAN MARGOLIES

Fitzgerald and Hollywood

While Fitzgerald's experiences in Hollywood during the last years of the 1930s contributed heavily to the planning and writing of *The Love of the Last Tycoon: A Western*, a glimpse at the novelist's earlier life and work suggests that this novel was almost foreordained. Fitzgerald had been interested in, maybe fascinated by, movie-making from a very early period in his life. He wrote film treatments and scripts and, in addition, used what he knew about Hollywood in several of his short stories as well as in *The Beautiful and Damned* and later in *Tender is the Night*. He had mixed feelings about film as an art form during these years, and yet was convinced of its power over its audience. With the advent of talking pictures, he mulled over the possibility – and felt sorrow – that someday it might replace the novel. In 1936, he wrote: "I saw that the novel, which at my maturity was the strongest and supplest medium for conveying thought and emotion from one human being to another, was becoming subordinated to a mechanical and communal art that, whether in the hands of Hollywood merchants or Russian idealists, was capable of only the tritest thought, the most obvious emotion" (*Crack-Up*, 78).

This gloominess reflected the beliefs of Oswald Spengler in his *Decline of the West*, a work Fitzgerald referred to a number of times in his writing. In addition, Fitzgerald's statement was written during a period of despondency. His writing during his last years in Hollywood suggests, however, that his pessimism about the future of film may have been wavering. Even though he planned to kill off movie man Monroe Stahr at the end of *The Last Tycoon*, he portrayed Stahr as a man who did not totally believe in "the tritest thought" and "the most obvious emotion." After meeting an educated black man who refuses to let his children go to the movies because of their trashy nature, the doomed Stahr changes his production plans. Elsewhere in the novel Stahr shocks his bosses when he tells them that he will make a quality film despite the fact that it will lose money: "[W]e have a certain duty to the public," he tells them (*LOTLT*, 48).

Some of Fitzgerald's earliest writing was for the silent screen. Before his first novel, among the many pieces that he unsuccessfully submitted for publication were movie scripts. After *This Side of Paradise* (1920) was published, his frustrations over not being able to begin a second novel caused him to think of becoming a screenwriter. He met famed film director D.W. Griffith at the Mamaroneck, NY, studios and made several suggestions for scripts. In 1920 he wrote a scenario for actress Dorothy Gish (who was then working for Griffith) but the film was not made. He also submitted a script idea to the young David Selznick, son of film magnate Lewis J. Selznick, but again nothing came of it.

In *The Beautiful and Damned* (1922), he drew his first major film character, Joseph Bloeckman, a movie executive and representative of the many European Jews who at the time had worked their way up in the film industry. In addition, Fitzgerald portrayed a film studio seen from the point of view of an outsider, Gloria Patch, who is given a screen test with the hopes of becoming a starlet although, unknown to her, she no longer retains her youthful bloom. Here Fitzgerald reflected ironically on the magic of film: "It cheered her that in some manner the illusion of beauty could be sustained, or perhaps preserved in celluloid after the reality had vanished" (307).

Soon after, Fitzgerald once again was involved in film projects. He wrote the titles for the 1923 Paramount Picture *The Glimpses of the Moon* (based on the Edith Wharton novel), and the scenario for the Film Guild's *Grit*, a gangster melodrama. On one hand the experience was disillusioning. "I'm too much of an egoist + not enough of a diplomat ever to succeed in the movies," he wrote his friend John Peale Bishop. On the other hand, there was money to be made in Hollywood. Just before *The Great Gatsby* was published, Fitzgerald wrote his editor Maxwell Perkins that if the novel did not make him enough money to support him as a serious writer, he would "go to Hollywood and learn the movie business." He complained: "I can't reduce our standard of living and I can't stand this financial insecurity. Anyhow there's no point in trying to be an artist if you can't do your best" (*Life in Letters*, 101, 107).

During this early period several of Fitzgerald's works were translated into film. "Head and Shoulders" (1920) became the 1920 Metro film *The Chorus Girl's Romance*; "Myra Meets His Family" (1920) was made into the 1920 Fox film *The Husband Hunter*; and "The Offshore Pirate" (1920) into the 1921 Metro film of the same name. Fitzgerald also sold the rights to "The Camel's Back" (1920) which loosely became the Warner Brothers' 1924 film *Conductor: 1492*. At least a few of these stories and others were written with Hollywood sale in mind. In the 1923 story "Dice, Brass-knuckles & Guitar," for example, after Fitzgerald introduced his beautiful heroine, the narrator gave tongue-in-cheek instructions for filming: "Now if this were a moving picture (as, of course, I hope it will be some day) I would take as many thousand of feet of her as I was allowed – then I would move the camera up close and show the yellow down on the back of her neck where her hair stopped and the warm color of her cheeks and arms" (*Price*, 48).

Other visits to the film studios followed. During the winter of 1924–5 in Rome, he became friendly with film actress Carmel Myers and went to the sets of the American film *Ben-Hur*. Later Fitzgerald was to use some of this experience first in the 1927 story "Jacob's Ladder" and then in slightly different form in *Tender is the Night* (1934), where actress Rosemary Hoyt is preparing for a scene in "The Grandeur that was Rome." In January 1927 he went to Hollywood to write "Lipstick," a silent film for actress Constance Talmadge. The plot was his own idea, the treatment somewhat silly and sufficiently poor to be turned down by the studio. It was to be one of those college films popular at the time, about a girl who goes to jail in the place of her uncle, her falling in love with a college student, and her magic lipstick guaranteed to give kisses. Fitzgerald made only $3,500 for his effort, the same amount that the *Saturday Evening Post* was paying him that year for each short story it published.

During this visit he became friendly with the youthful actress Lois Moran, who had lived abroad, spoke French, and read poetry. Moran was to be the prototype for Rosemary Hoyt as well as other young actresses in his fiction. For instance, in his 1928 story "The Bowl," a college story with a Princeton setting, Fitzgerald used some of his observations of Moran as the background for the eighteen-year-old actress Daisy Cary, who tells how, during the winter, with a fever of 102, she must fall six times into an open-air lagoon. He again used Moran's background in "Jacob's Ladder" for some of actress Jenny Prince's film experiences, but Moran was far more educated and sophisticated than Fitzgerald's heroine. In the 1928 story "Magnetism," Fitzgerald portrayed another Hollywood newcomer, this time Helen Avery, who falls in love with George Hannaford, a young movie veteran.

Other observations from this 1927 trip also eventually found their way into his fiction. In "Jacob's Ladder" he portrayed filmland's Sunday parties with guests inquiring about the health of others' children, while others were posing "immobile, statue-like, in a corner" (*Short Stories*, 361). In "Magnetism," he also drew upon the Hollywood parties, here contrasting the stars from the early Griffith films, thought of as the older crowd despite their youthfulness, with the newer stars. In both stories, the blackmail theme, a not unusual occurrence in Hollywood then, also appears, in "Jacob's Ladder," a failed attempt at revealing a young actress's relationship with her sister, a convicted murderer, and in "Magnetism," involving forged letters purportedly from Hannaford to a script girl. In the notes to *The Last Tycoon*, he considered using a blackmail situation once more.

Many of these stars during those silent days came from backgrounds that did not match their screen roles. In "Jacob's Ladder," the beautiful young Jenny Delahanty's lower-class New York accent and lack of polish ("Le' me alone, will you? Le' me alone. Geeze!" she implores an impatient reporter after her sister's conviction) do not disqualify her for a movie audition. Director Billy Farrelly of "Jacob's Ladder" comments, "They're all the same.... Shucks! Pick 'em out of the gutter today and they want gold plates tomorrow" (*Short Stories*, 351, 355). In "Magnetism," George Hannaford's success as a film actor is one of fortuity: "After a year in a small technical college he had taken a summer job with an electric company, and his first appearance in a studio was in the rôle of repairing a bank of Klieg lights. In an emergency he played a small part and made good" (*Stories*, 224).

Sets also seemed to fascinate him. In "Magnetism," he drew a portrait of "the white cracking glow of a stage with two people motionless upon it" and "apparently from afar, the gentle tremolo of a small organ" and then was to reuse the situation in *Tender is the Night*. And he paid more attention in "Magnetism" to Hollywood's geography with its "interminable boulevard[s]," and "hilly country" (*Stories*, 222). He was to return to this in *The Last Tycoon*.

Fitzgerald also used film imagery here to enhance his subject, once when Hannaford has a movie-like overly romantic dream about his wife whom he suspects of having an affair. The scene is in a garden with a river flowing past and stars twinkling above: "The grass was damp, and Kay came to him on hurried feet; her thin slippers were drenched with dew. She stood upon his shoes, nestling close to him..." Fitzgerald then added sentimental dialogue reminiscent of the titles in silent films:

> "Think how you love me," she whispered. "I don't ask you to love me always like this, but I ask you to remember."
> "You'll always be like this to me."
> "Oh, no; but promise me you'll remember." Her tears were falling. "I'll be different, but somewhere lost inside of me there'll always be the person I am tonight."

At this point Hannaford wakes up and the film imagery ends: "The scene dissolved slowly" (*Stories*, 230–1).

Fitzgerald returned to California in November 1931 for another brief period. Now he was working at MGM studios on the film *Red Headed Woman*. It was based on Katherine Brush's short story and he was not the first writer at the studio to struggle with it. He was anxious to learn about film technique, according to writer Dwight Taylor, who later recalled: "I remember he was always worried about camera angles, but I pointed out that it was his dialogue and characterizations that they were after" (Taylor, "Scott Fitzgerald in Hollywood," 68). Despite this advice, Fitzgerald's work was rejected and novelist Anita Loos given the assignment. Loos's version, a racy concoction about a sexy stenographer who seduces her boss, kills her husband, and winds up in Paris with a marquis and a chauffeur, was one of the films of the early 1930s that resulted in the eventual greater enforcement of the Motion Picture Producers and Distributors of America Production Code.

During this 1931 Hollywood trip, a tipsy Fitzgerald participated in the impromptu entertainment at one of the well-known Sunday afternoon parties given by filmmaker Irving Thalberg and his wife actress, Norma Shearer. Fitzgerald's innocuous but boring song about a dog was an embarrassing flop. Shearer, however, reacted with kindness and an abashed Fitzgerald pasted his hostess's magnanimous message, "I THOUGHT YOU WERE ONE OF THE MOST AGREEABLE PERSONS AT OUR TEA," in his scrapbook. Soon after, he used this experience in "Crazy Sunday" (1932) when writer Joel Coles entertains at a similar party, commits a *faux pas*, apologizes to his hostess, and receives a very similar telegram. But Coles's blunder is not so innocent as Fitzgerald's. It is a burlesque imitation of a Jewish independent producer, Mr. Dave Silverstein, known for his malapropisms. (Fitzgerald probably modeled him on famed producer Samuel Goldwyn.) The result is silence and "Boo! Boo!" from one of the more famous Hollywood actors: "It was the resentment of the professional toward the amateur, of the community toward the stranger, the thumbs-down of the clan" (*Short Stories*, 702).

"Crazy Sunday" is another of Fitzgerald's Hollywood stories that prefigures *The Last Tycoon*. Miles Calman is somewhat like Monroe Stahr, especially when Fitzgerald tells us that "Calman was the only director on the lot who did not work under a supervisor and was responsible to the money men alone"; when he reminds us that "he was the only American-born director with both an interesting temperament and an artistic conscience"; and when Joel Coles tells Calman's mother that Calman has become "a legend... Oracle and a Man of Destiny." Further, Calman's death in an airplane crash reminds us of Fitzgerald's plan for Stahr's demise. But despite this praise, and possibly because, unlike Monroe Stahr, he is never shown in action at the studio, Fitzgerald never convinces the reader that Calman is as great a man as his *Last Tycoon* hero (*Short Stories*, 699, 712, 700).

Further, the two stories are different. "Crazy Sunday" is mainly a study of character, the talented Calman with his need to be unfaithful to his wives and his jealousy of them, the weak Stella, and Joel Coles himself, who is introduced as an incipient weak character – "He was twenty-eight and not yet broken by Hollywood" – who seems to grow by the end of the story, and yet may be the most lost when he decides after Calman's death that he will continue his relationship with Stella. "Oh yes, I'll be back – I'll be back!" he says (*Short Stories*, 698, 713).

After completing *Tender is the Night*, Fitzgerald worked without success on several movie scripts. One was a sanitized film treatment of *Tender is the Night*, written in late 1934 with a young protégé, Bill Warren. The incest theme was omitted, obviously because of the Hollywood censorship of the time. Here Nicole Warren's mental disorder results from a physical injury. Dick Diver, now a brain surgeon rather than a psychiatrist, cures her, eventually marries her as in the novel, but a separation ensues because of actress Rosemary Hoyt's attraction for the doctor and Baby Warren's interference in her sister's marriage. Presumably to satisfy Hollywood and movie audiences, Fitzgerald and Warren wrote a happy ending to the plot, reuniting Dick and Nicole. Although Warren traveled to Hollywood and claimed to make many attempts to sell the treatment, nothing ever came of it.

That same year, Fitzgerald collaborated (with writer Robert Spafford) on the comedy *Gracie at Sea*, a treatment for entertainers George Burns and Gracie Allen. Allen played a wealthy yachtsman's daughter who must find a husband before her sisters can marry and Burns played the publicity man hired to find the husband. A number of slapstick episodes ending with a slapstick yacht race tempered by scenes involving Allen and an abandoned baby made for an extremely weak plot that, despite all, "damn near went over" with Hollywood, according to Fitzgerald (*Life in Letters*, 265).

As the 1930s progressed and the economy worsened, Fitzgerald's life was in free-fall. He was seemingly written out as a fiction writer. He had suffered a breakdown partly due to his drinking; his wife was in and out of hospitals because of her mental illness; and he desperately needed money for her upkeep, his daughter's education, and to repay heavy debts. Then, in 1937, Fitzgerald's agent wangled a twelve-month contract with Metro-Goldwyn-Mayer Pictures which was renewed for six more months the following year.

Fitzgerald's last Hollywood period occurred during one of the most exciting periods in the history of American film. *Lost Horizon* was released in 1937; *You Can't Take it With You* and *Bringing Up Baby* in 1938. Then came the great watershed years of 1939 and 1940: *Stagecoach*, *Mr. Smith Goes to Washington*, *Ninotchka*, *The Wizard of Oz*, and *Gone With the Wind* in 1939; *The Philadelphia Story, His Girl Friday, Foreign Correspondent, The Great Dictator, The Shop Around the Corner,* and *The Grapes of Wrath* in 1940. And there were two other great films in production while Fitzgerald was alive but released in 1941, *Citizen Kane* and *The Maltese Falcon.* This is a partial list. The reader may disagree with some and will want to substitute other favorites. For those who believe in the *auteur* theory, note the names of the directors of these films and others (including some soon-to-be directors) who were working in Hollywood during the last four years of Fitzgerald's life: Busby Berkeley, Frank Capra, Charlie Chaplin, George Cukor, Cecil B. De Mille, Allan Dwan, John Ford, Howard Hawks, Alfred Hitchcock, John Huston, Ernst Lubitsch, Lewis Milestone, Preston Sturges, George Stevens, King Vidor, Billy Wilder, William Wyler. Here too some may want to substitute other favorites. This was a golden period and this is what Fitzgerald was exposed to in his last years. Obviously he did not see all of the films mentioned nor did he socialize with everyone here, far from it. It was merely a wonderful time to be in Hollywood, especially for a novelist who was witnessing events that were to become material for *The Last Tycoon.*

And Fitzgerald was determined this third time to become a success. Once more he attempted to learn the technical side of film-making. He studied films, read books, and talked with other writers. "Pictures have a private and complex grammar," he wrote (*F. Scott Fitzgerald: Manuscripts, The Last Tycoon*; Part 1, 133). He called the work "a sort of tense crossword puzzle game" (*Letters,* 443). At first he was entranced with his new situation and extremely optimistic. "I love it here," he wrote. "It's nice work if you can get it and you can get it if you try about three years. The point is once you've got it – Screen Credit 1st, a Hit 2nd, and the Academy Award 3d – you can count on it forever" (*Life in Letters,* 341).

He even believed that some day he might have full control over a film as both writer and director, possibly similar to Preston Sturges. In 1940, a few months before Fitzgerald died, he saw the film *The Great McGinty,* starring Brian Donlevy as a vagrant who becomes governor with the help of crooked politicos. This was Sturges's first directorial job and he was to go on to make such wonderful comedies as *Sullivan's Travels* (1941) and *Hail the Conquering Hero* (1944). Although Fitzgerald said that *The Great McGinty* was "inferior in pace" and an "old story," he liked the film because (he wrote) "it had not suffered from compromises, polish jobs, formulas and that familiarity which is so falsely consoling to producers." Soon after this statement he wrote his wife: "They've let a certain writer here direct his own pictures and he has made such a go of it that there may be a different feeling about that soon. If I had that chance, I would attain my real goal in coming here in the first place" (*Life in Letters*, 459, 464).

Fitzgerald was not being realistic. His health was not getting any better and his alcoholism was a threat. And based on his track record, he did not have the constitution to work with and guide his associates. While working on *Red Headed Woman*, he had quarreled with a writing collaborator, Michael de Sano, over changes in the script, and partly blamed de Sano for Irving Thalberg's rejection of his work. He was to react in a similar way in 1937 when producer Joseph M. Mankiewicz interfered with his *Three Comrades* script. From today's vantage point, Thalberg's and Mankiewicz's decisions seem correct. Both films received critical accolades at the time and are still highly regarded.

Fitzgerald's first job at MGM during July 1937 was to revise part of the script of *A Yank at Oxford*, shot in England with the English actress Vivien Leigh but featuring the Americans Robert Taylor, Lionel Barrymore, and Maureen O'Sullivan, directed by the American Jack Conway (who had started his career with D. W. Griffith), and written by a team of writers in the United States. The plot was about an American student at Oxford who first feels disdain for his surroundings but eventually experiences a change in attitude. Fitzgerald's assignment included the rewriting of two scenes, some of which was used in the released film. He felt that the script needed more justification for the American's reversal of character, possibly a scene that dramatized these new feelings. He also believed that dialogue in the earlier version of the script made the American's soon-to-be girlfriend, Molly, seem too passive, even dull. Thus he changed her lines when she first spots her brother sitting with Lee, the American, from "I thought I'd have some coffee with you," to the more outgoing "Room for one more?" He also changed a line in response to Lee's query whether he would see her in Oxford. In the older script, she replied: "Possibly. I'm a student there – St. Cynthia's College." Fitzgerald's revision gave a coyness that she lacked originally: "If you want to be sure, you'd better come along with me right now" (Margolies, "F. Scott Fitzgerald's Work in the Film Studios," 83–4).

Fitzgerald was off to a good start, good enough for MGM next to assign him to prepare a script based on Erich Maria Remarque's novel *Three Comrades*, a tale of three German World War I veterans trying to survive the German recession of the 1920s. The film was to be directed by Frank Borzage and produced by Joseph M. Mankiewicz. Both were eminently qualified to work on a film set in post-World War I Germany. Borzage had directed the 1934 *Little Man, What Now*, one of the earliest anti-Nazi films. Mankiewicz had worked in Berlin as a *Chicago Tribune* reporter and as a film translator.

Among his MGM productions was Fritz Lang's 1936 *Fury*, a film about lynching and mob hysteria.

Fitzgerald did a workmanlike job converting the novel to film, emphasizing both the hardships the three heroes face in their automobile repair business as well as the doomed love affair of one of the comrades. But Fitzgerald's script also emphasized the political rumblings of the late 1920s in Germany. At one point Fitzgerald had one of the three heroes of the story, after a fight with a Nazi, say, "The country's mad. Little kids in soldier suits strutting around shrieking that they represent the Fatherland." Fitzgerald also wrote into the story the minor role of a Jewish cab driver, who, early in the film naively praises Germany as a homeland for Jews, but, later, finding himself jobless, says ironically: "There seems to be a little – prejudice around lately. But I must have struck the wrong people...I thought I had a job today – but the man wouldn't give it to me...because it was Christmas" (*F. Scott Fitzgerald's Screenplay for "Three Comrades,"* 48, 211, 213).

While most of the writing was acceptable, some of it seems mawkish today. When the three heroes, Erich, Koster, and Lenz, fight the Vogt brothers, owners of a competing repair shop, the dialogue becomes uncomfortably metaphoric:

21 KOSTER AND LENZ –
– approaching the wreck.
Biggest Vogt (to Bobby)
Don't talk tripe or you'll need repairs yourself.
  Koster and Lenz range themselves beside Bobby.
Koster
We've got permission from the owner to do the job.
Another Vogt Brother (producing a tire wrench from behind his back)
How would you like another scar on your fat face?
Koster
That took a machine gun.
Biggest Vogt (still sure of himself)
Three of you, eh?
Lenz
No, four.
Another Brother (looking around)
Go on – He's kidding.
Lenz (dryly)
You can't see him – his name is Justice. (*Screenplay*, 11)

At another point when Bobby, near the noisy repair shop, phones Pat, the heroine of the film, for a date, Fitzgerald called for angels and satyrs at the switchboard, and once again the dialogue became precious:

> Bobby waits for the connection with a
> beatific smile. The banging dies away as
> we –
>   CUT TO:
> 54   A SWITCHBOARD –
>   – with a white winged angel sitting at it.
> *Angel* (sweetly)
> One moment, please – I'll connect you with heaven.
>   CUT TO:
> 55   THE PEARLY GATES
>   St. Peter, the caretaker, sitting beside
>   another switchboard.
> *St. Peter* (cackling)
> I think she's in.
>   CUT TO:
> 56   BOBBY'S FACE –
>   – still ecstatic, changing to human
>   embarrassment as Pat's voice says:
> *Pat*
> Hello. (*Screenplay*, 43–4)

Among the visual devices in the script were a number of montages, nothing new at the time, as well as another extremely old, clichéd effect, a double exposure retained at the end of the film showing the two remaining comrades marching side by side with their dead friends.

Producer Mankiewicz felt that Fitzgerald needed help and he brought in writer E. E. Paramore, Jr., an old acquaintance of Fitzgerald, to co-author the second version of the script. And eventually there was a third version with Mankiewicz as well as at least one other writer, David Hertz, getting into the act. By this time, the overt anti-Nazi scenes had been removed. The ending, where originally the two remaining comrades return to fight the fascists, was changed. Now apparently they left for South America. Fitzgerald disliked the final script because of the maudlin dialogue he believed had been added. He told Mankiewicz that the German-English Pat had been transformed into "a sentimental girl from Brooklyn." In his copy of the final script "OKed by Joseph Mankiewicz" on the cover page, Fitzgerald crossed out "OKed" and wrote "scrawled over." And he wrote Mankiewicz that he had produced "a flop" (*Life in Letters*, 343–4).

In 1967, twenty-seven years after Fitzgerald's death, Mankiewicz, in an interview for *Cahiers du Cinéma in English*, criticized Fitzgerald's film-writing.

He said:

> I personally have been attacked as if I had spat on the American flag because it
> happened once that I rewrote some dialogue by F. Scott Fitzgerald. But indeed
> it needed it! The actors, among them Margaret Sullavan, absolutely could not
> read the lines. It was very literary dialogue, novelistic dialogue that lacked all
> the qualities for screen dialogue. The latter must be "spoken." Scott Fitzgerald
> really wrote very bad spoken dialogue. (Bontemps and Overstreet, "Measure,"
> 31)

Mankiewicz was exaggerating. The released film had retained Fitzgerald's
basic outline as well as at least one-third of the dialogue from his first script.
Further, the film was a success. Frank S. Nugent, for example, film reviewer
of the *New York Times*, wrote that the film was "a beautiful and memorable
film." In more recent days, reviewer Leonard Maltin's *Movie and Video
Guide* has consistently rated it superior, calling it a "beautifully poignant
film" with "excellent performances all around."

Fitzgerald's next boss was producer Hunt Stromberg, another film-maker
who had been involved in films since the silents and one whom Fitzgerald
liked. Among his credits were *Our Dancing Daughters* (1928), *The Thin Man*
(1934), and *The Great Ziegfeld* (1936). Now Fitzgerald was transforming
for the screen and for actress Joan Crawford, Ursula Parrott's magazine short
story, "Infidelity." Beginning in February 1938, Fitzgerald prepared extensively. He viewed several of Crawford's films, noting her acting strengths and
weaknesses. He outlined the major sequences of three films, *The Divorcee*
(1930), *Possessed* (1931), and *Chained* (1934), all with themes similar to that
of *Infidelity* and the last two starring Crawford. He also divided the films into
acts and noted montages in particular. He then made a comparable plan for
Infidelity, first arranging the story into nine sequences and then into scenes
with the proposed date of completion of each scene. Once again he also
broke up the story into acts. He was to make a similar outline for *The Last
Tycoon*.

Fitzgerald's script contained many more visual devices than his previous
efforts, including, besides montages and dissolves, two-shots, wipes, and
even one shot which appeared as if the viewer were looking through opera
glasses. However, these visual devices did not necessarily originate with
Fitzgerald. Stromberg had sent Fitzgerald a long memo detailing many of
them and Fitzgerald followed the director's advice.

Similar to his earlier work on *Three Comrades*, Fitzgerald's contribution
was good in part but nothing exceptional, and at times the prose again was
too precious. For example, when Althea Gilbert is leaving for Europe to visit

her ill mother, the following dialogue ensues between her and her husband, Nicolas:

> NICOLAS Listen. Did you read in the paper about the dog they froze up in a cake of ice.
> ALTHEA Poor dog.
> NICOLAS Wait a minute.
> ALTHEA I'm afraid I'm going to weep over that dog.
> NICOLAS Wait! They thawed him out after a month, and he came to life again. That's how it'll be with us.
> ALTHEA But what'll I think about in my cake of ice?
> NICOLAS Oh, you look out and see the Italian scenery and watch your mother get well and write me letters. (Margolies, "F. Scott Fitzgerald's Work in the Film Studios," 94–5)

But the film was never made. Though they made many attempts, Fitzgerald and Stromberg failed to solve the problem of how to reunite the married couple and eventually they gave up. The story had dealt with a happily married man who commits adultery while his wife is in Europe and the movie censors of the time had decreed that adultery had to be punished in some way. Among the many attempts to solve the problem was one when Fitzgerald, hoping to find a suitable ending, viewed scenes from the 1938 film *Test Pilot*. At another time he thought of a situation where each character might be placed in the role of another; thus Althea might understand and forgive the adulterous transgression. This too was unsuccessful. But Fitzgerald was to reuse the idea in *The Last Tycoon*, where the novelist Boxley, confronted with a script problem, solves it for the moment when he suggests: "Let each character see himself in the other's place ... You could almost call the thing 'Put Yourself in My Place'" (*LOTLT*, 108).

Next Fitzgerald worked briefly on the script for *Marie Antoinette*, including the scene in the film where Marie (played by Norma Shearer) bids farewell to Count Axel de Fersen (played by Tyrone Power). Again Stromberg was the producer. The director was W. S. Van Dyke II, who had made, among other films, the 1936 *San Francisco* with actors Clark Gable, Spencer Tracy, and Jeanette MacDonald.

During the second half of 1938, Fitzgerald was assigned to work with director Sidney Franklin on Donald Ogden Stewart's script of *The Women*, based on Claire Booth's humorous play. Several scenes needed revision. This was to be a film with a large cast of only women and with many more stars than usual. For background, Fitzgerald reviewed the classic 1932 film *Grand Hotel*. It too had many stars and a plot with many characters. (*The Women* was later produced using different writers.)

He also wrote a complete script, for Franklin, about the life of Polish physicist Marie Curie, who married famed physicist Pierre Curie and was known for her work on radioactivity. *Madame Curie* was based on Eve Curie's biography of her mother. Fitzgerald looked at the 1934 MGM film, *The Barretts of Wimpole Street*. He conceived of his script as mainly a story of courtship – similar to *The Barretts* – and as "a comparatively quiet picture." "It is," he wrote, "a relief to be working on something the censors have nothing against" (*Letters*, 102). But there was disagreement over Fitzgerald's conception and the project was postponed.

While at MGM he also submitted a number of ideas for scripts that he hoped he could work on alone. One of these was about an amateur theatre group for MGM child stars Mickey Rooney, Judy Garland, and Freddie Bartholomew. Fitzgerald thought of using some episodes from three short stories, "He Thinks He's Wonderful" (1928), "The Captured Shadow" (1928), and "The Perfect Life" (1929), all part of his series about the youngster Basil Duke Lee. Once again he diagrammed the plot and broke it up into sequences from these stories. Then he thought of it as a novel, dividing it into seven chapters and then three acts. But nothing came of this venture. At the end of 1938 MGM released Fitzgerald. He had worked for eighteen months, had been paid a large sum of money, $1,000 a week for the first six months and $1,250 for the next year, and had managed to repay most of his debts.

In early 1939 he worked for David Selznick for two weeks polishing one of the many versions of the script of *Gone With the Wind*. He was very lukewarm about the novel. He noted its lack of originality and criticized it for making "no new examination into human emotions." Yet, "on the other hand," he wrote, "it is interesting, surprisingly honest, consistent and workmanlike throughout, and I felt no contempt for it but only a certain pity for those who considered it the supreme achievement of the human mind" (*Life in Letters*, 383). His portion of the script begins with Scarlett's first meeting with Rhett Butler and continues to the burning of Atlanta. Fitzgerald's copy with pencil changes in his hand as well as other typed changes suggest that his contribution was extremely minor, mainly the shortening and cutting of lines and, once in a while, restoring a line from the book. He wrote Max Perkins: "Do you know in that 'Gone With the Wind' job I was absolutely forbidden to use any words except those of Margaret Mitchell, that is, when new phrases had to be invented one had to thumb through as if it were Scripture and check out phrases of her's which would cover the situation!" (*Dear Scott/Dear Max*, 255). His script with its pointed references to specific pages in the novel is verification.

That winter, Fitzgerald worked with writer Budd Schulberg on Walter Wanger's production of *Winter Carnival*, set at Dartmouth College. The two traveled to the school where a crew was filming background footage. After a brief period, however, Fitzgerald, drinking heavily, was fired. Later, while working on an early version of *The Last Tycoon*, Fitzgerald thought of using some of the Dartmouth material. In one note, he wrote: "I would like this episode to give a picture of the work of a cutter, camera man or second unit director in the making of such a thing as *Winter Carnival*" (*LOTLT*, 144). And although he warned himself, presumably for legal reasons, not to use anything specific that he had written for Wanger, he then went on to suggest a scene at a telegraph desk that is in the *Winter Carnival* treatment.

In 1939 and 1940, as his health deteriorated, Fitzgerald worked briefly at Paramount Pictures for a never-to-be-made film called *Air Raid*; one week for Universal Pictures writing a treatment titled *Open that Door*, based on Charles Bonner's novel *Bull By the Horns*; a week or so for producer Samuel Goldwyn and director Sam Wood on *Raffles*; briefly on the Sonja Henie film *Everything Happens at Night*; and again briefly for Twentieth-Century-Fox writing a treatment about the construction of the Brooklyn Bridge, *Brooklyn Bridge* (another film never made). In addition he wrote a complete script based on Emlyn Williams's play, *The Light of Heart*, and once again his script was not used.

During 1940, Fitzgerald was also completing a script for independent producer Lester Cowan based on one of his greatest short stories, "Babylon Revisited" (1931). In an author's note to the screenplay, Fitzgerald wrote, "This is an attempt to tell a story from a child's point of view *without* sentimentality" (*Babylon Revisited: The Screenplay*, 189). Unfortunately, the attempt failed. In the original version, Charlie Wales, who suffers a nervous breakdown and becomes an alcoholic after the death of his wife, returns to Paris to get back his daughter, who is now living with his sister-in-law and her husband, the child's legal guardians. In the screenplay, Wales has been drugged by a canny doctor who has been employed by Wales's unethical partner. The purpose is to get Wales to sign over his daughter's trust fund so the partner can use the money to cover stock market losses. Wales is helped by a pretty nurse whom we assume he will later marry. Wales's partner then hires a hit-man to track down Wales in Switzerland. Fitzgerald had taken a story which contrasted the frenzied twenties with the more austere thirties, a story of loss and emptiness, and had turned it into a trite melodrama.

Furthermore, the dialogue at times was far too sentimental. A scene near the end of the film when Charlie Wales thinks he will not be able to regain custody of his daughter, and two friends, somewhat drunk, appear, is only one of many examples. Wales dances with his daughter and tells her that the friends are parasites and that their annoying behavior is the result of their loneliness:

VICTORIA
(gravely)
It looks as if nobody wants us to have fun together, doesn't it, Daddy.
Wales concentrates on making her have a good time.
WALES
Those people are just lonesome, honey.
(in tones of pathos)
They haven't found any-body to annoy *all-l-l* day.
She looks at him, takes her cue, and laughs.
WALES
So they had to annoy *some*body – just to practice.
VICTORIA
Who are they?
WALES
(in a stage whisper)
Parasites.
VICTORIA
From Paris?
WALES
No, a parasite is something you find everywhere.
(whispers again)
They want something you've got.
VICTORIA
What do they want?
WALES
Sometimes it's your happiness.
VICTORIA
(looks around with interest)
How do they get to be that?
WALES
Oh, they begin by not doing their lessons.
VICTORIA
(with a sigh)
I knew there'd be a moral in it.
(pause)
I wish there was some person who could talk to you without always ending up with a moral.
WALES
Darling, from now on, word of honor, that'll be me.
(Babylon Revisited: The Screenplay, 178–9)

Budd Schulberg has written in an introduction to the published script:

> To read the short story and then study this screenplay is to understand the terrible contortions of an artist driven to turn himself inside out and upside down in one last desperate reach for Hollywood status...Despite his theory that the novel would become passé, replaced by the new art of the motion picture, Fitzgerald the novelist lives, while Fitzgerald the movie man remains an almost-forgotten footnote to literary history. (*Babylon Revisited: The Screenplay*, 13–14)

But all of this was material for the fiction that he would write in 1939 and 1940. The seventeen Pat Hobby stories published in *Esquire* are brief, very funny vignettes. Pat is a broken-down, alcoholic, forty-nine-year-old Hollywood writer. When Pat's script is based on a novel or short story, he never reads the source. He has been working in the studios for twenty years in both the publicity departments and as a scriptwriter. He may have been a success at one time, but now he scrounges for work. He has been married and divorced twice. He earns $250 a week. He steals from other writers. Once he took money from sightseers and took them on a phony tour. None of this, except for the drinking, was Fitzgerald. One wonders, however, if at times he felt like a Pat Hobby, and that these stories were a reflection of his insecurity.

While some of the Pat Hobby stories refer back to an earlier Hollywood period (the murder of director William Desmond Taylor in 1922, for example), the stories were contemporaneous. Subjects included tours of Hollywood stars' homes as well as the studios, going to previews, the arrival of Orson Welles, the use of script clichés, and sucking up to film bosses, in this instance giving a Civil War film "a Jewish touch." A few times, Fitzgerald once again employed film imagery in his writing. For example, in "A Patriotic Short" (1940), Pat recalls meeting the president of the United States: "Pat's mind dissolved once more into the glamorous past." Later Pat takes a break from his work and goes to a studio water fountain where once again he daydreams about this meeting. Then to bring the reader back to the present, Fitzgerald uses the equivalent of a match cut, in which the camera cuts from one object or shot to another that is similar in shape or content:

> The president glanced over into Pat's property.
> "I suppose – " he said, " – that you get lots of inspiration sitting by the side of that fine pool."
> "Yes," said Pat, "Yes I do."
> [Fitzgerald then returns to the present and writes]
> ...Pat filled his cup at the cooler in the hall.   (*PH*, 116, 118–19)

And in "Pat Hobby's Christmas Wish" (1940) where Pat has a blackmail scheme and hopes to cash in, Fitzgerald writes, "Cash, cars, girls, swimming pools swam in a glittering montage before Pat's eye" (*PH*, 7).

The Pat Hobby stories are funny. However, the plots are not subtle and the prose style is spare. They were written quickly for the $250 each that would give Fitzgerald the leisure to write *The Last Tycoon*. But they were written with thought and care, the evidence in the numerous letters and telegrams to *Esquire* editor Arnold Gingrich including revisions or requests at times that the order of publication be changed.

Other Hollywood stories written about this time include "Last Kiss" (1940), a gloomy story – Fitzgerald found it "Unpleasant as hell except the end" (*Short Stories*, 757) – about a young, pretty, talented but temperamental and ill-advised actress who loses her chance for stardom. After *Cosmopolitan* rejected the story Fitzgerald stripped it intending to use it in *The Last Tycoon*. But other than an English heroine whom producer Jim Leonard sees at a dance and a scene in a drugstore, there are few similarities. A second Hollywood story, "Director's Special," written in 1939, about Academy Award-winning actress Dolly Borton, who loses her husband to another actress, becomes penniless, and then wins a starring role, was rejected by *Collier's* magazine because of what was felt to be its elliptical nature.

Had Fitzgerald lived to complete *The Last Tycoon*, it seems obvious that the reaction would have been far different. At the time of publication, while a few critics were not overly impressed, most felt that it would have been counted among Fitzgerald's best work. J. Donald Adams in the *New York Times Book Review* wrote that "uncompleted though it is, one would be blind indeed not to see that it would have been Fitzgerald's best novel and a very fine one." James Thurber in the *New Republic* wondered about this extreme judgment, especially since he felt that it was a work in progress and some rewriting would have been needed. And yet it "would have been another book in the fine one-color mood of 'The Great Gatsby,' with that book's sure form and sure direction." Stephen Vincent Benét in the *Saturday Review of Literature* wrote: "Had Fitzgerald been permitted to finish the book, I think there is no doubt that it would have added a major character and a major novel to American fiction. As it is, 'The Last Tycoon' is a great deal more than a fragment. It shows the full powers of the author, at their height and at their best" (Bryer, *Critical Reception*).

For the structure of this last novel, Fitzgerald returned partly to his own past. He had always been aware of his literary models. For *Gatsby*, for example, he wrote that he had been influenced by those who were writing the dramatic novel, a novel of selectivity. *Tender is the Night*, he said, was more like the longer novels of the past, which he called the philosophical or psychological novel. *The Last Tycoon* was to be similar to *Gatsby* with a similar number of chapters, similar number of words, and so on. The published plans show us how much it intentionally resembled *Gatsby* in form. "It is a novel *à la Flaubert* without 'ideas' but only people moved singly and in mass through what I hope are authentic moods... The resemblance is rather to 'Gatsby' than to anything else I've written," he wrote his wife in 1940 (*Life in Letters*, 470–1).

Fitzgerald was writing a love story, about a great leader, and about Hollywood. He researched his subject. The notes to *The Last Tycoon* include references to Terry Ramsaye's two-volume history of the silent screen, *A Million and One Nights*, director William deMille's autobiography, *Hollywood Saga*, and articles in *Fortune* about MGM and Thalberg. Other notes include requests to his secretary, Frances Kroll, to go to the Pickwick, a Hollywood bookstore, to purchase film books as well as getting others from the public library and doing research there about Thalberg's life.

Cecilia Brady was based partly on Fitzgerald's daughter. His relationship with Sheilah Graham was translated partly into the relationship between Kathleen Moore and Stahr. The notes to the novel as well as Fitzgerald's correspondence also give us clues to the sources of a few of the other characters. Irving Thalberg, head of the studio at MGM in the late 1920s and early 1930s, for example, is mentioned a number of times. To Kenneth Littauer, of *Collier's* magazine, Fitzgerald wrote: "Stahr... is Irving Thalberg – and *this is my great secret*..." Others mentioned include actor Harry Carey as a model for Johnny Swanson, studio boss Marcus Loew as a model for Mr. Marcus, producer Harry Rapf as a model for Leanbaum, Joseph M. Mankiewicz for Jacques La Borwitz, novelist Aldous Huxley as a model for the writer Boxley, and so on. But Fitzgerald was writing fiction. This is what he wrote Littauer and what is most obvious in his portrayal of Monroe Stahr, who has some of the characteristics of Fitzgerald's friend, director King Vidor, some of theater impresario Florenz Ziegfeld, and probably those of a half dozen others, including, of course, Fitzgerald himself. He told Littauer that "he [Thalberg] may be recognized – but it will also be recognized that *no single fact is actually true*." Fitzgerald even explained this in an inscription intended for Norma Shearer. He wrote: "Though the story is purely imaginary perhaps you could see it as an attempt to preserve something of Irving" (*Life in Letters*, 409, 468).

Stahr was meant to be the exemplification of the great leader as Thalberg had been for Fitzgerald. But Thalberg was only one of the great leaders he admired or read about. Fitzgerald was a history buff. His library contained many historical works, in particular about the French Revolution, the Civil

War, and World War I, and he had always been interested in the lives of great men. In the late 1920s, he had even discussed with King Vidor the possibility of collaborating on a film about Napoleon.

It is also not too fruitful to attempt to accurately date the events in the novel. According to the letter to Littauer it was set during four or five months in 1935. Many of the songs mentioned in the novel come from 1934–5. Cecilia Brady, his narrator, says the events take place five years earlier. Does this mean five years before the intended date of publication, 1941, that is 1936? At another time, Fitzgerald suggested that it was set in approximately 1932. Some of the films alluded to in the novel were being made during Fitzgerald's 1931–2 trip to Hollywood; others were being made during his final years there. As with his characterizations, here too the films are mixed up. For example, the film that the English scriptwriter Boxley is working on – the writers feel it has too many characters and Boxley suggests that it needs even more – not only has characteristics of *Infidelity* but also the 1932 *Grand Hotel* and the 1939 *Stagecoach*, both of which Fitzgerald mentioned in his notes. The film that Broaca, Riemmund, and the others are discussing has characteristics of *Red Headed Woman* (Stahr says, "The premise of this story is that the girl did have dumb admiration for her boss"), and possibly *Three Comrades* and director W. S. Van Dyke II's *San Francisco* (*LOTLT*, 39).

Of course, some events are based partly on actual occurrences, such as the famous earthquake in the studios in 1936. But Fitzgerald was not in Hollywood in that year and there had been other earthquakes. And while the rivalry between Stahr and Brady is based on the rivalry between Thalberg and head of MGM Louis B. Mayer, Mayer and Thalberg, so far as we know, never attempted to murder each other as was planned for the novel.

Part of the greatness of this final novel is how well it reflects Fitzgerald's ambiguous feelings about Hollywood. And the description of what happens in the film studios has yet to be equaled.

But above all there is the exceptional rhythmic prose style. The description of a kiss at Kathleen's door is only one example. Stahr asks Kathleen if she has her key and she replies that she does. Then Fitzgerald writes:

> This was the moment to go in but she wanted to see him once more and she leaned her head to the left, then to the right trying to catch his face against the last twilight. She leaned too far and too long and it was natural when his hand touched the back of her upper arm and shoulder and pressed her forward into the darkness of his throat. She shut her eyes feeling the bevel of the key in her tight clutched hand. She said "Oh" in an expiring sigh and then "Oh" again as he pulled her in close and his chin pushed her cheek around gently. They

were both smiling just faintly and she was frowning too as the inch between them melted into darkness. (*LOTLT*, 86)

In short, the film work was beneficial. It extricated Fitzgerald from a period in which he had been depressed and incapable of writing successfully. It enabled him to repay most of his debts and it gave him the time to start his last novel. It provided him with a plot. His unfinished novel captured a unique portrayal of the film industry. He left us with a wonderful work in progress. Undoubtedly, the final version would have been greater.

NOTE

All references to *The Last Tycoon* in this chapter are from *The Love of the Last Tycoon*, ed. Bruccoli. The quotation from *The Beautiful and Damned* is from the 1998 edition.

11

JACKSON R. BRYER

The critical reputation of F. Scott Fitzgerald

1940–1949

F. Scott Fitzgerald's familiar and often-quoted observation that "there are no second acts in American lives" (*LT*, 163; it had a certain vogue during Bill Clinton's impeachment proceedings in 1999) is certainly belied by the history of Fitzgerald's own critical reputation. A celebrity and acclaimed literary figure at age twenty-three in 1920, when his first novel, *This Side of Paradise*, became a bestseller (it went through twelve printings in two years and sold 49,075 copies; Bruccoli, *Some Sort of Epic Grandeur*, 137) his short fiction eventually commanded a price of $4,000 per story from the *Saturday Evening Post* (he published nineteen at that rate between June 1929 and April 1931; Mangum, *A Fortune Yet*, 179). But at his death on December 21, 1940, he had not published a book in five years, his fee for a story had dipped to $250 (Mangum, *A Fortune Yet*, 181), and during the last year of his life, seventy-two copies of his nine books were sold (Maimon, "F. Scott Fitzgerald's Book Sales," 166). His letters to his longtime editor Maxwell Perkins during 1939 and 1940 were filled with ideas on how to resuscitate what he felt was his forgotten name with the American reading public. Typically and ironically, the last two sentences he ever wrote to Perkins, on December 13, were "How much will you sell the plates of *This Side of Paradise* for? I think it has a chance for a new life" (*Letters*, 291). Another revealing anecdote is Budd Schulberg's admission that when, in early 1939, as a fledgling screenwriter he was asked to collaborate with Fitzgerald (whose fiction he admired greatly) on a film about the Dartmouth Winter Carnival, Schulberg thought Fitzgerald was dead (Bruccoli, *Some Sort of Epic Grandeur*, 454). In twenty years, Fitzgerald's career and reputation had literally gone from the top to virtual obscurity.

Indications of the "second act" Fitzgerald was to experience, albeit posthumously, began to appear literally within days of his death. Newspapers across the country and overseas, which had totally ignored Fitzgerald at least since 1934 and 1935, when his last two books had appeared, ran editorials on his passing (Bryer, *Critical Reputation*, [1967], 202–9). While several of these asserted that he had outlived his career – Fitzgerald, said the Raleigh *News and Observer*, "did not die before his time. His time was already gone before he began to be old" (Bryer, *Critical Reputation*, 202) – there was abundant praise as well. The Los Angeles *Times* hailed him as "a brilliant, sometimes profound writer," the Indianapolis *News* predicted that his fiction "will have a permanent place in American literature," and the New York *World-Telegram* called him "the Gibbon of the jazz age, the Boswell of 'all the sad young men,' of 'the beautiful and damned' " (Bryer, *Critical Reputation*, 204, 203, 206). Then, in two issues of the venerable *New Republic* (March 3 and March 17, 1941), a group of Fitzgerald's most respected literary colleagues – John Peale Bishop, Malcolm Cowley, John Dos Passos, John O'Hara, and Glenway Wescott – weighed in with more substantial appreciations which almost a half-century later are still regarded as key documents in the restoration of Fitzgerald's critical reputation.

This flurry of attention accorded Fitzgerald shortly after his death was not only a harbinger of what was to come; it also was a reprise, if abbreviated and more limited, of the sort of coverage Fitzgerald and his wife Zelda had received during the 1920s and early 1930s, when they were among the most famous couples in the world. Their celebrity is graphically documented in the clippings which both Fitzgeralds carefully preserved in their scrapbooks. Generous excerpts from these scrapbooks are reproduced in *The Romantic Egoists: A Pictorial Autobiography From the Scrapbooks and Albums of Scott and Zelda Fitzgerald* (1974), edited by Matthew J. Bruccoli, Scottie Fitzgerald Smith, and Joan P. Kerr, surely one of the most underrated and overlooked works of Fitzgerald scholarship. There, alongside clippings of articles by and about both Fitzgeralds and memorabilia (which start with Fitzgerald's baby book) and letters (beginning with one written to his mother from summer camp when he was eight), are excerpts from Fitzgerald's published writings (arranged by the editors so that they are placed most appropriately chronologically) and hundreds of photographs. This compilation not only documents the Fitzgeralds' celebrity but also their own relishing of that attention. The contemporary critical scrutiny which Fitzgerald received is more fully represented in Jackson R. Bryer's *F. Scott Fitzgerald: The Critical Reception* (1978), which reprints 338 contemporary reviews which Fitzgerald's books received between 1920 and 1941. Taken together, these two books show the heights from which his reputation and visibility had descended in 1940. For a brief but comprehensive survey of Fitzgerald's critical reception during his lifetime, one can also consult pp. 292–5 in

Bryer's bibliographical essay on Fitzgerald in *Sixteen Modern American Authors* (1974).

After the obituary tributes of late 1940 and early 1941, the next major event in the history of Fitzgerald's literary reputation was the publication, on October 27, 1941, of a volume which included the incomplete text of *The Last Tycoon*, the novel Fitzgerald was working on when he died, along with *The Great Gatsby* and four of his best short stories – "May Day," "The Diamond as Big as the Ritz," "Absolution," and "Crazy Sunday." Reviewers greeted this publication with more uniformly positive responses than they had directed at any of his books during his lifetime. J. Donald Adams in the *New York Times Book Review* asserted that *The Last Tycoon* "would have been Fitzgerald's best novel and a very fine one"; Fanny Butcher in the Chicago *Tribune* hailed it as "the first major novel of Hollywood"; and W. T. Scott in the Providence *Journal* called it "a book of real writing – a living memorial" (Bryer, *Critical Reception*, 99, 100, 104). Most eloquent and prophetic, however, were the words of famed poet and essayist Stephen Vincent Benét, writing in the *Saturday Review of Literature*: "You can take off your hats now, gentlemen, and I think perhaps you had better. This is not a legend, this is a reputation – and, seen in perspective, it may well be one of the most secure reputations of our time" (Kazin, *F. Scott Fitzgerald*, 131–2).

Most commentators agree that, despite this immediate recognition in 1940–1, the first significant date in the "second act" of the history of Fitzgerald's critical reputation is 1945. In that year, two major books appeared: Edmund Wilson's edition of *The Crack-Up*, which contained essays, notebook entries, and letters to and from Fitzgerald, along with critical essays about him (including reprintings of three of the 1941 *New Republic* tributes – by Bishop, Dos Passos, and Wescott); and *The Portable F. Scott Fitzgerald*, selected by Dorothy Parker, which contained the full texts of two novels, *The Great Gatsby* and *Tender is the Night*, and nine short stories. The publication of these two collections, especially Wilson's, prompted several of America's leading men of letters to write extensive review-essays which used the occasion to reevaluate Fitzgerald's career and his place in American literary history. These assessments – by, among others, J. Donald Adams, Malcolm Cowley, Alfred Kazin, Joseph Wood Krutch, John O'Hara, J. F. Powers, Mark Schorer, Lionel Trilling, William Troy, and Andrews Wanning – represented the first and remain some of the best serious critical essays directed at Fitzgerald's work.[1]

With this impetus, other writers, critics, and academics began to turn their attention to Fitzgerald. These early articles set patterns for much later commentary. John Berryman wrote a major piece in the *Kenyon Review*

(Winter 1946), which praised *The Great Gatsby* as "a masterpiece" but had harsher words for the later work. His assessment reverberated for many years as *Gatsby* became the focus of much of the Fitzgerald criticism which followed. Milton Hindus inaugurated what became a long-running controversy in Fitzgerald studies with a consideration of "F. Scott Fitzgerald and Literary Anti-Semitism"; Martin Kallich did the same with respect to Fitzgerald's ambivalence towards wealth in "F. Scott Fitzgerald: Money or Morals"; and the first extended essays on Fitzgerald by British critics were written by Alan Ross in *Horizon* ("Rumble Among the Drums: F. Scott Fitzgerald [1896–1940] and the Jazz Age") and D. S. Savage in *World Review* ("Scott Fitzgerald, the Man and His Work").

1950–1959

The late 1940s had seen the appearance of a series of important articles on Fitzgerald by Arthur Mizener, who was a Professor of English at Carleton College in Minnesota. These culminated with the publication, in 1951, of Mizener's critical biography, *The Far Side of Paradise*, the first book on Fitzgerald. That same year, the second important date of what soon came to be called the "Fitzgerald Revival," also saw the publication of the first comprehensive gathering of Fitzgerald's short fiction, *The Stories of F. Scott Fitzgerald*, twenty-eight stories selected by Malcolm Cowley, and the first collection of Fitzgerald criticism, Alfred Kazin's *F. Scott Fitzgerald: The Man and His Work*. It is one of the oddities of Fitzgerald's critical reputation that to date, nearly a half-century later, two of these books have not really been superseded. Mizener's biography, a model balance of a detailed and carefully documented account of the life and an informed, sensitive, and authoritative analysis of the work, remains the best single biographical source (although, inevitably, new information has surfaced in subsequent biographies) as well as one of the most reliable critical studies. Similarly, while since 1951 there have been many collections of reprinted and of original essays and reviews about Fitzgerald's works, Kazin's regrettably and rather surprisingly remains the most comprehensive such gathering of reprinted materials (besides a four-volume British anthology which is prohibitively expensive and virtually unobtainable).

Mizener's biography did remarkably well commercially; within five days of its January publication date it had sold an astonishing 20,000 copies and by the end of the year, the total was over 70,000 (Maimon, "F. Scott Fitzgerald's Book Sales," 170, 172). It, along with the Cowley story collection and the Kazin anthology of criticism, also elicited many of the same kind of review-essays which had been generated by *The Crack-Up* and

The Portable F. Scott Fitzgerald in 1945 – in this instance by William Barrett, Joseph Warren Beach, Horace Gregory, Charles Jackson, R. W. B. Lewis, V. S. Pritchett, Delmore Schwartz, James Thurber, Perry Miller, Lionel Trilling, and Charles Weir, Jr.[2]

The decade of the 1950s also saw the publication of major critical essays in leading literary journals and book chapters. Three of the best of the former were written by Malcolm Cowley, a contemporary and friend of Fitzgerald's who was to become one of his most articulate and astute critics. The first, "The Scott Fitzgerald Story," registered its author's dissatisfaction with Mizener's biography and offered Cowley's own account, placing the emphasis on "the moral atmosphere of the period in which Fitzgerald flourished and declined." In "Fitzgerald: The Double Man," Cowley reiterated a thesis that he had first introduced in his 1941 review-essay on *The Last Tycoon* and which became one of the benchmarks of Fitzgerald criticism, that his "distinguishing mark as a writer" was his double vision, "the maximum of critical detachment...combined with the maximum of immersion in the drama." Cowley's third essay (*New Republic*, August 20, 1951) dealt with the composition of *Tender is the Night* and presented the idea that Fitzgerald had wanted to revise the novel by reversing the order of its first two books, an intention realized when, later in 1951, Scribners reissued the novel in revised form – with Cowley's essay as an introduction. Thus began one of the major controversies in Fitzgerald scholarship: while virtually all subsequent editions of *Tender* have used the original 1934 text, there are still scholars who feel that the revised version should also be available.

During this period Fitzgerald began to be the subject of major sections of critical books on American literature. Chief among these were John W. Aldridge's examination of Fitzgerald's five novels, "Fitzgerald – The Honor and the Vision of Paradise" (*After the Lost Generation* [1951]); Leslie Fiedler's "Some Notes on F. Scott Fitzgerald" (*An End to Innocence* [1955]); Frederick J. Hoffman's discussion of *Tender is the Night* (*Freudianism and the Literary Mind* [1957]); Hoffman's extended analyses of *This Side of Paradise* and *Gatsby* (*The Twenties* [1955]); Wright Morris's discussion of "The Crack-Up" essays (*The Territory Ahead* [1958]); Lionel Trilling's essay on "The Crack-Up" and *Gatsby* (*The Liberal Imagination* [1950]); and Colin Wilson's consideration of Fitzgerald as "the modern outsider" (*Religion and the Rebel* [1957]).

As noted above, in this first phase, *Gatsby* received by far the greatest attention of Fitzgerald's works. Perhaps the most influential early study was Marius Bewley's "Scott Fitzgerald's Criticism of America," probably the first and certainly one of the best analyses of *Gatsby* as a critique of the American experience and the American Dream and as a work with universal themes and appeal.

Despite this activity, the first full-length critical book on Fitzgerald did not appear until 1957 and it was published abroad. James E. Miller, Jr.'s *The Fictional Technique of Scott Fitzgerald*, largely neglected until its republication (in somewhat revised form) in the U.S. in 1964 as *F. Scott Fitzgerald: His Art and His Technique*, was an important and intelligent study which emphasized the literary influences to which Fitzgerald was subject (Wells, Mencken, James, Conrad, Cather, Keats, Wharton) and focused on the literary techniques in the novels. Another important book which came out at the end of the 1950s was *Beloved Infidel* (1958), Sheilah Graham's autobiography, which, for the first time, revealed that she had been Fitzgerald's lover during his last years in Hollywood. Unjustifiably ignored as a major contribution to Fitzgerald studies, *Beloved Infidel* was praised by Edmund Wilson, in a *New Yorker* review, as the best portrait of Fitzgerald in print. It included, besides Graham's reminiscences, many heretofore undiscovered Fitzgerald letters and poems. It was also the most prominent of yet another species of Fitzgerald commentary which began to appear in the 1950s, personal memories of Fitzgerald by his friends and associates. Among those who wrote this sort of piece were Struthers Burt, Lawrence Stallings, James Thurber, Andrew Turnbull, Shane Leslie, George Jean Nathan, and Frances Kroll Ring.

The late 1950s also saw new collections of Fitzgerald's works, as well as reprinted ones. Most important of the former was Mizener's edition of *Afternoon of an Author* (1957), which presented twenty previously uncollected essays and stories, most drawn from the late years of Fitzgerald's career. And in 1958 alone, Scribners reprinted *The Beautiful and Damned*, Fitzgerald's second novel, reissued *The Great Gatsby* in a single volume for the first time, published *The Last Tycoon* on its own, and issued a trade edition of *Afternoon of an Author* (it had originally been published by the Princeton University Library, the repository of Fitzgerald's papers). In 1959, Scribners brought out a new edition of *Flappers and Philosophers*, Fitzgerald's first short story collection. Besides generating more reviews and review-essays, these books played a big role in sharply increasing the sales figures of Fitzgerald titles: in 1955, the five Fitzgerald books in print at Scribners sold 6,992 copies; by 1960, with twelve titles in print, total sales were 177,849 (Maimon, "F. Scott Fitzgerald's Book Sales," 170, 172). In Great Britain, the Bodley Head publishing firm issued Volumes I (1958) and II (1959) of what would eventually become a six-volume edition of Fitzgerald's fiction. And just to punctuate the end of the decade, in 1958, Matthew J. Bruccoli, destined to become the most influential and productive Fitzgerald scholar/critic, founded the *Fitzgerald Newsletter*, a modest but important quarterly publication, which, for the next decade, included brief articles and notes and, in each issue, an invaluable extensive checklist of recent material by and about Fitzgerald. In 1951, John Abbot Clark had exclaimed, "It would seem that all Fitzgerald had broken loose" (Quoted in Bryer, *Sixteen Modern American Authors*, 299). One can only imagine what he would have said at the end of the decade!

1960–1969

Fitzgerald scholarship and criticism in the 1960s featured publication of still more "new" works by Fitzgerald, the first spate of significant full-length critical studies, the beginnings of bibliographical scholarship on Fitzgerald, important personal reminiscences, the founding of a substantial annual journal entirely devoted to Fitzgerald and Hemingway, and a continuing blizzard of critical essays and book chapters.

In 1960, Scribners published *Six Tales of the Jazz Age and Other Stories*, which collected nine Fitzgerald stories which had long been out of print. *The Pat Hobby Stories*, published by Scribners in 1962, exhumed from the pages of *Esquire* seventeen stories about a Hollywood hack screenwriter which Fitzgerald had published in the late 1930s. Arthur Mizener's selections for *The Fitzgerald Reader* (1963) featured a diverse and judicious sampling (*Gatsby*, chapters I–VI of *Tender*, chapters I and IV of *The Last Tycoon*, and a generous gathering of stories and essays). John Kuehl's editions of *The Apprentice Fiction of F. Scott Fitzgerald, 1909–1917* (1965) and the *Thoughtbook of Francis Scott Key Fitzgerald* (1965) both afforded early glimpses of Fitzgerald's talent. The former published for the first time in book form fifteen short stories and two plays he published at St. Paul Academy, the Newman School, and Princeton University; while the *Thoughtbook* was his diary, begun in August 1910, when he was fourteen, and ending in February 1911. Two briefer previously unpublished items surfaced as well: "Dearly Beloved" (*Fitzgerald/Hemingway Annual*, 1969), which was notable principally as Fitzgerald's only fiction focused on a black character; and "My Generation" (*Esquire*, October 1968), a 1939 essay defending his age group, which had recently been criticized by his daughter in an article in *Mademoiselle*.

While, up until 1960, there had been only one book-length critical study of Fitzgerald, the decade of the 1960s saw eight books and two pamphlets, as well as the American edition of Miller's book, alluded to earlier. Several of these remain important and frequently consulted critical resources. In the latter category are Richard D. Lehan's *F. Scott Fitzgerald and the Craft of Fiction* (1966), which provided excellent explications of the novels and expertly placed Fitzgerald among his contemporaries; Robert Sklar's *F. Scott Fitzgerald: The Last Laocoön* (1967), which was notable for its locating of Fitzgerald at the end of the genteel tradition, for its sections on the influences of Twain, Tarkington, and Joyce on Fitzgerald's female characters, and for its explications of the short stories; and Sergio Perosa's *The Art of F. Scott Fitzgerald* (1965), which stressed "the interdependent links" between the stories and novels and ranged over the full extent of Fitzgerald's career. Of the briefer volumes, Kenneth Eble's *F. Scott Fitzgerald* (1963; rev. edn., 1977), K. G. W. Cross's *F. Scott Fitzgerald* (1964), and Milton Hindus's *F. Scott Fitzgerald: An Introduction and Interpretation* (1968) were useful although somewhat superficial in their analyses. The same was true for the two pamphlets, Charles E. Shain's *F. Scott Fitzgerald* (1961) and Edwin M. Moseley's *F. Scott Fitzgerald: A Critical Essay* (1967). The other two books, William Goldhurst's *F. Scott Fitzgerald and His Contemporaries* (1963) and Henry Dan Piper's *F. Scott Fitzgerald: A Critical Portrait* (1965), while intermittently of interest, were superseded by later research and scholarship.

Important bibliographical research on Fitzgerald began in the 1960s. Jackson R. Bryer's *The Critical Reputation of F. Scott Fitzgerald* (1967) was an exhaustive, mostly annotated, listing of over 2,000 reviews, essays, book sections, newspaper articles, and graduate theses on Fitzgerald. Bryer also wrote two bibliographical essays surveying Fitzgerald research and criticism: "F. Scott Fitzgerald: A Review of Research and Scholarship" and "F. Scott Fitzgerald" in his edition of *Fifteen Modern American Authors: A Survey of Research and Criticism* (1969). In 1963, the American Literature Section of the Modern Language Association began publishing *American Literary Scholarship*, an annual survey of the year's work on American literature. Each volume in this continuing series has contained a chapter devoted to Fitzgerald and Hemingway, written over the years by such major scholars as Frederick J. Hoffman, William White, Jackson R. Bryer, Scott Donaldson, Michael S. Reynolds, Gerry Brenner, Susan F. Beegel, and Albert J. DeFazio III; it remains the single best ongoing source for reliable evaluation of research on Fitzgerald.

The decade of the 1960s also saw the publication of several worthwhile important personal reminiscences. The most important of these was Andrew Turnbull's memoir/biography, *Scott Fitzgerald* (1962), which combined Turnbull's own memories of Fitzgerald (whom he knew when Turnbull was eleven and the Fitzgeralds rented a house on the grounds of Turnbull's parents' Baltimore estate) with a scrupulously researched biography. One year later, Turnbull edited the first volume of Fitzgerald's correspondence, *The Letters of F. Scott Fitzgerald*, which, while highly selective (according to its editor, he published only half of the letters then available), rather clumsily arranged by recipient rather than chronologically, and unscholarly in its editing, nonetheless gave us our first comprehensive glimpse of Fitzgerald's important correspondences – with Maxwell Perkins, with Hemingway, with his wife and daughter, and with Edmund Wilson, among many others.

Ernest Hemingway's posthumous *A Moveable Feast* (1964) provided a devastating portrait of Fitzgerald during a disastrous motor trip from Lyon to Paris in the spring of 1925 and much criticism of Zelda Fitzgerald. Morley Callaghan's *That Summer in Paris* (1963) was a much less vituperative account of Fitzgerald in Paris in 1929; while Calvin Tompkins's *New Yorker* profile of Fitzgerald's friends Gerald and Sara Murphy ("Living Well is the Best Revenge," July 28, 1962; reprinted in 1971 as a book with the same title) contained much about the Fitzgeralds. Laura Hearne, in "A Summer with F. Scott Fitzgerald," published her detailed diary of her time as Fitzgerald's secretary in 1935; and Sheilah Graham's second book about Fitzgerald, *College of One* (1967), focused on the two-year liberal arts course Fitzgerald designed to educate her. In "Old Scott: The Mask, the Myth, and the Man," Budd Schulberg recounted his memories of Fitzgerald in Hollywood in the late 1930s.

Four volumes of reprinted Fitzgerald criticism appeared in the 1960s. The most comprehensive was Arthur Mizener's *F. Scott Fitzgerald: A Collection of Critical Essays* (1963), whose nineteen selections duplicated some of those in Kazin's 1951 collection but also added more recent essays and book chapters. The three other collections were more narrowly focused. Frederick J. Hoffman's *"The Great Gatsby": A Study* (1962) included ten reprinted pieces on the novel, two previously unpublished essays, selections from Fitzgerald's letters and fiction, and relevant background materials. Ernest H. Lockridge's *Twentieth Century Interpretations of "The Great Gatsby"* (1968) duplicated many of the selections in the Mizener and/or Hoffman collections, although it did contain an excellent new piece, "Dream, Design, and Interpretation in *The Great Gatsby*," by David L. Minter. Marvin J. LaHood's *"Tender Is the Night": Essays in Criticism* (1969) was an early indication of a shift in Fitzgerald studies away from the exclusive focus on *Gatsby* among the novels in that it reprinted the best of the early essays and book sections on *Tender*.

In 1969, Matthew J. Bruccoli founded the *Fitzgerald/Hemingway Annual* as a successor to the *Fitzgerald Newsletter*. From its inception until its cessation in 1979, this substantial hardbound volume, which often contained over 350 pages per issue, was the source of valuable critical essays, bibliographical and textual pieces, newly discovered letters and texts by Fitzgerald, reviews of recent publications, and an annual checklist of new primary and secondary materials.

1970–1979

The 1970s saw the continuation and expansion of the trends established in the 1960s: significant bibliographical studies; even more "new" Fitzgerald works, principally collections of stories and of letters; a major biography of Zelda Fitzgerald, along with two book-length biographical studies of her husband and more personal reminiscences; five collections of reprinted essays and reviews; seven full-length critical books; and the usual torrent of critical essays and book chapters.

The decade of the 1970s is notable in the history of Fitzgerald studies for the abundance of bibliographical and textual work it produced. Matthew J. Bruccoli's *F. Scott Fitzgerald: A Descriptive Bibliography* (1972), along with its *Supplement* (1980) and revised edition (1987), came to represent the definitive primary listing of Fitzgerald's writings. Exhaustive and meticulously detailed, it included everything that any researcher could conceivably want to know about Fitzgerald's works and dwarfed all previous and subsequent bibliographical research on Fitzgerald primary sources. Bruccoli's "'A Might Collation': Animadversions on the Text of F. Scott Fitzgerald" (*Editing Twentieth Century Texts* [1972]) was a similarly definitive examination of the highly corrupt texts of *Gatsby* and *Tender* then in common use; and his *"The Last of the Novelists": F. Scott Fitzgerald and "The Last Tycoon"* (1977) was a careful reconstruction of the composition process and posthumous publication of Fitzgerald's last novel which convincingly showed that Edmund Wilson, as editor of the 1941 edition, obscured "the gestational nature of Fitzgerald's work" and misled "readers into judging work-in-progress as completed stages."

Three other books published during the 1970s provided valuable resources for textual study of *Gatsby*: Bruccoli's edition of *"The Great Gatsby": A Facsimile of the Manuscript* (1973), Andrew T. Crosland's *A Concordance to F. Scott Fitzgerald's "The Great Gatsby"* (1975), and Bruccoli's *Apparatus for F. Scott Fitzgerald's "The Great Gatsby" [Under the Red, White, and Blue]* (1974). The latter was designed so that, using the collations, emendations, and revisions Bruccoli provided, any reader could mark up his own copy of *Gatsby* and prepare a definitive text.

More "new" books by Fitzgerald were published in the 1970s than had appeared during his entire lifetime. The first half of Matthew J. Bruccoli and Jackson R. Bryer's *F. Scott Fitzgerald in His Own Time* (1971) brought back into print obscure works by Fitzgerald (selected by Bruccoli) which spanned his entire career – from verse, lyrics, and humorous sketches he wrote as an undergraduate through book reviews and newspaper articles on love, marriage, and sex he wrote in the 1920s, down to blurbs, public statements, and letters to the editor from the 1930s. Bruccoli, alone and with collaborators, was also responsible for presenting several other volumes of importance. His edition of *The Price Was High: The Last Uncollected Stories of F. Scott Fitzgerald* (1979) performed the extremely valuable task of reprinting from the magazines in which they originally appeared thirty-nine previously uncollected stories and one ("On Your Own") never before published (plus ten previously collected stories), thus greatly facilitating study of Fitzgerald as a writer of short fiction. *Bits of Paradise* (1973), edited by Bruccoli and the Fitzgeralds' daughter, Scottie Fitzgerald Smith, similarly presented eleven previously uncollected stories by Scott (including "The Swimmers," which is one of his best), nine fictional sketches by Zelda, and one they wrote together. *The Basil and Josephine Stories*, edited by Jackson R. Bryer and John Kuehl, was the first book publication of these two series of stories about adolescents (eight about Basil, five about Josephine) which Fitzgerald had originally published in the *Saturday Evening Post* between 1928 and 1931; only three of the stories in the Bryer and Kuehl volume had never been collected but this was the first time the two series had ever appeared together (also included was one Basil story which the *Post* had not published).

During the 1970s, Bruccoli also edited editions of *F. Scott Fitzgerald's Screenplay for "Three Comrades" by Erich Maria Remarque* (1978), the only film assignment during his three sojourns in Hollywood for which Fitzgerald received screen credit; of *The Notebooks of F. Scott Fitzgerald* (1978); of *F. Scott Fitzgerald's Ledger: A Facsimile* (1973), the author's record of his and his wife's publications and how much they were paid for each and his "Outline Chart of My Life" from 1896 to 1935; and, in collaboration with Scottie Fitzgerald Smith and Joan P. Kerr, of *The Romantic Egoists* (1974), the expertly prepared gathering from the Fitzgeralds' scrapbooks mentioned at the beginning of this essay.

During the 1970s, Fitzgerald's career as a playwright, short-lived as it was, received increased exposure – with Alan Margolies's edition of *F. Scott Fitzgerald's St. Paul Plays: 1911–1914* (1978), which was the first publication of the four plays Fitzgerald wrote as a teenager for the Elizabethan Dramatic Club in his hometown; and the reissuing in 1976 by Scribners of Fitzgerald's one published play, *The Vegetable* (1923), with appendices which included scenes cut from the manuscript during its author's final revisions.

Two of Fitzgerald's most significant and long-standing business and personal relationships were those with his literary agent Harold Ober and his editor Maxwell Perkins. Excerpts from his correspondence with Ober and Perkins had appeared in Turnbull's 1963 volume of selected letters; but the publication early in the 1970s of *Dear Scott/Dear Max: The Fitzgerald–Perkins Correspondence*, edited by John Kuehl and Jackson R. Bryer (1971), and *As Ever, Scott Fitz: Letters Between F. Scott Fitzgerald and His Literary Agent, Harold Ober – 1919–1940*, edited by Matthew J. Bruccoli, with the assistance of Jennifer McCabe Atkinson (1972), presented much more complete pictures of these key friendships. Each book included a generous selection from both sides of the correspondence, as well as a scholarly introduction and notes provided by the editors.

Nancy Milford's *Zelda* (1970) managed to tell the story of Zelda Fitzgerald's life and work and of the Fitzgeralds' marriage in a manner which pleased both academics and a general public which found attractive Milford's depiction of Zelda as a pre-Women's Liberation liberated woman. While this highly readable biography emphasized telling Zelda's story at the expense of in-depth analysis and evaluation, it was an undeniably influential book whose effect is still being felt in Fitzgerald studies. Compared to it, Sara Mayfield's *Exiles from Paradise* (1971), which, despite the fact that its author knew Zelda for forty years and Scott for twenty, was strident and unconvincing in its determination to blame Scott for what befell Zelda during their marriage and in its insistence that she was the "natural" and "original" writer that neither he nor Hemingway were. Similarly, Aaron Latham's *Crazy Sundays* (1971), while it was a lively anecdote-filled reconstruction of Fitzgerald's Hollywood years, was devoid of any analysis of Fitzgerald's movie work and contained a number of factual and interpretive errors and omissions. Only Milford's book, of the three biographical accounts published in the 1970s, was a substantial full-length contribution.

There were several briefer biographical volumes and essays published during the decade. Arthur Mizener's *Scott Fitzgerald and His World* (1972) was worthwhile less for its largely familiar biographical account than for its numerous photographs of the Fitzgeralds and of persons and places associated with them. John F. Koblas's *F. Scott Fitzgerald in Minnesota* (1978) was a fifty-page booklet which combined a superficial biographical account with more valuable descriptions, discussions, and photographs of thirty-five locations in and around St. Paul with Fitzgerald associations. Matthew J. Bruccoli's *Scott and Ernest: The Authority of Failure and the Authority of Success* (1978) gathered all the available documentary evidence – letters, reminiscences, interviews, published autobiographical accounts by both principals, and previous research – and presented a very detailed and authoritative account of what was undoubtedly the most complex and troubling relationship Fitzgerald had, aside from his marriage, a relationship also examined by Ruth Prigozy in " 'A Matter of Measurement': The Tangled Relationship Between Fitzgerald and Hemingway."

The most important of the personal reminiscences published during the decade was Anthony Buttitta's *After the Good Gay Times* (1974), which was a remarkably vivid and full recreation of Buttitta's encounters with Fitzgerald in the summer of 1935 when the latter visited Buttitta's Asheville, North Carolina, bookstore. Sheilah Graham's third book on Fitzgerald, *The Real F. Scott Fitzgerald* (1976), while worthwhile as a first-hand account, did not add very much to what she had said in her two previous books.

But by far the most articulate and authoritative personal memories of the Fitzgeralds written in the 1970s were those offered by their daughter Scottie – in her "Foreword" to *Bits of Paradise* (1973), her "Introduction" to *The Romantic Egoists* (1974), in her "Foreword" to *As Ever, Scott Fitz* (1972), in her "Où Sont Les Soleils d'Antan? François 'Fijeralde'?" in Bruccoli and Clark's *F. Scott Fitzgerald and Ernest M. Hemingway in Paris* (1972), in "Notes About My Now-Famous Father" (*Family Circle*, May 1974), and in an interview with Christiane Johnson (*Etudes Anglaises*, January–March 1976).

Of the five collections of Fitzgerald criticism published during the decade, two were of permanent importance. The second half of Bruccoli and Bryer's *F. Scott Fitzgerald in His Own Time* (1971) emphasized material (selected by Bryer) written during Fitzgerald's lifetime, reprinting (in most cases for the first time) fifteen interviews and forty-six contemporary reviews, essays, and editorials, parodies, and obituary tributes. Mentioned earlier in this survey, Bryer's *F. Scott Fitzgerald: The Critical Reception* (1978) reprinted a generous sampling of the reviews Fitzgerald books received (often in local newspapers) from *This Side of Paradise* in 1920 to *The Last Tycoon* in 1941. By comparison, the other three collections of the 1970s – Kenneth E. Eble's *Scott Fitzgerald: A Collection of Criticism* (1973), which chose its twelve reprinted essays from the 1950s and 1960s; Matthew J. Bruccoli's *Profile of F. Scott Fitzgerald* (1971), and Henry Dan Piper's *Fitzgerald's "The Great Gatsby": The Novel, The Critics, The Background* (1970) – were much slighter.

There were ten critical books on Fitzgerald published during the 1970s; and while three were slim monographs, several of the others were significant full-length studies which have continued to command respect. Two of the latter, Milton R. Stern's *The Golden Moment: The Novels of F. Scott Fitzgerald* (1970) and John F. Callahan's *The Illusions of a Nation: Myth and History in the Novels of F. Scott Fitzgerald* (1972), both viewed Fitzgerald's work through the lens of the American experience. Stern saw at "the center of Fitzgerald's imagination" the "uses of history, the American identity, the moral reconstruction of the American past," and examined the four completed novels in that context. Callahan's book focused heavily on *Tender is the Night*, with briefer sections on *Gatsby* and *The Last Tycoon*, and described their author as "a novelist who captured the complexity of the American idealist, the frailty of his historical and psychic awareness together with his 'willingness of the heart.' "

John A. Higgins's *F. Scott Fitzgerald: A Study of the Stories* (1971) was the first book to focus exclusively on Fitzgerald's short fiction. Because Higgins covered virtually every story, his analyses were often superficial; but, in many instances, his comments stood for many years as the only attention a story received. Just as Higgins's volume established the bases for serious study of Fitzgerald's short stories, Joan M. Allen's *Candles and Carnival Lights* (1978) did the same for the equally important topic of the ways, both positive and negative, in which Fitzgerald's Catholic education and upbringing "formed his moral consciousness" and influenced his fiction.

Of the other critical books of the decade, Thomas J. Stavola's *Scott Fitzgerald: Crisis in an American Identity* (1979) was hampered by its author's tendency to read Fitzgerald's fiction as autobiography but did use Erik Erikson's psychoanalytic theories interestingly in looking at Fitzgerald's life and marriage. William A. Fahey's *F. Scott Fitzgerald and the American Dream* (1973), Rose Adrienne Gallo's *F. Scott Fitzgerald* (1978), and Eugene Huonder's *The Functional Significance of Setting in the Novels of Francis Scott Fitzgerald* (1974) were not very significant contributions. There were also two full-length studies of *Gatsby*, Robert Emmet Long's *The Achieving of "The Great Gatsby"* (1979), which did an excellent job of tracing how Fitzgerald's pre-*Gatsby* fiction led to the novel and of examining its "structure of interwoven detail and nuance," and John S. Whitley's *F. Scott Fitzgerald: "The Great Gatsby"* (1976), a sixty-four-page monograph which focused on Nick and Gatsby.

1980–1989

The 1980s saw substantial book-length updated revisions of the two major bibliographical resources on Fitzgerald, the first bibliography of foreign criticism, and a detailed composition study of *This Side of Paradise*; the first edition of Fitzgerald's poetry and the most comprehensive collection to date of his short stories; the largest and most comprehensive volume of Fitzgerald correspondence we have ever had; four new book-length biographies; three collections of original essays, one the first to be devoted exclusively to the short stories; seven full-length critical studies, including the first one on Fitzgerald's women characters and another a significant second one on the short stories.

As noted earlier in this essay, Matthew J. Bruccoli issued two subsequent editions of his 1972 bibliography of Fitzgerald's works – *Supplement to "F. Scott Fitzgerald: A Descriptive Bibliography"* (1980) and *F. Scott Fitzgerald: A Descriptive Bibliography – Revised edition* (1987). The first corrected and updated the original volume and added valuable new sections on translations and republications; while the *Revised Edition* incorporated these changes but condensed the two earlier versions by eliminating several sections found in them.

Jackson R. Bryer's *The Critical Reputation of F. Scott Fitzgerald: A Bibliographical Study – Supplement One through 1981* (1984), similarly to Bruccoli's updated bibliography, both picked up items inadvertently omitted from Bryer's 1967 volume, added items on stage and screen adaptations of Fitzgerald's fiction and a section of reviews of Zelda Fitzgerald's *Save Me the Waltz*, and – most importantly – enumerated in annotated form the some 2,200 reviews, essays, books and book sections, and graduate theses which had appeared in the seventeen years since the earlier book. Linda C. Stanley's *The Foreign Critical Reputation of F. Scott Fitzgerald: An Analysis and Annotated Bibliography* (1980) provided accounts of Fitzgerald's reception in, principally, France, Great Britain, Germany, Italy, and Japan – with briefer sections on Australia, Canada, Denmark, India, the Low Countries, Norway, Brazil, Russia, South Africa, Spain, and Sweden.

James L. W. West III, in *The Making of "This Side of Paradise"* (1983), provided a detailed reconstruction of the process which Fitzgerald employed in, literally, piecing together his first novel from his first draft, already published poems, stories, and playlets, and even letters from friends. West also looked at the post-publication textual history of Fitzgerald's most carelessly written and sloppily proofread book. Milton R. Stern's *"Tender is the Night*: The Text Itself"* (*Critical Essays on F. Scott Fitzgerald's "Tender is the Night"* [1986]) reviewed the novel's composition history and argued persuasively for the efficacy of Fitzgerald's second thoughts on and revision of the 1934 edition.

The seemingly indefatigable Matthew J. Bruccoli gave us two new collections of material by Fitzgerald and a new edition of Fitzgerald's correspondence. Bruccoli's edition of Fitzgerald's *Poems 1911–1940* (1981) collected in book form for the first time 149 poems, jingles, and doggerel verses, plus the fifty-five lyrics he wrote for three Triangle Club musicals at Princeton. His edition of *The Short Stories of F. Scott Fitzgerald: A New Collection* (1989) was – and remains – the single largest collection of Fitzgerald's short fiction, containing forty-three stories, twenty more than in Cowley's 1951 collection. In a similar fashion, Bruccoli and Margaret M. Duggan's edition of *Correspondence of F. Scott Fitzgerald* (1980) was and still is the largest and most comprehensive collection of Fitzgerald letters we have had. It does not include any letters previously published but it does contain a generous selection of letters to Fitzgerald, most notably the first appearance in print of some of Zelda Fitzgerald's marvelous letters to her husband.

It is hardly surprising that Mizener's magisterial 1951 Fitzgerald biography stood virtually alone for three decades; but the 1980s did produce four new biographies, none of which displaced Mizener's work but all of which were worthwhile as supplements to it. Chief among them was Matthew J. Bruccoli's *Some Sort of Epic Grandeur* (1981), which succeeded best as a documentary account utilizing the many new published and unpublished materials which had surfaced since 1951 and remains a valuable resource for all manner of information about Fitzgerald's life. André Le Vot's *F. Scott Fitzgerald* (1983), which had appeared in French in 1979, was notable primarily for its fresh (perhaps because its author was not American) views of Fitzgerald and his era; his sections on Princeton, on America in 1920, on the Jazz Age, on Prohibition, and, predictably, on Paris in the 1920s were especially rewarding. Scott Donaldson, in *Fool for Love* (1983), eschewed a chronological approach and presented a mosaic of chapters on various facets of Fitzgerald's career and personality – his childhood, his Princeton years, his drinking, his womanizing, his attitudes toward Jews and blacks, his crack-up – with a healthy reliance on letters to Fitzgerald as well as on other primary documents. *Invented Lives: F. Scott and Zelda Fitzgerald* (1984) by James R. Mellow, while a beautifully written account which brought to life the social and literary worlds of the Fitzgeralds, had very little new to offer and was colored by Mellow's admitted lack of sympathy for his subjects. Frances Kroll Ring's memoir of her time as Fitzgerald's secretary during the last twenty months of his life, *Against the Current* (1985), was a poignant and respectful portrait of a professional writer bravely persevering against great internal and external obstacles.

For the first time, in the 1980s, collections of critical material about Fitzgerald began to consist entirely of new essays. Three such collections appeared: Bruccoli's *New Essays on "The Great Gatsby"* (1985), Bryer's *The Short Stories of F. Scott Fitzgerald: New Approaches in Criticism* (1982), and A. Robert Lee's *Scott Fitzgerald: The Promises of Life* (1989). To speak of the last first, remarkably enough, this volume, published in England originally and containing essays by British and Continental scholars, was the first gathering of original essays on the full range of Fitzgerald's career to be published – and it remained the only such collection for eleven years. It included essays on *This Side of Paradise* (Andrew Hook), on *Gatsby* (Lee), on *Tender is the Night* (Harold Beaver), on *The Last Tycoon* (Robert Giddings), on women in the novels (Elizabeth Kaspar Aldrich), on Fitzgerald and Spengler (John S. Whitley), on Fitzgerald's "Ethics and Ethnicity" (Owen Dudley Edwards), and two essays on the short stories (Brian Harding and Herbie Butterfield). All were sensible and worthwhile. The same high standard applied to the five original essays on *Gatsby* in the Bruccoli collection. Two were usefully concerned with the novel's structure and style – Kenneth E. Eble's "*The Great Gatsby* and the Great American Novel" and novelist George Garrett's "Fire and Freshness: A Matter of Style in *The Great Gatsby*." Two others, Roger Lewis's "Money, Love and Aspiration in *The Great Gatsby*" and Susan Resneck Parr's "The Idea of Order at West Egg," focused on theme through close readings of the text; while Richard Anderson's "Gatsby's Long Shadow: Influence and Endurance" traced the novel's impact on American literature and culture.

Bryer's collection contained twenty-two new essays (this total probably just about equalled the number of serious critical essays devoted to Fitzgerald's short fiction prior to 1982) and an extensive checklist of criticism on Fitzgerald's short stories. It was divided into two basic sections: "Overviews" included general pieces on groups of stories, considered either from the point of view of their subject matter (fantasy [Lawrence Buell], the use of place [Richard Lehan], the Southern Belle [C. Hugh Holman], money and marriage [Scott Donaldson], alcoholism and mental illness [Kenneth E. Eble]), and Basil Duke Lee [Joseph Mancini, Jr.]) or the period in which they were written (stories written for the movie market [Alan Margolies], stories written during the Depression [Ruth Prigozy], stories written for *Esquire* [James L. W. West III], and stories written during Fitzgerald's last years in Hollywood [Robert A. Martin]). The second half of the book consisted of essays on individual stories, ranging from well-known ones like "The Ice Palace" (John Kuehl), "May Day" (James W. Tuttleton), "Winter Dreams" (Neil D. Isaacs), "Absolution" (Irving Malin), "The Rich Boy" (Peter Wolfe), "Babylon Revisited" (Carlos Baker), and "Crazy Sunday" (Sheldon Grebstein) to more obscure stories such as "Rags Martin-Jones and the Pr-nce of W-les" (Victor Doyno), "The Adjuster" (Christiane Johnson), "The Swimmers" (Melvin J. Friedman), "The Bridal Party" (James J. Martine), and "Financing Finnegan" (George Monteiro). In the case of this latter group, these were the first essays published on these stories.

Two of the other collections published in the 1980s contained both reprinted and original essays, with a preponderance of the former. Both were in the G. K. Hall Critical Essays on American Literature Series. Scott Donaldson's *Critical Essays on "The Great Gatsby"* (1984) was a well organized combination of a judicious selection of the best previously published commentary on *Gatsby* and five substantial new essays. The latter included Robert Roulston's on literary influences on the novel, Jackson R. Bryer's study of small stylistic units in the text, Donaldson's own discussion of "The Trouble with Nick," Alan Margolies's definitive examination of the three films and one stage play based on *Gatsby*, and Ross Posnack's exploration of its Marxist elements. Milton R. Stern's *Critical Essays on F. Scott Fitzgerald's "Tender is the Night"* (1986) also combined reprinted reviews and critical essays chronologically arranged with new pieces. In this instance, there were three of the latter: Stern's own comparison of the 1934 and 1951 texts, alluded to above; James W. Tuttleton's study of the "motif of female vampirism latent" in the novel; and Joseph Wenke's useful cross-referenced bibliography of criticism of *Tender*. The other two collections published in the 1980s are composed entirely of reprinted materials and both appeared in Harold Bloom's massive Chelsea House project: *F. Scott Fitzgerald's "The Great Gatsby"* (1986) and *F. Scott Fitzgerald* (1985).

Of the eight books on Fitzgerald published in English during the 1980s, the most worthwhile was the shortest, British scholar Brian Way's *F. Scott Fitzgerald and the Art of Social Fiction* (1980). Way sensibly avoided a biographical interpretation and concentrated on skilled close readings of the novels and stories of "a novelist more subtly responsive to the cultural and historical aura that surrounded him than any American contemporary save Faulkner, a social observer more intelligent and self-aware than any since Henry James." Sarah Beebe Fryer's *Fitzgerald's New Women* (1988) went well beyond previous commentary on Fitzgerald's female characters, with individual chapters devoted to Clara, Rosalind, and Eleanor of *This Side of Paradise*; Gloria of *The Beautiful and Damned*; Daisy Buchanan; Nicole of *Tender is the Night* compared to Alabama of *Save Me the Waltz*; Nicole alone; and Kathleen and Cecelia of *The Last Tycoon*.

Alice Hall Petry's *Fitzgerald's Craft of Short Fiction: The Collected Stories 1910–1935* (1989), while – as its title suggested – limited to the stories contained in the four collections published in Fitzgerald's lifetime, provided excellent close readings of many stories which had not previously been treated this seriously and extensively. Dan Seiters's concern, in *Image Patterns in the Novels of F. Scott Fitzgerald* (1986), was with how Fitzgerald's use of "transportation imagery, communication imagery, light–dark imagery, dirt–disease–decay imagery, and water imagery" became "more sophisticated and more skillfully integrated into his fiction with each succeeding novel."

Two of the other full-length studies dealt in very different ways with Fitzgerald's relationship to the movies. *Fiction, Film, and F. Scott Fitzgerald* (1986) by Gene D. Phillips, S.J., was divided into three sections, one each on

Fitzgerald as screenwriter, on films made from Fitzgerald's stories, and on films made from his novels. Wheeler Winston Dixon's focus in *The Cinematic Vision of F. Scott Fitzgerald* (1986) was much narrower, concentrating on Fitzgerald's film work between 1937 and 1940 and on *The Last Tycoon* – although he did devote brief chapters to *Gatsby* and *Tender* in order to discern "the connections between the style and structure of these earlier works and Fitzgerald's later work as a film scenarist."

John B. Chambers's *The Novels of F. Scott Fitzgerald* (1989) was another study by a British scholar which presented close readings of the four completed novels in an effort to examine the "intellectual coherence" they show. Benita Moore, in *Escape into a Labyrinth: F. Scott Fitzgerald, Catholic Sensibility, and the American Way* (1988), concentrated on Fitzgerald's life and writing through the publication of *Gatsby* in 1925 in examining how his Catholic background contributed to his feelings of alienation and his sense of himself as an outsider.

1990–1999

By any measure, the 1990s was probably the most eventful period in the history of Fitzgerald's critical reputation. Punctuated in 1996 by the celebration of the centenary of the author's birth and the numerous publications which it occasioned, the decade also saw the founding of the F. Scott Fitzgerald Society, which sponsored four international Fitzgerald conferences, thereby generating dozens of potentially publishable essays; the first three volumes of an ongoing standard edition of Fitzgerald's complete works; an eighteen-volume facsimile edition of Fitzgerald manuscripts and typescripts; the most comprehensive collection of reprinted secondary material we are ever likely to have; some twenty full-length studies (including two groundbreaking books on *Gatsby*); and a comprehensive collection of twenty-four original essays on Fitzgerald's least studied stories.

F. Scott Fitzgerald: Manuscripts (1990–1), edited by Matthew J. Bruccoli, with Alan Margolies as associate editor and Alexander P. Clark and Charles Scribner III as consulting editors, reproduced in eighteen volumes facsimiles of the manuscripts and typescripts of Fitzgerald's five novels, one play, short stories, and essays. As Bruccoli noted in his introduction, this set "democratized" Fitzgerald scholarship by affording all the opportunity previously available only to those able to access collections at Princeton and a few other libraries. These volumes also should greatly assist future textual scholarship and forever lay to rest what Bruccoli called "the myth of Fitzgerald's irresponsibility" by demonstrating that "he was a painstaking reviser of his work-in-progress."

Bruccoli's prediction that the *Fitzgerald Manuscripts* "will provide the basis for definitive editions of Fitzgerald's work" was realized when, in 1991, Cambridge University Press inaugurated the Cambridge Edition of the Works of F. Scott Fitzgerald with Bruccoli's edition of *The Great Gatsby*, followed in 1993 by *The Love of the Last Tycoon*, also edited by Bruccoli. James L. W. West III assumed the editorship of the series with the publication of *This Side of Paradise* in 1995. In each case, the texts in the Cambridge Edition were subsequently published in paperback by Scribners.

The Fitzgerald centennial in 1996 was the occasion for the publication of a facsimile edition of the 1914 acting script of *Fie! Fie! Fi-Fi!*, the Princeton Triangle Show for which Fitzgerald wrote the book and lyrics; and for Chip Deffaa's edition of *F. Scott Fitzgerald: The Princeton Years – Selected Writings 1914–1920*, a useful chronologically arranged reprinting of a generous sampling of the verse, fiction, and humor pieces Fitzgerald contributed to *The Tiger* and the *Nassau Lit* – with an excellent introduction by the editor. Budd Schulberg found a copy of Fitzgerald's film adaptation of his story "Babylon Revisited" (it was called "the most perfect motion-picture scenario I ever read" by a screenwriter asked to revise it [it was never used]), in a carton in his house. It was published as *Babylon Revisited: The Screenplay* (1993), with a marvelous introduction by Schulberg. A scholarly edition of the screenplay version of *Tender is the Night* by Canadian novelist Malcolm Lowry, edited by Miguel Mota and Paul Tiessen, appeared in 1990. *F. Scott Fitzgerald on Authorship* (1996), edited by Bruccoli with Judith S. Baughman, was a valuable collection of Fitzgerald's comments on his craft and his writing peers assembled from letters, notebook entries, and published essays and reviews. Again, as with the *Manuscripts* volumes, the intention was to challenge the misconception that Fitzgerald wrote brilliantly but did not know what he was doing and "squandered his genius."

In 1994, Bruccoli and his wife sold their immense Fitzgerald collection to the Thomas Cooper Library at the University of South Carolina. The occasion was observed by a 1996 exhibition of highlights from the collection and the issuing in the same year of an illustrated catalogue of the exhibition, entitled *F. Scott Fitzgerald Centenary Exhibition*. The catalogue featured seven essays written by advanced graduate students on aspects of Fitzgerald's career documented with material from the Bruccoli Collection. A detailed catalogue of the full collection, edited by Park Bucker, appeared in 1997.

The most valuable reference work published during the decade – and an indispensable one – was *F. Scott Fitzgerald A to Z* (1998) by Mary Jo Tate. With individual entries for every novel, story, play, essay, and book review Fitzgerald wrote, for the characters in his fiction, for persons associated with him, for places he lived, organizations with which he was involved, and publications in which his work appeared – along with longer entries on such specialized topics as "Biographical Studies," "Editing Fitzgerald's Texts" (written by Matthew J. Bruccoli), "Jazz Age," and "Hollywood, California" – the volume functioned both as an introduction to Fitzgerald's life and work for general readers and an invaluable source for specialists. Compared to Tate's compilation, Robert L. Gale's similar *An F. Scott Fitzgerald Encyclopedia* (1998) seemed elementary and incomplete.

The only new volume of Fitzgerald correspondence, Bruccoli's *F. Scott Fitzgerald: A Life in Letters* (1994), brought together in one chronological arrangement letters already available in earlier collections, as well as a number previously uncollected. In a few cases, Bruccoli printed a full accurate text of a letter silently corrected or excerpted in a previous edition.

Jeffrey Meyers's *F. Scott Fitzgerald: A Biography* (1994) contained very little new information and was a mean-spirited and gratuitously negative portrait which often seemed to emphasize the most damaging details at the expense of a more balanced assessment. By comparison, Bruccoli's new edition of his 1978 exploration of the Fitzgerald–Hemingway relationship, retitled *Fitzgerald and Hemingway: A Dangerous Friendship* (1994), and Scott Donaldson's book on the same subject, *Hemingway vs. Fitzgerald: The Rise and Fall of a Literary Friendship* (1999), both were carefully researched and helpful studies. Similarly, two other key relationships in Fitzgerald's life were responsibly examined in Eleanor Lanahan's biography of her mother, *Scottie: The Daughter of . . .: The Life of Frances Scott Fitzgerald Lanahan Smith* (1995) and Robert Westbrook's account of his mother's affair with Fitzgerald, *Intimate Lies: F. Scott Fitzgerald and Sheilah Graham* (1995).

The decade of the 1990s produced some seventeen book-length critical studies of Fitzgerald, just about twice as many as the number of his own books that he published in his lifetime. Interestingly and probably not surprisingly, the majority of them were not general in scope but tended to focus on a single work. The best of the more broadly focused books, Robert and Helen H. Roulston's *The Winding Road to West Egg* (1995), examined Fitzgerald's fiction published prior to 1925, principally the short stories, in order to "explore how Fitzgerald's previous works do – and in some cases do not – anticipate *Gatsby*." Next to this knowledgeable study, Elizabeth A. Weston's *The International Theme in F. Scott Fitzgerald's Literature* (1995), with its examination of Fitzgerald's fiction alongside works by Wharton, James, Twain, Hawthorne, and Hemingway, seemed unoriginal and thin; as did Aiping Zhang's *Enchanted Places* (1997), although the latter did deal with technique rather than theme. Zhang looked at "the five most frequently adopted and most essential settings" in Fitzgerald's works – home, bars, schools, cities, and Hollywood – and explored how each functions "suggestively as a microcosm of the whole American society." Andrew Hook's *F. Scott Fitzgerald* (1992) devoted individual chapters to each of the five novels in what Hook described as a "psycho-biographical" study which contended that "Fitzgerald discovered that the kind of man he was, and the kind of writer he needed to be, were difficult to reconcile."

Two other general studies found new and rather unusual Fitzgerald sources. Deborah Davis Schlacks's *American Dream Visions: Chaucer's Surprising Influence on F. Scott Fitzgerald* (1994) centered on "The Offshore Pirate," "The Ice Palace," "The Diamond as Big as the Ritz," *The Vegetable*, and *Gatsby* in juxtaposition with Chaucer's four dream visions. The parallels Schlacks suggested, while not always compelling, were often intriguing and certainly gave convincing evidence of Fitzgerald's knowledge and use of the medieval period. Theodora Tsimpouki's *F. Scott Fitzgerald's Aestheticism: His Unacknowledged Debt to Walter Pater* (1992), by comparison, was puerile and superficial.

At just about the point in Fitzgerald studies when one would have expected that there surely was no more to say about *The Great Gatsby*, Ronald Berman, who had never previously published a word on Fitzgerald, produced two entirely original and seminal books. The first, *"The Great Gatsby" and Modern Times* (1994), placed the novel within the context of its time, as viewed principally in newspaper columns and editorials, advertisements, popular fiction, and other manifestations of the mass culture of the day. This was a genuinely new approach to *Gatsby*, an approach which reflected Berman's vast familiarity with American culture and literature. His second book, *"The Great Gatsby" and Fitzgerald's World of Ideas* (1997), combined close reading of *Gatsby* with knowledgeable discussion of what Berman called the "firsthand cultural and intellectual sources" upon which Fitzgerald drew – William James, H. L. Mencken, George Santayana, Josiah Royce, Walter Lipmann, and John Dewey. Again, the result was as insightful as it was fresh.

Of the decade's three other books on *Gatsby*, Richard Lehan's *"The Great Gatsby": The Limits of Wonder* (1990) was the work of one of our most perceptive Fitzgerald critics and was, predictably, unfailingly authoritative. It dealt with both such external matters as the novel's historical context and critical reception as well as with various aspects of the text. In *I'm Sorry About the Clock: Chronology, Composition, and Narrative Technique in "The Great Gatsby"* (1993), Thomas Pendleton concentrated on "the continual incoherences in Fitzgerald's management of the chronology" in *Gatsby*, concluding, in what was at best a debatable assertion, that these "incoherences" limit the achievement of the novel. Stephen Matterson's slim volume, *"The Great Gatsby"* (1990), was redundant in its review of common approaches to the novel (which occupied two-thirds of his study) and his brief examination of such well-studied aspects of it as time, women, social class, and history.

Both books on *Tender is the Night* were the work of seasoned Fitzgerald scholar/critics. Milton R. Stern's *"Tender is the Night": The Broken Universe* (1994), while it drew heavily – and admittedly – on Stern's important previous work on *Tender*, was an excellent first full-length study of what Stern saw as "the great novel about American history." Matthew J. Bruccoli and Judith S. Baughman's *Reader's Companion to F. Scott Fitzgerald's "Tender is the Night"* (1996) seemed directed at specialists rather than at the general reader in that more than half of it was a scholar's guide to the editorial specifics necessary to establish a fair text of the novel, although it did also contain over 100 pages of "Explanatory Notes" which were valuable to those teaching and reading *Tender*.

The title of Jack Hendricksen's *"This Side of Paradise" as a Bildungsroman* (1993) indicated its premise that Fitzgerald's first novel followed in the tradition of Goethe's *Wilhelm Meisters Lehrjahre* (1796) and Joyce's *A Portrait of the Artist as a Young Man* (1916) and thus was far more than the immature autobiographical work that most critics consider it to be. Hendricksen's careful literary study was part of the continuing tendency in Fitzgerald studies to show that he was a skilled craftsman who read widely.

Another positive direction which Fitzgerald studies took in the 1990s was toward greater attention to the short stories. Besides the Roulstons' book already mentioned, which contained considerable analysis of many pre-1925 stories, the decade saw three critical books and a collection of original essays devoted to Fitzgerald's short fiction. John Kuehl's *F. Scott Fitzgerald: A Study of the Short Fiction* (1991) was yet another book by a veteran Fitzgerald critic which provided an overview of his short story career, a long section on his prep school and college stories, and brief but insightful analyses of individual stories – "The Ice Palace," "May Day," "Absolution," "Majesty," and "Two Wrongs." Bryant Mangum, in *A Fortune Yet: Money in the Art of F. Scott Fitzgerald's Short Stories* (1991), concentrated on how Fitzgerald tailored his stories to the particular requirements and readership of the magazines in which he published them. This enabled Mangum to account plausibly for both the strengths and weaknesses of a great number of Fitzgerald stories and to provide worthwhile analyses of many obscure ones. Stephen W. Potts's *The Price of Paradise: The Magazine Career of F. Scott Fitzgerald* (1993) went over much of the same ground as Mangum but less authoritatively, blaming the mediocrity of many of the more than 170 stories he looked at on what he rather vaguely characterized as "personal factors."

Jackson R. Bryer's *New Essays on F. Scott Fitzgerald's Neglected Stories* (1996) included twenty-four original pieces, many of them by leading Fitzgerald critics (Alan Margolies, Bryant Mangum, Robert Roulston, Scott Donaldson, John Kuehl, Ruth Prigozy, James L. W. West III, Alice Hall Petry, and Milton R. Stern) and several of them on stories which had never before been examined in such detail ("The Spire and the Gargoyle," "Dalrymple Goes Wrong," "Benediction," "The Camel's Back," "John Jackson's Arcady," "Jacob's Ladder," "The Bowl," "Outside the Cabinet-Maker's," "The Rough Crossing," "Two Wrongs," "One Trip Abroad," "The Hotel Child," "The Rubber Check," "What a Handsome Pair!," "Her Last Case," "An Alcoholic Case," and "The Lost Decade").

There were three other collections of new essays published in the 1990s. J. Gerald Kennedy and Jackson R. Bryer's *French Connections: Hemingway and Fitzgerald Abroad* (1998) published seventeen essays, most of them expanded versions of papers delivered at the 1994 Hemingway/Fitzgerald International Conference in Paris. Three (by John F. Callahan, Felipe Smith, and Jacqueline Tavernier-Courbin) dealt with *Tender is the Night*; while there were five comparative studies – of *The Garden of Eden, A Moveable Feast,* and *The Great Gatsby* by Jacqueline Vaught Brogan; of *The Sun Also Rises* and *The Great Gatsby* by James Plath; of "The Fitzgeralds, Hemingway, and the Matter of Modernism" by Nancy R. Comley; of Hemingway and *Tender is the Night* by Robert E. Gajdusek; and of "The Snows of Kilimanjaro" and "Babylon Revisited" by J. Gerald Kennedy. Compared with these uniformly informed and informative pieces (the book also included an essay on Fitzgerald and Paris by Ruth Prigozy), the briefer selections (mostly unrevised conference papers) gathered in two Indian centennial collections, Somdatta Mandal's two-volume *F. Scott Fitzgerald: A Centennial Tribute* (1997) and Mohan Ramanan's *F. Scott Fitzgerald: Centenary Essays from India* (1998), were much less valuable. The Fitzgerald centennial also produced two gatherings of brief tributes to Fitzgerald by leading contemporary writers, *F. Scott Fitzgerald at 100: Centenary Tributes by American Writers* (1996) and *F. Scott Fitzgerald – 24 September 1896 to 21 December 1940: 24 September 1996 Centenary Celebration* (1996).

It is safe to say that Henry Claridge's four-volume collection of reprinted Fitzgerald criticism, *F. Scott Fitzgerald: Critical Assessments* (1992), is likely to remain the most comprehensive such volume for many years to come. While the price (approximately $500) and the fact that only 600 copies were printed limited the set's distribution, it is an indispensable resource. It included 226 selections, ranging from contemporary book reviews of the 1920s and 1930s and review-essays from the 1940s and 1950s through a section of "Memories and Reminiscences" and early scholarly essays down to a sensibly chosen gathering of critical pieces from the 1960s, 1970s, and 1980s (the book's terminal point seemed to be the mid-1980s). The only other general collection published in the 1990s, Katie de Koster's *Readings of F. Scott Fitzgerald* (1998), which reprinted some worthwhile pieces, was insignificant in comparison to Claridge's book.

The other collections of reprinted material were all more narrowly focused. Five dealt with *The Great Gatsby*. Dalton and Maryjean Gross's *Understanding "The Great Gatsby": A Student Casebook to Issues, Sources, and Historical Documents* (1998) included a variety of materials relevant to the novel; while Nicolas Tredell, in *F. Scott Fitzgerald: "The Great Gatsby"* (1997), traced the novel's critical reputation from 1925 into the 1990s, interweaving Tredell's narrative with generous excerpts from reviews and critical essays. Katie de Koster's *Readings on "The Great Gatsby"* (1998) and Harold Bloom's *Major Literary Characters: Gatsby* (1991) and *F. Scott Fitzgerald's "The Great Gatsby"* (1999) were more conventional collections of largely familiar materials. Bloom's *F. Scott Fitzgerald* (1999) reprinted pieces on the short stories.

The 1990s also witnessed continuing interest in Zelda Fitzgerald. A valuable and comprehensive volume of her *Collected Writings* (1991), edited by Matthew J. Bruccoli, included the full text of her novel *Save Me the Waltz*, her stories, her essays (only two had previously been collected), and a generous selection of her letters to her husband. Koula Svokos Hartnett's *Zelda Fitzgerald and the Failure of the American Dream for Women* (1991) was a sloppily written and poorly researched study which was rendered implausible by its tendency to place all the blame for Zelda's personal and literary difficulties on her husband.

2000 and beyond

As this chapter is being written, the first six months of the year 2000 have already produced an edition of *Flappers and Philosophers*, edited by James L. W. West III for the Cambridge Edition; two editions of *Trimalchio* (the previously unpublished first version of *Gatsby*), one a scholarly text edited by James L. W. West III for the Cambridge Edition and the other a facsimile of the unrevised galley proofs in the Bruccoli Collection at the University of South Carolina Library, with an afterword by Bruccoli; *F. Scott Fitzgerald: New Perspectives*, edited by Jackson R. Bryer, Alan Margolies, and Ruth Prigozy, a collection of twenty-one original essays expanded from papers delivered at the 1992 International F. Scott Fitzgerald Conference at Hofstra University; Linda C. Pelzer's *Student Companion to F. Scott Fitzgerald*; and worthwhile periodical essays by Morris Dickstein (*American Scholar*,

Spring 2000), Christopher Hitchens (*Vanity Fair*, May 2000), and James L. W. West III (*American Scholar*, Spring 2000). All indications are that critical and scholarly scrutiny of Fitzgerald will continue unabated into the new millennium and that his critical reputation will have many more "lives," to end with the quotation with which this survey began.

NOTES

1 See Bryer, *Critical Reputation*, 211–12, for citations. The Cowley, Kazin, Powers, Schorer, Trilling, Troy, and Wanning essays are reprinted in Kazin, *F. Scott Fitzgerald*.
2 See Bryer, *Critical Reputation*, 300–1, 304–6, for citations of these essays.

BIBLIOGRAPHY

This list includes all works cited in the chapters in this collection, as well as a selection – by Jackson R. Bryer – of significant periodical articles about Fitzgerald and books with sections on Fitzgerald.

Acland, Charles. *Youth, Murder, Spectacle: The Cultural Politics of "Youth in Crisis."* Boulder, CO: Westview Press, 1995.

Adams, J. Donald. "Scott Fitzgerald's Last Novel." *New York Times Book Review* November 9, 1941: 1.

Aldridge, John W. *After the Lost Generation.* New York: McGraw-Hill, 1951.

Classics and Contemporaries. Columbia: University of Missouri Press, 1992.

Allen, Joan M. *Candles and Carnival Lights: The Catholic Sensibility of F. Scott Fitzgerald.* New York: New York University Press, 1978.

American Literary Scholarship: An Annual. Durham, NC: Duke University Press, 1963–.

Ames, Christopher. *The Life of the Party: Festive Vision in Modern Fiction.* Athens: University of Georgia Press, 1991.

Anderson, Hilton. "*Daisy Miller* and 'The Hotel Child': A Jamesian Influence on F. Scott Fitzgerald." *Studies in American Fiction* 17 (Autumn 1989): 213–18.

Anderson, W[illiam] R[ichard, Jr.]. "Rivalry and Partnership: The Short Fiction of Zelda Sayre Fitzgerald." *Fitzgerald/Hemingway Annual* 9 (1977): 19–42.

Arnold, Edwin T. "The Motion Picture as Metaphor in the Works of F. Scott Fitzgerald." *Fitzgerald/Hemingway Annual* 9 (1977): 43–60.

Astro, Richard. "*Vandover and the Brute* and *The Beautiful and Damned*: A Search for Thematic and Stylistic Reinterpretations." *Modern Fiction Studies* 14 (Winter 1968–69): 397–413.

Atkinson, Jennifer McCabe. "Lost and Unpublished Stories by F. Scott Fitzgerald." *Fitzgerald/Hemingway Annual* 3 (1971): 32–63.

Auchincloss, Louis. *The Style's the Man: Reflections on Proust, Fitzgerald, Wharton, Vidal and Others.* New York: Charles Scribner's, 1994.

Babb, Howard S. "'The Great Gatsby' and the Grotesque." *Criticism* 5 (Fall 1963): 336–48.

Baldwin, Marc. "F. Scott Fitzgerald's 'One Trip Abroad': A Metafantasy of the Divided Self." *Journal of the Fantastic in the Arts* 4 (No. 3, 1991): 69–78.

Banning, Margaret Culkin. "Scott Fitzgerald in Tryon, North Carolina." *Fitzgerald/Hemingway Annual* 5 (1973): 151–4.

Barbour, Brian M. "*The Great Gatsby* and the American Past." *Southern Review* n.s.9 (Spring 1973): 288–99.

Barrett, Laura. "'Material Without Being Real': Photography and the End of Reality in *The Great Gatsby*." *Studies in the Novel* 30 (Winter 1998): 540–57.

Beard, George Miller. *American Nervousness*. New York: G. P. Putnam's, 1981.

Bender, Bert. "'His Mind Aglow': The Biological Undercurrent in Fitzgerald's *Gatsby* and Other Works." *Journal of American Studies* 32 (December 1998): 399–420.

Benét, Stephen Vincent. "Fitzgerald's Unfinished Symphony." *Saturday Review of Literature*, 24 (December 6, 1941): 10.

Berman, Jeffrey. *The Talking Cure: Literary Representations of Psychoanalysis*. New York: New York University Press, 1985.

Berman, Ronald. *"The Great Gatsby" and Fitzgerald's World of Ideas*. Tuscaloosa: University of Alabama Press, 1997.

   "The Great Gatsby" and Modern Times. Urbana: University of Illinois Press, 1994.

Berryman, John. "F. Scott Fitzgerald." *Kenyon Review* 8 (Winter 1946): 103–12.

Bewley, Marius. "Scott Fitzgerald's Criticism of America." *Sewanee Review* 62 (Spring 1954): 223–46.

Bicknell, John W. "The Waste Land of F. Scott Fitzgerald." *Virginia Quarterly Review* 30 (Autumn 1954): 556–72.

Bigsby, C. W. E. "The Two Identities of F. Scott Fitzgerald." *The American Novel and the Nineteen Twenties*. Ed. Malcolm Bradbury and David Palmer. London: Edward Arnold, 1971. 129–49.

Bishop, John Peale. "The Missing All." *Virginia Quarterly Review* 13 (Winter 1937): 106–21.

Blake, Nelson M. *Novelist's America: Fiction as History, 1910–1940*. Syracuse, NY: Syracuse University Press, 1969.

Blanchard, Phyllis, and Carlyn Manasses. *New Girls for Old*. New York: Macaulay, 1930.

Bliven, Bruce. "Flapper Jane." *New Republic* 44 (September 9, 1925): 65–7.

Bloom, Harold, ed. *F. Scott Fitzgerald*. New York: Chelsea House, 1985.

   F. Scott Fitzgerald. New York: Chelsea House, 1999.

   F. Scott Fitzgerald's "The Great Gatsby." New York: Chelsea House, 1986.

   F. Scott Fitzgerald's "The Great Gatsby." New York: Chelsea House, 1999.

   Major Literary Characters: Gatsby. New York: Chelsea House, 1991.

Bloom, James D. "Out of Minnesota: Mythography and Generational Poetics in the Writings of Bob Dylan and F. Scott Fitzgerald." *American Studies* 40 (Spring 1999): 5–21.

Bontemps, Jacques, and Richard Overstreet. "Measure for Measure: Interview with Joseph L. Mankiewicz." *Cahiers du Cinéma in English* 18 (February 1967): 28–41.

Bradbury, Malcolm. *Dangerous Pilgrimages: Transatlantic Mythologies and the Novel.* New York: Viking Press, 1996.

Bradsher, Earl L. "Age and Literature." *North American Review* 220 (November 1924): 546–53.

Breitwieser, Mitchell. "*The Great Gatsby*: Grief, Jazz and the Eye-Witness." *Arizona Quarterly* 47 (Autumn 1991): 17–70.

Brondell, William J. "Structural Metaphors in Fitzgerald's Short Fiction." *Kansas Quarterly* 14 (Spring 1982): 95–112.

Brooks, Van Wyck. *The Writer in America.* New York: E. P. Dutton, 1953.

Brown, Dorothy M. *Setting a Course: American Women in the 1920s.* Boston: Twayne, 1987.

Bruccoli, Matthew J. *Apparatus for F. Scott Fitzgerald's "The Great Gatsby" [Under the Red, White, and Blue].* Columbia: University of South Carolina Press, 1974.

"Bibliographical Notes on F. Scott Fitzgerald's *The Beautiful and Damned.*" *Studies in Bibliography* 13 (1960): 258–61.

"A Collation of F. Scott Fitzgerald's *This Side of Paradise.*" *Studies in Bibliography* 9 (1957): 263–5.

The Composition of "Tender Is the Night": A Study of the Manuscripts. Pittsburgh: University of Pittsburgh Press, 1963.

Fitzgerald and Hemingway: A Dangerous Friendship. New York: Carroll & Graf, 1994.

F. Scott Fitzgerald: A Descriptive Bibliography. Pittsburgh: University of Pittsburgh Press, 1972.

F. Scott Fitzgerald: A Descriptive Bibliography. Revised edition. Pittsburgh: University of Pittsburgh Press, 1987.

"Getting It Right: The Publishing Process and the Correction of Factual Errors – With Reference to 'The Great Gatsby.' " *Library Chronicle of the University of Texas,* 21 (No. 3–4, 1991): 40–59.

"The Last of the Novelists": F. Scott Fitzgerald and "The Last Tycoon." Carbondale: Southern Illinois University Press, 1977.

"Material for a Centenary Edition of *Tender Is the Night.*" *Studies in Bibliography* 17 (1964): 177–93.

" 'A Might Collation': Animadversions on the Text of F. Scott Fitzgerald." *Editing Twentieth Century Texts.* Ed. Francis G. Halpenny. Toronto: University of Toronto Press, 1972. 28–50.

Scott and Ernest: The Authority of Failure and the Authority of Success. New York: Random House, 1978.

Some Sort of Epic Grandeur: The Life of F. Scott Fitzgerald. New York: Harcourt Brace Jovanovich, 1981.

Supplement to "F. Scott Fitzgerald: A Descriptive Bibliography." Pittsburgh: University of Pittsburgh Press, 1980.

"Where They Belong: The Acquisition of the F. Scott Fitzgerald Papers." *Princeton University Library Chronicle* 50 (Autumn 1988): 30–7.

and Judith S. Baughman. *Reader's Companion to F. Scott Fitzgerald's "Tender Is the Night."* Columbia: University of South Carolina Press, 1996.

Bruccoli, Matthew J., ed. *"The Great Gatsby": A Facsimile of the Manuscript.* Washington, DC: Microcard Editions, 1973.

New Essays on "The Great Gatsby." Cambridge, UK: Cambridge University Press, 1985.

Profile of F. Scott Fitzgerald. Columbus, OH: Charles E. Merrill, 1971.

with Judith S. Baughman. *F. Scott Fitzgerald on Authorship.* Columbia: University of South Carolina Press, 1996.

Bruccoli, Matthew J., ed., with the assistance of Jennifer McCabe Atkinson. *As Ever, Scott Fitz: Letters Between F. Scott Fitzgerald and His Literary Agent, Harold Ober 1919–1940.* Philadelphia: J. B. Lippincott, 1972.

Bruccoli, Matthew J., and Jackson R. Bryer, eds. *F. Scott Fitzgerald in His Own Time: A Miscellany.* Kent, OH: Kent State University Press, 1971.

Bruccoli, Matthew J., and C. E. F[razer] C[lark, Jr.], eds. *F. Scott Fitzgerald and Ernest M. Hemingway in Paris: An Exhibition at the Bibliothèque Benjamin Franklin.* Bloomfield Hills, MI and Columbia, SC: Bruccoli Clark, 1972.

Bruccoli, Matthew J., and Margaret M. Duggan, eds., with the assistance of Susan Walker. *Correspondence of F. Scott Fitzgerald.* New York: Random House, 1980.

Bruccoli, Matthew J., Scottie Fitzgerald Smith, and Joan P. Kerr, eds. *The Romantic Egoists: A Pictorial Autobiography from the Scrapbooks and Albums of Scott and Zelda Fitzgerald.* New York: Charles Scribner's, 1974.

Bryer, Jackson R. *The Critical Reputation of F. Scott Fitzgerald: A Bibliographical Study.* Hamden, CT: Archon, 1967.

The Critical Reputation of F. Scott Fitzgerald: A Bibliographical Study – Supplement One through 1981. Hamden, CT: Archon, 1984.

Bryer, Jackson R., ed. "Four Decades of Fitzgerald Studies: The Best and the Brightest." *Twentieth Century Literature* 26 (Summer 1980): 247–67.

Fifteen Modern American Authors: A Survey of Research and Criticism. Durham, NC: Duke University Press, 1969.

F. Scott Fitzgerald: The Critical Reception. New York: Burt Franklin, 1978.

New Essays on F. Scott Fitzgerald's Neglected Stories. Columbia: University of Missouri Press, 1996.

The Short Stories of F. Scott Fitzgerald: New Approaches in Criticism. Madison: University of Wisconsin Press, 1982.

Sixteen Modern American Authors: A Review of Research and Criticism. Durham, NC: Duke University Press, 1974.

Sixteen Modern American Authors – Volume 2: A Survey of Research and Criticism Since 1972. Durham, NC: Duke University Press, 1990.

Bryer, Jackson R., Alan Margolies, and Ruth Prigozy, eds. *F. Scott Fitzgerald: New Perspectives.* Athens: University of Georgia Press, 2000.

Bucker, Park, ed. *Catalog of the Matthew J. and Arlyn Bruccoli F. Scott Fitzgerald Collection at the Thomas Cooper Library, the University of South Carolina.* Columbia: University of South Carolina Press, 1997.

Bufkin, E. C. "A Pattern of Parallel and Double: The Function of Myrtle in *The Great Gatsby.*" *Modern Fiction Studies* 15 (Winter 1969–70): 517–24.

Burhans, Clinton S., Jr. "'Magnificently Attune to Life': The Value of 'Winter Dreams.'" *Studies in Short Fiction* 6 (Summer 1969): 401–12.

"Structure and Theme in *This Side of Paradise.*" *Journal of English and Germanic Philology* 68 (October 1969): 605–24.

Burnam, Tom. "The Eyes of Dr. Eckleburg: A Re-examination of 'The Great Gatsby.'" *College English* 14 (October 1952): 7–12.

Burroughs, Catherine B. "Of 'Sheer Being': Fitzgerald's Aesthetic Typology and the Burden of Transcription." *Modern Language Studies* 22 (Winter 1992): 102–9.

Burt, Struthers. "Scott Fitzgerald, Whose Novels Are the Work of an Unreconciled Poet." *New York Herald Tribune Book Review,* July 8, 1951: 2, 10.

Burton, Mary E. "The Counter-Transference of Dr. Diver." *ELH* 38 (September 1971): 459–71.

Buttitta, Tony. *After the Good Gay Times: Asheville – Summer of '35 – A Season With F. Scott Fitzgerald.* New York: Viking Press, 1974.

Callaghan, Morley. *That Summer in Paris.* New York: Coward-McCann, 1963.

Callahan, John F. "F. Scott Fitzgerald's Evolving American Dream: The 'Pursuit of Happiness' in *Gatsby, Tender Is the Night,* and *The Last Tycoon. Twentieth Century Literature* 42 (Fall 1996): 374–95.

The Illusions of a Nation: Myth and History in the Novels of F. Scott Fitzgerald. Urbana: University of Illinois Press, 1972.

Canby, Henry Seidel. *College Sons and College Fathers.* New York: Harper & Brothers, 1915.

Cardwell, Guy A. "The Lyric World of Scott Fitzgerald." *Virginia Quarterly Review* 38 (Spring 1962): 299–323.

Carey, John. *The Intellectuals and the Masses: Pride and Prejudice Among the Literary Intelligentsia, 1880–1939.* New York: St. Martin's Press, 1993.

Carpenter, Humphrey. *Geniuses Together: American Writers in Paris in the 1920s.* Boston: Houghton Mifflin, 1988.

Carter, John F. "These Wild Young People." *Atlantic Monthly* 126 (September 1920): 301–4.

Cartwright, Kent. "Nick Carraway as an Unreliable Narrator." *Papers on Language & Literature* 20 (Spring 1984): 218–32.

Cary, Meredith. "*Save Me the Waltz* as a Novel." *Fitzgerald/Hemingway Annual* 8 (1976): 65–78.

Cashill, Jack. "The Keeper of the Faith: Mogul as Hero in *The Last Tycoon.*" *Revue Française d'Etudes Américaines* 19 (February 1984): 33–8.

Cass, Colin S. "Fitzgerald's Second Thoughts About 'May Day': A Collation and Study." *Fitzgerald/Hemingway Annual* 2 (1970): 69–95.

Casty, Alan. "'I and It' in the Stories of F. Scott Fitzgerald." *Studies in Short Fiction* 9 (Winter 1972): 47–58.

Chambers, John B. *The Novels of F. Scott Fitzgerald.* New York: St. Martin's Press, 1989.

Chan, K. K. Leonard. "Molecular Story Structures: Lao She's *Rickshaw* and F. Scott Fitzgerald's *The Great Gatsby.*" *Style* 25 (Summer 1991): 240–50.

Chard, Leslie F., II. "Outward Forms and the Inner Life: Coleridge and Gatsby." *Fitzgerald/Hemingway Annual* 5 (1973): 189–94.

Charvat, William. *The Profession of Authorship in America, 1800–1870.* Ed. Matthew J. Bruccoli. Columbus: Ohio State University Press, 1968.

Chase, Richard. *The American Novel and Its Tradition.* Garden City, NY: Doubleday, 1957.

Chudacoff, Howard. *How Old Are You?: Age Consciousness in American Culture.* Princeton, NJ: Princeton University Press, 1989.

Claridge, Henry, ed. *F. Scott Fitzgerald: Critical Assessments.* 4 vols. Robertsbridge, UK: Helm, 1992.

Clark, Suzanne. *Sentimental Modernism: Women Writers and the Revolution of the Word.* Bloomington: Indiana University Press, 1991.

Clemens, Anna Valdine. "Zelda Fitzgerald: An Unromantic Revision." *Dalhousie Review* 62 (Summer 1982): 196–211.

Cohen, Milton A. "Fitzgerald's Third Regret: Intellectual Pretense and the Ghost of Edmund Wilson." *Texas Studies in Literature and Language* 33 (Spring 1991): 64–88.

Cole, Thomas. *The Journey of Life: A Cultural History of Aging.* New York: Cambridge University Press, 1991.

Coleman, Dan. "'A World Complete in Itself': *Gatsby*'s Elegiac Narration." *Journal of Narrative Technique* 27 (Spring 1997): 207–33.

Coleman, Tom C., III. "Nicole Warren Diver and Scott Fitzgerald: The Girl and the Egotist." *Studies in the Novel* 3 (Spring 1971): 34–43.

Corson, Richard. *Fashions in Eyeglasses.* London: Peter Owen, 1980.

Cotkin, George. *William James, Public Philosopher.* Baltimore: Johns Hopkins University Press, 1990.

Cowart, David. "Fitzgerald's 'Babylon Revisited.'" *Lost Generation Journal* 8 (Spring 1987): 16–19.

Cowley, Malcolm. *Exile's Return: A Literary Odyssey of the 1920s.* 1924. New York: Penguin, 1976.

"Fitzgerald: The Double Man." *Saturday Review of Literature* 34 (February 24, 1951): 9–10, 42–4.

"The Fitzgerald Revival, 1941–53." *Fitzgerald/Hemingway Annual* 6 (1974): 11–13.

"Fitzgerald's 'Tender': The Story of a Novel." *New Republic* 125 (August 20, 1951): 18–20. Reprinted as Introduction to *Tender Is the Night.* Revised edition. New York: Charles Scribner's, 1951. ix–xviii.

"F. Scott Fitzgerald: The Romance of Money." *Western Review* 17 (Summer 1953): 245–55.

"The Scott Fitzgerald Story." *New Republic* 124 (February 12, 1951): 17–20.

A Second Flowering: Works and Days of the Lost Generation. New York: Viking Press, 1973.

Think Back on Us...A Contemporary Chronicle of the 1930s. Carbondale: Southern Illinois University Press, 1967.

"Third Act and Epilogue." *New Yorker* 21 (June 30, 1945): 53–8.

Crosland, Andrew T. *A Concordance to F. Scott Fitzgerald's "The Great Gatsby."* Detroit: Gale/Bruccoli Clark, 1975.

Cross, K. G. W. *F. Scott Fitzgerald.* Edinburgh: Oliver and Boyd, 1964; New York: Grove Press, 1964.

Curry, Ralph, and Janet Lewis. "Stephen Leacock: An Early Influence on F. Scott Fitzgerald." *Canadian Review of American Studies* 7 (Spring 1976): 5–14.

Curry, Stephen, and Peter L. Hays. "Fitzgerald's *Vanity Fair.*" *Fitzgerald/Hemingway Annual* 9 (1977): 63–75.

Dahlie, Hallvard. "Alienation and Disintegration in 'Tender Is the Night.'" *Humanities Association Bulletin* 22 (Fall 1971): 3–8.

"The Dangerous Teens." *San Francisco Chronicle* August 22, 1920: 2E.

Daniels, Thomas E. "Pat Hobby: Anti-Hero." *Fitzgerald/Hemingway Annual* 5 (1973): 131–9.

"The Texts of 'Winter Dreams.'" *Fitzgerald/Hemingway Annual* 9 (1977): 77–100.

"Toward a Definitive Edition of F. Scott Fitzgerald's Short Stories." *Publications of the Bibliographical Society of America* 71 (Third Quarter 1977): 295–310.

Dardis, Tom. *Some Time in the Sun.* New York: Charles Scribner's, 1976.

Davis, Simone Weil. "'The Burden of Reflecting': Effort and Desire in Zelda Fitzgerald's *Save Me the Waltz.*" *Modern Language Quarterly* 56 (September 1995): 327–61.

Decker, Jeffrey Louis. "Gatsby's Pristine Dream: The Diminishment of the Self-Made Man in the Tribal Twenties." *Novel* 28 (Fall 1994): 52–71.

Deffaa, Chip, ed. *F. Scott Fitzgerald: The Princeton Years – Selected Writings 1914–1920.* Fort Bragg, CA: Cypress House Press, 1996.

de Koster, Katie, ed. *Readings on F. Scott Fitzgerald.* San Diego, CA: Greenhaven, 1998.

Readings on "The Great Gatsby." San Diego, CA: Greenhaven, 1998.

DeKoven, Marianne. *Rich and Strange: Gender, History, Modernism.* Princeton, NJ: Princeton University Press, 1991.

Dell, Floyd. "Why They Pet." *Parent's Magazine* 6 (October 6, 1931): 60–3.

de Mille, William. *Hollywood Saga.* New York: E. P. Dutton, 1939.

Dessner, Lawrence Jay. "Photography and *The Great Gatsby.*" *Essays in Literature* (Macomb, IL) 6 (Spring 1979): 79–90.

DiBattista, Maria. "The Aesthetic of Forbearance: Fitzgerald's *Tender Is the Night*." *Novel* 11 (Fall 1977): 26–39.

Dickstein, Morris. "The Authority of Failure." *American Scholar* 69 (Spring 2000): 69–81.

"Fitzgerald's Second Act." *South Atlantic Quarterly* 90 (Summer 1991): 555–78.

Dixon, Wheeler Winston. *The Cinematic Vision of F. Scott Fitzgerald*. Ann Arbor, MI: UMI Research Press, 1986.

Dolan, Marc. *Modern Lives: A Cultural Re-Reading of "The Lost Generation."* West Lafayette, IN: Purdue University Press, 1996.

Donaldson, Scott. "The Crisis of Fitzgerald's 'Crack-Up.'" *Twentieth Century Literature* 26 (Summer 1980): 171–88.

Fool for Love: F. Scott Fitzgerald. New York: Congdon & Weed, 1983.

Hemingway vs. Fitzgerald: The Rise and Fall of a Literary Friendship. Woodstock, NY: Overlook Press, 1999.

" 'No, I Am Not Prince Charming': Fairy Tales in *Tender Is the Night*." *Fitzgerald/ Hemingway Annual* 5 (1973): 105–12.

"The Political Development of F. Scott Fitzgerald." *Prospects* 6 (1981): 313–55.

"Scott Fitzgerald's Romance With the South." *Southern Literary Journal* 5 (Spring 1973): 3–17.

"A Short History of *Tender Is the Night*." *Writing the American Classics*. Ed. James Barbour and Tom Quirk. Chapel Hill: University of North Carolina Press, 1990. 177–208.

Donaldson, Scott, ed. *Critical Essays on "The Great Gatsby."* Boston: G. K. Hall, 1984.

Drake, Constance. "Josephine and Emotional Bankruptcy." *Fitzgerald/Hemingway Annual* 1 (1969): 5–13.

Dudley, Juanita Williams. "Dr. Diver, Vivisectionist." *College Literature* 2 (Spring 1975): 128–34.

Eble, Kenneth. "The Craft of Revision: *The Great Gatsby*." *American Literature* 36 (November 1964): 315–26.

F. Scott Fitzgerald. New York: Twayne, 1963; revised edition New York: Twayne, 1977.

"*The Great Gatsby*." *College Literature* 1 (Winter 1974): 34–47.

Eble, Kenneth, ed. *F. Scott Fitzgerald: A Collection of Criticism*. New York: McGraw-Hill, 1973.

Elias, Amy J. "The Composition and Revision of Fitzgerald's *The Beautiful and Damned*." *Princeton University Library Chronicle* 51 (Spring 1990): 245–66.

Ellis, James. "Fitzgerald's Fragmented Hero: Dick Diver." *University Review* 32 (October 1965): 43–9.

Elmore, A[lbert] E. "Color and Cosmos in *The Great Gatsby*." *Sewanee Review* 78 (Summer 1970): 427–43.

"*The Great Gatsby* as Well-Wrought Urn." *Modern American Fiction: Form and Function.* Ed. Thomas Daniel Young. Baton Rouge: Louisiana State University Press, 1989. 57–92.

"Nick Carraway's Self-Introduction." *Fitzgerald/Hemingway Annual* 3 (1971): 130–47.

Emmitt, Robert J. "Love, Death and Resurrection in *The Great Gatsby.*" *Aeolian Harps: Essays in Literature in Honor of Maurice Browning Cramer.* Ed. Donna G. Fricke and Douglas C. Fricke. Bowling Green, OH: Bowling Green University Press, 1976. 273–89.

Epstein, Joseph. "F. Scott Fitzgerald's Third Act." *Commentary* 98 (November 1994): 52–7.

Evans, Oliver H. "'A Sort of Moral Attention': The Narrator of *The Great Gatsby.*" *Fitzgerald/Hemingway Annual* 3 (1971): 117–29.

Fahey, William A. *F. Scott Fitzgerald and the American Dream.* New York: Thomas Y. Crowell, 1973.

Fain, J. T. "Recollections of F. Scott Fitzgerald." *Fitzgerald/Hemingway Annual* 7 (1975): 133–9.

Fairey, Wendy. "*The Last Tycoon*: The Dilemma of Maturity for F. Scott Fitzgerald." *Fitzgerald/Hemingway Annual* 11 (1979): 65–78.

Fass, Paula S. *The Damned and the Beautiful: American Youth in the 1920's.* New York: Oxford University Press, 1977.

Fedo, David. "Women in the Fiction of F. Scott Fitzgerald." *Ball State University Forum* 21 (Spring 1980): 26–33.

Felski, Rita. *The Gendering of Modernity.* Cambridge, MA: Harvard University Press, 1995.

Ferguson, Robert A. "The Grotesque in the Novels of F. Scott Fitzgerald." *South Atlantic Quarterly* 78 (Autumn 1979): 460–77.

Fetterley, Judith. *The Resisting Reader: A Feminist Approach to American Fiction.* Bloomington: Indiana University Press, 1978.

"Who Killed Dick Diver? The Sexual Politics of *Tender Is the Night.*" *Mosaic* 17 (Winter 1984): 111–28.

Fiedler, Leslie. *An End to Innocence.* Boston: Beacon Press, 1955.

Fitzgerald, F. Scott. *Afternoon of an Author: A Selection of Uncollected Stories and Essays.* Princeton, NJ: Princeton University Library, 1957; New York: Charles Scribner's, 1958.

The Apprentice Fiction of F. Scott Fitzgerald, 1909–1917. Ed. John Kuehl. New Brunswick, NJ: Rutgers University Press, 1965.

"An Author's Mother." *Esquire* 6 (September 1936): 36.

Babylon Revisited: The Screenplay. New York: Carroll & Graf, 1993.

"'Ballet Shoes': A Movie Synopsis." *Fitzgerald/Hemingway Annual* 8 (1976): 3–7.

The Basil and Josephine Stories. Ed. Jackson R. Bryer and John Kuehl. New York: Charles Scribner's, 1973.

The Beautiful and Damned. New York: Charles Scribner's, 1922.

The Beautiful and Damned. New York: Charles Scribner's, 1995.

The Beautiful and Damned. Ed. Alan Margolies. Oxford, UK: Oxford University Press, 1998.

The Bodley Head Scott Fitzgerald, Volume I. London: Bodley Head, 1958.

The Bodley Head Scott Fitzgerald, Volume II. London: Bodley Head, 1959.

The Bodley Head Scott Fitzgerald, Volume III. London: Bodley Head, 1960.

The Bodley Head Scott Fitzgerald, Volume IV. London: Bodley Head, 1961.

The Bodley Head Scott Fitzgerald, Volume V. London: Bodley Head, 1963.

The Bodley Head Scott Fitzgerald, Volume VI. London: Bodley Head, 1963.

The Crack-Up. Ed. Edmund Wilson. New York: New Directions, 1945.

The Cruise of the Rolling Junk. Bloomfield Hills, MI: Bruccoli Clark, 1976.

"Dearly Beloved." *Fitzgerald/Hemingway Annual* 1 (1969): 1–3.

"'The Defeat of Art.'" *Fitzgerald/Hemingway Annual* 9 (1977): 11–12.

"'The Feather Fan.'" *Fitzgerald/Hemingway Annual* 9 (1977): 3–5.

The Fitzgerald Reader. Selected by Arthur Mizener. New York: Charles Scribner's, 1963.

Flappers and Philosophers. New York: Charles Scribner's, 1920.

Flappers and Philosophers. Ed. James L. W. West III. New York: Cambridge University Press, 2000.

F. Scott Fitzgerald: Manuscripts. 18 vols. Ed. Matthew J. Bruccoli. New York: Garland, 1990–1.

F. Scott Fitzgerald's Ledger: A Facsimile. Washington, DC: NCR/Microcard, 1973.

F. Scott Fitzgerald: A Life in Letters. Ed. Matthew J. Bruccoli. New York: Charles Scribner's, 1994.

"F. Scott Fitzgerald's Memo on the Typescript of *A Farewell to Arms*." *Fitzgerald/Hemingway Annual* 8 (1976): 146–52.

F. Scott Fitzgerald's St. Paul Plays 1911–1914. Ed. Alan Margolies. Princeton, NJ: Princeton University Library, 1978.

F. Scott Fitzgerald's Screenplay for "Three Comrades" by Erich Maria Remarque. Ed. Matthew J. Bruccoli. Carbondale: Southern Illinois University Press, 1978.

The Great Gatsby. New York: Charles Scribner's, 1925.

The Great Gatsby. Ed. Matthew J. Bruccoli. New York: Cambridge University Press, 1991.

The Great Gatsby. Ed. Ruth Prigozy. Oxford, UK: Oxford University Press, 1998.

"Imagination and a Few Mothers." *"Ladies' Home Journal" Treasury*. New York: Simon & Schuster, 1956. 180–1.

"Last Kiss." *Collier's* 123 (April 16, 1949): 16–17, 34, 38, 41, 43–4.

The Last Tycoon: An Unfinished Novel Together With "The Great Gatsby" and Selected Stories. New York: Charles Scribner's, 1941.

"Letter to Ernest Hemingway." *Fitzgerald/Hemingway Annual* 2 (1970): 10–13.

The Letters of F. Scott Fitzgerald. Ed. Andrew Turnbull. New York: Charles Scribner's, 1963.

"*Lipstick.*" *Fitzgerald/Hemingway Annual* 10 (1978): 3–35.

The Love of the Last Tycoon: A Western. Ed. Matthew J. Bruccoli. New York: Cambridge University Press, 1993.

"My Generation." *Esquire* 70 (October 1968): 119, 121.

The Notebooks of F. Scott Fitzgerald. Ed. Matthew J. Bruccoli. New York: Harcourt Brace Jovanovich/Bruccoli Clark, 1978.

"'Oh, Sister, Can You Spare Your Heart.'" *Fitzgerald/Hemingway Annual* 4 (1972): 114–15.

The Pat Hobby Stories. New York: Charles Scribner's, 1962.

Poems 1911–1940. Ed. Matthew J. Bruccoli. Bloomfield Hills, MI and Columbia, SC: Bruccoli Clark, 1981.

The Portable F. Scott Fitzgerald. Selected by Dorothy Parker. New York: Viking Press, 1945.

"Preface to *This Side of Paradise.*" *Fitzgerald/Hemingway Annual* 4 (1972): 1–2.

The Price Was High: The Last Uncollected Stories of F. Scott Fitzgerald. Ed. Matthew J. Bruccoli. New York: Harcourt Brace Jovanovich/Bruccoli Clark, 1979.

The Short Stories of F. Scott Fitzgerald: A New Collection. Ed. Matthew J. Bruccoli. New York: Charles Scribner's, 1989.

Six Tales of the Jazz Age and Other Stories. New York: Charles Scribner's, 1960.

"'Sleep of a University': An Unrecorded Fitzgerald Poem." *Fitzgerald/Hemingway Annual* 2 (1970): 14–15.

The Stories of F. Scott Fitzgerald. New York: Charles Scribner's, 1951.

Taps at Reveille. New York: Charles Scribner's, 1935.

Tender Is the Night. New York: Charles Scribner's, 1934.

Tender Is the Night. Rev. edition New York: Charles Scribner's, 1951.

Tender Is the Night. New York: Charles Scribner's, 1995.

Tender Is the Night. Ed. Matthew J. Bruccoli. Everyman Centennial Edition. London: J. M. Dent, 1996.

This Side of Paradise. New York: Charles Scribner's, 1920.

This Side of Paradise. New York: Charles Scribner's, 1995.

This Side of Paradise. Ed. James L. W. West III. New York: Cambridge University Press, 1995.

Thoughtbook of Francis Scott Key Fitzgerald. Princeton, NJ: Princeton University Library, 1965.

Three Novels of F. Scott Fitzgerald. New York: Charles Scribner's, 1953.

Trimalchio: An Early Version of "The Great Gatsby." Ed. James L. W. West III. New York: Cambridge University Press, 2000.

Trimalchio by F. Scott Fitzgerald: A Facsimile Edition of the Original Galley Proofs for "The Great Gatsby." Columbia: University of South Carolina Press, 2000.

The Vegetable. 1923. New York: Charles Scribner's, 1976.

Fitzgerald, F. Scott, and Zelda Fitzgerald. *Bits of Paradise: 21 Uncollected Stories by F. Scott and Zelda Fitzgerald.* Selected by Scottie Fitzgerald Smith and Matthew J. Bruccoli. London: Bodley Head, 1973; New York: Charles Scribner's, 1974.

Fitzgerald, F. Scott, D. D. Griffin, A. L. Booth, and P. B. Dickey. *Fie! Fie! Fi-Fi!: A Facsimile of the 1914 Acting Script and the Musical Score.* Columbia: University of South Carolina Press for the Thomas Cooper Library, 1996.

Fitzgerald, Zelda. *The Collected Writings.* Ed. Matthew J. Bruccoli. New York: Charles Scribner's, 1991.

Scandalabra. Columbia, SC: BC Research, 1980.

Fitzgerald/Hemingway Annual, 1969–1979.

Flahiff, F[rederick] T. "*The Great Gatsby*: Scott Fitzgerald's Chaucerian Rag." *Figures in a Ground: Canadian Essays on Modern Literature Collected in Honor of Sheila Watson.* Ed. Diane Bessai and David Jackel. Saskatoon: Western Producer Prairie, 1978. 87–98.

Flügel, John C. *The Psychology of Clothes.* London: Hogarth Press, 1930.

Forrey, Robert. "Negroes in the Fiction of F. Scott Fitzgerald." *Phylon* 28 (Third Quarter 1967): 293–8.

Foster, Richard. "Time's Exile: Dick Diver and the Heroic Idea." *Mosaic* 8 (Spring 1975): 89–108.

Friedman, Jean E., *et al.*, eds. *Our American Sisters: Women in American Life and Thought.* 4th edn. Lexington, MA: D. C. Heath, 1987.

Frohock, W. M. "Morals, Manners, and Scott Fitzgerald." *Southwest Review* 40 (Summer 1955): 220–8.

Fryer, Sarah Beebe. *Fitzgerald's New Women: Harbingers of Change.* Ann Arbor, MI: UMI Research Press, 1988.

F. Scott Fitzgerald at 100: Centenary Tributes by American Writers. Rockville, MD: Quill & Brush, 1996.

F. Scott Fitzgerald Centenary Exhibition: September 24, 1896 – September 24, 1996 – The Matthew J. and Arlyn Bruccoli Collection, The Thomas Cooper Library. Columbia: University of South Carolina Press for the Thomas Cooper Library, 1996.

F. Scott Fitzgerald – 24 September 1896 to 21 December 1940 – 24 September 1996 Centenary Celebration. Columbia: Thomas Cooper Society, Thomas Cooper Library, University of South Carolina, 1996.

Fussell, Edwin S. "Fitzgerald's Brave New World." *ELH* 19 (December 1952): 291–306.

Gale, Robert L. *An F. Scott Fitzgerald Encyclopedia.* Westport, CT: Greenwood Press, 1998.

Gallo, Rose Adrienne. *F. Scott Fitzgerald.* New York: Frederick Ungar, 1978.

Gamio, Manuel. *Mexican Immigration to the U.S.: A Study of Human Migration and Adjustment.* 1930. New York: Arno, 1969.

Gervais, Ronald J. " 'Sleepy Hollow's Gone': Pastoral Myth and Artifice in Fitzgerald's *The Beautiful and Damned*." *Ball State University Forum* 22 (Summer 1981): 75–9.

"The Snow of Twenty-nine: 'Babylon Revisited' as *ubi sunt* Lament." *College Literature* 7 (Winter 1980): 47–52.

"The Socialist and the Silk Stockings: Fitzgerald's Double Allegiance." *Mosaic* 15 (June 1982): 79–92.

Gibbens, Elizabeth Pennington. *The Baby Vamp and the Decline of the West: Biographical and Cultural Issues in F. Scott Fitzgerald's Portrayals of Women.* Ann Arbor, MI: UMI Research Press, 1994.

Giles, Paul. *American Catholic Arts and Fictions.* New York: Cambridge University Press, 1992.

Gilman, Charlotte Perkins. "Vanguard, Rear-Guard, and Mud-Guard." *Century Magazine* 104 (July 1922): 348–53.

Gilmore, Thomas B. *Equivocal Spirits: Alcoholism and Drinking in Twentieth-Century Literature.* Chapel Hill: University of North Carolina Press, 1987.

Giltrow, Janet, and David Stouck. "Style as Politics in *The Great Gatsby.*" *Studies in the Novel* 29 (Winter 1997): 476–90.

Gindin, James. "Gods and Fathers in F. Scott Fitzgerald's Novels." *Modern Language Quarterly* 30 (March 1969): 64–85.

Glicksberg, Charles I. *The Sexual Revolution in Modern American Literature.* The Hague: Martinus Nijhoff, 1971.

Godden, Richard. "Money Makes Manners Make Man Make Woman: *Tender Is the Night,* a Familiar Romance?" *Literature and History* 12 (Spring 1986): 16–37.

Goldhurst, William. *F. Scott Fitzgerald and His Contemporaries.* Cleveland: World, 1963.

Goldman, Arnold. "F. Scott Fitzgerald: The 'Personal Stuff.'" *American Studies: Essays in Honor of Marcus Cunliffe.* Ed. Brian Holden Reid, John White, and Arthur M. Schlesinger, Jr. New York: St. Martin's Press, 1991. 210–30.

Gollin, Rita K. "The Automobiles of *The Great Gatsby.*" *Studies in the Twentieth Century* 6 (Fall 1970): 63–83.

"Modes of Travel in *Tender Is the Night.*" *Studies in the Twentieth Century* 8 (Fall 1971): 103–14.

Good, Dorothy Ballweg. "'A Romance and a Reading List': The Literary References in *This Side of Paradise.*" *Fitzgerald/Hemingway Annual* 8 (1976): 35–64.

Graham, Sheilah. *College of One.* New York: Viking Press, 1967.

The Real F. Scott Fitzgerald: Thirty-Nine Years Later. New York: Grosset & Dunlap, 1976.

The Rest of the Story. New York: Coward–McCann, 1964.

Graham, Sheilah, and Gerald Frank. *Beloved Infidel.* New York: Henry Holt, 1958.

Greenwald, Fay T. "Fitzgerald's Female Narrators." *Mid-Hudson Language Studies* 2 (1979): 116–33.

Grenberg, Bruce L. "Fitzgerald's 'Figured Curtain': Personality and History in *Tender Is the Night.*" *Fitzgerald/Hemingway Annual* 10 (1978): 105–36.

Gross, Barry [Edward]. "The Dark Side of Twenty-five: Fitzgerald and *The Beautiful and Damned.*" *Bucknell Review* 16 (December 1968): 40–52.

"Fitzgerald in the Fifties." *Studies in the Novel* 5 (Fall 1973): 324–35.

"Fitzgerald's Midwest: 'Something Gorgeous Somewhere' – Somewhere Else." *Midamerica* 6 (1979): 111–16.

"Jay Gatsby and Myrtle Wilson: A Kinship." *Tennessee Studies in Literature* 8 (1963): 57–60.

"Success and Failure in *The Last Tycoon.*" *University Review* 31 (June 1965): 273–6.

"*This Side of Paradise*: The Dominating Intention." *Studies in the Novel* 1 (Spring 1969): 51–9.

"'Would 25-Cent Press Keep *Gatsby* in the Public Eye – Or Is the Book Unpopular?'" *Seasoned Authors for a New Season: The Search for Standards in Popular Writing*. Ed. Louis Filler. Bowling Green, OH: Bowling Green University Press, 1980. 51–7.

Gross, Dalton, and Maryjean Gross. *Understanding "The Great Gatsby": A Student Casebook to Issues, Sources, and Historical Documents*. Westport, CT: Greenwood Press, 1998.

Gross, Seymour L. "Fitzgerald's 'Babylon Revisited.'" *College English* 25 (November 1963): 128–35.

Gross, Theodore L. "F. Scott Fitzgerald: The Hero in Retrospect." *South Atlantic Quarterly* 67 (Winter 1968): 64–77.

Grube, John. "*Tender Is the Night*: Keats and Scott Fitzgerald." *Dalhousie Review* 44 (Winter 1964–5): 433–51.

Gruber, Michael P. "Fitzgerald's 'May Day': A Prelude to Triumph." *Essays in Literature* (Denver), 2 (No. 1, 1973): 20–35.

Gunn, Giles. "F. Scott Fitzgerald's *Gatsby* and the Imagination of Wonder." *Journal of the American Academy of Religion* 41 (June 1973): 171–83.

Haber, Carole, and Brian Gratton. *Old Age and the Search for Security: An American Social History*. Bloomington: Indiana University Press, 1989.

Haegert, John. "Repression and Counter-Memory in *Tender Is the Night.*" *Essays in Literature* 21 (Spring 1994): 97–115.

Hagemann, E. R. "Should Scott Fitzgerald Be Absolved for the Sins of 'Absolution?'" *Journal of Modern Literature* 12 (March 1985): 169–74.

Hall, G. Stanley. *Adolescence and Its Psychology and Its Relations to Psychology, Anthropology, Sociology, Sex, Crime, Religion, and Education*. 2 vols. New York: Appleton, 1904.

"Flapper Americana Novissima." *Atlantic Monthly* 129 (June 1922): 771–80.

Hall, William F. "Dialogue and Theme in *Tender Is the Night.*" *Modern Language Notes* 76 (November 1961): 616–22.

Hamblin, Dora Jane. "What a Spectacle." *Smithsonian Magazine* 13 (March 1983): 100.

Hansl, Eva V. B. "Parents in Modern Fiction." *The Bookman* 62 (September 1925): 21–7.

Hanzo, Thomas A. "The Theme and the Narrator of 'The Great Gatsby.'" *Modern Fiction Studies* 2 (Winter 1956–7): 183–90.

Harding, D. W. "Scott Fitzgerald." *Scrutiny* 18 (Winter 1951–2): 166–74.

Hart, Jeffrey. "Anything Can Happen: Magical Transformation in *The Great Gatsby.*" *South Central Review* 25 (Spring 1993): 37–50.

Hart, John E. "Fitzgerald's *The Last Tycoon*: A Search for Identity." *Modern Fiction Studies* 7 (Spring 1961): 63–70.

Hartnett, Koula Svokos. *Zelda Fitzgerald and the Failure of the American Dream for Women.* New York: Peter Lang, 1991.

Harvey, W. J. "Theme and Texture in *The Great Gatsby.*" *English Studies* 38 (February 1957): 12–20.

Hays, Peter L. "*Gatsby*, Myth, Fairy Tale, and Legend." *Southern Folklore Quarterly* 41 (1977): 213–23.

Haywood, Lynn. "Historical Notes for *This Side of Paradise.*" *Resources for American Literary Study* 10 (Autumn 1980): 191–208.

Hearn, Charles R. "F. Scott Fitzgerald and the Popular Magazine Formula Story of the Twenties." *Journal of American Culture* 18 (Fall 1995): 33–40.

Hearne, Laura Guthrie. "A Summer With F. Scott Fitzgerald." *Esquire* 62 (December 1964): 160–5, 232, 236, 237, 240, 242, 246, 250, 252, 254–8, 260.

Heilbrun, Carolyn G. *Toward a Recognition of Androgyny.* New York: Alfred A. Knopf, 1973.

Hemingway, Ernest. *A Moveable Feast.* New York: Charles Scribner's, 1964.

The Sun Also Rises. New York: Charles Scribner's, 1926.

Hendriksen, Jack. *"This Side of Paradise" as a Bildungsroman.* New York: Peter Lang, 1993.

Higgins, Brian, and Hershel Parker. "Sober Second Thoughts: The 'Author's Final Version' of *Tender Is the Night.*" *Proof* 4 (1975): 111–34.

Higgins, John A. *F. Scott Fitzgerald: A Study of the Stories.* Jamaica, NY: St. John's University Press, 1971.

Hindus, Milton. "F. Scott Fitzgerald and Literary Anti-Semitism." *Commentary* 3 (June 1947): 508–16.

F. Scott Fitzgerald: An Introduction and Interpretation. New York: Holt, Rinehart and Winston, 1968.

"The Mysterious Eyes of Doctor T. J. Eckleburg." *Boston University Studies in English* 3 (Spring 1957): 22–31.

Hitchens, Christopher. "The Road to West Egg." *Vanity Fair* No. 477 (May 2000): 76, 80, 84, 86.

Hochman, Barbara. "Disembodied Voices and Narrating Bodies in *The Great Gatsby.*" *Style* 28 (Spring 1994): 95–118.

Hoffman, Frederick J. *Freudianism and the Literary Mind.* 2nd edition. Baton Rouge: Louisiana State University Press, 1957.

The Twenties. New York: Viking Press, 1955.

Hoffman, Frederick J., ed. *"The Great Gatsby": A Study.* New York: Charles Scribner's, 1962.

Hoffman, Madelyn. "*This Side of Paradise*: A Study of Pathological Narcissism." *Literature and Psychology* 28 (Number 3 and 4, 1978): 178–85.

Hoffman, Nancy Y. "*The Great Gatsby*: *Troilus and Cressida* Revisited?" *Fitzgerald/Hemingway Annual* 3 (1971): 148–58.

Hook, Andrew. *F. Scott Fitzgerald*. London: Edward Arnold, 1992.

Hughes, G. I. "Sub Specie Doctor T. J. Eckleburg: Man and God in 'The Great Gatsby.'" *English Studies in Africa* 15 (September 1972): 81–92.

Hunt, Jan, and John M. Suarez. "The Evasion of Adult Love in Fitzgerald's Fiction." *Centennial Review* 17 (Spring 1973): 152–69.

Huonder, Eugen. *The Functional Significance of Setting in the Novels of Francis Scott Fitzgerald*. Bern: Herbert Lang, 1974.

Huyssen, Andreas. *After the Great Divide*. Bloomington: Indiana University Press, 1986.

Irwin, John T. "Compensating Visions: *The Great Gatsby*." *Southwest Review* 77 (Autumn 1992): 536–45.

"Is Fitzgerald a Southern Writer?" *Raritan* 16 (Winter 1997): 1–23.

Ishikawa, Akiko. "From 'Winter Dreams' to *The Great Gatsby*." *Persica* No. 5 (January 1978): 79–92.

Jacobs, Deborah F. "Feminist Criticism/Cultural Studies/Modernist Texts: A Manifesto for the '90s." *Rereading Modernism: New Directions in Feminist Criticism*. Ed. Lisa Rado. New York: Garland, 1994. 273–95.

James, William. *The Will to Believe*. Ed. Frederick H. Burkhardt. Cambridge, MA: Harvard University Press, 1979.

Johnson, Christiane. "Daughter and Father: An Interview with Mrs. Frances Scott Fitzgerald Smith – Washington, D.C., August 29, 1973." *Etudes Anglaises* 29 (January–March 1976): 72–5.

"*The Great Gatsby*: The Final Vision." *Fitzgerald/Hemingway Annual* 8 (1976): 108–15.

Johnston, Kenneth. "Fitzgerald's 'Crazy Sunday': Cinderella in Hollywood." *Literature/Film Quarterly* 6 (Summer 1978): 214–21.

Jones, Nard. "Protest at Thirty." *Esquire* 85 (March 1976): 74, 136.

Jonson, Ben. *Poems*. Ed. Ian Donaldson. London: Oxford University Press, 1975.

Joy, Neill R. "*The Last Tycoon* and Max Eastman: Fitzgerald's Complete Political Primer." *Prospects* 12 (1987): 365–92.

Kahn, Sy. "*This Side of Paradise*: The Pageantry of Disillusion." *Midwest Quarterly* 7 (Winter 1966): 177–94.

Kallich, Martin. "F. Scott Fitzgerald: Money or Morals." *University of Kansas City Review* 15 (Summer 1949): 271–80.

Kane, Patricia. "F. Scott Fitzgerald's St. Paul: A Writer's Use of Material." *Minnesota History* 45 (Winter 1976): 141–8.

Kaplan, Caren. *Questions of Travel: Postmodern Discourses of Displacement*. Durham, NC: Duke University Press, 1996.

Kazin, Alfred, ed. *F. Scott Fitzgerald: The Man and His Work*. 1951. New York: Collier Books, 1967.

Kennedy, J. Gerald. *Imagining Paris: Exile, Writing, and American Identity*. New Haven, CT: Yale University Press, 1993.

Kennedy, J. Gerald, and Jackson R. Bryer, eds. *French Connections: Hemingway and Fitzgerald Abroad*. New York: St. Martin's Press, 1998.

Kerr, Frances. "Feeling 'Half-Feminine': Modernism and the Politics of Emotion in *The Great Gatsby*." *American Literature* 68 (June 1996): 405–31.

Kett, Joseph F. *Rites of Passage: Adolescence in America 1790 to the Present*. New York: Basic Books, 1973.

Kirkby, Joan. "Spengler and Apocalyptic Typology in F. Scott Fitzgerald's *Tender Is the Night*." *Southern Review* (Australia) 12 (November 1979): 246–61.

Knodt, Kenneth S. "The Gathering Darkness: A Study of the Effects of Technology in *The Great Gatsby*." *Fitzgerald/Hemingway Annual* 8 (1976): 130–8.

Koblas, John J. *F. Scott Fitzgerald in Minnesota: His Homes and Haunts*. St. Paul: Minnesota Historical Society Press, 1978.

Kopf, Josephine Z. "Meyer Wolfsheim [*sic*] and Robert Cohn: A Study of a Jewish Type and Stereotype." *Tradition* 10 (Spring 1969): 93–104.

Korenman, Joan S. "'Only Her Hairdresser...': Another Look at Daisy Buchanan." *American Literature* 46 (January 1975): 574–8.

"A View from the (Queensboro) Bridge." *Fitzgerald/Hemingway Annual* 7 (1975): 93–6.

Kuehl, John. *F. Scott Fitzgerald: A Study of the Short Fiction*. Boston: Twayne, 1991.

"Scott Fitzgerald: Romantic and Realist." *Texas Studies in Literature and Language* 1 (Autumn 1959): 412–26.

Kuehl, John, and Jackson R. Bryer, eds. *Dear Scott/Dear Max: The Fitzgerald–Perkins Correspondence*. New York: Charles Scribner's, 1971.

Kuhnle, John H. "*The Great Gatsby* as Pastoral Elegy." *Fitzgerald/Hemingway Annual* 10 (1978): 141–54.

LaHood, Marvin J., ed. *"Tender Is the Night": Essays in Criticism*. Bloomington: Indiana University Press, 1969.

Lanahan, Eleanor. *Scottie: The Daughter of...: The Life of Frances Scott Fitzgerald Lanahan Smith*. New York: HarperCollins, 1995.

Langman, F. H. "Style and Shape in *The Great Gatsby*." *Southern Review* (Australia) 6 (March 1973): 48–67.

Lasch, Christopher. *The Revolt of the Elites*. New York: W. W. Norton, 1995.

Latham, Aaron. *Crazy Sundays: F. Scott Fitzgerald in Hollywood*. New York: Viking Press, 1971.

Lauricella, John A. "The Black Sox Signature Baseball in *The Great Gatsby*." *Aethlon* 10 (Fall 1992): 83–98.

Lears, T. J. Jackson. "From Salvation to Self-Realization: Advertising and the Therapeutic Roots of the Consumer Culture, 1880–1930." *The Culture of Consumption*. Ed. Richard Wightman Fox and T. J. Jackson Lears. New York: Pantheon, 1983. 3–38.

No Place of Grace: Antimodernism and the Transformation of American Culture, 1880–1920. 1983. Chicago: University of Chicago Press, 1994.

Lee, A. Robert, ed. *Scott Fitzgerald: The Promises of Life*. London: Vision Press, 1989; New York: St. Martin's Press, 1989.

LeGates, Charlotte. "Dual-Perspective Irony and the Fitzgerald Short Story." *Iowa English Bulletin: Yearbook* 26 (1977): 18–20.

Lehan, Richard D. *F. Scott Fitzgerald and the Craft of Fiction*. Carbondale: Southern Illinois University Press, 1966.

"F. Scott Fitzgerald and Romantic Destiny." *Twentieth Century Literature* 26 (Summer 1980): 137–56.

"The Great Gatsby": The Limits of Wonder. Boston: Twayne, 1990.

Lena, Alberto. "Deceitful Traces of Power: An Analysis of the Decadence of Tom Buchanan in *The Great Gatsby*." *Canadian Review of American Studies* 28 (No. 1, 1998): 19–41.

"The Seducer's Stratagems: *The Great Gatsby* and the Early Twenties." *Forum for Modern Language Studies* 34 (October 1998): 303–13.

Leslie, Shane. "Some Memories of F. Scott Fitzgerald." *Times Literary Supplement* (London) October 31, 1958: 632.

Le Vot, André. *F. Scott Fitzgerald: A Biography*. Trans. William Byron. New York: Doubleday, 1983.

Lewis, Janet. " 'The Cruise of the Rolling Junk': The Fictionalized Joys of Motoring." *Fitzgerald/Hemingway Annual* 10 (1978): 69–81.

"Fitzgerald's 'Philippe, Count of Darkness.' " *Fitzgerald/Hemingway Annual* 7 (1975): 7–32.

Lewis, Wyndham. *The Doom of Youth*. New York: McBride, 1932.

Lhamon, W. T., Jr. "The Essential Houses of *The Great Gatsby*." *Markham Review* 6 (Spring 1977): 56–60.

Lippmann, Walter. *Drift and Mastery*. New York: Mitchell Kennerly, 1914.

Lisca, Peter. "Nick Carraway and the Imagery of Disorder." *Twentieth Century Literature* 13 (April 1967): 18–28.

Lockridge, Ernest H. "F. Scott Fitzgerald's *Trompe l'Oeil* and *The Great Gatsby*'s Buried Plot." *Journal of Narrative Technique* 17 (Spring 1987): 163–83.

Lockridge, Ernest [H], ed. *Twentieth Century Interpretations of "The Great Gatsby": A Collection of Critical Essays*. Englewood Cliffs, NJ: Prentice-Hall, 1968.

Loeb, Harold, Morrill Cody, Florence Gilliam, and André Chamson. "Fitzgerald and Hemingway in Paris." *Fitzgerald/Hemingway Annual* 5 (1973): 33–76.

Long, Robert Emmet. *The Achieving of "The Great Gatsby": F. Scott Fitzgerald, 1920–1925*. Lewisburg, PA: Bucknell University Press, 1979.

"Fitzgerald and Hemingway on Stage." *Fitzgerald/Hemingway Annual* 1 (1969): 143–4.

"The Great Gatsby and the Tradition of Joseph Conrad: Part I." *Texas Studies in Literature and Language* 8 (Summer 1966): 257–76.

"The Great Gatsby and the Tradition of Joseph Conrad: Part II." *Texas Studies in Literature and Language* 8 (Fall 1966): 407–22.

Lowry, Malcolm. *The Cinema of Malcolm Lowry: A Scholarly Edition of Lowry's "Tender Is the Night."* Ed. Miguel Mota and Paul Tiessen. Vancouver: University of British Columbia Press, 1990.

Lowry, Malcolm, and Margerie Bonner Lowry. *Notes on a Screenplay for F. Scott Fitzgerald's "Tender Is the Night."* Bloomfield Hills, MI and Columbia, SC: Bruccoli Clark, 1976.

Lucas, John. "In Praise of Scott Fitzgerald." *Critical Quarterly* 5 (Summer 1963): 132–47.

Lutes, Della T. "The Art of Not Growing Old." *Forum Magazine* 43 (September 24, 1923): 353–61.

Lynd, Robert S., and Helen Merrell Lynd. *Middletown.* New York: Harcourt Brace, 1929.

McCall, Dan. " 'The Self-Same Song That Found a Path': Keats and *The Great Gatsby.*" *American Literature* 42 (January 1971): 521–30.

Mccay, Mary A. "Fitzgerald's Women: Beyond Winter Dreams." *American Novelists Revisited: Essays in Feminist Criticism.* Ed. F. Fleischmann. Boston: G. K. Hall, 1982. 311–24.

McGilligan, Patrick. *George Cukor: A Double Life.* New York: St. Martin's Press, 1991.

McGovern, James R. "The American Woman's Pre-World War I Freedom in Manners and Morals." *Our American Sisters.* Ed. Jean E. Friedman *et al.* 4th edition. Lexington, MA: D. C. Heath, 1987. 426–46.

MacKie, Elizabeth Beckwith. "My Friend Scott Fitzgerald." *Fitzgerald/Hemingway Annual* 2 (1970): 16–27.

MacLeish, Archibald. *Collected Poems, 1917–52.* Boston: Houghton Mifflin, 1952.

McMaster, John D. "As I Remember Scott (Memoir)." *Confrontation* 7 (Fall 1973): 3–11.

McNally, John J. "Boats and Automobiles in *The Great Gatsby*: Symbols of Drift and Death." *Husson Review* 5 (No. 1, 1971): 11–17.

McNicholas, Mary Verity, O. P. "Fitzgerald's Women in *Tender Is the Night.*" *College Literature* 4 (Winter 1977): 40–70.

MacPhee, Laurence E. "*The Great Gatsby*'s 'Romance of Motoring': Nick Carraway and Jordan Baker." *Modern Fiction Studies* 18 (Summer 1972): 207–12.

Maimon, Elaine P. "F. Scott Fitzgerald's Book Sales: A Look at the Record." *Fitzgerald/Hemingway Annual* 5 (1973): 165–73.

Male, Roy R. " 'Babylon Revisited': A Story of the Exile's Return." *Studies in Short Fiction* 2 (Spring 1965): 270–7.

Maltin, Leonard. *Leonard Maltin's Movie and Video Guide: 2000 Edition.* New York: Signet-New American Library, 1999.

Mandal, Somdatta, ed. *F. Scott Fitzgerald: A Centennial Tribute.* 2 vols. New Delhi: Prestige, 1997.

Mangum, Bryant. *A Fortune Yet: Money in the Art of F. Scott Fitzgerald's Short Stories.* New York: Garland, 1991.

Marchalonis, Shirley. *College Girls: A Century in Fiction*. New Brunswick, NJ: Rutgers University Press, 1995.

Marchand, Roland. *Advertising the American Dream: Making Way for Modernity*. Berkeley: University of California Press, 1984.

Margolies, Alan. "F. Scott Fitzgerald and *The Wedding Night*." *Fitzgerald/Hemingway Annual* 2 (1970): 224–5.

"F. Scott Fitzgerald's Work in the Film Studios." *Princeton University Library Chronicle* 32 (Winter 1971): 81–110.

"The Maturing of F. Scott Fitzgerald." *Twentieth Century Literature* 43 (Spring 1997): 75–93.

" 'Particular Rhythms' and Other Influences: Hemingway and *Tender Is the Night*." *Hemingway in Italy and Other Essays*. Ed. Robert W. Lewis. New York: Praeger, 1990. 69–75.

Marquand, John P. "Looking Backwards – 1. Fitzgerald: 'This Side of Paradise.' " *Saturday Review of Literature* 22 (August 6, 1949): 30–1.

Martin, Marjory. "Fitzgerald's Image of Woman: Anima Projections in *Tender Is the Night*." *English Studies Collections* 1 (September 1976): 1–17.

Martin, Robert A. "Fitzgerald's Climatology." *Lost Generation Journal* 8 (Spring 1987): 9–11, 23.

"The Hot Madness of Four O'Clock in Fitzgerald's 'Absolution' and *Gatsby*." *Studies in American Fiction* 2 (Autumn 1974): 230–8.

Martin, Robert K. "Sexual and Group Relationships in 'May Day': Fear and Longing." *Studies in Short Fiction* 15 (Winter 1978): 99–101.

Matterson, Stephen. *"The Great Gatsby."* London: Macmillan, 1990.

May, Rollo. *The Cry for Myth*. New York: W. W. Norton, 1991.

Mayfield, Sara. *Exiles from Paradise: Zelda and Scott Fitzgerald*. New York: Delacorte Press, 1971.

Mazzella, Anthony J. "The Tension of Opposites in Fitzgerald's 'May Day.' " *Studies in Short Fiction* 14 (Fall 1977): 379–85.

Mellow, James R. *Invented Lives: F. Scott and Zelda Fitzgerald*. Boston: Houghton Mifflin, 1984.

Mencken, H. L. *A Mencken Chrestomathy*. New York: Vintage, 1982.

A Second Mencken Chrestomathy. Ed. Terry Teachout. New York: Alfred A. Knopf, 1995.

Merrill, Robert. *"Tender Is the Night* as a Tragic Action." *Texas Studies in Literature and Language* 25 (Winter 1983): 597–615.

Merz, Charles. *The Great American Band Wagon*. New York: Literary Guild, 1928.

Messent, Peter. *New Readings in the American Novel: Narrative Theory and Its Application*. New York: St. Martin's Press, 1990.

Meyers, Jeffrey. *F. Scott Fitzgerald: A Biography*. New York: HarperCollins, 1994.

Michaels, Walter Benn. *Our America: Nativism, Modernism, and Pluralism*. Durham, NC: Duke University Press, 1995.

Michelson, Bruce. "The Myth of Gatsby." *Modern Fiction Studies* 26 (Winter 1980–1): 563–77.

Milford, Nancy. *Zelda: A Biography.* New York: Harper & Row, 1970.

Millay, Edna St. Vincent. *Collected Sonnets.* New York: Harper & Row, 1941.

Miller, James E., Jr. *The Fictional Technique of F. Scott Fitzgerald.* The Hague: Martinus Nijhoff, 1957.

"Fitzgerald's *Gatsby*: The World as Ash Heap." *The Twenties: Fiction, Poetry, Drama.* Ed. Warren French. Deland, FL: Everett/Edwards, 1975. 181–202.

F. Scott Fitzgerald: His Art and His Technique. New York: New York University Press, 1964.

Millgate, Michael. "Scott Fitzgerald as Social Novelist: Statement and Technique in *The Great Gatsby.*" *Modern Language Review* 57 (July 1962): 335–9.

"Scott Fitzgerald as Social Novelist: Statement and Technique in 'The Last Tycoon.'" *English Studies* 43 (February 1962): 29–34.

Minter, David. *A Cultural History of the American Novel: Henry James to William Faulkner.* Cambridge, UK: Cambridge University Press, 1994.

Mizener, Arthur. "Arthur Mizener on F. Scott Fitzgerald." *Talks With Authors.* Ed. Charles F. Madden. Carbondale: Southern Illinois University Press, 1968. 23–38.

The Far Side of Paradise: A Biography of F. Scott Fitzgerald. Boston: Houghton Mifflin, 1951; revised edition. New York: Vintage, 1959.

"The Maturity of F. Scott Fitzgerald." *Sewanee Review* 67 (Autumn 1959): 658–75.

Scott Fitzgerald and His World. New York: G. P. Putnam's, 1972.

"Scott Fitzgerald and the 1920's." *Minnesota Review* 1 (Winter 1961): 161–74.

Twelve Great American Novels. New York: New American Library, 1967.

Mizener, Arthur, ed. *F. Scott Fitzgerald: A Collection of Critical Essays.* Englewood Cliffs, NJ: Prentice-Hall, 1963.

Modell, John. *Into One's Own: From Youth to Adulthood in the United States, 1920–75.* Berkeley: University of California Press, 1989.

Monk, Craig. "The Political F. Scott Fitzgerald: Liberal Illusion and Disillusion in *This Side of Paradise* and *The Beautiful and the* [sic] *Damned.*" *American Studies International* 33 (October 1995): 60–70.

Monk, Donald. "Fitzgerald: The Tissue of Style." *Journal of American Studies* 17 (April 1983): 77–94.

Monteiro, George. "Fitzgerald vs. Fitzgerald: 'An Alcoholic Case.'" *Literature & Medicine* 6 (1987): 110–16.

"James Gatz and John Keats." *Fitzgerald/Hemingway Annual* 4 (1972): 291–4.

"The Limits of Professionalism: A Sociological Approach to Faulkner, Fitzgerald, and Hemingway." *Criticism* 15 (Spring 1973): 145–55.

Moore, Benita A. *Escape into a Labyrinth: F. Scott Fitzgerald, Catholic Sensibility, and the American Way.* New York: Garland, 1988.

Moreland, Kim. *The Medievalist Impulse in American Literature: Twain, Adams, Fitzgerald, and Hemingway.* Charlottesville: University Press of Virginia, 1996.

Morris, Wright. *The Territory Ahead.* New York: Harcourt Brace, 1958.

Moseley, Edwin M. *F. Scott Fitzgerald: A Critical Essay.* Grand Rapids, MI: William B. Eerdmans, 1967.

Moses, Edwin. "F. Scott Fitzgerald and the Quest to the Ice Palace." *CEA Critic* 36 (January 1974): 11–14.

"Tragic Inevitability in *The Great Gatsby*." *College Language Association Journal* 21 (September 1977): 51–7.

Moyer, Kermit W. "Fitzgerald's Two Unfinished Novels: The Count and the Tycoon in Spenglerian Perspective." *Contemporary Literature* 15 (Spring 1974): 238–56.

"*The Great Gatsby*: Fitzgerald's Meditation on American History." *Fitzgerald/ Hemingway Annual* 4 (1972): 43–57.

Murphy, George D. "The Unconscious Dimension of *Tender Is the Night*." *Studies in the Novel* 5 (Fall 1973): 314–23.

Murphy, Patrick D. "Illumination and Affection in the Parallel Plots of 'The Rich Boy' and 'The Beast in the Jungle.'" *Papers on Language & Literature* 22 (Fall 1986): 406–16.

Nanney, Lisa. "Zelda Fitzgerald's *Save Me the Waltz* as Southern Novel and *Künstlerroman*." *The Female Tradition in Southern Literature*. Ed. Carol S. Manning. Urbana: University of Illinois Press, 1993. 220–32.

Nathan, George Jean. "Memories of Fitzgerald, Lewis and Dreiser – The Golden Boys of the Twenties." *Esquire* 50 (October 1958): 148–9.

Nattermann, Udo. "Nicole Diver's Monologue: A Close Examination of a Key Segment." *Massachussetts Studies in English* 10 (Fall 1986): 213–28.

Nelson, Gerald B. *Ten Versions of America*. New York: Alfred A. Knopf, 1972.

Nettels, Elsa. "Howells's 'A Circle in the Water' and Fitzgerald's 'Babylon Revisited.'" *Studies in Short Fiction* 19 (Summer 1982): 261–7.

Nowlin, Michael. "The World's Rarest Work: Modernism and Masculinity in Fitzgerald's *Tender Is the Night*." *College Literature* 25 (Spring 1998): 58–77.

Nugent, Frank S. "Remarque's 'Three Comrades' Comes to the Capitol in a Brilliant Film Edition." *New York Times* June 3, 1938: 12.

O'Meara, Lauraleigh. "Medium of Exchange: The Blue Coupé Dialogue in *The Great Gatsby*." *Papers on Language & Literature* 30 (Winter 1994): 73–87.

Ornstein, Robert. "Scott Fitzgerald's Fable of East and West." *College English* 18 (December 1956): 139–43.

Owen, Guy. "Imagery and Meaning in 'The Great Gatsby.'" *Essays in Modern American Literature*. Ed. Richard E. Langford. DeLand, FL: Stetson University Press, 1963. 46–54.

Parker, Dorothy. "Professional Youth." *Saturday Evening Post* 195 (April 28, 1923): 14, 156–7.

Patterson, Richard North. *Escape the Night*. New York: Ballantine, 1984.

Payne, Michelle. "5′4″ × 2": Zelda Fitzgerald, Anorexia Nervosa, and *Save Me the Waltz*." *Bucknell Review* 39 (No. 1, 1995): 39–56.

Peeples, Edwin A. "Twilight of a God: A Brief, Beery Encounter With F. Scott Fitzgerald." *Mademoiselle* 78 (November 1973): 170–1, 209–12.

Pelzer, Linda C. *Student Companion to F. Scott Fitzgerald*. Westport, CT: Greenwood Press, 2000.

Pendleton, Thomas. *I'm Sorry About the Clock: Chronology, Composition, and Narrative Technique in "The Great Gatsby."* Selingsgrove, PA: Susquehanna University Press, 1993.

Perlis, Alan. "The Narrative Is All: A Study of F. Scott Fitzgerald's 'May Day.'" *Western Humanities Review* 33 (Winter 1979): 65–72.

Perlmutter, Ruth. "Malcolm Lowry's Unpublished Filmscript of *Tender Is the Night.*" *American Quarterly* 28 (Winter 1976): 561–74.

Perloff, Marjorie. *The Futurist Moment.* Chicago: University of Chicago Press, 1986.

Perosa, Sergio. *The Art of F. Scott Fitzgerald.* Trans. Charles Matz and the author. Ann Arbor: University of Michigan Press, 1965.

Person, Leland S., Jr. "Fitzgerald's 'O Russet Witch!': Dangerous Women, Dangerous Art." *Studies in Short Fiction* 23 (Fall 1986): 443–8.

"'Herstory' and Daisy Buchanan." *American Literature* 50 (May 1978): 250–7.

Peterman, Michael A. "A Neglected Source for *The Great Gatsby*: The Influence of Edith Wharton's *The Spark.*" *Canadian Review of American Studies* 8 (Spring 1977): 26–35.

Petry, Alice Hall. *Fitzgerald's Craft of Short Fiction: The Collected Stories 1910–1935.* Ann Arbor, MI: UMI Research Press, 1989.

"F. Scott Fitzgerald's 'A Change of Class' and Frank Norris." *Markham Review* 12 (Spring 1983): 49–52.

"Love Story: Mock Courtship in F. Scott Fitzgerald's 'The Jelly-Bean.'" *Arizona Quarterly* 39 (Autumn 1983): 251–60.

"Women's Work: The Case of Zelda Fitzgerald." *LIT* 1 (December 1989): 69–83.

Phelan, James. *Narrative as Rhetoric.* Columbus: Ohio State University Press, 1996.

Phillips, Gene D., S.J. *Fiction, Film, and F. Scott Fitzgerald.* Chicago: Loyola University Press, 1986.

Pike, Gerald. "Four Voices in 'Winter Dreams.'" *Studies in Short Fiction* 23 (Summer 1986): 315–20.

Piper, Henry Dan. "Frank Norris and Scott Fitzgerald." *Huntington Library Quarterly* 19 (August 1956): 393–400.

F. Scott Fitzgerald: A Critical Portrait. New York: Holt, Rinehart and Winston, 1965.

Piper, Henry Dan, ed. *Fitzgerald's "The Great Gatsby": The Novel, The Critics, The Background.* New York: Charles Scribner's, 1970.

Pizer, Donald. *American Expatriate Writing and the Paris Moment: Modernism and Place.* Baton Rouge: Louisiana State University Press, 1995.

Podis, Leonard A. "*The Beautiful and Damned*: Fitzgerald's Test of Youth." *Fitzgerald/Hemingway Annual* 5 (1973): 141–7.

"Fitzgerald's 'The Diamond as Big as the Ritz' and Hawthorne's 'Rappaccini's Daughter.'" *Studies in Short Fiction* 21 (Summer 1984): 243–50.

"'The Unreality of Reality': Metaphor in *The Great Gatsby.*" *Style* 11 (Winter 1977): 56–72.

Poffenberger, Albert T. *Psychology in Advertising.* New York: Shaw, 1925.

Potts, Stephen W. *The Price of Paradise: The Magazine Career of F. Scott Fitzgerald*. San Bernardino, CA: Borgo Press, 1993.

Powell, Anthony. "Hollywood Canteen: A Memoir of Scott Fitzgerald in 1937." *Fitzgerald/Hemingway Annual* 3 (1971): 71–80.

Pratt, Mary Louise. *Imperial Eyes: Travel Writing and Transculturation*. London: Routledge, 1992.

Prigozy, Ruth. "From Griffith's Girls to *Daddy's Girl*: The Masks of Innocence in *Tender Is the Night*." *Twentieth Century Literature* 26 (Summer 1980): 189–221.

"'A Matter of Measurement': The Tangled Relationship Between Fitzgerald and Hemingway." *Commonweal* 95 (October 29, 1971): 103–6, 108–9.

"'Poor Butterfly': F. Scott Fitzgerald and Popular Music." *Prospects* 2 (1976): 41–67.

Qualls, Barry V. "Physician in the Counting House: The Religious Motif in *Tender Is the Night*." *Essays in Literature* (Macomb, IL) 2 (Fall 1975): 192–208.

Quirk, Tom. "Fitzgerald and Cather: *The Great Gatsby*." *American Literature* 54 (December 1982): 576–91.

Raeburn, John. *Fame Became of Him: Hemingway as Public Writer*. Bloomington: Indiana University Press, 1984.

Raleigh, John Henry. "Fitzgerald's *The Great Gatsby*." *University of Kansas City Review* 13 (June 1957): 283–91.

"F. Scott Fitzgerald's *The Great Gatsby*: Legendary Bases and Allegorical Significances." *University of Kansas City Review* 4 (October 1957): 55–8.

Ramanan, Mohan, ed. *F. Scott Fitzgerald: Centenary Essays from India*. New Delhi: Prestige, 1998.

Ramsaye, Terry. *A Million and One Nights: A History of the Motion Picture*. 2 vols. New York: Simon and Schuster, 1926.

Rand, William E. "The Structure of the Outsider in the Short Fiction of Richard Wright and F. Scott Fitzgerald." *College Language Association Journal* 40 (December 1996): 230–45.

Rapp, Rayna, and Ellen Ross. "The 1920s Feminism, Consumerism, and Political Backlash in the United States." *Women in Culture and Politics: A Century of Change*. Ed. Judith Friedlander *et al*. Bloomington: Indiana University Press, 1986. 52–61.

"The Release of Youth." *The Nation* 10 (May 22, 1920): 674.

Reynolds, Guy. *Willa Cather in Context: Progress, Race, Empire*. New York: St. Martin's Press, 1996.

Rhodes, Robert E. "F. Scott Fitzgerald: 'All My Fathers.'" *Irish-American Fiction*. Ed. Robert E. Rhodes and Daniel J. Casey. New York: AMS Press, 1979. 29–51.

Riddel, Joseph N. "F. Scott Fitzgerald, the Jamesian Inheritance, and the Morality of Fiction." *Modern Fiction Studies* 11 (Winter 1965–6): 331–50.

Riley, Glenda. *Inventing the American Woman: A Perspective on Women's History*. Arlington Heights, IL: Harlan Davidson, 1987.

Ring, Frances Kroll. *Against the Current: As I Remember F. Scott Fitzgerald*. Berkeley, CA: Creative Arts, 1985.

"Footnotes on Fitzgerald." *Esquire* 52 (December 1959): 149–50.

"The Resurrection of F. Scott Fitzgerald." *The F. Scott Fitzgerald Society Newsletter* (October 1995): 1–4.

Roberts, Ruth E. "Nonverbal Communication in *The Great Gatsby*." *Language and Literature* 7 (Nos. 1–3, 1982): 107–29.

Robson, Vincent. "The Psychosocial Conflict and the Distortion of Time: A Study of Diver's Disintegration in *Tender Is the Night*." *Language and Literature* (Copenhagen) 1 (Winter 1972): 55–64.

Roethke, Theodore. *Straw for the Fire: The Notebooks of Theodore Roethke, 1943–63*. Ed. David Wagoner. Garden City, NY: Anchor, 1974.

Ross, Alan. "Rumble Among the Drums: F. Scott Fitzgerald (1896–1940) and the Jazz Age." *Horizon* 18 (December 1948): 420–35.

Roulston, Robert. "*The Beautiful and Damned*: The Alcoholic's Revenge." *Literature and Psychology* 27 (No. 3, 1977): 156–63.

"Dick Diver's Plunge Into the Roman Void: The Setting of *Tender Is the Night*." *South Atlantic Quarterly* 77 (Winter 1978): 85–97.

"Fitzgerald's 'May Day': The Uses of Irresponsibility." *Modern Fiction Studies* 34 (Summer 1988): 207–15.

"Rummaging through F. Scott Fitzgerald's 'Trash': Early Stories in the *Saturday Evening Post*." *Journal of Popular Culture* 21 (Spring 1988): 151–63.

"Slumbering With the Just: A Maryland Lens for *Tender Is the Night*." *Southern Quarterly* 16 (January 1978): 125–37.

"*This Side of Paradise*: The Ghost of Rupert Brooke." *Fitzgerald/Hemingway Annual* 7 (1975): 117–30.

"Tom Buchanan: Patrician in Motley." *Arizona Quarterly* 34 (Summer 1978): 101–11.

"Traces of *Tono-Bungay* in *The Great Gatsby*." *Journal of Narrative Technique* 10 (Winter 1980): 68–76.

"Whistling 'Dixie' in Encino: *The Last Tycoon* and F. Scott Fitzgerald's Two Souths." *South Atlantic Quarterly* 79 (Autumn 1980): 355–63.

Roulston, Robert, and Helen H. Roulston. *The Winding Road to West Egg: The Artistic Development of F. Scott Fitzgerald*. Lewisburg, PA: Bucknell University Press, 1995.

Rowe, Joyce A. *Equivocal Endings in Classic American Novels*. Cambridge, UK: Cambridge University Press, 1988.

Royce, Josiah. *The Basic Writings of Josiah Royce*. 2 vols. Ed. John J. McDermott. Chicago: University of Chicago Press, 1969.

Sander, Barbara Gerber. "Structural Imagery in *The Great Gatsby*: Metaphor and Matrix." *Linguistics in Literature* 1 (Fall 1975): 53–75.

Santayana, George. *Character and Opinion in the United States*. New York: Doubleday Anchor, 1956.

Saposnik, Irving S. "The Passion and the Life: Technology as Pattern in *The Great Gatsby*." *Fitzgerald/Hemingway Annual* 11 (1979): 181–8.

Sarotte, Georges-Michel. *Like a Brother, Like a Lover: Male Homosexuality in the American Novel and Theater*. Garden City, NY: Doubleday, 1978.

Savage, D. S. "Scott Fitzgerald, the Man and His Work." *World Review* No. 6 (August 1949): 65–7, 80.

Scharnhorst, Gary. "Scribbling Upward: Fitzgerald's Debt to Horatio Alger, Jr." *Fitzgerald/Hemingway Annual* 10 (1978): 161–9.

Schlacks, Deborah Davis. *American Dream Visions: Chaucer's Surprising Influence on F. Scott Fitzgerald*. New York: Peter Lang, 1994.

Schneider, Daniel J. "Color-Symbolism in *The Great Gatsby*." *University Review* 31 (October 1964): 13–17.

Schoenwald, Richard L. "F. Scott Fitzgerald as John Keats." *Boston University Studies in English* 3 (Spring 1957): 12–21.

Schorer, Mark. *The World We Imagine*. New York: Farrar, Straus and Giroux, 1968.

Schulberg, Budd. *The Disenchanted*. New York: Random House, 1950.

  The Four Seasons of Success. Garden City, NY: Doubleday, 1972.

  "Old Scott: The Mask, the Myth, and the Man." *Esquire* 55 (January 1961): 97–101.

Scribner, Charles III. "Celestial Eyes: From Metamorphosis to Masterpiece." *Princeton University Library Chronicle* 53 (Winter 1992): 140–55.

Scrimgeour, Gary J. "Against 'The Great Gatsby.'" *Criticism* 8 (Winter 1966): 75–86.

Sealts, Merton M., Jr. "Scott Fitzgerald and *The Great Gatsby*: A Reappraisal." *Colorado Quarterly* 25 (Fall–Winter 1998): 137–52.

Seiters, Dan. *Image Patterns in the Novels of F. Scott Fitzgerald*. Ann Arbor, MI: UMI Research Press, 1986.

Settle, Glenn. "Fitzgerald's Daisy: The Siren Voice." *American Literature* 57 (March 1985): 115–24.

Shain, Charles E. *F. Scott Fitzgerald*. Minneapolis: University of Minnesota Press, 1961.

Showalter, Elaine. *Sister's Choice: Tradition and Change in American Women's Writing*. Oxford, UK: Clarendon Press, 1991.

Silhol, Robert. "*Tender Is the Night* or the Rape of the Child." *Literature & Psychology* 40 (No. 4, 1994): 40–63.

Sipiora, Phillip. "Vampires in the Heart: Gender Trouble in *The Great Gatsby*." *The Aching Hearth: Family Violence in Life and Literature*. New York: Plenum, 1991. 199–220.

Skinner, John. "The Oral and the Written: Kurtz and Gatsby Revisited." *Journal of Narrative Technique* 17 (Winter 1987): 131–40.

Sklar, Robert. *F. Scott Fitzgerald: The Last Laocoön*. New York: Oxford University Press, 1967.

Smith, Frances Scott Fitzgerald. "Notes About My Now-Famous Father." *Family Circle* 84 (May 1974): 118, 120.

Solomon, Barbara H., ed. *Ain't We Got Fun?: Essays, Lyrics, and Stories of the Twenties*. New York: New American Library, 1980.

Sontag, Susan. *On Photography*. New York: Farrar, Straus and Giroux, 1977.

Speer, Roderick S. "*The Great Gatsby*'s 'Romance of Motoring' and 'The Cruise of the Rolling Junk.'" *Modern Fiction Studies* 20 (Winter 1974–5): 540–3.

Spindler, Michael. *American Literature and Social Change*. Bloomington: Indiana University Press, 1983.

Stallings, Laurence. "The Youth in the Abyss." *Esquire* 36 (October 1951): 107–11.

Stallman, Robert Wooster. "Conrad and *The Great Gatsby*." *Twentieth Century Literature* 1 (April 1955): 5–12.

Stanley, Linda C. *The Foreign Critical Reputation of F. Scott Fitzgerald: An Analysis and Annotated Bibliography*. Westport, CT: Greenwood Press, 1980.

Stark, Bruce R. "The Intricate Pattern in *The Great Gatsby*." *Fitzgerald/Hemingway Annual* 6 (1974): 51–61.

Stark, John. "The Style of *Tender Is the Night*." *Fitzgerald/Hemingway Annual* 4 (1972): 89–95.

Stavola, Thomas J. *Scott Fitzgerald: Crisis in an American Identity*. New York: Barnes & Noble, 1979.

Steinbrink, Jeffrey. "'Boats Against the Current': Mortality and the Myth of Renewal in *The Great Gatsby*." *Twentieth Century Literature* 26 (Summer 1980): 157–70.

Stern, Milton R. *The Golden Moment: The Novels of F. Scott Fitzgerald*. Urbana: University of Illinois Press, 1970.

"Tender Is the Night": The Broken Universe. New York: Twayne, 1994.

Stern, Milton R., ed. *Critical Essays on F. Scott Fitzgerald's "Tender Is the Night."* Boston: G. K. Hall, 1986.

Stevens, A. Wilber. "Fitzgerald's *Tender Is the Night*: The Idea as Morality." *Brigham Young University Studies* 3 (Spring and Summer 1961): 95–104.

Stewart, Donald Ogden. "Recollections of F. Scott Fitzgerald and Hemingway." *Fitzgerald/Hemingway Annual* 3 (1971): 177–88.

Stewart, Lawrence D. "'Absolution' and *The Great Gatsby*." *Fitzgerald/Hemingway Annual* 5 (1973): 181–7.

Storey, John. *An Introductory Guide to Culture Theory and Popular Culture*. Athens: University of Georgia Press, 1993.

Stouck, David. "White Sheep on Fifth Avenue: *The Great Gatsby* as Pastoral." *Genre* 4 (December 1971): 335–47.

Tarkington, Booth. *Seventeen*. New York: Grosset & Dunlap, 1916.

Tate, Mary Jo. *F. Scott Fitzgerald A to Z: The Essential Reference to His Life and Work*. New York: Facts on File, 1998.

Tavernier-Courbin, Jacqueline. "Sensuality as Key to Characterization in *Tender Is the Night*." *English Studies in Canada* 9 (December 1983): 452–67.

Taylor, Dwight. "Scott Fitzgerald in Hollywood." *Harper's* 218 (March 1959): 67–71.

Thornton, Lawrence. "Ford Madox Ford and *The Great Gatsby.*" *Fitzgerald/Hemingway Annual* 7 (1975): 57–74.

Thurber, James. "'Scott in Thorns.'" *The Reporter* 4 (April 17, 1951): 35–8.

"Taps at Assembly." *New Republic* 106 (February 9, 1942): 211–12.

Toklas, Alice B. *What is Remembered.* New York: Holt, Rinehart and Winston, 1963.

Toles, George. "The Metaphysics of Style in *Tender Is the Night.*" *American Literature* 62 (September 1990): 423–44.

Tolmatchoff, V. M. "The Metaphor of History in the Work of F. Scott Fitzgerald." *Russian Eyes on American Literature.* Ed. Sergei Chakovsky and M. Thomas Inge. Jackson: University Press of Mississippi, 1992. 126–41.

Tompkins, Calvin. "Living Well Is the Best Revenge." *New Yorker* 38 (July 28, 1962): 31–2, 34, 36, 38, 43–4, 46–7, 49–50, 52, 54, 56–9.

Living Well Is the Best Revenge. New York: Viking Press, 1971.

Toor, David. "Guilt and Retribution in 'Babylon Revisited.'" *Fitzgerald/Hemingway Annual* 5 (1973): 155–64.

Trachtenberg, Alan. "The Journey Back: Myth and History in *Tender Is the Night.*" *Experience in the Novel: Selected Papers From the English Institute.* Ed. Roy Harvey Pearce. New York: Columbia University Press, 1968. 133–62.

Tredell, Nicholas, ed. *F. Scott Fitzgerald: "The Great Gatsby."* New York: Columbia University Press, 1997.

Trilling, Lionel. *The Liberal Imagination.* New York: Viking Press, 1950.

Trouard, Dawn. "Fitzgerald's Missed Moments: Surrealistic Style in His Major Novels." *Fitzgerald/Hemingway Annual* 11 (1979): 189–205.

Tsimpouki, Theodora. *F. Scott Fitzgerald's Aestheticism: His Unacknowledged Debt to Walter Pater.* Athens: Parousia, 1992.

Turnbull, Andrew W. "Further Notes on Fitzgerald at La Paix." *New Yorker* 32 (November 17, 1956): 153–65.

Scott Fitzgerald. New York: Charles Scribner's, 1962.

"Scott Fitzgerald at La Paix." *New Yorker* 32 (April 7, 1956): 98–109.

Tuttleton, James W. "'Combat in the Erogenous Zone': Women in the American Novel Between the Two World Wars." *What Manner of Woman: Essays on English and American Life and Literature.* Ed. Marlene Springer. New York: New York University Press, 1977. 271–96.

"F. Scott Fitzgerald & the Magical Glory." *New Criterion* 13 (November 13, 1994): 24–31.

The Novel of Manners in America. Chapel Hill: University of North Carolina Press, 1972.

Twitchell, James B. "'Babylon Revisited': Chronology and Characters." *Fitzgerald/Hemingway Annual* 10 (1978): 155–60.

Vaill, Amanda. *Everybody Was So Young: Gerald and Sara Murphy – A Lost Generation Love Story.* Boston: Houghton Mifflin, 1998.

Varet-Ali, Elizabeth M. "The Unfortunate Fate of Seventeen Fitzgerald 'Originals': Toward a Reading of *The Pat Hobby Stories* 'On Their Own Merits Completely.'" *Journal of the Short Story in English* 14 (Spring 1990): 87–110.

Wagner, Joseph B. "*Gatsby* and John Keats: Another Version." *Fitzgerald/Hemingway Annual* 11 (1979): 91–8.

Wagner, Linda W. "*Save Me the Waltz*: An Assessment in Craft." *Journal of Narrative Technique* 12 (Fall 1982): 201–9.

Wakefield, Dan. *New York in the Fifties*. Boston: Houghton Mifflin, 1992.

Wasiolek, Edward. "The Sexual Drama of Nick and Gatsby." *International Fiction Review* 19 (No. 1, 1992): 14–22.

Way, Brian. *F. Scott Fitzgerald and the Art of Social Fiction*. London: Edward Arnold, 1980; New York: St. Martin's Press, 1980.

"Scott Fitzgerald." *New Left Review* No. 21 (October 1963): 36–51.

West, James L. W. III. *American Authors and the Literary Marketplace since 1900*. Philadelphia: University of Pennsylvania Press, 1988.

"Annotating Mr. Fitzgerald." *American Scholar* 69 (Spring 2000): 83–91.

"Did F. Scott Fitzgerald Have the Right Publisher?" *Sewanee Review* 100 (Fall 1992): 644–56.

The Making of "This Side of Paradise." Philadelphia: University of Pennsylvania Press, 1983.

"Notes on the Text of F. Scott Fitzgerald's 'Early Success.'" *Resources for American Literary Study* 3 (Spring 1973): 73–99.

"Prospects for the Study of F. Scott Fitzgerald." *Resources for American Literary Study* 23 (No. 2, 1997): 147–58.

West, James L. W. III., and J. Barclay Inge. "F. Scott Fitzgerald's Revision of 'The Rich Boy.'" *Proof* 5 (1977): 127–46.

West, Suzanne. "Nicole's Gardens." *Fitzgerald/Hemingway Annual* 10 (1978): 85–95.

Westbrook, Robert. *Intimate Lies: F. Scott Fitzgerald and Sheilah Graham: Her Son's Story*. New York: HarperCollins, 1995.

Westbrook, Wayne W. "Portrait of a Dandy in *The Beautiful and Damned*." *Fitzgerald/Hemingway Annual* 11 (1979): 147–9.

Weston, Elizabeth A. *The International Theme in F. Scott Fitzgerald's Literature*. New York: Peter Lang, 1995.

White, Eugene. "The 'Intricate Destiny' of Dick Diver." *Modern Fiction Studies* 7 (Spring 1961): 55–62.

Whitley, John S. *F. Scott Fitzgerald: "The Great Gatsby."* London: Edward Arnold, 1976.

Wickes, George. *Americans in Paris*. 1969. New York: Da Capo, 1980.

Williams, Tennessee. *Clothes for a Summer Hotel*. New York: New Directions, 1983.

Wilson, B. W. "The Theatrical Motif in *The Great Gatsby*." *Fitzgerald/Hemingway Annual* 7 (1975): 107–13.

Wilson, Colin. *Religion and the Rebel*. Boston: Houghton Mifflin, 1957.

Wilson, Edmund. "The Delegate from Great Neck." *The Shores of Light*. New York: Farrar, Straus and Young, 1952. 141–55.

"Sheilah Graham." *New Yorker* 34 (January 24, 1959): 16–17.

Letters on Literature and Politics: 1912–1972. Ed. Elena Wilson. New York: Farrar, Straus and Giroux, 1977.

Wilson, Raymond J. "Henry James and F. Scott Fitzgerald: Americans Abroad." *Research Studies* 45 (June 1977): 82–91.

Wilson, Robert N. *The Writer as Social Seer*. Chapel Hill: University of North Carolina Press, 1979.

Wilt, Judith. "The Spinning Story: Gothic Motifs in *Tender Is the Night*." *Fitzgerald/ Hemingway Annual* 8 (1976): 79–95.

Winters, Keith. "Artistic Tensions: The Enigma of F. Scott Fitzgerald." *Research Studies* 37 (December 1969): 285–97.

Witham, W. Tasker. *The Adolescent in the American Novel, 1920–1960*. New York: Frederick Ungar, 1964.

Wood, Mary E. "A Wizard Cultivator: Zelda Fitzgerald's *Save Me the Waltz* as Asylum Autobiography." *Tulsa Studies in Women's Literature* 11 (Fall 1992): 247–64.

Woodward, Jeffrey Harris. *F. Scott Fitzgerald: The Artist as Public Figure, 1920– 1940*. Ann Arbor, MI: University Microfilms, 1973.

Young, Philip. "Scott Fitzgerald's Waste Land." *Kansas Magazine* 23 (1956): 73–7.

"Youth's Greatest Problem: Wait or Mate." *True Confessions* 12 (October 1928): 113.

Zhang, Aiping. *Enchanted Places: The Use of Setting in F. Scott Fitzgerald's Fiction*. Westport, CT: Greenwood Press, 1997.

Zwerdling, Alex. *Improvised Europeans: American Literary Expatriates and the Siege of London*. New York: Basic Books, 1998.

INDEX

Note: Novels by F. Scott Fitzgerald, collections of his stories, and (major) collections of criticism of him, are entered in the index directly under their titles. His shorter works and plays are listed under his name. The abbreviation FSF is used in the index to stand for F. Scott Fitzgerald.

Adams, J. Donald 205, 211
advertising xviii, 5, 7, 9, 41–2, 164–5, 177
Afternoon of an Author (FSF) 214
age consciousness 9, 28–46
alcoholism 6, 16, 54–6, 64, 70, 174, 178–9, 186, 196
Alcott, Louisa May: *Little Women* 150, 151
Aldridge, John W. 213
Alger, Horatio 32, 80, 87
All the Sad Young Men (FSF) xix, 57, 68, 69–70, 74; promotion 81; reception 58; *see also titles of stories under* Fitzgerald, F. Scott
Allen, Gracie 194
Allen, Joan M. 222
American Booksellers Association 6, 164–5
American Dream, the 67, 69, 84–7
American Literary Scholarship 216
American Mercury 68
androgyny 162
army, U.S. xviii, 148, 165
Ashford, Daisy: *The Young Visiters* 166
Atlantic 17

Ballet mécanique (film) 93
Baltimore xx, 185
Basil and Josephine Stories, The (FSF) 219; *see also titles of stories under* Fitzgerald, F. Scott
Beard, George Miller 44
Beautiful and Damned, The (FSF) xix, 45, 95, 167, 214; cluster stories 57, 65, 66, 67; film-making in 26, 190; reviewed by Zelda 8, 152; vocation in 48–56; women in 38, 152–4, 226

Beegel, Susan F. 60
Before I Wake (play by Trevor Reese) 18
Benét, Stephen Vincent 205, 211
Berman, Ronald xi, 25–6, 155, 230
Berryman, John 211–12
Bewley, Marius 213
Bishop, John Peale xvii, 29, 147, 190, 210, 211
Bits of Paradise (FSF) 219
Bloom, Harold 233
Bodley Head 214
Bookman 32
Booth, Claire: *The Women* 200
Borzage, Frank 196
Boyd, Thomas 6
Breit, Harvey 17
Bridges, Robert 168
"Broken Soil" (film) 13
Brooks, Van Wyck 46, 80, 168
Broun, Heywood 166
Bruccoli, Matthew 59, 80, 91, 119, 138, 214–15, 217, 218–19, 220, 221, 223, 224, 225, 227, 228, 229, 231, 233; *Fitzgerald and Hemingway* 16, 23; *Some Sort of Epic Grandeur* 224; and *Tender is the Night* 116, 117
Bruccoli Collection 228, 233
Brush, Katherine 192
Bryer, Jackson R. xi, 27, 59, 60, 63, 211, 216, 218, 223, 224, 225, 226, 232; *The Critical Reputation of F. Scott Fitzgerald* 210, 216; *F. Scott Fitzgerald: The Critical Reception* 210, 221; *The Short Stories of F. Scott Fitzgerald* (ed.) 59, 225, 226
Buell, Lawrence 60

Buffalo, New York xvii
Butcher, Fanny 211
Buttita, Anthony 221

Cain, James M. 17
Callaghan, Morley 217
Callahan, John F. 221, 222
Cambridge Edition of the Works of F. Scott
Fitzgerald 228, 233
Canby, Henry Seidel 42
Carey, Harry 206
Carnegie, Dale 183
Cather, Willa 154, 214
Cendrars, Blaise 82
Chambers, John B. 227
Charvat, William 61
Chicago Tribune 66, 196, 211
Chorus Girl's Romance, The (film) 190
Chudacoff, Howard 45
Claridge, Henry 232
Clark, John Abbot 215
College Humor 9, 157
Collier's 66, 75, 77, 205, 206
colors 90–1
Conductor (film) 190
Conrad, Joseph 54, 79, 87, 214; *Almayer's
Folly* 80, 82
Cosmopolitan 205
Cowan, Lester 202
Cowley, Malcolm 16, 17, 62, 118, 119,
210, 211, 213; and *Tender is the Night*
117
Crack-Up essays 10, 13, 29, 30, 61,
178–85, 186, 188; *see also essay titles
under* Fitzgerald, F. Scott
Crack-Up, The (ed. Wilson) 211, 212
Crawford, Joan 199
Cross, K. G. W. 216
Cukor, George 12
Curie, Marie 201
Curnutt, Kirk xi, 25

Daily Mirror 18
Daily News 18
Dana, Viola 12
Dartmouth College xxi, 201–2, 209
de Sano, Michael 196
Dewey, John 83, 84, 85
Dickstein, Morris 180, 233
Dixon, Wheeler Winston 227
Donahoe, Sap 182
Donaldson, Scott xi, 2, 13, 26, 80, 147,
224, 225–6, 229
Dos Passos, John 10, 178, 210, 211
Dreiser, Theodore 54, 66, 110

Eble, Kenneth 216, 221, 225
Egorova, Lubov 156
Eliot, T. S. 79; *The Waste Land* 80,
82, 92
Ellerslie, Delaware xix, 23
Ellis, Havelock 161
Epstein, Joseph 184
Esquire 18, 19, 26, 27, 74, 75–7, 96, 178,
179, 184, 186, 204, 205
Europe xviii, xix, 94, 118–41; World War I
103–5, 106, 117, 145; *see also* France
expatriates 96, 118–41

F. Scott Fitzgerald: A Descriptive Bible 218
F. Scott Fitzgerald: Critical Assessments
232–3
F. Scott Fitzgerald: Manuscripts 227–8
F. Scott Fitzgerald: New Perspectives 233
F. Scott Fitzgerald A to Z 228–9
F. Scott Fitzgerald Centenary Exhibition
228
F. Scott Fitzgerald in His Own Time 218–19
F. Scott Fitzgerald on Authorship 228
F. Scott Fitzgerald Society 227
F. Scott Fitzgerald's Ledger 219
Fabian, Warner: *Flaming Youth* 42–3
Fass, Paula 36
Faulkner, William 98, 226
feminism 19–21, 39
Fetterley, Judith 158, 160
Fiedler, Leslie 16, 46, 213
film-making 12–13, 26–7, 114, 189–208,
219; books on FSF's 226–7
Fitzgerald, Annabel (sister of FSF) xvii,
149, 150
Fitzgerald, Edward (father of FSF) xvii, xx,
147
Fitzgerald, F. Scott: ARTICLES AND ESSAYS BY:
"An Alcoholic Case" 186; "Author's
House" 184–5; "An Author's Mother"
184, 186; "The Crack-Up" 13, 180–1,
186; "Crazy Sunday" 193–4, 211; "The
Cruise of the Rolling Junk" 9, 169;
"Early Success" 29, 187–8; "Echoes of
the Jazz Age" 30, 135, 175; "Handle
with Care" 179, 182–4; "How I Would
Sell My Books If I Were a Bookseller"
167; "How to Live on $36,000 a Year"
11, 168–9; "How to Live on
Practically Nothing a Year" 11, 119,
120–1, 138, 169, 170; "I Didn't Get
Over" 186; "Imagination and a Few
Mothers" 171–2, 175; "The Long Way
Out" 186–7; "Looking Back Eight
Years" 9; "Making Monogamy Work"

171; "My Generation" 215; "My Lost City" 4, 11, 166, 174; "My Old New England House on the Erie" 169; "One Hundred False Starts" 175–6; "Outline Chart of My Life" 219; "Pasting It Together" 181–2; "Ring" 176–7; "A Short Autobiography" 6, 174; "Sleeping and Waking" 177; "Wait Till You Have Children of Your Own!" 172; "What Became of Our Flappers and Sheiks" 9; "What I Think and Feel at Twenty-Five" 167, 170; "What Kind of Husbands Do 'Jimmies' Make?" 172–3; "Who's Who – and Why" 10–11, 165; "Why Blame It on the Poor Kiss…" 47, 171; CRITICISM OF: 1940–1949 209–12; 1950–1959 212–15; 1960–1969 215–18; 1970–1979 218–22; 1980–1989 222–7; 1990–1999 227–33; 2000– 233–4; PLAYS: *The Debutante* 148; *Fie! Fie! Fi-Fi!* 228; "Lipstick" (screenplay) xix, 156, 191; *The Vegetable* xix, 12, 57, 68, 168, 219; SHORT STORIES: "Absolution" 68, 70, 211; "The Adjuster" 38, 59, 60, 70; "The Adolescent Marriage" 38, 71; "Afternoon of an Author" 184, 185; "At Your Age" 28, 71, 157; "The Author's Apology" 6, 43; "Babes in the Woods" 63; "The Baby Party" 70; "Babylon Revisited" 35, 38, 56, 58, 70, 71, 74, 120, 132–3, 140, 158, 175; film script 202–3, 228; "Basil and Cleopatra" 34; "Benediction" 59, 65; "Bernice Bobs Her Hair" 36, 60, 64, 65, 151–2; "The Bowl" 71–2, 74, 191; "The Bridal Party" 70, 129–30; "The Camel's Back" 66, 166: filmed 190; "The Captured Shadow" 72, 201; "The Curious Case of Benjamin Buttons" 44, 60, 66; "The Cut Glass Bowl" 65; "Dalrymple Goes Wrong" 59, 65; "Dearly Beloved" 215; "Design in Plaster" 76; "The Diamond as Big as the Ritz" 53, 58, 59, 60, 64, 66, 67, 80, 91, 211; "Diamond Dick and the First Law of Woman" 79; "Dice, Brassknuckles & Guitar" 43, 68, 70, 73, 190–1; "Director's Special" 205; "Discard" 77–8; "Emotional Bankruptcy" 34, 72, 73, 158, 175; "Experiments in Convalescence" 55; "Family in the Wind" 74, 75; "Fiend, The" 74–5; "Financing Finnegan" 76, 187; "First Blood" 34–5; "Flight and Pursuit" 134; "The Four Fists" 65; "Girls Believe in Girls" 173; "Gretchen's Forty Winks" 68, 70; "He Thinks He's Wonderful" 201; "Head and Shoulders" 12, 64, 65, 161: filmed 190; "Her Last Case" 73; "His Russet Witch" 66; "Hot & Cold Blood" 70; "The Hotel Child" 70, 135–6; "The Ice Palace" 40, 58, 59, 60, 64, 65, 67, 73; "Image on the Heart" 139–40; "Indecision" 71, 136–8, 140–1; "The Intimate Strangers" 75, 138–9; "Jacob's Ladder" 59, 71, 157, 191, 192; "The Jelly-Bean" 40, 60, 66, 73; "Jemina" 66; "John Jackson's Arcady" 68; "Last Kiss" 77, 205; "The Last of the Belles" 35, 60, 73, 74; "The Lees of Happiness" 65, 66; "The Lost Decade" 76; "The Love Boat" 71; "Love in the Night" 38, 70–1, 121–3; "Luckless Santa Claus, A" 62; "Magnetism" 71, 191–2; "Majesty" 70, 71, 74, 126, 135, 138, 141; "May Day" 48, 53, 58, 59, 64, 65, 66, 67, 104, 211; "More Than Just a House" 73; "Myra Meets His Family" 13, 53: filmed 190; "The Mystery of the Raymond Mortgage" xvii, 61–2; "A New Leaf" 71, 72, 133–4; "News of Paris – Fifteen Years Ago" 140; "The Night Before Chancellorsville" 74, 75; "Not in the Guidebook" 68, 123–4; "The Offshore Pirate" 13, 38, 62, 64, 65: filmed 190; "On Schedule" 71; "On Your Own" 219; "One Interne" 73, 74, 75; "One of My Oldest Friends" 68; "One Trip Abroad" 38, 71, 72, 74, 130–2, 140; "The Ordeal" 63, 65; "Outside the Cabinet Maker's" 59; "The Passionate Eskimo" 75; "Pat Hobby's Christmas Wish" 205; "Pat Hobby's Secret" 76; "A Patriotic Short" 76–7, 204–5; "A Penny Spent" 70, 124–5; "The Perfect Life" 201; "The Pierian Springs and the Last Straw" 62; "Porcelain and Pink" 66; "Presumption" 71; "The Pusher in the Face" 68; "Rags Martin-Jones and the Pr-nce of W-les" 38, 62; "The Rich Boy" 45, 56, 58, 67, 70, 80, 125, 173; "The Room with the Green Blinds" 62; "The Rough Crossing" 71, 72, 74, 126, 130; "The Sensible Thing" 35, 68, 69, 70, 79; "Sentiment and the Use of Rouge" 63; "Shaggy's Morning" 76; "A Short Trip Home" 71, 74; "The Smilers" 64, 65; "The Spire and the Gargoyle" 59, 63; "The Swimmers" 71, 72, 74, 85, 126–8, 219; "Tarquin of Cheepside" 63, 66;

Fitzgerald, F. Scott (*cont.*)
  "The Third Casket" 68; "The Trail of the
  Duke" 62–3; " 'Trouble' " 71, 75; "Two
  for a Cent" 66; "Two Wrongs" 71, 74,
  128–9, 141; "The Unspeakable Egg" 38,
  68; "What a Handsome Pair!" 38, 157;
  "Winter Dreams" 35, 58, 64, 67, 69, 70,
  79, 184; "Zone of Accident" 73, 75
Fitzgerald, Frances Scott ("Scottie"; daughter
  of FSF) xviii, 18, 20, 132, 152, 160, 171,
  176, 177, 180, 182, 206, 210; biography
  229; writes of FSF 215, 219, 221
Fitzgerald, Mollie McQillan (mother of FSF)
  xvii, 147, 172, 184, 186
Fitzgerald (*née* Sayre), Zelda 2, 5, 7, 8, 9,
  10, 11, 12, 13–14, 16, 18, 19–23, 48,
  96–7, 118, 125, 139, 141, 143, 148–9,
  152–3, 166, 168, 169, 170, 171, 172, 181,
  210, 217; early life 148; meets FSF
  xviii, 148; marriage xviii, 37; biographies
  19–20, 22–3, 80–1, 148, 220, 233; FSF's
  letters to 13, 14, 19–20, 140, 154;
  mental illness xix, xx, xxi, 14, 17, 20,
  138, 157, 173, 178, 186–7; writing 8,
  19–21, 75, 144, 148–9, 152, 156–7, 219:
  "Eulogy on the Flapper" 146–7, 149; of
  FSF, posthumously 144; letters 4, 19,
  224; *McCall's* article 39–40 ; publication
  and criticism, posthumous 233; reviews
  B&D 8, 152; *Save Me the Waltz* 5, 21,
  23, 138, 139, 157, 233
Fitzgerald centennial 227, 232
Fitzgerald/Hemingway Annual 217–18
Fitzgerald Newsletter 214–15, 217
Fitzgerald Theater, St. Paul 24
Flagg, James Montgomery 9
flappers 12, 20, 26, 39–43, 65, 143,
  145–50, 152, 166, 167, 170–1, 173
Flappers and Philosophers (FSF) xviii, 57,
  65, 66, 67, 166, 214; *see also titles of
  stories under* Fitzgerald, F. Scott
Flügel, John C. *The Psychology of Clothes*
  39
Fort Leavenworth, Kansas xviii, 165
Fortune 206
Forum Magazine 43, 45
France xviii, xix, 118, 119–29, 131–4,
  139–40; Riviera xix, 119–22, 125, 154,
  169, 175
Franklin, Sidney 200, 201
*French Connections: Hemingway and
  Fitzgerald Abroad* 232
Freud, Sigmund 146
Friedman, Melvin J. 141
Fryer, Sarah Beebe 60, 159, 226

Gale, Robert L. 229
Gellhorn, Martha 2
Germany 196–8
Getting Straight (film) 1, 23
Gibson, Charles Dana 146
Gibson Girl 39, 145–6
Gilman, Charlotte Perkins 29, 39
Gingrich, Arnold 18, 75, 77, 178, 205
Gish, Dorothy 190
Glimpses of the Moon (film) 190
Goldhurst, William 216
Goldwyn, Samuel 193, 202
Gone With the Wind (film) 201
Gordon, Mary 3, 20
Gracie at Sea (film) 194
Graham, Sheilah xx, xxi, 7–8, 14, 18, 20,
  94, 147, 206, 221, 229; *Beloved Infidel*
  14, 15, 19, 214; *College of One* 217; *The
  Rest of the Story* 15
Grand Hotel (film) 200, 207
Great Gatsby, The (FSF) 79–94, 173;
  criticism of 212, 213–14, 217, 218, 222,
  224, 225–6, 230–1, 233; cluster stories
  57, 67, 68–70, 71; Gatsby's death 115,
  184; play (by Owen Davis) 12; structure
  95, 205–6; time in 91; and vocation 56;
  women in 41, 154–6
Great McGinty, The (film) 195–6
Great Neck, Long Island xix, 168
Greenwich Village Follies 10
Griffith, D. W. 12, 190
Grit (film) 190
Gross, Barry 135

Hall, G. Stanley 40; *Adolescence* 32, 33,
  34, 35, 36
Handy, W. C. 94
Harper's Bazaar 77
Hearne, Laura 217
Hearst's International 9
Heilbrun, Carolyn G. 162
Held, John: cartoons by 9, 39, 166
Hemingway, Ernest xix, 2, 3, 5, 17–18,
  19, 21, 22–3, 61, 98, 110, 119, 178,
  182, 216, 217, 229; *A Farewell to Arms*
  82; *In Our Time* 176; *A Moveable
  Feast* 57, 217
Hersey, Marie 147
Hertz, David 198
Higgins, John A. 59, 222
Highland Hospital, North Carolina xxi
Hindus, Milton 178, 212, 216
history 100–16, 206–7
Hitchcock, Alfred 13
Hoffman, Frederick J. 213, 217

Hollywood xix, xx, xxi, 9, 12, 13, 26–7, 189–207, 219
Holman, C. Hugh 60
homosexuality 23, 138, 156, 161
Hook, Andrew 230
Horizon 212
Hotchner, A. E. 23
Husband Hunter, The (film) 190
Huxley, Aldous 206

Immigration Bills 94, 136
Infidelity (proposed film) 199–200, 207
Italy xviii, xix

James, Henry 98, 123, 141, 154, 226; *The Ambassadors* 126
James, William 83, 84, 85–6, 87, 92, 230
jazz 93, 175
Johnson, Owen: *Stover at Yale* 31
Joyce, James 31, 125, 231
Jozan, Edouard xix, 118, 139, 154, 156
Jung, Carl 161

Kallich, Martin 212
Kaplan, Caren 118–19
Kazin, Alfred 17, 178, 211, 212
Keillor, Garrison 24
Kennedy, J. Gerald xi–xii, 26
King, Ginevra xvii, 141, 147–8, 150, 158, 188
Kissel, Howard 21
Knopf, Edwin H. 13
Koblas, John F. 220
Kuehl, John 62, 131, 142, 215, 231

Ladies' Home Journal 171
Lanahan, Eleanor 229
Lardner, Ring 106, 166, 176–7
Last Tycoon, The (FSF) 189, 192, 195, 199, 200, 202, 205–8, 226; cluster stories 74, 77, 96, 193; publication 57, 211
Latham, Aaron 220
Lawrence, D. H. 145, 161
Le Vot, André 224
Lehan, Richard 80, 159, 215–16, 230
Letters of F. Scott Fitzgerald, The 216–17
Lewis, Sinclair 81
Lewis, Wyndham 145
Liberty 68, 75
Life 17, 18, 146
Lincoln, Abraham 106
Lippmann, Walter 83, 84, 92
Littauer, Kenneth 206, 207
Loew, Marcus 206
Long, Robert Emmet 90, 222

Loos, Anita 193
Love of the Last Tycoon, The: A Western (FSF) 189; *see also Last Tycoon, The*
Lowell, Robert 179
Lowry, Malcolm 228

MacLeish, Archibald 141
Madame Curie (film) 201
Maltin, Leonard 199
Mangum, Bryant xii, 25, 231
Mankiewicz, Joseph M. 196–7, 198–9, 206
Marchand, Roland 42
Margolies, Alan xii, 13, 26–7, 219, 226
Marie Antoinette (film) 200
Marks, Percy 42
Marsh, Reginald 10
Matterson, Stephen 230–1
Mayer, Louis B. 207
Mayfield, Sara 20, 23, 220
McCall's 9, 39–40, 75
McKaig, Alex 4
McQuillan, Mollie *see* Fitzgerald
Mellow, James: *Invented Lives* 4, 22–3, 80–1, 224
Mencken, H. L. 54, 58, 65, 81, 82, 98, 145, 167, 214, 230
Metro-Goldwyn-Mayer (MGM) xx, 190, 192, 194, 196–201, 206
Metropolitan Magazine 7, 48, 66, 67, 149
Metropolitan Newspaper Service 171
Meyers, Jeffrey 7, 23, 24, 229
Milford, Nancy: *Zelda: a Biography* 3, 19–20, 220
Millay, Edna St. Vincent 147
Millay, Kathleen 42
Miller, James A. 69
Miller, James E., Jr. 214
Minter, David L. 217
Mizener, Arthur 18, 212, 214, 215, 217, 220; *The Far Side of Paradise* 3, 15, 16, 17, 59, 212, 224
Modell, John 47
Modernism 82, 93, 118, 161–2
Mok, Michel 6, 14
Montgomery, Alabama xviii, xx, xxi
Montross, Lynn and Lois: *Town and Gown* 42
Moore, Benita 227
Moran, Lois xix, 13, 156, 157, 191
Morris, Wright 213
Motor 9
Murphy, Gerald 19, 93, 96, 118, 134, 182, 183, 217
Murphy, Sarah 19, 96, 118, 134, 217
Myers, Carmel 191

Nassau Literary Magazine xvii, 62, 63, 65, 228
New Essays on F. Scott Fitzgerald's Neglected Stories 232
New Leader 17
New Republic 15, 43, 168, 205, 210, 211
New Woman 107–14, 144–6, 153–4, 173
New York City xviii, xxi, 10, 81, 82–3, 93–4, 166, 171, 174
New York Evening World 7
New York Post 14
New York Times 15, 17, 36, 44, 174, 199
New York Times Book Review 17, 205, 211
New York Tribune 165, 168
New Yorker 6, 16, 17, 23, 174, 214, 217
Newman School, Hackensack xvii, 215
Newman School News xvii, 62
News (Indianapolis) 210
News and Observer (Raleigh) 210
Norris, Frank 66
Now and Then, St. Paul Academy xvii, 61, 62
Nugent, Frank S. 199

Ober, Harold 12, 13, 57, 58, 64, 70, 72, 77, 169, 170, 178, 219–20
O'Hara, John 186, 210, 211
Osler, William 44

Paramore, E. E. 198
Paramount Pictures 190, 202
Paris xix, 123–7, 129–34, 140
Parker, Dorothy 62, 147, 211; "Professional Youth" 43
Parrott, Ursula: "Infidelity" 199
Patterson, Richard North: *Escape the Night* 1
Pendleton, Thomas 230
perfectibility 104
Perkins, Maxwell 5, 12, 13, 14, 33, 48, 57, 69, 74, 81, 88, 97, 148, 164, 169–70, 177, 178, 190, 201, 209, 217, 220
Perosa, Sergio 178, 216
Petry, Alice Hall 59, 69, 80, 141, 226
Piper, Henry Dan 216, 221
Pirie, John 188
Poe, E. A. 16
Poems 1911–1940 (FSF) 223
popular culture 2–4, 8, 15, 21–5, 113–14
Portable F. Scott Fitzgerald, The 211, 213

Potts, Stephen W. 231
Pound, Ezra 82
Powell, Anthony 14
Price Was High, The (FSF stories) 59, 219
Prigozy, Ruth xii, 136, 139, 154, 159, 221, 232, 233
Princeton Tiger, The xvii, 228
Princeton University, New Jersey xvii, xviii, 10, 29, 49, 53, 62, 63, 88, 164, 168, 181, 215, 224, 228; Triangle Club xvii, 148, 223, 228
Printer's Ink 44
psychiatry/psychology 7, 159, 161
Public Philosophy 84–5, 91

Raffles (film) 202
Ramsaye, Terry 206
Rapf, Harry 206
Rascoe, Burton 31, 168
Red Headed Woman (film) 192, 196, 207
Ring, Frances Kroll 7–8, 19, 22, 24, 206, 214; *Against the Current* 224
Romanoff, Michael 16
Romantic Egoists, The 8, 63, 210, 219
Rooney, Mickey 201
Roosevelt, Franklin 103
Rosaldo, Renato 121
Ross, Alan 212
Ross, Lillian 16
Roulston, Robert 226, 229, 231
Royce, Josiah 84–5

Salinger, J. D. 3, 17
San Francisco Chronicle 33
Sanderson, Rena xii, 26
Santayana, George 84, 85, 230; "Materialism and Idealism in American Life" 86–7
Saturday Evening Post xviii, 10, 11, 28, 33, 43, 58, 63, 64, 65, 67, 68, 69, 70, 71, 72, 73, 75, 76, 77, 119, 120, 127, 157–8, 161, 165, 166, 168, 170, 178, 191, 209, 219
Saturday Review of Literature 42, 205, 211
Savage, D. S. 212
Sayre, Anthony xviii, 148
Sayre, Zelda *see* Fitzgerald
Schlacks, Deborah Davis 230
Schulberg, Budd xxi, 27, 201–2, 209, 217; on "Babylon Revisited" film script 204, 228; *The Disenchanted* 3, 15, 16, 17–18: dramatic version 18; *Four Seasons* 4, 12, 15, 17, 19; in *New Republic* 15
Scott, W. T. 211

Scott Fitzgerald: The Promises of Life
  224–5
Scribner's Magazine 9, 64, 65, 97, 168
Scribner's Sons, Charles xviii, 5, 48, 49, 57,
  58, 148, 165, 177, 213, 214, 215, 228
Seiter, Dan 226
Seldes, Gilbert 10
Selznick, David 190, 201
Shearer, Norma 193, 200, 206
Shiel, Lily *see* Graham, Sheilah
Short Stories of F. Scott Fitzgerald, The
  (ed. Bryer) 225, 226
Siegel, Joel 21–2
Sklar, Robert 166, 216
Smart Set xviii, 58, 63, 64, 65, 68
Sontag, Susan 82
Spafford, Robert 194
Spengler, Oswald 7, 145, 161, 189
St. Louis Post-Dispatch 31
St. Paul, Minnesota xvii, xviii, 24, 185,
  186, 219
St. Paul Academy, Minnesota xvii, 61,
  215
Stagecoach (film) 207
Stavola, Thomas J. 222
Stein, Gertrude 46
Steinach operation 44
Stern, Milton R. xii, 26, 69, 84–5, 89, 161,
  221–2, 223, 226, 231
Stewart, Donald Ogden 10
Stories of F. Scott Fitzgerald, The 212
Stromberg, Hunt 199, 200
Sturges, Preston 195
Switzerland xix, 135–6, 138

Tales of the Jazz Age (FSF) xviii, 57, 58, 66,
  67, 68, 69, 166; *see also titles of stories
  under* Fitzgerald, F. Scott
Talmadge, Constance, 191
Taps at Reveille (FSF) 57, 64, 70, 71, 73,
  74, 75; reception 58; *see also titles of
  stories under* Fitzgerald, F. Scott
Tarkington, Booth: *Penrod* 33; *Seventeen*
  31, 33, 34–5, 38, 41
Tate, Mary Jo 228–9
Taylor, Dwight 192–3
television 3, 19, 22
Tender is the Night (FSF) 47, 56, 57, 118,
  183, 191, 205–6; cluster stories 57, 64,
  70–1, 72–4, 77, 131; criticism of 26,
  213, 231; and history 95–116;
  promotion 9–10, 177; screenplay 194,
  228; women in 39, 40–1, 45, 156–61,
  173, 226; writing 20, 138

Thalberg, Irving 193, 196, 206, 207
This Side of Paradise (FSF) 28, 31, 32–3,
  36, 95, 176; cluster stories 57, 61, 63,
  66, 67, 69, 72; criticism 223, 231, 265;
  film planned 13; vocation in 48–56;
  women in 40, 148, 149–51, 167, 226;
  writing and publication xviii, 61, 164–5,
  187, 209, 223
Thoughtbook of Francis Scott Key Fitzgerald
  215
Three Comrades (film) xx, 196–9, 207,
  219
Thurber, James 205
Time 14
Times (Los Angeles) 210
Toklas, Alice B. 46
Tompkins, Calvin 19, 217
Triangle Club, Princeton xvii, 148, 223,
  228
Trilling, Lionel 80, 211, 213
Trimalchio 233; *see also Great Gatsby, The*
  (FSF)
Tsimpouki, Theodora 230
Turnbull, Andrew 19, 27, 216–17
Turnbull, Frances 176
Turner Network Television 22
Twain, Mark 81
Twentieth-Century Fox 202

Universal Pictures 202
University of South Carolina Thomas
  Cooper Library 228, 233

Vaill, Amanda 93
Vanity Fair 7
Vidor, King 13, 206, 207
vocation 50–4

Wakefield, Dan 16, 17, 19
Wanger, Walter xxi, 201–2
war 103–7, 117, 145
Warren, Bill 194
Way, Brian 226
Wedding Night, The (film) 13
Welles, Orson 204
Wescott, Glenway 15, 178, 210, 211
West, James L. W. III xiii, 25, 223, 228,
  233, 234
Westbrook, Robert 229
Weston, Elizabeth A. 229
Westport, Connecticut xviii, 9
Wharton, Edith xix, 51, 110, 190,
  214, 229
Wickes, George 118

Wilde, Oscar 149
Wilkinson, Burke 17
Williams, Emlyn: *The Light of Heart* 202
Williams, Tennessee 21: *Clothes for a Summer Hotel* 21
Wilson, Colin 213
Wilson, Edmund xvii, 48, 57, 81, 143, 147, 182, 214; ed. *The Crack-up* 211; "The Delegate from Great Neck" 168; ed. *The Last Tycoon* 218
Winter Carnival (film) xxi, 201–2
Wodehouse, P. G. 103
Woman: American 9, 160; New 107–14, 144–6, 153–4, 173
Woman's Home Companion 68, 172

women 143–62, 176, 226; feminism 19–21, 39; flappers 12, 20, 26, 39–43, 65, 143, 145–50, 152, 166, 167, 170–1, 173
Women, The (film) 200
Women's Liberation 20, 39
World-Telegram 210
World War I 103–5, 106, 117, 145

Yank at Oxford, A (film) 196
youth culture 25, 28–46, 160

Zelda (TV drama) 1–2
Zhang, Aiping 229–30
Ziegfeld, Florenz 206
Zwerdling, Alex 136, 141

44608185R00165

Made in the USA
Lexington, KY
03 September 2015